CRIMINAL INJURIES COMPENSATION

STATE AND OFFENDER COMPENSATION FOR VIOLENT CRIME

CRIMINAL INJURIES COMPENSATION

State and Offender Compensation for Violent Crime

DR DAVID MIERS

Consultant Editors

BEN COLLINS QC

JUDGE NICHOLAS WIKELEY

Foreword by

SIR ERNEST RYDER

OXFORD
UNIVERSITY PRESS

OXFORD
UNIVERSITY PRESS

Great Clarendon Street, Oxford, OX2 6DP,
United Kingdom

Oxford University Press is a department of the University of Oxford. It furthers the University's objective of excellence in research, scholarship, and education by publishing worldwide. Oxford is a registered trade mark of Oxford University Press in the UK and in certain other countries

First Edition published in 2018

Impression: 1

Published in the United States of America by Oxford University Press
198 Madison Avenue, New York, NY 10016, United States of America

British Library Cataloguing in Publication Data
Data available

Library of Congress Control Number: 2018948329

ISBN 978–0–19–880662–2

Printed and bound by
CPI Group (UK) Ltd, Croydon, CR0 4YY

FOREWORD

I am delighted to have this opportunity to write the foreword to this invaluable new work on criminal injuries compensation by Emeritus Professor David Miers. It is axiomatic that one of the fundamental functions of the modern State is to protect its citizens from harm. Recent years have also seen increasing emphasis in Government policy on both the role and the voice of the victim in the criminal justice system. In that context the extent to which it is right and proper that the State should provide a system of financial redress for the victims of violent crime and sexual offences has become a matter of intense public debate.

The difficult public policy choices that have to be made are evidenced by the fact that since the first criminal injuries compensation scheme was established under the Royal Prerogative in 1964 it has undergone several important transformations. Most notably the old system based on personal injuries awards in civil litigation was abandoned for a tariff approach in 1996, which has since been further refined in the 2001, 2008 and 2012 Schemes. At the same time, although without quite the same level of public debate, there have been a series of changes to sentencing practice and to the duties on the criminal courts that place greater emphasis on the use of compensation orders for victims of crimes of violence.

Professor Miers's magisterial new book adopts a holistic approach, examining in detail both the Criminal Injuries Compensation Scheme 2012 in Part 1, which helpfully places its analysis of the 2012 scheme in the context of its predecessor schemes, and the parallel sentencing options available to the criminal courts in Part 2. As Senior President of Tribunals, I hope I will be forgiven for focussing on the issues raised by Part 1 of this impressive work. The publication of this book is especially timely as we approach the 10th anniversary of the implementation of the reforms to the tribunal system enshrined in the Tribunals, Courts and Enforcement Act (TCEA) 2007 (which came into force for most purposes on 3 November 2008). Before November 2008 an appeal against a decision by the Authority lay to the Criminal Injuries Compensation Appeal Panel (CICAP), with onward challenge by way of judicial review in the Administrative Court. Under TCEA the CICAP was subsumed into the new First-tier Tribunal (or FtT), subject to judicial review in the Upper Tribunal. This major structural reform has had two important consequences.

The first, and little remarked on in the literature to date, has been in terms of access to justice for the citizen – before 2008 there were only a handful of judicial reviews in the Administrative Court each year. Since 2008, however, the Upper Tribunal has seen between 50 and 80 applications for judicial review each year from decisions of the FtT in criminal injuries compensation cases, an increase in the judicial review caseload in this area which may be as much as tenfold. For my part, I am happy to emphasise that it may now be time to revisit whether a statutory appeal under the TCEA, rather than judicial review, is not the more appropriate route of challenge.

The second is that this increase in caseload, combined with the TCEA reforms, has enabled the Administrative Appeals Chamber of the Upper Tribunal to develop a coherent body of jurisprudence on the operation of the various criminal injuries compensation schemes, reviewed in detail throughout the text.In doing so the Upper Tribunal has demonstrated the statutory hallmark of specialist, innovative and accessible justice at the apex of the reformed tribunal system which has put into practice the philosophy of the Leggatt Report. Notably the Supreme Court in *Jones v First Tier Tribunal & Criminal Injuries Compensation Authority* [2013] UKSC 19 has recognised the importance of both the pre-eminent fact-finding function of the First-tier Tribunal and the specialist judicial expertise of the Upper Tribunal. As Professor Miers' book was going to press, the Court of Appeal published its decisions in the two appeals concerning the exclusionary effect of unspent convictions on a claimant's eligibility, and the lawfulness of the 'same roof' rule. Shortly thereafter the government announced that it is to hold a full review of the Scheme as part of a cross-government Victims Strategy, expected to report in 2019. This review will address such matters as the time lime limits for applications, the scope of the central definition of 'a crime of violence' and the implications of the Court of Appeal's decisions in these two appeals. Their conclusions on the interpretation of these significant aspects of the 2012 Scheme are summarized in his text.

As we enter the second decade of the reformed tribunal system, and as tribunals develop new ways of working, the need for authoritative and scholarly analysis of the law will remain foremost. For all those involved in criminal injuries compensation cases, from user through practitioner to judge, Professor Miers's new book will be a vital companion on that journey. I warmly endorse its use and thank him for his scholarly attention to detail.

Ernest Ryder
Royal Courts of Justice, Strand, London
September 2018

PREFACE

This book is intended for those who rely upon, work with, or seek to understand the statutory, judicial, and administrative rules that govern state and offender payment of compensation to victims of sexual offences, and of crimes of violence. My principal audience is those private and public sector practitioners who advise on making an application under the Criminal Injuries Compensation Scheme 2012 (the 2012 Scheme), and who appear before the First-tier and the Upper Tribunals, or who pursue on the victim's behalf a compensation order from offenders. There are, furthermore, many voluntary and charitable bodies for whom the possibilities for compensation that are offered by restorative justice may be of value to their clients. While the 2012 Scheme applies throughout Great Britain, my focus is the law of England and Wales, as it applies also in respect of offender compensation.

The state and offender compensation arrangements analysed in this book sit within a political context that seeks to ensure that victims of crime are better served by the criminal justice system; it will be of interest to those who study or are otherwise concerned with the state's responses to, and with its remedies for, those affected by violent and sexual crime. Other academics, in particular those who have an interest in tort and personal injury law, may note that the scheme has, since its creation, constituted a unique taxpayer funded arrangement for the victims of intentional torts to the person. In addition, there are instructive points of similarity and difference between these two compensating systems' response to claimants who suffer mental injury upon witnessing violent crime, or who contributed to their own injuries.

Between 1964 and 1996, the scheme was largely based on common law principles governing personal and fatal injury actions. This approach was replaced in 1996 by a statutory scheme that, administered by the Criminal Injuries Compensation Authority, retained the occasions for compensation but broke the link with common law general damages, providing instead for payment to be made on the basis of a tariff of awards. The Criminal Injuries Compensation Act 1995 also provided for appeals to be heard by the Criminal Injuries Compensation Appeals Panel, arrangements that were changed by the Tribunals, Courts and Enforcement Act 2007. This provided for appeals to be heard by a First-tier Tribunal, and for the Upper Tribunal to hear applications for judicial review of that tribunal's decisions. The Upper Tribunal's own decisions now form a substantial jurisprudence concerning the scheme's interpretation, examined in detail in the text. This statutory scheme was the subject of my earlier analysis, *State Compensation for*

Criminal Injuries (1997). The government's continuing concern to exert greater control over its burden on the taxpayer, and over the criteria of eligibility, led to the major revisions made in the 2012 Scheme, which are the subject matter of Part I of this book.

The proposition that the criminal justice system should make arrangements whereby those who commit offences against others should be required to compensate them is largely uncontroversial. This finds statutory expression in the compensation orders that criminal courts may make following a conviction, introduced in 1972. Of more recent origin, restorative justice offers consenting victims and offenders an opportunity to meet, in order that the victim can describe the impact of the offence, which the offender can acknowledge, and for which the offender can accept responsibility. 'Making amends' may indeed involve making compensation. As is the case with the 2012 Scheme, the government sees offender compensation and restorative justice as practical methods by which the state can address and possibly meet victims' expectations that their injuries are 'recognized' in some way. These concerns are the subject matter of Part II.

Chapter 1 amplifies by way of introduction the themes touched on in the preceding paragraphs. Part I, *State Compensation*, comprises a detailed analysis of the operation of the 2012 Scheme. The text is written from its point of view, but many of its provisions are of equivalent effect to those of its predecessors, including some that date from the common law schemes. Their similarities and differences are highlighted as appropriate. Chapters 2–4 deal in turn with the criteria for applicant eligibility: the scope of the defining elements of a criminal injury, the definition and proof of the resulting personal injury, the identification of those eligible for compensation, and the conditions under which applicants may be refused or be made a reduced award on account of their criminal record, conduct, or character. Chapter 5 deals with the assessment of compensation, and Chapter 6 addresses its procedural aspects: the rules on applications, the making and review of awards, appeals before the First-tier Tribunal, and the jurisdiction of the Upper Tribunal.

Part II, *Offender Compensation*, deals first with the law and implementation of compensation orders. Chapters 7–9 principally concern the provisions in sections 130–34 of the Powers of Criminal Courts (Sentencing) Act 2000. They cover the injuries for which, and the persons for whom an order may be made, the assessment of compensation, and the status of a compensation order as a sentence of the court. Chapter 10 reviews the wide range of statutory and administrative provisions governing those restorative justice responses to offending behaviour that may lead to the compensation of the victim.

I owe a profound debt of gratitude to my two consultant editors, Upper Tribunal Judge Nicholas Wikeley, and Ben Collins QC. They read and commented on draft and revised chapters, making many suggestions for better, or more accurate, ways in which to set out the applicable law and its interpretation. I have greatly valued their continued encouragement and advice. Neither has any responsibility for the opinions in the text, nor for any remaining errors. I would also like to thank the OUP production team, and Catherine Rogers, Liana Green, and Zoe Tustin at Oxford University Press for their enthusiastic and helpful support from start to finish.

David Miers
June 2018

CONTENTS

TABLE OF CONTENTS

PART II

TABLE OF CASES

Throughout the book the phrases '(*Social Entitlement Chamber*)' and '(*Criminal Injuries Compensation*)', as they appear in case citations, are abbreviated to (*SEC*) and to (*CIC*), respectively.

EUROPEAN COURT OF HUMAN RIGHTS

TABLE OF LEGISLATION

STATUTES

SUBORDINATE LEGISLATION

OTHER LEGISLATION

EUROPEAN LEGISLATION

INTERNATIONAL INSTRUMENTS

1

COMPENSATING VICTIMS OF VIOLENT CRIME

Context and Purpose

I Introduction

For some years, a central claim of criminal justice policy in England and Wales has been to 'make sure that the victim's voice is heard at the heart of Government'.[1] This is a claim that for many critics remains unfulfilled, but which in practice presents a number of challenges to an even-handed criminal justice system. As in other areas where it has been alert to popular criticism of its treatment of crime victims, the government's proposals in *Getting it Right for Victims and Witnesses*, the consultation paper that led to the 2012 Criminal Injuries Compensation Scheme (the 2012 Scheme),[2] struck an implicit but combative note in favour of what has frequently been characterized as a 'rebalancing' of that policy in favour of the victim's interests.[3] This aim was clearly evident in the thinking that lay behind the government's introduction of the common law Scheme in 1964. **1.01**

[1] Home Office (2005) 8.

[2] Ministry of Justice (2012a).

[3] Home Office (1959) 7 and (2006). There is a substantial literature concerning the relationship between victims and the criminal justice system, see references in David Miers, 'Compensating Deserving Victims of Violent Crime: The Criminal Injuries Compensation Scheme 2012' (2014) 34 *Legal Studies* 242–78.

Its instrumental purpose was to make *unique* provision for the compensation of victims of violent crime, distinct from any resources directed to offenders;[4] its symbolic purpose was clearly to *differentiate* victims from offenders in the distribution of public funds.

1.02 This demonstrable difference continues to be central to its political legitimacy. The 2012 Scheme is intended to ensure that the taxpayer is asked to compensate only those who are 'blameless victims of serious crimes',[5] a 'payment trigger' whose primary function is 'to select worthy claimants from the less deserving and to make payments only to the former'.[6] In *R (McNiece) v (1) Criminal Injuries Compensation Authority (2) The Lord Chancellor and Secretary of State for Justice* and *R (1) A (2) B v (1) Criminal Injuries Compensation Authority (2) The Lord Chancellor and Secretary of State for Justice,* the Administrative Court, and in the subsequent appeal by A and B, the Court of Appeal, confirmed that the government's stated objectives pursue 'a legitimate aim to seek to ensure that the limited funds devoted to a taxpayer funded expression of public sympathy should be directed towards those who are considered "blameless", that is, who have themselves obeyed the law and not cost society money through their offending behaviour'.[7]

1.03 *Getting it Right for Victims and Witnesses* also sought to give more effective meaning to the government's view that as the guilty party is the offender, 'in an ideal world, it should be the offender who compensates the victim',[8] and, by implication, not the taxpayer. In order to make offenders take greater moral and financial responsibility for their actions, the consultation proposed to extend the use of restorative justice, to require offenders more frequently to make reparation for 'low level' crime, and to strengthen the court's power to order the offender to pay compensation to the victim.

1.04 This chapter comprises two sections. The first, *Establishing the Criminal Injuries Compensation Schemes*, traces their development to the introduction of the 2012 Scheme. The second, *Making Offenders Pay for their Crimes*, gives a brief overview of the making of compensation orders against offenders, and of the more recent promotion of restorative justice, in which victim compensation may play a role.

---

4 Home Office (1961) and (1964).

5 Ministry of Justice (2012b) Foreword 4.

6 Sonia Macleod and Christopher Hodges, *Redress Schemes for Personal Injuries* (Hart Publishing 2017) 640.

7 [2017] EWHC 2, 2017 WL 11799 [92] (QB) (Wilkie J); *A and B v Criminal Injuries Compensation Authority and Secretary of State for Justice* [2018] EWCA Civ 1534, 2018 WL 03224139 [92] (CA) Gross LJ).

8 Home Office (2005) 14; David Miers, 'Offender and State Compensation for Victims of Crimes: Two Decades of Development and Change' (2014) 20 *International Review of Victimology* 145–68.

II Establishing the Criminal Injuries Compensation Schemes

A Justifications

When introduced in 1964, the scheme was one of many established throughout the common law world during the 1960s and 1970s to correct what critics saw as an unjustifiable imbalance between the treatment of victims and of offenders. One aspect of that imbalance was the gap between the 'ideal world' in which offenders compensated their victims, and the unreality of the practical enforcement of the theoretical civil remedy. While the rebalancing agenda was sufficient to justify the further imposition of financial burdens on offenders, the introduction of these state schemes generated a substantial literature that sought to justify this novel allocation of public funds. Much of this literature sought to locate the juridical basis of criminal injuries compensation schemes in analogies with contract law, or with state liability, but neither was convincing.[9] **1.05**

The contract analogy relied on the premise that in consideration for the acceptance of laws regulating the private use of force in the pursuit of grievances, and of its effective monopoly over the prosecution, trial, and disposal of offenders, the state promises to compensate citizens should they suffer criminal injuries. One objection is that citizens gain far more than they lose as a result of gun control and of the state's intervention in policing and the prosecution of offences. The argument also overstates the force of recognizing citizens' rights. Allowing that it does have an obligation to protect them, this says no more than that the state has an obligation to provide health care or education. This does not imply a right to compensation as measured by damages for breach of contract, but only to the allocation of a fair share of the public funds that might reasonably be allocated to such a scheme, or to other public goods. **1.06**

Nor does the common law entail the proposition that its law enforcement agencies promise to protect all people at all times, or that by negligently failing to prevent injurious criminal activity, the state assumes the role of a tortfeasor. The government's long held position is entirely consistent with the courts' repeated decisions that, in the absence of a 'special distinctive risk' of harm to the victim, it would not be fair, just, or reasonable to impose liability in negligence on a police authority for another's offences.[10] In Lord Kerr's words in *Commissioner of Police of the Metropolis v DSD and Another*, 'to re-visit such matters step by step by way of litigation with a view to private compensation would inhibit the robust **1.07**

[9] These justifications are discussed in David Miers, *State Compensation for Criminal Injuries* (Blackstone Press 1997) 2–13.

[10] *Hill v Chief Constable for West Yorkshire* [1989] AC 53 (HL) 62 (Lord Keith).

operation of police work, and divert resources from current inquiries; it would be detrimental to, not a spur to, law enforcement'.[11]

1.08 Funded by general taxation, these schemes may be the state's way of acknowledging the hardship that arises from this rule of public policy.[12] They may also be seen as its way of insuring citizens against the statistically determinable risk that each one has of being a victim of crime, a risk that, in common with road traffic, industrial and other accidents, falls unevenly across the population.[13] The argument for public insurance resonates with some conceptions of the functions of tort law; that it is socially more just and economically more sensible to distribute losses occasioned by criminal activity at large, rather than letting them fall on the particular victim.[14]

1.09 But this could not justify treating victims of violent crime more favourably than those injured on the roads, as was the case when the scheme was introduced. Until it was replaced in 1996 by the tariff scheme, its provision for victims of violent crime went well beyond the confines of welfare payments, in essence providing the measure of compensation that would be payable in a civil action against the offender. Forced to the point, the government could find 'no constitutional or social principle on which state compensation could be justified'.[15] As it later candidly accepted, '[w]e have to ask ourselves whether we can say that victims of crime are intrinsically different from other disabled people in the community'.[16]

1.10 More recently, the government has placed greater emphasis on the notion of 'civic trust':[17] 'justice depends on the public having trust in the system'.[18] To experience crime is to experience a failure in civic trust; that is, in the trust that citizens have, and that the state encourages them to have, in the capacity of the criminal justice system to protect them. As citizens, victims are the gatekeepers to that system; their

---

[11] [2018] UKSC 11, [2018] 2 WLR 895 [132] (HL); *Robinson v Chief Constable of West Yorkshire Police* [2018] UKSC 4, [2018] 2 WLR 595 [31]–[71] (SC) (Lord Reed).

[12] *Rathbland v Chief Constable of the Northumbria Constabulary* [2016] EWHC 181 [152], 2016 WL 00386311 (QB) (Males J); Home Office (2005) 21.

[13] Iain Brennan, Simon Moore, and Jonathan Shepherd, 'Risk Factors for Violent Victimisation and Injury from Six Years of the British Crime Survey' (2010) 17 *International Review of Victimology* 209–29.

[14] Simon Deakin, Angus Johnston, and Basil Markesinis, *Markesinis and Deakin's Tort Law* (7th edn, Oxford University Press 2013) 99–121.

[15] Home Office (1961) para 18.

[16] Hansard HL vol 395 col 306 (18 July 1978 WA). This inconsistency was forcefully argued at the time in Patrick Atiyah, *Accidents, Compensation and the Law* (Weidenfeld & Nicolson 1970) 324. 'Such payments are no different in principle from, for example, benefits payable to persons who have suffered industrial injuries . . . or to people who have disabilities. Awards of compensation under the criminal injuries scheme are not made because the state is responsible for causing the victim's injuries, any more than the state is responsible if an accident occurs at work or if a person is or becomes disabled'; *JT v First-tier Tribunal, Criminal Injuries Compensation Authority, and Equality and Human Rights Commission* [2018] EWCA Civ 1755, 2018 WL 03537078 [65] (CA) (Leggat LJ) (JT v CICA 2).

[17] Pablo de Greiff, 'Justice and reparations' in Pablo de Greiff (ed), *The Handbook of Reparations* (Oxford University Press 2006) 461–64; Miers, 'Compensating Deserving Victims of Violent Crime' (n 3) 246–47.

[18] Ministry of Justice (2012a) para 63.

willingness to report offences and to engage with its agencies rests upon their trust that it will reliably produce the outcomes they reasonably expect: 'The Government owes it to victims of crime to ensure as far as possible that offenders are caught, that they are punished, and that they are dealt with in a way that reduces the likelihood of their re-offending and creating more victims'.[19] In its recognition of these mutual obligations of citizens and of the state,[20] the notion of civic trust resonates with some elements of the doctrinal arguments derived from contract and tort.

B The common law scheme

Administered by the Criminal Injuries Compensation Board (CICB), the *ex gratia* scheme came into effect on 1 August 1964 by means of a written parliamentary answer.[21] The reliance on executive rather than legislative authority gave effect to the government's view that the state had no legal liability for the personal injuries caused by offenders.[22] But the denial of a right to sue the state was of little practical moment. In *R v Criminal Injuries Compensation Board, ex parte Lain*, Diplock LJ held that the CICB's quasi-judicial procedures were amenable to review; if an applicant's claim fell within the scheme's provisions, it would be unlawful to withhold payment.[23] In practice, the CICB always regarded itself as bound to award compensation to anyone who met its conditions.[24] **1.11**

A more pragmatic reason for the choice of executive action was that the government intended the scheme to be an experiment that could be easily amended,[25] which necessarily precluded any move to establish it on a statutory basis. By the early 1980s the pressure for legislation had grown, leading to the enactment of the recommendations of the 1986 Home Office Working Party as sections 108–117 of the Criminal Justice Act 1988 (CJA 1988). However, it became clear during 1989 that their introduction would only exacerbate the serious difficulties that the CICB was then experiencing. **1.12**

Three factors had combined to present the CICB and the Home Office with an increasingly difficult task. First, in the decade between 1979–80 and 1988–89, the number of applications had nearly quadrupled, which meant that 'in simple terms, most victims can now expect to wait at least a year until their claim is met'.[26] Secondly, these increasing numbers were matched by the government's **1.13**

---

[19] ibid para 1.

[20] Ian Loader, 'In Search of Civic Policing: Recasting the 'Peelian' Principles' (2016) 10 *Criminal Law and Philosophy* 427–40. The state's obligations are formally recognized in the *Code of Practice for Victims of Crime* (Ministry of Justice 2015a).

[21] Hansard HC vol 697 cols 89–94 (24 June 1964).

[22] Home Office (1961) para 17.

[23] [1967] 2 QB 864, 883–88; *R v Criminal Injuries Compensation Board, ex parte P* [1994] 1 All ER 80 (CA).

[24] Home Office (1986) para 2.2.

[25] Home Office (1964) para 29; Home Office (1978).

[26] Home Affairs Select Committee (1990) para 5.

growing concern about its relative lack of financial control over the scheme's burgeoning cost. Expenditure was, in essence, demand led, and claims risk free. Based on the common law, the primary reason why the scheme would continue to be expensive was the virtually complete parallel between the levels set by judicial decisions governing the assessment of damages in personal injury litigation, and its awards for pain and suffering. Decision-making was complex and time-consuming, obscuring for applicants the basis on which their claims were resolved, and generating disparities between victims presenting similar injuries.[27] Accordingly, no commencement order was made, although some substantial procedural changes were made.[28]

1.14 The Home Office's 1993 review concluded that, as then structured, the scheme was 'inherently incapable of delivering the standard of service claimants should now reasonably expect—that is, a service which produces awards reasonably quickly, and in an understandable and predictable manner',[29] in particular where the application was refused or reduced. The remedy was to substitute for common law general damages, a tariff of awards that grouped injuries of comparable severity in payment bands, to which single fixed amounts could be allocated. Decisions in straightforward claims could be made speedily against publicly accessible injury descriptions and compensation levels. The absence of any discretion meant that decisions could be taken by relatively junior officials, and being no longer tied to increases in common law damages, the government could control exactly the tariff sums payable for each injury, which would be capped at £250,000. Its expectation was that this substitution would substantially meet its concerns about the scheme's management, transparency, and costs.

1.15 Undeterred by the immediate and widespread hostility that these and its associated proposals attracted, the government introduced a tariff scheme with effect from 1 April 1994. As this scheme contemplated a wholly different measure of compensation from that provided by sections 108–117 of the CJA 1988, its introduction made it impossible for the government to exercise its discretion under section 171(1) to bring them into force. In *R v Secretary of State for the Home Department, ex parte Fire Brigades Unions and Others,* the House of Lords held by a majority that it had acted unlawfully.[30]

C The statutory scheme

1 Administration and workload

1.16 The immediate consequence of the House of Lords' decision was the enactment of the Criminal Injuries Compensation Act 1995 (CICA 1995). Its purpose was

[27] Home Office (1993) para 11.
[28] These came into force on 1 April 1990, Hansard HC vol 163 cols 411–17 (8 December 1989).
[29] Home Office (1993) paras 2, 10–12.
[30] [1995] 2 AC 513 (HL).

to set 'the framework for an enhanced tariff scheme', that would provide 'the right balance between the needs of victims while protecting the interests of taxpayers'.[31] The reference to an 'enhanced' scheme signalled the government's retreat from its proposed exclusion of special damages for long term care;[32] it would instead continue to provide as compensation, 'additional payments' for loss of earnings, special expenses, and in fatal cases, for bereavement and loss of dependency.

Administered by the Criminal Injuries Compensation Authority (CICA),[33] a non-departmental public body sponsored then by the Home Office, and currently by the Ministry of Justice, the tariff scheme took effect from 1 April 1996. Replacing the unsatisfactory arrangement under which the CICB exercised both original and appellate jurisdiction, the Criminal Injuries Compensation Appeals Panel (CICAP) was established to hear appeals from the CICA's decisions. The CICAP's decisions were in turn, like the CICB's, subject to judicial review. These amendments were superseded in 2008 to provide for the more fundamental changes brought about by the Tribunals, Courts and Enforcement Act 2007, which transferred a reconstituted CICAP to the Tribunals Service in April 2006, as a part of the First-tier Tribunal (FTT, Social Entitlement Chamber (SEC)). A second major change was to bring the scheme's administrative officers' decisions within the jurisdiction of the Parliamentary and Health Service Ombudsman.[34] **1.17**

Applications and appeals lodged by 1 April 1996 continued to be heard by the CICB until it was wound up on 31 March 2000, when some 6,000 unresolved cases were transferred to the new statutory bodies. Following the 2001 revisions that gave effect to the National Audit Office's procedural recommendations,[35] the number of applications stood at just over 78,000, including both tariff and legacy common law scheme claims. Over the following five years, the CICA gradually managed to bring into balance the number of applications it received, which declined to just over 60,000 in 2006–2007, and the number of those it decided. But as the National Audit Office noted in its follow-up review in 2007, the time taken to reach those decisions remained stubbornly high.[36] Despite some improvements in the following years,[37] the 2012 consultation was also critical of the continuing delays in claims resolution.[38] **1.18**

2 Rethinking the purpose of compensation

So far as the levels of award were concerned, it had been clear since the introduction of the statutory scheme that the word 'compensation' should not be taken **1.19**

31 Hansard HL vol 566, col 292 (19 July 1995).
32 Home Office (1993) paras 21 and 25.
33 See now the 2012 Scheme, para 135.
34 CICA 1995 s 10; Parliamentary Commissioner Act 1967 s 11(b); CICA (2015) 11; (2016) 12.
35 National Audit Office (2000).
36 National Audit Office (2007).
37 CICA (2012) 9–10.
38 Ministry of Justice (2012a) Foreword 3.

to imply awards commensurate with those available in civil proceedings.[39] The logic of the tariff's disengagement from common law principles of assessment was explicit in the 2012 consultation's fundamental questioning of the purpose of compensation, at least for less serious criminal injuries, where immediate support would be more effective than payments that would take time to assess.[40] Concerned about the scheme's recurring costs, the government undertook reviews of its scope and tariff levels in 1999 and 2005. Their purpose was to radically simplify it, and to focus 'on the most serious cases'.[41]

1.20 Made chiefly for reasons of financial exigency, the immediate thrust of the proposals in the 2005 consultation was to reinforce the scheme's long-standing policy of compensating only innocent ('blameless') victims of crime, to remove some of the uncertainties concerning its scope, and to concentrate its reduced budget on injuries that had a more severe or long-lasting impact. Its publication coincided with the bombings on the London Underground and on a bus in Tavistock Square on 7 July 2005, which killed fifty-two people and injured some 700, but with the prospect of the inevitable criticism that would greet any proposals to curtail the scheme, there was little political appetite to progress its proposals.[42]

1.21 The questions that these reviews addressed were what ought to be the extent of the burden on the taxpayer in respect of the injuries, the persons, the heads of damage, and the levels of award that would be payable to qualifying applicants?[43] There is no single right answer here,[44] but the government's was that a revised scheme should be limited primarily to those injuries that directly arise from crimes of violence to the person, and not extend to those that are compensated under other statutory arrangements.

1.22 In order to protect payments to those most seriously affected by their injuries, to recognize public concern for particularly vulnerable groups and for those who have been the victims of particularly distressing crimes,[45] and to make the required £50 million cut in its expenditure, the 2012 consultation proposed radical changes. These envisaged the elimination of the lowest tariff bands (£1,000–£2,000), and the substitution of statutory sick pay for capped actual income as the rate at which the loss of earnings, of earning capacity, and dependency would be calculated.

---

[39] Home Office (1999) para 46.

[40] Ministry of Justice (2012b) Introduction para 4.

[41] Home Office (2005) 3, 18.

[42] David Miers, 'Rebuilding Lives: Operational and Policy Issues in the Compensation of Victims of Violent and Terrorist Crimes' [2006] *Criminal Law Review* 695.

[43] Ministry of Justice (2012b) para 2; Miers, 'Compensating Deserving Victims of Violent Crime' (n 3) 244.

[44] See the range of provision across the EU; European Commission Directorate-General Justice Freedom & Security (2008).

[45] Ministry of Justice (2012a) para 172; (2012b) para 150.

Given the essentially contested nature of criminal justice policy, these proposals were inevitably controversial, approved at the second attempt.[46] The 2012 Scheme was made on 13 November 2012, applying to all applications received on or after the date on which it came into force: 27 November 2012; that is, including applications relating to criminal injuries sustained before that date. Paragraphs 141–44 make transitional arrangements in the case of an application arising before that date which, according to the date on which it was received, fell within the terms of an earlier statutory, or the common law scheme. **1.23**

In terms of their operational impact, the cumulative effect of these reforms has substantially reduced the number of applicants eligible for compensation. In its first full year, 2013/2014, the number of applications had nearly halved, to 33,668, and in the succeeding two years, 32,595 and 32,415. Although it will fluctuate, depending on the level of violent crime, the number has stabilized: 32,280 in 2017–2018.[47] This 'steady decrease' in applications has led to a corresponding reduction in the number of appeals received.[48] Notwithstanding the elimination of those 'simple claims' that were valued at £2,000 or less, the average time taken to resolve claim remains at just over a year.[49] **1.24**

The 2012 reforms signalled a further shift in the scheme's evolving philosophy, limiting its scope primarily to the provision of a form of enhanced social security for seriously injured victims of violent crime: 'Eligible applicants will receive a clear, predictable sum that will supplement other amounts that they may receive from other sources, such as state benefits'.[50] CICA's mission 'is to provide a sensitive, efficient, and fair service to blameless victims of violent crime'.[51] In an echo of its earlier justifications, the 2012 Guide says: 'Although the size of the award varies to reflect the seriousness of the injury, we know that it will never fully compensate you for what you have suffered or lost—it is just society's way of recognizing that you have been a victim'.[52] This is a recognition that may be perceived as a 'dignified equivalent' for what has been lost, but that is not susceptible of economic assessment.[53] **1.25**

D Interpretation of the 2012 Scheme

When interpreting the common law scheme, the courts repeatedly said that it should not be approached as though it were a statute, but that the CICB members 'ought to be free to deal with [these] eventualities when they arise in a flexible **1.26**

---

[46] Hansard HC vol 552, col 940 (7 November 2012) and vol 553, cols 141 and 161 (12 and 13 November 2012).

[47] CICA (2014) 9; (2015) 9; CICA (2016) 9; (2018) 7.

[48] Senior President of Tribunals' Annual Report 2017, 38.

[49] CICA (2016) 9; (2017) 10.

[50] Hansard HC vol 553, col 161 (13 November 2012).

[51] CICA 2020 and 2017-18, *Business Plan.*

[52] CICA (2012 Guide).

[53] Viviana Zelizer, *The Social Meaning of Money* (Princeton University Press 1997) 20.

manner having regard to the whole object of the scheme'; it should be interpreted 'so as to give effect to its underlying policy, adopting the interpretation of a reasonable and literate man'.[54]

1.27 In common with its predecessors made under the CICA 1995, the 2012 Scheme is subordinate legislation within the meaning of section 21(1) of the Interpretation Act 1978. As the Court of Appeal emphasized in *Criminal Injuries Compensation Authority and First-tier Tribunal (SEC) (CIC) v Y*, whatever might have been its origins, it is important to underline that it 'must now be governed by the rules of statutory construction which apply to all such instrument and the observations that some different standard should be deployed no longer apply'.[55]

1.28 In essence, the 2012 Scheme is to be interpreted *sui generis*. Where its provisions touch upon common law principles or authority the Upper Tribunal has been clear that it is not appropriate to try to fit the scheme 'into a pre-conceived "common law" model', a view unequivocally endorsed by the Court of Appeal. The CICA 1995 expressly requires compensation to be determined in accordance with the scheme;[56] in common with any other provision in a statutory scheme, it is to be interpreted 'at least as a starting point, by reference to the ordinary meaning of the words used', and should 'be construed both in the context of the Scheme as a whole, and with due regard to its evident purpose'.[57]

1.29 This 'does not require the exercise to be conducted in a straitjacket or mean that no help can be gained where appropriate from the wisdom reflected in authorities at the highest level dealing with similar issues'.[58] There may be instructive analogies to be drawn from that model, but care should be exercised in doing so, as both the Upper Tribunal and the Court of Appeal have cautioned. In *Criminal Injuries Compensation Authority v First-tier Tribunal and AS*, the Upper Tribunal held that in construing the meaning of 'intent' in Annex B paragraph 4(1)(b), the criminal law authorities 'may provide assistance but only insofar as these illuminate the natural meaning of the words in the 2012 Scheme'.[59] It should be interpreted 'without being distracted by an inappropriate endeavour to fit the statutory scheme within the confines of some analogous legal context, either at common law or (as in this case) under the Limitation Acts'.[60]

---

54 *R v Criminal Injuries Compensation Board, ex parte Schofield* [1971] 2 All ER 1011 (CA) (Bridge J); *R v Criminal Injuries Compensation Board, ex parte Webb* [1987] QB 74, 77 (CA) (Lawton LJ); *Cozens v Brutus* [1973] AC 854 (HL).

55 [2014] EWCA Civ 139, [2017] 4 WLR 60 [24] (CA) (Leveson P) (*CICA v Y*).

56 ibid [25].

57 *Colefax v FTT and CICA* [2014] EWCA Civ 945, [2015] 1 WLR 35 [16]–[17] (CA) (Briggs LJ) (*Colefax v CICA*).

58 *Rust-Andrews v First-tier Tribunal* [2011] EWCA Civ 1548, [2012] AACR 33 [34] (CA) (Carnwath LJ).

59 [2017] UKUT 43 (AAC) [57], [70] (Judge Knowles QC).

60 *Colefax v CICA* (n 57) [16].

Similarly, on the value of any analogy with the principles of the law of tort governing liability to secondary victims, Laws LJ observed: 'I consider with respect that some caution needs to be exercised in drawing assistance from the common law cases in tort in relation to "immediate aftermath". It is important that the decision maker should not be distracted from applying the ordinary meaning of the scheme's words'.[61] While the court's task is to interpret the scheme on its own terms, and there are different public interests in play as between tort and criminal law, there can, in its interpretation nevertheless, be 'merit of providing coherence between the civil and criminal law'.[62] **1.30**

The 2012 Scheme contains five appendices, which, in addition to setting out the full tariff, provide detailed interpretation of some of its defining terms. The scheme initially required the CICA to publish a guide to its operation, which, in addition to explaining the procedures for dealing with applications, 'will set out, where appropriate, the criteria by which decisions will normally be reached'. The guide is now digital, available on its website. Its details, and those of the guides to the earlier schemes, can be found in section 1.2 of the Bibliography. **1.31**

The guide's status as an interpretive document was considered by the Upper Tribunal in *AA v First-tier Tribunal (CIC)* in connection with the 2008 Scheme, and it is suggested that its conclusions equally apply to the 2012 Guide. As an explanation of how the CICA deals with claims, the guide can be 'an aid to transparent and consistent decision making'. Its guidance sets out the way claims officers should exercise their discretion, but 'at the very most' this can only be a starting point; consistent with ordinary principles of public law it cannot fetter that discretion. The guide is not part of the scheme and does not bind the CICA; still less courts or tribunals. It follows that '[w]here there is a difference between the Scheme and the Guidance, the Scheme prevails'.[63] It may assist a lay audience, but its terms cannot supplant those of the scheme.[64] **1.32**

E Precedent in the Upper Tribunal

In hearing appeals from the CICA's decisions and in deciding issues raised by way of judicial review, the First-tier Tribunal and the Upper Tribunal are necessarily bound on those issues by decisions of the Court of Appeal and the Supreme Court. The Upper Tribunal is bound by decisions of the High Court when exercising its supervisory jurisdiction over that tribunal, but not where the tribunal is effectively exercising a jurisdiction formerly exercised by the High Court, or a division of the High Court is dealing with an analogous but not exact equivalent **1.33**

[61] *Criminal Injuries Compensation Authority v RS* [2013] EWCA Civ 1040, [2014] 1 WLR 1313 [19] (CA).

[62] *CP v First-tier Tribunal (CIC)* [2014] EWCA Civ 1554, [2015] QB 459 [47] (CA) (Treacy LJ).

[63] *AA v First-tier Tribunal (CIC)* [2014] UKUT 211 [12]–[15] (Judge Lane).

[64] *AG v First-tier Tribunal and CICA* [2013] UKUT402 (AAC) [21] (Judge Jacobs).

issue.[65] It is a court of coordinate jurisdiction with the Outer House of the Court of Session hearing a petition for judicial review, with the effect that their decisions are entitled 'to equal respect'.[66]

1.34 Upper Tribunal decisions are reported in the Administrative Appeals Chamber Reports (AACR), but only if they command the general assent of the majority of the permanent judges of the Administrative Appeals Chamber of the Upper Tribunal (AAC). The tribunal generally follows its own decisions on matters of legal principle; more accurately, that part of its decision that is both on a point of legal principle and vital to the decision reached. Other comments are to be regarded as merely persuasive, although the weight to be attached to them will depend on the customary factors relating to their cogency, and the reliance that the tribunal placed upon them.

1.35 A single judge of the Upper Tribunal will not follow a decision of another single judge if satisfied that it was wrong, but must follow a decision of a three-judge panel. This is a panel appointed in a case where the Senior President of Tribunals or the Chamber President considers that the matter involves a question of law of special difficulty or an important point of principle or practice, or it is otherwise appropriate so to be decided.[67] A three-judge panel will generally follow a decision of another three-judge panel but will not do so if satisfied that it was wrong.

1.36 The application of the scheme necessarily includes its susceptibility to any one of its provisions being found to be incompatible with the UK's obligations under the European Convention on Human Rights. In *Secretary of State for Work and Pensions v Carmichael and Sefton MBC (HB)*, a three-judge panel of the Upper Tribunal held that

> courts and tribunals ultimately have the power to determine and so order or direct that to the extent that subordinate legislation is incompatible with a person's Convention rights it should not be given effect to in determining the person's lawful entitlement, or should be otherwise applied or disapplied in a way that does not breach the person's Convention rights.[68]

There have been a number of challenges based on the Convention that are discussed in the text.

1.37 As is the case for all domestic courts, when 'determining a question which has arisen in connection with a Convention right' the Upper Tribunal 'must take into

---

[65] *H v First-tier Tribunal and Criminal Injuries Compensation Authority* [2014] UKUT 338 (AAC) (Judge Levenson). These sections draw on Mark Rowland and Robin White, *Social Security Legislation 2017/18, Volume III: Administration, Adjudication and the European Dimension* (Sweet & Maxwell 2017) 1530–35.

[66] *MM v Criminal Injuries Compensation Authority* [2018] CSOH 63, 2018 WL 02942739 [8].

[67] Tribunals Judiciary, *Practice Statement* (2014).

[68] [2017] UKUT 174 (AAC) [62] (Charles J, Judge Lloyd-Davies, and Judge Wikeley); see *JT v CICA* 2 (n 16) [123]–[128].

account' decisions of the European Court of Human Rights, but is not bound by them. At the time of writing it continues to be bound by decisions of the Court of Justice of the European Union where European Union law impinges on the scheme's provisions.

III Making Offenders Pay for Their Crimes

A Justifications

Unlike taxpayer funded compensation for criminal injuries, there has been relatively little controversy concerning the principle that the state should maintain, and amend to their benefit, arrangements designed to promote a greater incidence of offender funded compensation for victims of crime. The legal and moral norms that justify this principle are typically questioned only where they are indeterminate, for example as to the definition of the harm in question, or where the offender offers some relevant excusing condition. Otherwise it has generally been accepted that victims have a right to be compensated by those who cause them personal injury, and that the courts (or other specified bodies) have both the authority and the obligation to enforce that right where the offender's liability is determined according to law. This right sounds most strongly in private law, where intentional crimes of violence against the person can be pursued as civil actions for damages, as an intentional tort to the person.[69] **1.38**

B Compensation orders

While the principle of offender compensation to the victim is clear, the issue has always been with its implementation. Successful personal injury litigation against an offender is rare, not least because he is likely to be impecunious. It was to fill the gap between the victim's theoretical private remedy and its enforcement that the state committed public funds. But even where the possibility arises, victims' objectives may be as much to achieve a finding of responsibility against their offenders, as to secure an award of damages. Even where they can pay only a limited amount, victims may prefer offender compensation to financial compensation by the state, because it nevertheless constitutes the offender's recognition of the harm done. **1.39**

Alongside the private remedy, courts of criminal jurisdiction have since 1972 had powers to require offenders convicted of offences causing personal injury **1.40**

[69] David Miers, 'State Compensation for Victims of Violent Crime' in Inge Vanfraechem, Anthony Pemberton, and Felix Ndahinda (eds), *Justice for Victims: Perspectives on Rights, Transition and Reconciliation* (Routledge 2014) 105–39.

to compensate their victims. These arrangements have not been without their share of contentious issues, which centre on a number of inter-connected considerations.

1.41 First, whose should be the responsibility to collate and present the victim's claim at the trial, and upon what quality of evidence should the court proceed to order compensation? Secondly, upon what basis is the level of compensation to be determined and, in particular, given that a lack of means is a condition that equally affects the making of a compensation order, what ought to be the relationship between the ideal assessment of the victim's loss or injury, and the amount of compensation that the offender can afford? A third consideration, which reflects the common law's traditional understanding that the award of financial compensation for injuries wrongfully inflicted, is, classically, a domain of tort law,[70] is the Court of Appeal's continued cautionary advice to trial judges, not to make compensation orders in any other than simple and straightforward cases. Lastly, what is the place of victim compensation by the offender within the full range of the penal system's objectives, and how should conflicts between them be resolved as a matter both of theory and sentencing practice?

C Restorative justice

1.42 Compensation orders give effect to the traditional common law conception of a monetary payment for the injuries that the offender has caused. This conception, which relies on the sufficiency of the offender's financial circumstances, can be distinguished from a broader understanding of offender compensation that involves the reallocation of the offender's time and labour, typically to be found in restorative justice outcomes. There is good evidence that victims place value on what offenders can *do* by way of compensating behaviour, rather than what they can afford to pay.[71] Offenders' time and labour could be monetized, but the distinction is not simply instrumental. Victims may perceive money payments, like fines, simply as a tax on conduct, but which, because they are not normatively equivalent to the redistribution of the offender's wealth as measured by their time and labour, do not 'compensate' for the moral harm implicit in the offence.[72] This is a disposal that deprives offenders of the freedom to do as they please, and from which they cannot purchase their freedom. More bluntly, restorative justice's function is both to assert a moral rebalancing between their offending and the harm they caused, and for the state to show offenders that unpleasant actions have unpleasant consequences for them as well as for their victims.

---

[70] Mathew Dyson and John Randall, 'England's Splendid Isolation' in Matthew Dyson (ed), *Comparing Tort and Crime* (Cambridge University Press 2015) 54.

[71] Heather Strang, *Repair or Revenge: Victims and Restorative Justice* (Oxford University Press 2002) 8–24.

[72] Gerry Johnstone, *Restorative Justice: Ideas, Values, Debates* (Willan Publishing 2002) 74–76.

There is a very substantial literature that aims to trace the development of restorative justice across different times and communities, to identify the principles that underlie and that differentiate it from the conventional criminal justice responses to offensive behaviour, to agree its operating arrangements both outside and within existing legal structures, and to promote its values of mutual understanding and reconciliation as a more effective, and possibly transformative, means of addressing in particular ethnic or sectarian conflict. Closer to the themes in this book, restorative justice practice has been presented as a means whereby the victim's and offender's conflict could be wrested from a proprietorial and obtuse criminal justice system so that, as the parties to that conflict, they themselves enjoy the power to resolve it.[73] **1.43**

As is the case with compensation orders, a number of inter-connected issues arise for the courts, and for the other criminal justice agencies, that order restorative justice disposals. Operational issues centre on when, for what offences, and subject to what governance arrangements, restorative justice should be available. The theoretical issues have remained less tractable, centred primarily on the divergent values implicit in the public as distinct from the private resolution of offensive behaviours. It is not possible here even to begin a review of the literature that addresses these issues.[74] My aim in this book is more modest: to identify the limited possibilities for monetary compensation by the offender provided by the current law and practice on restorative justice. **1.44**

---

[73] Nils Christie, 'Conflicts as Property' (1977) 17 *British Journal of Criminology* 1.

[74] Joanna Shapland, 'Implications of Growth: Challenges for Restorative Justice' (2014) 20 *International Review of Victimology* 111; David Miers, 'Restorative Justice as a Boundary Object: Some Critical Reflections on the Rise and Influence of Restorative Justice in England and Wales' in Sandra Walklate and Dale Spencer (eds), *Critical Victimology: Reconceptualizations, Interventions, and Possibilities* (Lexington Books 2016) 95–110.

Part I

2

CRIMINAL INJURIES
Victimizing Events

I Introduction

Claims under the Criminal Injuries Compensation Scheme 2012 (the 2012 Scheme) are made in respect of 'a criminal injury'; that is, 'an injury which appears in Part A or B of the tariff in Annex E' (Annex A). These differentiate the tariff levels that apply respectively to 'the amount payable in respect of physical and mental injuries', and to 'the amount payable in respect of fatal injuries, sexual and physical abuse'. A criminal injury may be the result of a crime of violence (paragraph 4), an act of law enforcement in which the applicant was taking an exceptional and justifiable risk (paragraph 5), or being present at and witnessing an incident or its immediate aftermath in which an applicant's 'loved one' sustained a criminal injury (paragraph 6). **2.01**

In order to exert greater financial control over its costs, the government's objective was to confine eligibility to the scheme's 'core purpose': 'to provide payments to those who suffer serious physical or mental injury as the direct result of deliberate violent crime, including sexual offences, of which they are the innocent victim'.[1] **2.02**

[1] Ministry of Justice (2012a) para 178, (2012b) para 160.

To achieve this, the 2012 Scheme makes a number of substantial changes to the scope of its statutory predecessors.

II Paragraph 4: A Crime of Violence

2.03 Paragraph 4 provides: 'A person may be eligible for an award under this Scheme if they sustain a criminal injury which is directly attributable to their being a direct victim of a crime of violence committed in a relevant place'. None of the earlier schemes defined the phrase 'a crime of violence'. As the vast majority of claims are the result of indisputable instances of such offences, there may have seemed little point in undertaking a definitional exercise that presents some complexity.[2] But there are good reasons why the scheme should provide some certainty on this defining condition of eligibility. One is a matter of practical client advice: many applications are rejected precisely because the injury was not the result of a crime of violence. A second reason is that 'the need for a clear definition of a crime of violence' is a way of indicating that the scheme 'should not be regarded as underwriting any injury loosely connected with a breach of the criminal law'.[3] The broader the scope of the scheme, the greater the burden on the taxpayer; accordingly, any question concerning its scope is 'a matter of policy rather than something directly dictated by the criminal law'.[4]

2.04 As used in the common law scheme, this phrase was not a term of art, but as the Court of Appeal held in *R v Criminal Injuries Compensation Board, ex parte Webb*, a 'jury question'.[5] But in its interpretation within the statutory scheme it would, as Lord Hope said in *Jones v First-tier Tribunal (SEC)*, 'be more accurate to say that it is for the tribunal which decides the case to consider whether the words "a crime of violence" do or do not apply to the facts which have been proved'.[6] The generic answer distinguishes the 'nature' of a crime of violence from its 'consequences'. A more particular answer, and here it breaks with its predecessors, is the 2012 Scheme's categorization of those victimizing events that are either to be included in, or excluded from, its scope, and the omission of two long-standing criminal injuries.

A The nature and the consequences of a crime of violence

2.05 The definitional question, what constituted 'a crime of violence' under paragraph 4 of the common law scheme, was first confronted in *R v Criminal Injuries*

2 Ministry of Justice (2012a) para 176.
3 Home Office (1986) para 4.4.
4 Ministry of Justice (2012a) para 177.
5 [1987] 1 QB 74, 77G (CA) (*ex parte Webb*).
6 [2013] UKSC 192, [2013] 2 AC 48 [16] (SC) (*Jones*).

Compensation Board, ex parte Clowes.[7] The Criminal Injuries Compensation Board (CICB) rejected a claim based on injuries sustained in an explosion that followed the deceased's breaking open of a gas main, contrary to section 1(1) of the Criminal Damage Act 1971 (CDA 1971), in order to commit suicide. First, the scheme did not apply to crimes against property, notwithstanding that violence was used in their commission. Secondly, even if the facts of the applicant's injury could be regarded as being within the scope of an offence against the person, for example, sections 20 or 23 of the Offences Against the Person Act 1861 (OAPA 1861), the CICB concluded that the deceased had not formed, prior to his death, the requisite fault element for either of them. The Divisional Court agreed that the expression 'a crime of violence' connoted violence to a person, but also held by a majority that this could include an offence against property where its commission had violent *consequences* for the applicant. Provided that the 'assailant' had or could be inferred to have had the requisite fault element,[8] in this case of intending or being reckless as to whether the life of another would be endangered by the damage or destruction (CDA 1971 section 1(2)), the resulting injury could fall within the scheme. Dissenting on this point, Lord Widgery CJ preferred the CICB's approach, which he considered more closely gave effect to the scheme's purpose, to compensate for acts of criminal violence directed against the person. The phrase 'should mean a crime of which violence is an essential ingredient'.[9]

Whether paragraph 4 extended to a crime that had violent consequences, but in which violence to a person is not one of its 'essential ingredients', was the central issue in the test case, *ex parte Webb*. This concerned claims made by train drivers in respect of the mental injuries they sustained when witnessing persons who, theoretically guilty of an offence under section 34 of the OAPA 1881,[10] had committed, or were in the act of committing, suicide on the railway track. Encouraged by *dicta* in an earlier claim on similar facts, *R v Criminal Injuries Compensation Board, ex parte Parsons,* in which the Court of Appeal commented that 'it was perhaps stretching the phraseology a little to describe an offence under section 34 as a crime of violence',[11] the CICB refused their applications. The Divisional Court rejected the argument that 'what matters is the impact on the victim, not the intent of the offender', preferring the CICB's position, that a crime of violence is 'one where the definition of the crime itself involves either direct infliction of **2.06**

[7] [1977] 1 WLR 1353 (DC) (*ex parte Clowes*).

[8] By Annex A of the 2012 Scheme, 'assailant' means 'a person responsible for the criminal injury which is the subject of the application'.

[9] *Ex parte Clowes* (n 7) 1364.

[10] 'Whosoever, by any unlawful act, or by any wilful omission or neglect, shall endanger or cause to be endangered the safety of any person conveyed or being in or upon a railway, or shall aid or assist therein, shall be guilty of a misdemeanour.'

[11] See the Divisional Court judgment in *R v Criminal Injuries Compensation Board, ex parte Webb* [1986] QB 184, 191–93 (DC).

force on the victim, or at least a hostile act directed towards the victim or class of victim'.[12] The Court of Appeal agreed, but did not attempt a definition; it was for the CICB to decide 'whether unlawful conduct because of its nature, not its consequence, amounts to a crime of violence'.[13]

2.07 In *R v Criminal Injuries Compensation Appeal Panel, ex parte August and Brown,* the Court of Appeal expressly approved Lawton LJ's formulation in *ex parte Webb* as being applicable to the statutory scheme. The correct approach was not to classify particular offences as crimes of violence, but to decide in each case whether the events that occurred were (a) a crime, and (b) a crime of violence; for this purpose, 'it is necessary to look at the nature and not the consequences of the unlawful conduct'.[14] This distinction was central to the Supreme Court's decision in *Jones*, where Lord Hope expressly approved the Court of Appeal's formulation in these two decisions. Built into the phrase, 'a crime of violence', 'there are two questions that the tribunal must consider. The first is whether, having regard to the facts which have been proved, a criminal offence has been committed. The second is whether, having regard to the nature of the criminal act, the offence that was committed was a crime of violence'.[15]

2.08 In *Jones* the driver of an articulated lorry swerved in an unsuccessful attempt to avoid hitting a man who had suddenly run into the road, and stood in front of it in order to commit suicide. The man was killed and the lorry collided with another vehicle driven by the claimant, who suffered catastrophic injuries. The application was made under the 2001 Scheme, paragraph 8(a) of which simply provided that the 'criminal injury' be directly attributable to 'a crime of violence'. The Criminal Injuries Compensation Authority (CICA) rejected the claim, the First-tier Tribunal (FTT) agreeing that, as the deceased's primary aim had been to commit suicide, and there was no evidence that he had intended to cause harm or been reckless as to whether harm might be caused to others, there was no offence under section 20 of the OAPA 1861. The Upper Tribunal found no fault with the FTT's decision, but it was reversed by the Court of Appeal, which held that its emphasis on 'the need to demonstrate a hostile act directed towards the victim' expressed the test too narrowly'.[16]

2.09 *Jones* raised three issues, two substantive and one jurisdictional. The substantive issues were: in running into the road did the deceased commit the *actus reus* of a crime, and if so, was it a crime of violence, and, secondly, did he have the relevant *mens rea* of that crime? I deal with the former issue here, and the fault element below (2.66–2.68). I deal in Chapter 6.178–6.184 with the role of an

[12] ibid 195.
[13] *Ex parte Webb* (n 5) 79–80 (CA) (Lawton LJ).
[14] [2001] QB 774 [24] (CA) (Buxton LJ) (*ex parte August and Brown*).
[15] *Jones* (n 6) [16].
[16] [2011] EWCA Civ 400, [2012] QB 345 [28] (CA) (Patten LJ).

appeal court in dealing with issues of fact that have been left for determination of specialist appellate tribunals.

Giving the leading judgment, Lord Hope confirmed the distinction between the nature and the consequences of the act: **2.10**

> [t]he question whether a criminal offence has been committed is a question for the tribunal, having informed itself as to what the law requires for proof of that offence, to determine as a matter of fact. The question whether the nature of the criminal act amounted to a crime of violence may or may not raise an issue of fact for the tribunal to determine. This will depend on what the law requires for proof of the offence.[17]

For instance, the violent consequence that the frail and elderly householder suffered where, in *Watson*, he died from a heart attack shortly after his house had been burgled,[18] could not fall within the scheme if burglary were the only offence committed; it could be otherwise if there had been a threat (2.28–2.40) or the use of violence against him (2.17–2.22).

Jones decisively confirms, first, the 'well-established case law to the effect that it is the nature of the crime and not its consequences which need to be considered'.[19] In *HW v First-tier Tribunal (SEC)* the FTT allowed an appeal in which a taxi driver claimed for the anxiety and stress he suffered as a result of his arrest following a passenger's false allegation of rape. This was a conclusion that the Upper Tribunal could not support. The consequences of the passenger's perjury may have entailed a great deal of suffering, but 'the nature of the offence could not reasonably be described as a crime of violence'.[20] **2.11**

Secondly, *Jones* confirms that 'a crime does not become a crime of violence simply because it results in injury to the person'.[21] The distinction between the nature and the consequences of the offence has been central to a number of claims brought under the earlier tariff schemes, where personal injuries were caused by dog attacks in circumstances amounting to an offence under section 3(1) of the Dangerous Dogs Act 1991 (DDA 1991). Its owner, or person for the time being in charge, is guilty of an offence 'if a dog is dangerously out of control in a public place', and of an aggravated offence 'if the dog while so out of control injures any person'. The issue in these claims was whether the offence was, by virtue of the injuries the victim sustained, a crime of violence. **2.12**

---

[17] *Jones* (n 6) [17].

[18] [1989] 2 All ER 865 (CA).

[19] *Criminal Injuries Compensation Authority v First-tier Tribunal and AS* [2017] UKUT 43 (AAC) [58]–[59] (Judge Knowles QC) (*CICA v AS*).

[20] [2010] UKUT (AAC) 199 [27] (Nicol J) (*HW v FTT*).

[21] *Criminal Injuries Compensation Authority v First-tier Tribunal and FC (CIC)* [2014] UKUT 555 AAC [18] (Judge Wikeley).

2.13 The key point here is the Court of Appeal's clear restatement of the distinction in *Criminal Injuries Compensation Authority v First-tier Tribunal (SEC) and TS*,[22] and its application in *R (NJ) v First-tier Tribunal and Criminal Injuries Compensation Authority (CIC)*. There, the Upper Tribunal held that the Court of Appeal's decision is authority for the proposition that the simple offence in section 3(1) of the DDA 1991 'is not by its *nature* (as opposed to its *consequences*) necessarily a crime of violence' (original emphasis). The 'crux' of the question before the Upper Tribunal was whether, in Lord Hope's words in *Jones*, '*having regard to the nature of the criminal act*, the offence that was committed was a crime of violence' (emphasis added).[23] In contrast, the aggravated offence under section 3(1) does require that a person is injured; in this case, 'the consequences of the offence are "an integral element" of the definition of the respective offences under section 3(1) (and hence of their nature)', and thus may be a crime of violence.[24]

2.14 Finally, while acknowledging that it is for the CICA or the FTT to determine whether there was a crime of violence, Lord Hope held in *Jones* that 'the words of the statute admit of only one answer. They speak for themselves'; in short, 'the crime that s 20 defines will always amount to a crime of violence for the purposes of the scheme for compensation for criminal injury'. As Lord Hope commented, such categorical assertion may not be possible in the case of the quite loosely defined common law crimes known to the law of Scotland.[25] It may also be respectfully suggested that the same assertion in respect of the law of England and Wales appears to foreclose the very decision that the Supreme Court held falls to the tribunal of fact to decide.

B Annex B: specific instances of a crime of violence

2.15 The 2012 Guide says only: 'There is no legal definition of the term 'a crime of violence'. But in pursuit of the government's wish to control eligibility more tightly, Annex B paragraph 2(1) provides that 'a "crime of violence" is a crime which involves' any one of five specific victimizing events, and by paragraph 2(4), five injuries that will not be considered to have been the result of a crime of violence (2.65–2.94).

2.16 Three preliminary points concerning paragraph 2(1) may be noted. The use of the verb 'involves' rather than 'includes' suggests that the list is intended to be exhaustive. Secondly, by Annex B paragraph 1 'where a claims officer is satisfied that a crime has been committed it is still necessary for that crime to constitute a crime of violence in accordance with this Annex'. Thirdly, by paragraph 2(2), 'an

22 [2014] EWCA Civ 65, [2014] PIQR P10 [23] (CA) (*CICA v TS*).
23 [2015] AACR 42 [14] (Judge Wikeley) (*NJ v FTT*).
24 ibid [26].
25 *Jones* (n 6) [17]–[18].

act or omission under sub-paragraph (1) will not constitute a crime of violence unless it is done either intentionally or recklessly'.

1 Annex B paragraph 2(1)(a): 'A physical attack'

By paragraph 2(1)(a) 'a "crime of violence" is a crime which involves: "a physical attack"'. This is undefined, but as an ordinary phrase of the English language its scope is a matter for the tribunal of fact to determine in each case.[26] The vast majority of criminal injury claims are based on the assailant's physical attack on the victim, of more recent prominence, by means of an acid attack causing disfigurement or visual impairment.[27] Depending on the severity of the injury and the assailant's *mens rea*, these attacks will constitute an offence under sections 18, 20, or 47 of the OAPA 1861.[28] An offence under section 1(1) of the Female Genital Mutilation Act 2003 (FGMA 2003) should also be regarded as a physical attack; if not, then certainly as an act of 'a violent nature which causes physical injury to a person' under Annex B paragraph 2(1)(b) (2.23–2.27). **2.17**

A personal injury is not a criminal injury where it is caused by a breach of rules under which the 'offender' may be punished, if that breach cannot be construed as constituting the external elements of a crime of violence. If a prison officer strains his back trying to carry a heavy and uncooperative prisoner, there is no act or omission on the part of the prisoner which can render this a criminal injury, no matter how much the prisoner may desire the officer to hurt himself in the process, and irrespective of the fact that the prisoner's refusal to comply with the officer's instruction to move itself involved a breach of the prison rules.[29] But if the prisoner had made some move to obstruct the officer, intending to bring about the particular kind of harm that was in fact done, or foreseeing that some physical harm to some person, albeit of a minor character, might result, the risk of which he had then taken, he would have acted 'maliciously' for the purpose of section 20 of the OAPA 1861.[30] **2.18**

A person is guilty of assault if he intentionally or recklessly causes another to apprehend that the latter will suffer immediate and unlawful violence. While it is a crime, an assault alone, however threatening, will not constitute 'a physical attack', although it may, where the victim fears the application to him of that violence, fall within Annex B paragraph 2(1)(c). **2.19**

A battery does involve the application of unlawful force to another, and where it is directly inflicted, would constitute a physical attack. The slightest degree of **2.20**

[26] *Cozens v Brutus* [1973] AC 854 (HL); *Jones* (n 6) [17].
[27] OAPA 1861 s 29 (use of a corrosive fluid to burn, maim, disfigure, disable, or to do some grievous bodily harm to any person).
[28] Ministry of Justice (2012a) para 179.
[29] *R v Criminal Injuries Compensation Board, ex parte Penny* [1982] Crim LR 298.
[30] *Savage and Parmenter* [1992] 1 AC 699 (HL); *Jones* (n 6) [9]–[11].

force, such as grabbing a person's arm, is sufficient for the offence, although any resulting injury might well be insufficient to come within the tariff. As to the fault element in the case of a claim based on section 47 of the OAPA 1861,[31] it is sufficient that the CICA is satisfied that the assailant had the *mens rea* of assault; it is not necessary that the assailant intended or foresaw a risk of actual bodily harm to that person.[32] In determining whether the assailant was reckless for the purposes of assault or battery, or for offences under sections 20 and 47 of the OAPA 1861, the CICA is bound to follow *R v G and R*,[33] overruling *DPP v Caldwell*.[34]

2.21 An offence of murder by means of a physical attack will clearly constitute a crime of violence. Offences against the person that result in death, but in respect of which the assailant had no intention of causing death or grievous (or really serious) bodily harm,[35] may constitute an offence of manslaughter by the commission of an unlawful and dangerous act. On the assumption that the unlawful act is a 'physical attack', that the assailant had the *mens rea* of an offence, typically sections 20 or 47 of the OAPA 1861, and that the act was objectively dangerous,[36] an offence of constructive manslaughter will be a crime of violence. This form of involuntary manslaughter does not appear to require that the unlawful and dangerous act be directed at the victim,[37] but for the purpose of Annex B paragraph 2(a)(a), paragraph 4 of the 2012 Scheme requires the applicant to be 'a direct victim', suggesting in this case the contrary.

2.22 As Annex B paragraph 2(2)) provides, recklessness is the minimum level of fault. Although an injury is consistent with conduct constituting the external element of an offence such as sections 20 or 47 of the OAPA 1861, and could, if accompanied by the assailant's recklessness (or intention) amount to a physical attack, it will not constitute a criminal injury if it was only negligently inflicted. For example, applications that were heard by the CICB, in which applicants were knocked over by another skater, breaking their leg on the ice, had their fingers crushed by a hinged drainage gate another person had dropped, or were struck by a javelin thrown during a school sports day, all failed because the injuries were only negligently inflicted.[38]

---

[31] 'Bodily harm' in s 47 includes 'any hurt or injury calculated to interfere with the health and comfort of the victim', which must not be so trivial as to be insignificant; *BM* [2018] EWCA Crim 560, 2018 WL 01428152 [22] (CA) (*BM*).

[32] *Cunningham* [1957] 2 QB 396 (CA).

[33] [2003] UKHL 50, [2004] 1 AC 1034 (HL).

[34] [1982] AC 341 (HL).

[35] *Rahman* [2008] UKHL 45, [2009] 1 AC 129 (HL).

[36] *Church* [1966] 1 QB 59 (CA).

[37] Richard Card and Jill Molloy, *Card, Cross & Jones, Criminal law* (22nd edn, Oxford University Press 2016) 254–65 (Card and Molloy, *Criminal Law*).

[38] CICB, 22nd Report (Cm 42 1986) para 16; 25th Report (Cm 900 1989) paras 16.3–16.4; 21st Report (Cmnd 9684 1985) para 20, respectively.

2 Annex B paragraph 2(1)(b): 'Any other act or omission of a violent nature which causes physical injury to a person'

Having established in paragraph 2(1)(a) the paradigm case of a crime of violence, paragraph 2(1)(b) contemplates a limited extension upon it: physical injuries directly attributable to acts or omissions that constitute crimes which are violent in their 'nature', but which do not of themselves consist of 'a physical attack'. It is clear from the Upper Tribunal's decision in *CICA v AS* that 'the requirement from earlier case law and from *Jones* that it is the nature of the act or omission which is significant is incorporated into the wording of the 2012 Scheme'.[39] Paragraph 2(1)(b) does not extend to those offences that, although they have violent consequences, do not include them as an element of the *actus reus* of the offence; that is, as one of its 'essential ingredients'.[40] **2.23**

This paragraph also contemplates a wider range of (physical) injuries than those that might be caused by the 'physical attack' that is the subject of paragraph 2(1)(a). That phrase might be taken to imply a closer physical engagement between the victim and the assailant than an 'act or omission of a violent nature'; for example, an injury being caused by being struck at a distance by a catapulted stone,[41] by an object thrown at the victim from a moving car, by masonry being dropped from a bridge onto cars passing below,[42] or by 'a hostile act directed towards a class of victim', for example where the accused sprays acid over a number of people in a crowded space, or by his conduct causes them to be injured as they seek to escape.[43] These actions would all comprise offences under the OAPA 1861, and while the physical injuries sustained could be regarded as being directly attributable to acts or omissions 'of a violent nature', they might not necessarily comprise 'a physical attack'. **2.24**

The external elements of the crime that triggers paragraph 2(1)(b) will typically comprise acts rather than omissions, and it is perhaps difficult to envisage a wounding by omission.[44] But suppose an offender hid in his clothing a razor blade, an open knife, or a hypodermic needle, and when asked by a police officer conducting a 'pat down' search, either denied their presence or did not warn the police officer, the resulting injury could prompt a conviction under section 47 of the OAPA 1861, the offender being reckless as to whether the officer would injure himself.[45] Section 47 does not require a violent act or omission,[46] but where the offender's actions have created a dangerous situation, his denial, silence, or failure to correct it could, following *Miller*,[47] constitute the *actus reus* of a section **2.25**

[39] *CICA v AS* (n 19) [60] (Judge Knowles QC).
[40] Ministry of Justice (2012a) para 179.
[41] CICAP (2005) 19.
[42] *Webster and Warwick* [1995] 2 All ER 168 (CA).
[43] *Martin* (1881) 8 QBD 54.
[44] Card and Molloy, *Criminal Law* (n 37) 189 n 266.
[45] *Santana-Bermudez* [2003] EWHC 2908 (Admin), [2004] Crim LR 471 (DC).
[46] *DPP v Smith* [2006] EWHC 94 (Admin), [2006] 2 All ER 16 (DC).
[47] [1983] 2 AC 161 (HL).

47 offence where the offender had the relevant *mens rea* when he omitted to neutralize the danger.[48]

2.26 The criminal law punishes omissions where the definition of the offence specifies that it is committed by a failure to act, or where the offender is under a legal duty to act and failed to do so. For the purposes of the 2012 Scheme, where physical injury flows from these omissions, the failure must be either intentional or reckless. An offence of cruelty to children under the age of 16 in section 1 of the Children and Young Persons Act 1933 includes neglect and wilful assault 'in a manner likely to cause 'unnecessary suffering or injury to health including any mental derangement'. Physical injury caused by neglect of the child will not fall within paragraph 2(1)(b), but wilful assault causing physical or psychological injury will fall within paragraph 2(1)(a).[49]

2.27 The criminal injury in paragraph 2(1)(a) is defined by reference to the incident in which the injury is sustained—'a physical attack'. The criminal injury in paragraph 2(1)(b) is defined in part by reference to the incident—'any other act or omission of a violent nature'—and in part to the injury sustained, which must be 'a physical injury'. An offender who remotely detonates a bomb on a bus or a train, causing personal injuries to its passengers, would surely be regarded as committing an act 'of a violent nature', but there might be doubt as to whether, because the offender was not present at the scene, the passengers could be said to have been physically attacked by him. This is important, as a victim who is injured in 'a physical attack' will have sustained a criminal injury for which she could claim for either or both of a physical and a mental injury. Were this incident to be regarded as falling within paragraph 2(1)(b), a passenger who sustained a physical injury would similarly also be able to claim for a mental injury, but if she was physically unharmed, there will be no criminal injury under this paragraph, even though she sustains a mental injury caused by the thought of what might have been, had she been caught by the explosion.

3 Annex B paragraph 2(1)(c): 'A threat against a person, causing fear of immediate violence in circumstances which would cause a person of reasonable firmness to be put in such fear'

2.28 This formulation represents both a welcome simplification and some significant limitations on the equivalent criminal injury in the earlier tariff schemes. They made some arguably over-complex provision for cases where the only injury the victim sustained was mental injury; compensation would not be payable unless the applicant came within one of four specified categories. The first two of these reflected the 'fundamental distinction' between primary and secondary victims of

[48] *Fagan v Metropolitan Police Commissioner* [1969] 1 QB 439 (DC); *DPP v K* [1990] 1 All ER 331 (DC).

[49] *LM v First-tier Tribunal* [2011] UKUT 179 (AAC) [16]–[17].

psychiatric harm established by the House of Lords in *Page v Smith*.[50] As in their case, where liability at common law has sought 'to limit the financial liability that may be incurred by the state, private insurance companies or private individuals',[51] further control over the state's financial burden was similarly the 2012 Scheme's purpose.

Primary victims' eligibility was by paragraph 9(a) limited 'to those persons actually present at the scene of a crime of violence and put in fear of immediate physical injury to themselves'.[52] This remains a central condition of paragraph 2(1)(c), but is restricted by the 2012 Scheme to cases in which that fear was the result of 'a threat against a person'. Secondary victims' eligibility was limited by paragraph 9(b) to incidents in which they had witnessed a criminal injury to a primary victim defined as a 'loved one', where eligibility has been further limited by paragraph 6 of the 2012 Scheme (2.122–2.144). **2.29**

(a) **'A threat against a person'** Paragraph 2(1)(c) clearly covers incidents in which the claimant is himself threatened with violence, for example during a street robbery,[53] being threatened with an offensive weapon or a bladed article in a public place or on school premises,[54] or by a threat to kill him.[55] These would all have fallen within the scope of paragraph 9(a), but because they did not require any initial threat, it was sufficient that in the circumstances created by the offender the claimant was put in fear; for example, where the offender had committed the offences of having an offensive weapon, or of carrying a firearm, in a public place.[56] This is no longer the case; under paragraph 2(1)(c) it is necessary that the claimant's fear was caused by a threat. This in turn raises the question of whether that threat must be directed at the claimant or, as in the example of a street robbery which the claimant witnesses, and which puts her in fear, may be directed only against another person. **2.30**

Under paragraph 9(a) the answer would be affirmative, but not, it is suggested, under paragraph 2(1)(c). Eligibility under paragraph 4 of the 2012 Scheme depends upon the applicant sustaining a criminal injury 'which is directly attributable to their being a *direct* victim of a crime of violence' (emphasis added). As the crime of violence in paragraph 2(1)(c) involves 'a threat against a person', the phrase 'a person' must **2.31**

---

[50] [1996] 1 AC 155 (HL); Simon Deakin, Angus Johnston, and Basil Markesinis, *Markesinis and Deakin's Tort Law* (7th edn, Oxford University Press 2013) (Deakin, Johnston, and Markesinis, *Tort Law*) 125–35.

[51] *Sion v Hampstead HA* [1994] 5 Med LR 170, 173 (CA) (Staughton LJ).

[52] Home Office (1986) para 4.11.

[53] Theft Act 1968 s 8(1); CICA (2001) 10 (case summary 1: trauma following armed robbery). If the direct victim were in fact subject to violence, she would be the victim of 'a physical attack' (para 2(1)(a)).

[54] Criminal Justice Act 1988 s 139AA (CJA 1988).

[55] OAPA 1861 s 16.

[56] CJA 1988 s 139, Firearms Act 1968 s 19.

refer to the claimant, the 'direct victim' of the threat. Conversely, a claimant who was present when 'a person' other than him was threatened, cannot be the 'direct victim' of the threat, since the crime of violence was committed against that other person; he is instead the *indirect* victim of that threat. This interpretation of paragraph 2(1)(c) conforms, first, to the scheme's overall purpose, to impose new limitations on eligibility; and is supported, secondly, by the government's position that offences committed from a distance, for example by silent phone calls, will not normally be crimes of violence, 'unless there are *direct threats* which put the recipient in fear of immediate physical harm' (emphasis added).[57]

2.32 The answer to this question differs where the threat is made against a person with whom the claimant 'had a close relationship of love and affection' (paragraph 6(a) of the 2012 Scheme). If, in the example above, one of the robbers threatened the claimant's spouse or child with violence if the claimant did not comply with their demands, the claimant could not come within paragraph 2(1)(c) unless he himself was also threatened. It is not enough that the claimant only fears for the use of violence against another, even where that other person is 'a loved one'. But if the claimant's spouse or child was put in fear by the threat made against them, they would sustain a criminal injury within paragraph 2(1)(c), while the claimant could sustain a criminal injury by virtue of his witnessing the criminal injury sustained by his 'loved one' (paragraph 6).

2.33 In sum, paragraph 2(1)(c) excludes a person who, although in the circumstances was put in fear of immediate violence that a person of reasonable firmness would also experience, was put there otherwise than by him- or herself being threatened with violence.

2.34 **(b) Fear of immediate *violence*** The second change made by the 2012 Scheme is that the fear that the claimant experiences is of immediate 'violence', and not, as paragraph 9(a) provided, of immediate physical 'harm'. It was not clear why paragraph 9(a) of the earlier schemes identified 'harm' rather than 'injury'. It may be that 'harm' embraces a wider range of detrimental effects on the body than does 'injury'. A person fearful of being pushed to the ground by the offender, and thus suffering some minor and transitory shock, might be said to have been harmed, but it may be doubted whether the person had been injured. In specifying 'violence', paragraph 2(1)(c) gives effect to the government's stricter policy for this category of a crime of violence.

2.35 **(c) Fear of *immediate* violence** A common element of the current and the earlier versions of this criminal injury is that the fear the claimant experiences must be of 'immediate' harm or violence. As an ordinary word of the English language, 'immediate' implies an almost exact correspondence in time and place between the offender's actions and the victim's apprehension. This threat may

[57] Ministry of Justice (2012a) para 179.

be verbally explicit, or implicit in a gesture or movement on the offender's part, but paragraph 2(1)(c) requires that it must *actually*, and not merely hypothetically or possibly, inspire the fear that the claimant experienced. This is clear from *Criminal Injuries Compensation Authority v First-tier Tribunal and BW*.[58] The claimant had discovered that her stepfather had secretly filmed her on a number of occasions while she was naked in the family bathroom. It was accepted that voyeurism,[59] of which he was convicted, was not a crime of violence. The FTT found that the claimant came within paragraph 2(1)(c), in that she had a well-founded fear of immediate violence whenever her stepfather returned to the house and discovered that she knew of his actions. The Upper Tribunal disagreed. The claimant may subjectively have feared this scenario, but in its absence, the 'threat' from the stepfather was hypothetical.[60]

In actually causing fear of immediate violence, 'immediacy' does not, as *Smith v Chief Superintendent, Woking Police Station* indicates,[61] necessarily require proximity between the victim and the offender in the sense of physical presence. Immediacy was satisfied by close *visual* presence where, intending to frighten her, the offender stood in the victim's garden looking at her through the window. It is well established that an offender can commit an assault although there is no physical contact, as may occur where the victim is subjected, as in *Constanza*,[62] and *Ireland*, and *Burstow*,[63] to silent phone calls, text messages, emails, or other forms of harassment that are offences under section 1(1)(a) of the Malicious Communications Act 1988 (MCA 1988). Depending on the circumstances of this *aural* presence, the House of Lords confirmed in *Ireland* that causing psychiatric injury could constitute actual bodily harm under section 47 of the OAPA 1861. As in *Woking Police Station*, the decision in *Ireland* demonstrates the elasticity of the word 'immediate'; the offender puts the victim in fear by instilling in her uncertainty as to what he would do next, and whether that might involve 'the *possibility* of immediate personal violence' directed against her (original emphasis).[64] **2.36**

In its consultation the government was pressed to expand the definition of a crime of violence to cover explicit reference to harassment and stalking, but was unwilling to broaden its scope, for example to harassment by telephone, or electronically, insisting that there must be a direct threat of immediate physical harm.[65] Such immediacy may be satisfied by an offence under section 4A(1) **2.37**

58 [2017] UKUT 97 (AAC) (*CICA v BW*).
59 Sexual Offences Act 2003 ss 67–68 (SOA 2003).
60 *CICA v BW* (n 58) [20] (Judge Levenson).
61 (1983) 76 Cr App Rep 234 (CA).
62 [1997) 2 Cr App Rep 492 (CA).
63 [1998] AC 147 (HL).
64 ibid 162 (Lord Steyn).
65 Ministry of Justice (2012a) paras 178 and 179; Ministry of Justice (2012b) para 161.

of the Protection from Harassment Act 1997. This provides that a person (A) whose course of conduct amounts to stalking, and 'causes another (B) to fear, on at least two occasions, that violence will be used against B', is guilty of an offence if A 'knows or ought to know that A's course of conduct will cause B so to fear'. 'Stalking' is an offence under section 2A of that Act, so if the offender's repeated course of offensive conduct, for example under section 1 of the MCA 1988, which is not of itself a crime of violence, involves direct threats which put the recipient in fear of immediate physical harm on more than two occasions, there could be both a crime, and a crime of violence under paragraph 2(1)(c).

2.38 (d) **'In circumstances which would cause a person of reasonable firmness to be put in such fear'** Although it was not explicit, to come within paragraph 9(a) the applicant had to satisfy both a subjective and an objective test. This was demonstrated in the first of the three cases heard as *HW v FTT.* A police officer suffered post-traumatic stress disorder (PTSD) following an incident in which a man broke into a private room in a police station; although he did not directly threaten the victim or her colleague, he was behaving erratically and his right hand was clenched around an object that turned out to be a 12-inch kitchen knife. Because she was able to leave the room without hindrance, and return with other officers who arrested him, the Upper Tribunal concluded that, in applying these tests, her fear (even if immediate) was not reasonably held.[66]

2.39 The two tests are explicit in paragraph 2(1)(c). Whether the threat caused the victim to fear immediate violence is a subjective question of fact, and whether it would do so in circumstances that would cause 'a person of reasonable firmness' to be put in such fear is an objective test. This does not ask whether a person of reasonable firmness 'in the victim's shoes' would have been put in fear; the relevance of those shoes is that such factors as a disparity in stature between the victim and the offender, as in *HW v FTT*, or the victim's age, ethnic origin, disability, or other vulnerability, relates only to the subjective question: did the threat cause the victim to fear such violence?

2.40 In *Burstow* there was an offence under section 20 of the OAPA 1861, but because none of the offender's telephone calls involved *threats* of physical harm, paragraph 2(1)(c) would not apply, although the victim 'was fearful of personal violence'.[67] In *Chan-Fook* the victim was tied up in a first-floor room in a house he occupied with two others, including the offender.[68] On a claim under the 2012 Scheme based on his fear that he might be physically attacked at any time while so constrained, the offender's actions might be considered to amount to a threat

[66] *HW v FTT* (n 20) [10] (Nicol J).
[67] *Burstow* (n 63) 155 (Lord Steyn).
[68] (1994) 99 Cr App Rep 147 (CA).

of immediate violence that would cause a person of reasonable firmness to be put in such fear.

4 Annex B paragraph 2(1)(d): 'A sexual assault to which a person did not in fact consent'

(a) **General principles** Neither the common law nor the earlier tariff schemes specifically provided that personal injuries arising from non-consensual sexual offences constituted criminal injuries, although both the CICB and the CICA routinely treated the resulting injuries as falling with their scope.[69] While rape, unlawful sexual intercourse, and buggery did not require it as a matter of definition, these offences have typically been accompanied by violence, at the least by a battery, and those of indecent assault and assault with intent to commit buggery, by definition by an assault.[70] The 'personal injury' to which that assault gave rise included 'sexual abuse/assault', which provided the basis for claims for periods of physical or sexual abuse against children and adults. But a child that is born with disabilities caused by the incestuous rape of its mother did not sustain a personal injury because, as the Court of Appeal held in *Criminal Injuries Compensation Authority and First-tier Tribunal (SEC) (CIC) v Y*, at the time of the offence the foetus was not 'a person', nor was there an 'injury' for the purpose of the scheme.[71] **2.41**

By implication, the earlier schemes proceeded on the basis that in any application arising from a sexual offence the applicant had to be a non-consenting victim, otherwise there would be no crime of violence, irrespective of the extent of any physical or mental injuries that were sustained. This left open the eligibility of a victim who, as provided by paragraph 9(1)(c) of the earlier schemes, 'consented in fact but was deemed in law not to have consented', in particular a child under the age of 16. In the case of minors, even though there might have been a crime of violence, this paragraph provided that where the only injury the minor sustained was mental injury, compensation would not be payable if the minor did in fact consent. This did not therefore apply to those who suffered physical injury and possibly also mental injury, but there appear to have been no decisions arising from such applications, nor was it clear why the scheme distinguished the two injuries in this way. The policy could also apply to an adult who was suffering from mental incapacity and thus incapable of making the choice specified in section 74 of the SOA 2003,[72] or against a person with a mental disorder (SOA 2003 sections 30–41), either of whom consented in fact. **2.42**

The government's consultation noted that paragraph 9(1)(c) could particularly affect young people aged between 13 and 15 who had engaged in consensual **2.43**

[69] CICA (2008 Guide) s 2 para 5.
[70] Sexual Offences Act 1956 ss 1, 5, 6, 12, and 14–16 (SOA 1956).
[71] [2017] EWCA Civ 139, [2017] 4 WLR 60 (CA); ch 3.82-3.85.
[72] Mental Capacity Act 2005 ss 2 and 3.

sexual activity. But it concluded that, while 'there are good reasons why the law criminalises certain behaviour or deems those below a certain age unable to consent . . . eligibility for compensation from the State is different, and so we consider it is proportionate that where a person in fact consented to the behaviour, they should not then be able to benefit from state compensation for any injury which results'.[73] Its proposal 'to continue this practice in relation to consensual sexual activity' therefore sends a powerful message about how it conceives innocent victims behave when so engaged, and the injuries for which taxpayers may properly be called upon to compensate. There is clear judicial support for this approach. In *R (on the application of JE) v Criminal Injuries Compensation Appeal Panel*, Lord Woolf LCJ observed that

> [i]t would be an absurd result if a willing participant could obtain compensation for the injuries, the infliction of which had been welcomed. A willing participant is hardly a victim and the Scheme is intended to compensate victims. It is to avoid this absurdity that, as the authorities make clear, consent can be fatal to a claim for compensation for an offence of violence.[74]

2.44 Annex B paragraph 2(1)(d) of the 2012 Scheme provides that a "crime of violence" is a crime which involves: ... 'a sexual assault to which a person did not in fact consent'. This much simpler phraseology both eliminates the former distinction between the two forms of personal injury, and explicitly provides that a sexual assault is a crime of violence. As was the case under the earlier schemes, sexual offences that involve no physical contact with the victim do not fall within this paragraph. Offences of indecent exposure (SOA 2003 section 66),[75] and voyeurism (SOA 2003 sections 67–68),[76] are not criminal injuries for the purpose of paragraph 4 of the 2012 Scheme.

2.45 The SOA 2003 distinguishes non-consensual sexual offences among adults from those against children, which do not depend upon the presence or absence of consent but upon the victim's age. The following sections consider separately the scheme's application to these two groups of offences, but do not deal with the extensive law on the interpretation of their fault and external elements save as they bear upon its application.[77]

2.46 **(b) Non-consensual sexual offences among adults** A non-consenting victim aged 16 or over who sustains personal injuries directly attributable to the commission of an offence under sections 1–4 of the SOA 2003, that is, rape, assault by penetration, sexual assault, and, where it follows an assault, causing a person to engage in sexual activity without consent, will have been injured by a crime of violence under paragraph 2(1)(d), and will have sustained a criminal injury

[73] Ministry of Justice (2012c) paras 90 and 97.
[74] [2003] EWCA Civ 234, 2003 WL 270842 [17] (CA) (*JE v CICAP*).
[75] *C v Criminal Injuries Compensation Board* [1999] SC 551; *Jones* (n 6) [15].
[76] *CICA v BW* (n 58).
[77] Card and Molloy, *Criminal Law* (n 37) ch 9.

within paragraph 4 of the 2012 Scheme. These offences all require proof that the victim did not consent to the penetration, touching, or sexual activity, and that the defendant did not reasonably believe that she (or he) consented. Eligibility under paragraph 4 and Annex B paragraph 2(1)(d) therefore appears to be compromised where there was an acquittal because the jury was not persuaded beyond a reasonable doubt that the defendant did not so believe. This conclusion is considered in Chapter 3.27 in connection with paragraph 9 of the scheme, where on the civil standard of proof the CICA may find 'that a person may be eligible for an award whether or not the incident giving rise to the criminal injury to which their application relates has resulted in the conviction of an offender'.

It is clear that considerable weight hangs on the scope of 'consent' within the SOA 2003. By section 74, 'a person consents if he agrees by choice, and has the freedom and capacity to make that choice'. Capacity to choose may engage the law on mental capacity and mental disorder, where it is usually assessed by reference to the act for which capacity is needed. So an individual might, for example, have capacity to consent to sexual activity without having capacity to manage complex financial transactions.[78] Where there is incapacity or mental disorder, there normally will be an offence, but this could be otherwise where there is clear evidence that such a person did consent 'to this act of sex with this person at this time and in this place'.[79] In all of these situations, the CICA would need to examine the facts, make findings as to the ingredients of the offence, and then determine whether the applicant in fact consented, an exercise that necessarily would include considering whether the victim was capable of consenting to the specific act defined in the offence. **2.47**

Freedom to make that choice may be compromised by a variety of factors. Sections 76 and 77 provide, first, that there is a conclusive presumption that the victim did not consent to 'the relevant act' in sections 1–4 of the SOA 2003, where her consent was induced by deception or by impersonation. By section 76(2), the deception must go to 'the nature or purpose of the relevant act'. A claimant who consents to be touched by a medical practitioner for the purported purpose of a medical examination, or who is deceived into thinking that sexual intercourse will improve her singing voice, may for the purpose of an offence under section 3 of the SOA 2003 be presumed not to have consented to be sexually touched by the practitioner,[80] or to penetration (section 2) by the music teacher.[81] The issue for the scheme is whether these victims, or those induced into sexual activity in the **2.48**

---

[78] Department of Constitutional Affairs (2007), *Mental Capacity Act 2005 Code of Practice*, and Rebecca Jacob, Michael Gunn, and Anthony Holland (eds), *Mental Capacity Legislation: Principles and Practice* (The Royal College of Psychiatrists 2013).

[79] *C* [2009] UKHL 42, [2009] 1 WLR 1786 [27] (HL) (Baroness Hale).

[80] *Tabassum* [2000] 2 Cr App Rep 328 (CA).

[81] *Williams* [1923] KB 340 (CA).

rare cases of impersonation,[82] 'consented in fact' to these sexual assaults. In *JE v CICAP*, the Court of Appeal, reviewing its earlier decision in *ex parte August and Brown*, held that the test is whether there was 'real consent' on the victim's part. There may be consent in fact, but 'consent that is not real will not do'.[83]

2.49 The presumption in section 76 does not apply where the deception does not go to 'the nature or purpose of the relevant act'. Absent the conclusive presumption, it is necessary to show that the victim did not in fact consent, that is, did not give a 'real consent' to the particular sexual activity. This asks the question, to what *did* the victim consent? Bigamy is not a crime of violence, which means that a victim's consent to sexual intercourse on a promise to marry would not fall within the scheme. Although the victim's consent to sexual intercourse may have been obtained by fraud, it did not deceive her as to its nature or purpose.[84] Although the deception in *Konzani* concerned the commission of an offence under section 20 of the OAPA 1861, the Court of Appeal's decision illustrates the notion of a 'real consent'. It held that the victim had consented to sexual intercourse but not, given that the offender had deceived her as to his HIV condition, to the risk of being infected, and of suffering grievous bodily harm. This was because 'she cannot give an informed consent to something of which she is ignorant'.[85] Where a claim is made in respect of a sexual assault following some deception, for example as to gender,[86] the issue for the CICA is whether there was, in fact, no 'true',[87] 'real', or 'informed' consent to the assault.

2.50 There is, secondly, an evidential presumption that the victim did not consent to 'the relevant act' where it was obtained in any of the six circumstances set out in section 75(2) of the SOA 2003. This presumed consent may be rebutted where the offender adduces sufficient evidence to raise an issue as to whether the victim did consent,[88] and he reasonably believed that she did (section 75(1)). Section 75(2)(c)–(f) concern the victim's unlawful detention, unconsciousness,[89] disability, or non-consensual administration of a stupefying or overpowering substance, such as a 'date rape' drug. Section 75(2)(a)–(b) concerns circumstances in which, 'at the time of the relevant act or immediately before it began', violence was being used against the victim, or caused her to fear that it was being used against another person, or to fear that immediate violence would be used against

[82] SOA 2003 s 76(2)(b).

[83] *JE v CICAP* (n 74) 234 (Lord Woolf).

[84] *Gray v Criminal Injuries Compensation Board* (1999) SC 137.

[85] [2005] EWCA Crim 706, [2005] 2 Cr App R 14 [49] (CA) (Judge LJ).

[86] *Jheeta* [2007] EWCA Crim 1699, [2007] 2 Cr App R 477 (CA); *B* [2013] EWCA Crim 823, [2013] 2 Cr App R 307 (CA); *McNally* [2013] EWCA Crim 1051, [2014] 2 WLR 200 (CA).

[87] *Tabassum* (n 80) [38].

[88] *Ciccarellli* [2011] EWCA Crim 2665, [2012] 1 Cr App R 15 (CA).

[89] This could cover a claim under the common law scheme in which the applicant, placed under hypnosis, had been subject to rape and buggery; CICB 28th Report (Cm 2122 1993) para 27.5.

her or another person. For the purpose of section 75, the question of whether the victim was fearful of 'immediate violence' appears to be only a subjective matter; it is not necessary that it is reasonably held.

Suppose that the claimant consents to a sexual assault because the offender or an accomplice uses or threatens immediate violence against her or her child or spouse. Assuming that the presumption is not rebutted and the assailant is convicted, it is 'still necessary' (Annex B paragraph 2(1)) for the CICA to determine whether there was a crime of violence; that is, that there was a sexual assault to which the claimant 'did not in fact consent'. There is nothing in paragraph 2(1)(d) that corresponds to the circumstances in section 75 of the SOA 2003, but where they do obtain, and the offender is convicted, the claimant's unlawful detention or non-consensual drugged condition would suggest, on the balance of probabilities, that there was no 'real' consent in fact. The same decision must be made where violence was used or the claimant feared its immediate use, based on her actual state of mind when faced with the use, or threat, of violence to herself or another. Such factors as its nature or immediacy are, it is suggested, evidential matters that are relevant in assessing whether there was in fact consent, but not that paragraph 2(1)(d) calls for an objective test akin to that in paragraph 2(1)(c), of their effect upon 'a person of reasonable firmness'. **2.51**

(c) **Offences against children** A child is a person below the age of 16. The provisions in the SOA 2003 are complex. In short, any sexual assault in respect of a child under the age of 13 is an offence, and that is so also where the child is between 13 and 16 years of age and the offender does not reasonably believe the victim to be over 16 (sections 5–12); or, in the case of sexual activity with a child family member, over 18 years (sections 25–26). The absence of consent is irrelevant in law to the proof of any of these offences, but its absence in fact is relevant to paragraph 2(1)(d). As is the case of adult victims, the question of whether a child victim of a sexual assault 'did not in fact consent' to it asks whether there was a 'real' consent. In the frequently complex factual and legal circumstances surrounding claims arising from sexual abuse against children, the interpretation of this paragraph and its predecessors is more acute. **2.52**

The central question in *ex parte August and Brown* was whether repeated consensual acts of buggery with boys aged 12–14, causing them physical injury, constituted a 'crime of violence',[90] as required by paragraph 8(a) of the 2001 Scheme. In *ex parte August*, the Criminal Injuries Compensation Appeals Panel (CICAP) concluded that because the claimant had consented in fact, there was no crime of violence. His application to the Administrative Court for judicial review of that decision on the ground that he could not have consented in law to the offences **2.53**

[90] SOA 1956 s 12, for which the victim's consent was, as is now the case under SOA 2003 s 9 (sexual activity with a child), irrelevant.

was rejected. In *ex parte Brown*, the CICAP found that in the circumstances of the approved school in which the claimant lived, it was more likely that the various sexual acts were consensual, but the Court held that its conclusion, that because a child's consent was no defence to the crime of buggery, there could be no crime of violence, was wrong in law. Dismissing the claimant's appeal in *ex parte August* but allowing the CICAP's in *ex parte Brown*, the Court of Appeal held that the CICAP was right in thinking that the victim's consent was relevant, but that its presence or absence was not conclusive of the question of whether there was 'a crime of violence' for the purpose of the scheme. It was open to the CICAP to find in these cases that, on the facts, the victims' consent was freely and voluntarily given, but it did not follow that there could be no circumstances in which a sexual offence would be committed, notwithstanding that the victim consented. Whether they were non-consenting victims was relevant only for 'the different and limited question of when compensation will be payable' for the injury attributable to that crime of violence.[91]

2.54 Of more general significance is the interpretation that later courts have placed upon this decision, reflected in Lord Woolf's comment in *JE v CICAP* that 'properly understood, the court in *August* recognised that a crime could be a crime of violence as long as there was not "real consent" '.[92] This case concerned a highly suggestible 22 year old who lacked capacity who, while in prison, had been sexually abused by his older and more sexually experienced cellmate. Reviewing the circumstances of the abuse, the CICAP concluded that 'whilst the applicant could not give consent in law he did consent in fact'. The Court of Appeal quashed its decision, holding that the CICAP had made no allowance for the claimant's vulnerability; 'it was also necessary to ask whether, despite the fact he consented, that consent was real so as to prevent his being a victim'.[93] Lord Woolf CJ observed that 'submission is not the same thing as consent'; in each case, 'the Panel has to ask itself whether the proper conclusion on the facts is that the applicant was, in relation to what happened, a victim of a crime of violence. This will be the situation if there was no real consent'.[94]

2.55 The question of whether there was a 'real consent' was directly addressed in the two judicial review applications in *R (on the application of CD and JM) v Criminal Injuries Compensation Appeal Panel*.[95] In *CD v CICAP*, the High Court dismissed the application to quash the CICAP's decision that upheld the CICA's refusal of an award to a 12 year old girl who claimed to have been raped. Silber J drew a number of differences with *JE v CICAP*. In lacking capacity, the victim in that

91 *Ex parte August and Brown* (n 14) [39] and [81] (CA).
92 *JE v CICAP* (n 74) [28].
93 ibid [32]; CICAP (1999) 19 para 4.6.
94 *JE v CICAP* (n 74) [28].
95 [2004] EWHC 1674 (Admin).

case had been exploited by a sexually experienced man who was more than twice his age. Secondly, he had no interest in, and no experience of, the sexual activities complained of, and complained at the first opportunity; but in *CD v CICA* there was evidence of the victim's previous sexual experience and wholly voluntary participation, suggesting that she had consented in fact. Finally, the apportionment of liability in *CD v CICAP* was very different from that in *JE v CICAP*, where, if it had considered their relative responsibility for the abuse, the CICAP would have very likely concluded that the offender in *JE v CICAP* 'was substantially, if not entirely to blame for what occurred'.[96]

In *JM v CICAP* the applicant was 12 years of age who had been sexually abused over a period of years, and when placed in foster care was further abused for about twelve to eighteen months by her foster mother's son. In part because of her substantial delay in making a complaint, and its doubts about the unwanted nature of the son's actions, the CICAP upheld the CICA's refusal. But in determining whether there was a real consent, Silber J noted five points that the CICAP should have considered. These were the relative degrees of responsibility of the applicant and the son, her vulnerability because her natural mother was unavailable to support her at the time of the abuse, her weak position when exploited by her foster mother's son, the question of whether she *could* (original emphasis) have complained when the abuse occurred but did not, and, finally, her vulnerability as a result of her previous sexual abuse.[97] **2.56**

In proposing to continue its policy of refusing compensation where there had been consent in fact, the government noted that the CICA's practice then assumed 'that a child under 13 who is the victim of sexual assault will be eligible for compensation if an offence is reported to the police and the child cooperates so far as reasonably practicable' with the criminal justice system. This leaves open, as it must, the CICA's discretion to find on appropriate facts, that a child under 13 nevertheless gave a real consent. It also acknowledged that **2.57**

> [b]etween 13 and 15 a more difficult assessment must be made in each case. Consensual sexual activity between young people in this age group who are of similar age and circumstances should not attract criminal injuries compensation. However, the more unbalanced a sexual relationship involving a young person becomes, the more likely it is that he or she will suffer harm such that they should be compensated (whether they in fact consented or not).[98]

In assessing the claimant's vulnerability to sexual exploitation, the factors that were present in the decisions discussed above include the child's age and emotional maturity, the place of residence or otherwise in which the sexual assault took place, the child's history, in particular of any prior abuse, educational **2.58**

[96] ibid [38]–[39].
[97] ibid [70]–[74].
[98] Ministry of Justice (2012c) para 97.

attainment, the use of threats, coercion, or other pressure, and the nature of the relationship between the parties, including any disparity in age or experience, and any power imbalance between them: the CICA must consider all of these factors when determining whether consent was apparent rather than real. They are also likely to be relevant to claims arising from sexual grooming of a child over a period of time, and more particularly in the case of offences involving the abuse of a position of trust under sections 16–19 of the SOA 2003, which apply to children aged between 16 and 17, for example, by a school teacher, a priest, or a scout leader. The application of paragraph 2(1)(d) and its predecessors to claims made by children has always been controversial; it was confirmed in 2017 that the CICA was reviewing its guidance,[99] but at the time of writing this has not been published.

5 Annex B paragraph 2(1)(e): 'Arson and fire-raising'

2.59 By section 1(2) of the CDA 1971, it is an offence of aggravated criminal damage if the offender intended by that damage or destruction to endanger the life of another or was reckless as to whether the life of another would thereby be endangered, and will be charged as arson if the damage or destruction is caused by fire (CDA 1971 section 1(3)). A person who sustained personal injuries when the building he was in was fire bombed,[100] would sustain a criminal injury under this paragraph. Arson, and in Scotland, fire-raising, were included in the 2012 Scheme in line with the government's long-standing view that they might not otherwise be considered to be violent, in the sense of involving the direct application of physical force to the victim.[101]

C Unlawfulness: consent and self-defence

1 Consent

2.60 Where a person consents to an activity that comprises the external and fault elements of an offence, there will, subject to statutory or common law rules to the contrary, be no criminal liability if its performance does not go beyond the terms of that consent, or of what might reasonably be expected of the activity. This includes reasonable surgical interference, body piercing and tattooing for personal adornment, and rough horseplay. Where personal injury results there will be no criminal injury, because there will be no crime of violence as instanced in Annex B. In the case of properly conducted sports or games, the 2012 Scheme specifically excludes injuries sustained 'in the usual course of

[99] Hansard HC Debs vol 628 oral answers 5 September 2017; https://hansard.parliament.uk/Commons/2017-09-05/debates/9887B2D7-C9BF-40E6-B617-BAA3F3319CE6/ChildSexAbuseCompensation.

[100] *Dudley* [1989] Crim LR 57.

[101] Ministry of Justice (2012a) para 183.

sporting or other activity to which a person consented by taking part in the activity' (2.87–2.90).

Consent can be express or implied. But not all consents are valid for the purpose of criminal liability. A girl's consent to genital mutilation is irrelevant under the FGMA 2003, as is a child's consent to a sexual offence. As a matter of public policy, consent to bodily harm does not in general relieve the person inflicting it of criminal liability under the OAPA 1861,[102] but it does not follow that the injury that is caused will be compensable. In determining whether it is appropriate to make an award, the CICA may, by paragraph 25 of the 2012 Scheme, take into account the applicant's conduct at the time he sustained the criminal injury (Chapter 4.22–4.44). As consenting adults to the violence that was used to accompany sexual activity, the CICA would, as the government was clear should be the case,[103] surely reject applications based on the circumstances in *Brown*,[104] where the participants freely and voluntarily engaged in the sado-masochistic activities that caused their injuries. **2.61**

The claims that arise under paragraph 2(1)(d) where children or adults engage in consensual sexual activity illustrate the general point that, to be effective, any consent in fact must be a 'real' or a 'true' consent. Consent to what would otherwise constitute a violent offence, but which is obtained by coercion or by putting a person in fear of immediate violence that a person of reasonable firmness might experience, may well be ineffective, and any resulting personal injury a criminal injury. **2.62**

In the case of sexual offences, consent may also be vitiated by deception. More difficult is a case where there is no deception but the offender fails to disclose a fact that, had it been known, it might, or would, have caused the victim to withhold consent. In *Dica*, the Court of Appeal held that where a person knows that the other has a sexually transmissible disease but nevertheless engages in sexual intercourse, the risk of infection is a risk to which he consents;[105] in such a case there would be no crime, and no criminal injury. This will not be so where the other did not disclose the disease. In this case, there would be no defence to a charge under sections 47 or 20 of the OAPA 1861, but for the scheme, the question is, as the Court if Appeal put it in *Konzani*, whether the victim consented to sexual intercourse, or to the risk of contracting a disease. The CICA would need to decide whether the victim's ignorance of the assailant's condition meant that the victim's consent in fact was not 'genuine' or 'real'.[106] **2.63**

102 *A-G's Reference (No 6 of 1980)* [1981] QB 715 (CA); *BM* (n 31) [38–[45].
103 Ministry of Justice (2012a) para 186.
104 [1994] 1 AC 212 (HL); Card and Molloy, *Criminal Law* (n 37) 150–59.
105 [2004] EWCA Crim 706, [2004] 2 Cr App R (S) 95 (CA).
106 *Konzani* (n 85) [49].

2 *Self-defence*

2.64 As consent may render lawful conduct that prima facie constitutes the external elements of an offence, so the 'offender's' belief that he is entitled to use reasonable force in self-defence or defence of another (private defence), or to effect an arrest (public defence), may negative the fault elements. It will be apparent that a person who sustains a personal injury because another has used reasonable force against him in self-defence is unlikely to have the basis for a claim, both because there will be no crime of violence, and because the 'victim' will have contributed to the circumstances in which the other believed that such force was necessary. Moreover, even where the other's use of force in a 'householder case' is grossly disproportionate and thus an offence, the CICA may well still regard the victim as having contributed to his own injuries (Chapter 4.24).

D Annex B: specifically excluded injuries

2.65 In addition to specifying those injuries that it considered would give effect to the main purpose of the scheme, the government identified a number of circumstances in which, although technically involving the commission of a criminal offence, the use of taxpayers' money to compensate those injuries would be inconsistent with that purpose.[107] In seeking to confine the scope of the phrase 'a crime of violence' to the commission of 'deliberate violent crime', it addressed two broader policy issues raised by the earlier schemes. These were their formal extension to injuries arising from trespass on a railway, and the difficulties that have arisen in the interpretation of its exclusion of injuries 'attributable to the use of a vehicle', both of which were made more complex by virtue of the possible availability of other compensating arrangements. The following sections deal with the injuries that are listed in Annex B paragraph 4(2), followed by the two that are simply omitted from the 2012 Scheme.

1 *Annex B paragraph 4(1)(a): third party injuries arising from suicide or attempted suicide*

2.66 The second substantive issue that arose in *Jones* was whether, in running into the road, the deceased had formed the relevant *mens rea* of a crime of violence (2.08–2.09). The Supreme Court held that the question of whether harm might be caused to others by his suicidal actions was pre-eminently a matter of fact, which was for the FTT and not the Court of Appeal to decide. As there were no grounds for setting aside the FTT's finding that the facts disclosed no offence under section 20 of the OAPA 1861, it was not open to review either by the Upper Tribunal (which had dismissed the applicant's appeal from the FTT), or by the Court of Appeal. *Jones* therefore acknowledges that a person committing

---

[107] Ministry of Justice (2012a) paras 185–86.

suicide, who necessarily desires his own death, may or may not (depending on the facts) be subjectively reckless as to whether his actions may cause death or injury to others.[108]

On other facts, it may therefore be possible to reach the conclusion that the deceased had committed a crime of violence, but that must, as the Upper Tribunal emphasized in *R (Criminal Injuries Compensation Authority) v First-tier Tribunal,*[109] be based on a clear application of a subjective test. In a claim based on facts materially the same as in *Jones,* the FTT had allowed the claimant's appeal on the ground that the deceased '*should* have foreseen' (emphasis added) that some physical harm would come to another person. Applying the correct, subjective, test the FTT could still have found that the deceased did foresee harm to another, but the Upper Tribunal held that it had made a material error, in the sense that the application of an objective test *could* have made a difference to the outcome, but on the facts, not that it *would.* **2.67**

A suicide's recklessness as to other road users did not, however, square with the government's policy to limit the 2012 Scheme to a 'direct, hostile, physical attack against a person', of which the applicant is, as paragraph 4 provides, a 'direct victim'. By Annex B paragraph 4(1), 'a crime of violence will not be considered to have been committed for the purposes of this Scheme if, in particular, an injury: (a) resulted from suicide or attempted suicide, unless the suicidal person acted with intent to cause injury to another person'. This is intended to preclude claims under the 2012 Scheme by 'third parties injured inadvertently by an act the sole purpose of which is suicide (e.g. someone jumps off a building and someone below runs into another person, injuring them, in an attempt to get out of the way of the suicide)',[110] or runs into a busy road for that purpose. **2.68**

2 Annex B paragraph 4(1)(b): the use of a vehicle

The exclusion of personal injuries attributable to the use of a vehicle is a longstanding feature of both the common law and the tariff schemes; injuries sustained as a result of the principal driving offences under sections 1–3A and 28–29 of the Road Traffic Act 1988 (RTA 1988) will not be criminal injuries. The justification for their exclusion continues to be based on 'the purely practical consideration of avoiding the need for [the CICA] to embark upon detailed consideration of cases which are eligible for compensation under motor insurance arrangements, including the agreements between the Motor Insurers' Bureau and the Secretary of State for Transport'.[111] **2.69**

---

[108] *Jones* (n 6) [24]–[26].

[109] [2015] UKUT 299 (AAC) [24].

[110] Ministry of Justice (2012a) para 186; (ch 3.40–3.41).

[111] Home Office (1986) para 11.1; Andrew Ritchie and Jeremy Ford, *APIL Guide to MIB Claims: Uninsured and Untraced Drivers* (Jordan Publishing 2016).

2.70 To this general exclusion there has always been, in the words of paragraph 11 of the 2001 and 2008 Schemes, an exception in cases where 'the vehicle was used so as deliberately to inflict, or attempt to inflict, injury on any person'. In maintaining the underlying policy, the 2012 Scheme casts the exception in slightly different terms. By Annex B paragraph 4(1), 'a crime of violence will not be considered to have been committed for the purposes of this Scheme if, in particular, an injury: (b) resulted from the use of a vehicle, unless the vehicle was used with intent to cause injury to a person'. In such a case the offence that the driver committed would, depending on the extent of the victim's injury and of the driver's intention, most likely fall under sections 18, 20, or 47 of the OAPA 1861, or attempted murder.

2.71 Using the vehicle in this way could readily include driving at a police officer who is seeking to apprehend the driver, driving at another person in a fit of 'road rage', or in an act of terrorism driving at pedestrians with intent to kill or injure them, as in the incident on Westminster Bridge in March 2017; but an attack in person in a road rage incident will simply fall within paragraph 4(1)(a) as a 'physical attack'. As the tariff schemes have provided a broad definition of a vehicle, in Annex B paragraph 4(2), as 'any device which can be used to transport persons, animals or goods, whether by land, water or air', it may be that deliberately running into another person in a fit of 'shopper rage' with a pram or a shopping trolley could fall within the exception.

2.72 The question that arose in *Tait v Criminal Injuries Compensation Appeal Panel* was whether a finding that a vehicle had been deliberately used to ram a police car with the primary motive of disabling it, so as to enable the driver to make good his escape, was compatible with a second finding, that it had been used 'so as deliberately to inflict or attempt to inflict injury' on the policemen inside the car. The High Court held, first, that there was no inconsistency between these two states of mind and, secondly, that having identified the driver's primary motive, a finding that he foresaw that the claimant would be injured, and that he intended to injure him, was on the facts, 'inescapable'.[112]

2.73 Annex B paragraph 4(1)(b) replaces 'deliberately' in the exceptional circumstances set out in paragraph 11, with an 'intent' to cause injury to a person. This substitution is designed to exclude the dangerous or reckless driving associated with 'hit and run' road accidents, which the government emphasized 'will not give rise to a payment under the Scheme'.[113]

2.74 But this does not foreclose questions concerning the nature of a driver's intent. Suppose that the driver of a car drives at a person intending that the person

[112] [2009] EWHC 767 (Admin), [2010] RTR 6 [14] and [32] (Stadlen J) (QBD) (*Tait v CICAP*).
[113] Ministry of Justice (2012a) para 186.

should suffer a psychiatric injury as a result of the alarm that his driving causes, but contrary to his intention, the driver fails to steer away or loses control, striking and injuring that person. The driver may well be reckless, but it was not his intention to cause injury, which may fall outside the exceptional case.[114] The same question arises where an offender, intending to cause an accident in order to make an insurance claim for her 'whiplash' injury, also injures the driver of the car with which she intentionally collides. As in *Tait v CICAP*, and in *Jones*, the question is whether, on the facts, the CICA could find that in acting as he did, the offender could simultaneously intend these two different consequences.

Although they concerned earlier versions of the tariff scheme, both *Tait v CICAP* and *Jones* contemplated the possibility that an offender could do so. That in its turn depends on what is meant by 'intent' in Annex B paragraph 4(1)(b), which was a central issue in *CICA v AS*. Here, the CICA refused a claim arising from the injuries caused by a young cyclist who, riding at such speed as constituted an offence of dangerous cycling under section 28 of the RTA 1988, struck and severely injured the claimant using a pedestrian crossing. Although the FTT's reasons clearly stated that it 'had regard to the nature of the act and not its consequences', the Upper Tribunal held that it had failed adequately to distinguish them.[115] This error was in part attributable to its reliance on the House of Lords' approval in *Woollin* of the Court of Appeal's formulation in *Nedrick*,[116] that the necessary intention [in murder] may be found where (a) the outcome was a virtually certain consequence of the defendant's voluntary act and (b) that the defendant appreciated that fact.[117] The FTT had insufficiently focused on the cyclist's 'aim or purpose during the incident—put simply, what was in his mind'. It had accepted that, when he started out on his journey, the cyclist did not intend to cause injury to anyone, but when he did strike the claimant, 'what was required of the tribunal was an analysis of the point in time at which [he] *did* form the aim or purpose of causing injury' to the claimant (original emphasis).[118] **2.75**

Two final matters merit comment. The CICB received many applications arising from injuries sustained on the road, where the victim was pushed off her bike or forced into the path of an oncoming vehicle. Its driver being blameless for the ensuing injury, none of these injuries was attributable to the *use* of a vehicle; but under the 2012 Scheme the initial assault could be 'a physical attack' within Annex B paragraph 2(1)(a). Such an assault is materially indistinguishable from a case where the offender pushes the victim into a canal or river, over a cliff, or **2.76**

[114] *Waide, Re Judicial Review* [2008] NICA 1, discussed in *Tait v CICAP* (n 112) [15]–[19].
[115] *CICA v AS* (n 19) [8], [54]–[68].
[116] [1997] 1 Cr App R 97 (CA); (ch 1.29).
[117] [1999] 1 AC 82, 96 (HL).
[118] *CICA v AS* (n 19) [9] and [69]–[80].

other natural or artificial embankment, or off a railway platform, intending to cause death or personal injury, or being reckless as to whether these are caused.

2.77 The CICB also heard claims in which cyclists were injured when they struck objects deliberately placed in the road, and then possibly falling into the path of an oncoming vehicle. Neither were these excluded, and under the 2012 Scheme could fall within Annex B paragraph 2(1)(b) as acts of a violent nature, similar to *Martin*.[119]

3 Annex B paragraph 4(1)(c): animal attacks

2.78 The external elements of a crime of violence must be attributable to human action or omission. Under the common law scheme, the CICB regularly received applications from persons injured in attacks by animals, most frequently by dogs over which the person in charge had lost control, or had deliberately set upon the applicant. Claims falling under the latter category necessarily meant that the owner had taken some action prior to the attack that could be described as 'deliberate', as a crime which, depending on the extent of the victim's injury and the owner's intention, could be an offence under sections 18, 20, or 47 of the OAPA 1861, and a crime of violence. The obvious analogy were claims in which the applicant had been 'deliberately' injured by the use of a weapon.

2.79 But cases in which the owner's action or inaction concerning the control of her dog was not deliberate proved much more difficult to resolve,[120] leading to a sequence of claims that culminated in the Court of Appeal's decision in *CICA v TS*,[121] and its application in *NJ v CICA*.[122] Following the Supreme Court's decision in *Jones*, these decisions confirm that the approach to be taken in these cases and in any falling within what was paragraph 8(a) of the earlier tariff schemes, now paragraph 4 of the 2012 Scheme, is to ask whether the injury was directly attributable to (a) a crime that (b) having regard to its nature, was a crime of violence.

2.80 Both (a) and (b) may be satisfied where the tribunal of fact can find that the owner had committed an offence under section 20 of the OAPA 1861. As to (a), the Upper Tribunal held in *Criminal Injuries Compensation Authority v First-tier Tribunal and Doyle* that the question for the FTT was whether the owner had been subjectively reckless as to any risk of injury to a person that was posed by the dog. If the owner was, that finding must be clearly stated; it was wrong to say that the owner '*should have* foreseen that some physical harm' (emphasis added) to the claimant.[123] As to (b), the Supreme Court having determined that the section 20

[119] *Martin* (n 43); CICB, 22nd Report (Cm 42 1986) para 26; 28th Report (Cm 2122 1993) para 23.4; 31st Report (Cm 3169 1996) para 6.4, respectively; (ch 2.23–2.27).

[120] CICA (Guide 2001) para 7.20, (Guide 2008) para 23.

[121] *CICA v TS* (n 22).

[122] *NJ v CICA* (n 23).

[123] [2014] UKUT 556 (AAC) [19] (*CICA v Doyle*).

offence would always be a crime of violence for the purpose of the scheme, the Upper Tribunal did not disturb the FTT's conclusion that the claimant should succeed.

Section 3(1) of DDA 1991 provides that its owner or person for the time being in charge is guilty of an offence 'if a dog is dangerously out of control in a public place', and of an aggravated offence 'if the dog while so out of control injures any person'. As a crime of strict liability the dog owner's state of mind is irrelevant. 'The offence is committed simply by being the owner of a dog which is in a public place in circumstances giving rise to grounds for reasonable apprehension that it will injure someone' (DDA 1991 section 10(1)).[124] As to (a), there must be a finding on the facts that there was a crime, evidenced either by a conviction or the drawing of a reasonable inference from them, and as to (b), 'a crime does not become a crime of violence simply because it results in injury to the person'.[125] In determining (b), the offender's state of mind may form 'part of the wider factual matrix which needs to be considered in deciding whether what was committed was a crime of violence'.[126] **2.81**

The specific question of whether an offence under section 3(1) of the DDA 1991 could be a crime of violence was considered at length by the Court of Appeal in *CICA v TS*. The claimant, who was riding his bicycle, was severely injured when he swerved into the path of a car as he tried to avoid a small dog that had run into the road and was barking aggressively at him. His claim was rejected by the CICA but allowed by the FTT, which the Upper Tribunal upheld. On the facts, the Court of Appeal agreed that there was a crime under section 3(1), but applying Lord Hope's analysis in *Jones*, concluded that 'the offence in this case could only be described as a crime of violence if one were to have regard to its consequences rather than its nature'. Both the FTT and the Upper Tribunal had 'concentrated on the consequences of the crime rather than its essential nature';[127] accordingly, the CICA's decision was upheld. **2.82**

The application of the Court of Appeal's decision to claims made under the 2008 and the 2012 Schemes was analysed at length by the Upper Tribunal in *NJ v CICA*. The facts are similar to *CICA v TS*, save that in *NJ v CICA* the cyclist had been directly attacked and seriously injured by the dog,[128] a 'telling' distinction which suggests that in *CICA v TS* there was a break in the chain of causation.[129] The issue before the Upper Tribunal centred on the resolution of two propositions **2.83**

---

[124] *CICA v TS* (n 22) [9] (Moore-Bick LJ).
[125] *NJ v CICA* (n 23) [15] (Judge Wikeley).
[126] ibid [25]; *CICA v AS* (n 19) [65] 'consideration of the consequences of an act are not wholly excluded if that sheds light on the nature of the act itself' (Judge Knowles QC).
[127] *CICA v TS* (n 22) [22]–[24] (Moore-Bick LJ).
[128] *NJ v CICA* (n 23) [37].
[129] *CICA v Doyle* (n 123) [27]; (ch 3.35–3.36).

that flowed from the Court of Appeal's decision. These were, first, that the fact that an injury constitutes an offence under section 3(1) of the DDA 1991 does not of itself make it a crime of violence and, secondly, that it does not follow that that offence could never be such a crime. As the Upper Tribunal succinctly put the matter, 'the dog's owner was later convicted of an offence under the Dangerous Dogs Act 1991. But is that enough to make it a "crime of violence"? I conclude the short answer is that it may be'.[130]

2.84 The Upper Tribunal found that the FTT's summary of reasons, as in *CICA v Doyle*, could have been clearer on whether there was an offence under section 3(1), but that in its application of the second element of the two-stage test in *Jones*, its reasoning was flawed. Because it had not adequately analysed the offence, it did not ask all the factual questions relevant in deciding whether section 3(1) was a crime of violence. As it later observed in *Criminal Injuries Compensation Authority v First-tier Tribunal and CB*, the FTT must avoid the danger of conflating the existence of a reckless state of mind with a crime of violence, without identifying and analysing the particular crime of violence and its inherent nature.[131] It did not follow, because the consequence of the dog being 'so out of control' that it 'injures any person', that the aggravated offence was of its nature a crime of violence; the question in *NJ v CICA* was whether injury to any person was an 'integral element' of its definition.[132] Whether it is or not '*will depend on the particular circumstances of the case*';[133] in short, as *NJ v CICA* shows, an offence under section 3(1) of the DDA 1991 may be treated on its facts as a crime of violence.[134]

2.85 This question ceases to be an issue under the 2012 Scheme. Concerned that awards were being made in claims where the dog's owner was only reckless as to the risk of injury to another, the government tightened the condition under which this may be a criminal injury. Annex B paragraph 4(1) provides that 'a crime of violence will not be considered to have been committed for the purposes of this Scheme if, in particular, an injury: (c) resulted from an animal attack, unless the animal was used with intent to cause injury to a person', phraseology that mimics paragraph 4(1)(b) concerning claims arising from the use of a vehicle. And, as in that case, the fault element is now 'intent' instead of deliberation.[135] This, together with the phraseology, 'of this Scheme', indicate both that its wording is to be taken as distancing its interpretation from that reached in the case of the 2008 Scheme and, in retrospect, that it would have

---

[130] *NJ v CICA* (n 23) [1] (Judge Wikeley).

[131] [2015] UKUT 371 (AAC) [72].

[132] *NJ v CICA* (n 23) [25]–[27].

[133] *CICA v TS* (n 22) [24] (Moore-Bick LJ), emphasis added in *NJ v CICA* (n 23) [44].

[134] See Judge Wikeley's analysis in *NJ v CICA* (n 23) [41]–[42] of the approach to be taken to claims under the 2008 Scheme following the Court of Appeal's decision in *CICA v TS* (n 22).

[135] Ministry of Justice (2012a) para 186.

been inappropriate to have read that or earlier tariff schemes 'through the lens of the more restrictive 2012 Scheme'.[136]

Attacks by dogs remain a problem, but the government was clear that the scheme should extend only to cases where the dog was used as a weapon. The proper redress in these circumstances 'would be found elsewhere—through an insurance claim, a compensation order as a result of criminal proceedings or a civil claim'.[137] **2.86**

4 Annex B paragraph 4(1)(d): injuries sustained in sport and other activities

Contact sports and other activities that involve the possibility of serious injury give rise to no criminal liability where the participants consented, and any personal injury that is sustained, no matter how serious, occurred within the rules of the game or the agreed or implicit expectations about its conduct. In such cases, paragraph 4(1) of Annex B provides that a 'crime of violence will not be considered to have been committed for the purposes of this Scheme if, in particular, an injury: (d) was sustained in the usual course of sporting or other activity to which a person consented by taking part in the activity'. 'The usual course' will cover injuries sustained, for example, in boxing or wrestling matches, or in a game of rugby or football, where the participants were playing by the rules, possibly as judged by an official. **2.87**

In civil law, the question is whether the defendant 'failed to exercise that degree of care which was appropriate in all the circumstances, or that he acted in a way to which the plaintiff cannot be expected to have consented'.[138] But, for the purpose of the 2012 Scheme, the act or omission causing the injury must be done either intentionally, such as being punched after the bell in a boxing match, or in the case of a late or a high tackle in rugby or soccer, recklessly. These judgments are questions of fact, and where the fault element is found, may constitute an offence under section 20 of the OAPA 1861, and thus a crime of violence under paragraph 2(1)(a), as a 'physical attack', or under paragraph 2(1)(b), as an 'act or omission of a violent nature'. But an injury that is negligently inflicted, even though it is outwith the game's 'usual course' will not be a criminal injury, no matter how serious the injury, because there will be no crime of intention or recklessness. **2.88**

The key questions under Annex B paragraph 4(1)(d) are whether (a) there was a crime, and (b) the injury was outside the usual course of the activity. The second question was in issue in *AH v First-tier Tribunal and Criminal Injuries Compensation Authority*, a claim based on the 2008 Scheme.[139] The claimant had been blinded in one eye as the result of a 'hand-off' executed by an opposing **2.89**

[136] *NJ v CICA* (n 23) [35].
[137] Ministry of Justice (2012b) para 160; on compensation orders; (ch 7.09).
[138] *Condon v Basi* [1985] 1 WLR 866, 868E (CA) (Sir John Donaldson MR).
[139] JR/1184/2013 (*AH v CICA*).

player in a game of rugby union. If the player's actions constituted an offence under section 20 of the OAPA 1861, there would, as *Jones* had held, be a crime of violence. But as the FTT had, contrary to the RFU Disciplinary Panel, found that the player's hand-off was within the rules, the claimant could be said to have implicitly consented to the possibility of injury. If that were so, the question for the FTT was whether what occurred went 'beyond what a player can reasonably be regarded as having accepted by taking part in the sport'.[140] The FTT had not addressed this question, but while accepting that it was not bound by the Disciplinary Panel's findings of fact, the Upper Tribunal found that the FTT was wrong in law because it did not sufficiently set out the reasons why it had reached a contrary decision.[141]

2.90 The 'other activity' that carries a risk of injury to which a person consented may cover a wide variety of incidents. In a claim before the CICB, a professional escapologist sustained injury when he was unable to free himself from the rope with which two volunteers from the audience, one a climber and the other himself an escapologist, had bound him.[142] That activity might extend to 'horseplay', which, where it takes place amongst children, implicitly carries within it the notion of rule-bound behaviour.[143] In the case of adult participants, that behaviour may go beyond what is 'the usual course', and may comprise a crime of violence and a criminal injury, but because of the applicant's conduct,[144] the CICA might think it appropriate to refuse or reduce an award under paragraph 25 of the scheme (Chapter 4.22–4.44).

5 Annex B paragraph 4(1)(e): foetal injury caused by substance abuse

2.91 Under the common law scheme, the CICB had accepted and sometimes made awards in respect of children born with Foetal Alcohol Spectrum Disorder (FASD). The basis of such claims was that the mother had consumed so much alcohol during pregnancy that she had committed an offence under section 23 of the OAPA 1861, in that she had inflicted grievous bodily harm on 'any other person' by administering to that person 'any poison or other destructive or noxious thing'. In the successful claims, it was clear that FASD did constitute grievous bodily harm, and that as the mother had at least been reckless as to whether some harm should occur,[145] there was a crime of violence, for which paragraph 8(a) of the then tariff schemes specifically included 'an act of poisoning'.

[140] *Barnes* [2004] EWCA Crim 3246, [2005] 1 WLR 910 [12] (CA).
[141] *AH v CICA* (n 139) [22]–[24].
[142] CICB 25th Report (n 38) paras 16.7–9.
[143] *Blake v Galloway* [2004] EWCA Civ 814, [2004] 3 All ER 315 (CA); Ministry of Justice (2012a) para 181).
[144] *Richardson and Irwin* [1999] 1 Cr App R 192 (CA).
[145] *Cunningham* (n 32), *Savage and Parmenter* (n 30).

The CICA changed its approach to these claims following the decision in *Attorney General's Reference (No 3 of 1994)*. This concerned the prosecution of a defendant who stabbed a woman in the stomach, knowing her to be pregnant. She was treated in hospital and lived, but gave birth prematurely to child who, after a brief life, died as a result of the attack. In determining the defendant's liability for the murder or manslaughter of the child, the House of Lords identified a number of established rules relating to criminal liability. Rule 3 was that: 'Except under statute an embryo or foetus *in utero* cannot be the victim of a crime of violence'.[146] Consequently, the CICA took the view that a foetus could not satisfy the external element of section 23, that the poison or destructive or noxious thing was administered to or taken by 'any other person'. **2.92**

Its approach was challenged in *CP v First-tier Tribunal and Criminal Injuries Compensation Authority*. CP was born with FASD as a direct result of her mother's consumption of alcohol during pregnancy. A claim was made on her behalf under the 2008 Scheme. The CICA refused to make an award on the basis that she had not been the victim of a crime of violence, which was reversed on appeal to the FTT. The judicial review of the FTT's decision was heard after the Supreme Court's decision in *Jones*. Following the House of Lords' analysis, the Upper Tribunal held that as section 23 required the poison (the alcohol) to be administered to 'any other person', the *actus reus* could not be met because at the time that it was administered the foetus had no legal personality.[147] The Court of Appeal upheld this finding, rejecting as flawed the claimant's argument there was an unbroken causal connection between the mother's actions and the child's birth, at which point she acquired legal personality and could be a victim of the offence. The Court contrasted the offence of manslaughter, where the victim's death, which necessarily occurs at a time after birth, with the *actus reus* of section 23, which is completed once the poison has been administered.[148] **2.93**

Whatever the legal status of an unborn child, the government's view was that it would be inappropriate to use taxpayers' money in circumstances it considered to be inconsistent with the scheme's main purpose.[149] Paragraph 4(1) of the 2012 Scheme specifically excludes an injury that (e) 'was sustained *in utero* as a result of harmful substances willingly ingested by the mother during pregnancy, with intent to cause, or being reckless as to, injury to the foetus'. **2.94**

146 [1998] AC 245, 254 (HL) (Lord Mustill).

147 [2013] UKUT 638 (AAC) [15]–[16] (*CP v CICA*).

148 [2014] EWCA Civ 1554, [2015] QB 45 [63] (CA) (Lord Dyson).

149 Ministry of Justice (2012a) para 186.

E Omitted injuries

1 Poisoning

2.95 The absence of any definition of a 'crime of violence' from the common law or the earlier tariff schemes necessitated the specific inclusion of poisoning, which like arson is an offence that can be committed without violence being directed at the victim. Despite the government's clear assertion that, in common with arson, 'for the removal of any doubt', acts of poisoning would continue to be included, there is no reference to this offence in the 2012 Scheme.[150] In *CP v CICA*, Treacy LJ observed that as poisoning is an offence which may be committed intentionally or recklessly, its inclusion in paragraph 8(a) of the earlier scheme was not determinative of its status: '[it] may well be that those differing states of mind have a bearing on the question on whether the crime committed is a crime of violence', but his Lordship did not pursue the matter.[151] In the case of a victim with legal personality, it might be difficult to regard injuries caused by an offence under section 23 of the OAPA 1861 as a 'physical attack' under paragraph 2(1)(a), but Treacy LJ's comments leave open the question of whether it could constitute an act 'of a violent nature' under paragraph 2(1)(b).

2 Trespass on a railway

2.96 For many years, both the common law and the tariff schemes provided that an injury directly attributable to 'an offence of trespass on a railway' was a criminal injury. Introduced in paragraph 4(c) of the 1990 revision, this was the government's concession to train drivers over the matter of railway suicides,[152] which the Court of Appeal had held in *ex parte Webb* not to be attributable to the commission of a crime of violence.[153] The personal injuries that they sustained in these cases were typically mental rather than physical; but provided that the mental injury accompanied a physical injury, such as could occur if the driver applied the brakes on the train so hard that he injured himself by falling in his cab, there would be a criminal injury under paragraph 8(b) without more.

2.97 The condition that any mental injury had to be accompanied by a physical injury was the implicit consequence of paragraph 9(d) of the earlier tariff schemes, which, in common with paragraphs 9(a)–(c), limited both the scope of the criminal injury, and the range of potential applicants, where the only injury the applicant sustained was mental injury. Compensation in this case would not be payable unless the injury was sustained 'by a person employed in the business

---

150 Ministry of Justice (2012a) para 183; (2012b) para 29.17.

151 *CP v CICA* (n 147) [51].

152 Home Office (2005) 21; David Miers, 'Compensating Deserving Victims of Violent Crime: The Criminal Injuries Compensation Scheme 2012' (2014) 34 *Legal Studies* 242–78, 256–58.

153 *Ex parte Webb* (n 5).

of a railway', who 'either witnessed and was present on the occasion when another person sustained physical (including fatal) injury directly attributable to an offence of trespass on a railway, or was closely involved in its immediate aftermath'. These alternative conditions were the same as those which paragraph 9(b) applied to secondary victims who witnessed or were closely involved in the aftermath of a criminal injury sustained by a 'loved one'. Because the government concluded that the scheme was not designed to compensate injuries sustained in the course of a person's employment,[154] this criminal injury was omitted from the 2012 Scheme.

Its omission does not, however, entirely exclude personal injuries directly attributable to other violent crimes against the person that the offender may have committed while trespassing on a railway. Section 34 of the OAPA 1861 can cover personal injuries to the train driver or the passengers caused when the train strikes, or brakes suddenly to avoid striking, objects placed on the track by a trespasser. By analogy with the appeal in *Webster,* abandoning a car on a level crossing in order to cause, and that did cause, a passenger train to crash or derail, could also constitute an offence under section 20 of the OAPA 1861 and an act of a violent nature within Annex B paragraph 2(1)(b); or by analogy with *Warwick*,[155] personal injuries caused by a person standing on a trackside embankment throwing stones or other objects at or through the train's windows could come within that paragraph where the driver or a passenger was a 'direct victim' of a section 20 offence. **2.98**

III Paragraph 5: Law Enforcement

A Introduction

First introduced in the common law scheme, paragraph 5(1) continues to provide that injuries directly attributable to an act of law enforcement are criminal injuries for which an award may be made: **2.99**

> [a] person may be eligible for an award if they sustain a criminal injury 'which is directly attributable to their taking an exceptional and justified risk for the purpose, in a relevant place, of: (a) apprehending an offender or suspected offender; (b) preventing a crime; (c) containing or remedying the consequences of a crime; or (d) assisting a constable who is acting for one or more of the purposes described in paragraphs (a) to (c).

Although its terms have always extended to employees in the private sector, the principal beneficiaries of this provision have been, and will continue to be, the

[154] Ministry of Justice (2012b) para 160.
[155] *Webster and Warwick* (n 42).

police and other public sector personnel, such as teachers, prison officers, and medical staff criminally injured while at work.

2.100 Apart from the police, this category of criminal injury was designed to apply to injuries sustained by private citizens engaged in an act of the law enforcement, but in respect of which it might be difficult to say that the injuries were caused by a crime of violence. If during the struggle to apprehend him, the offender intentionally or recklessly injured the victim, it is likely that there would have been an offence under sections 20 or 47 of the OAPA 1861, or more particularly under section 18. These would also constitute a crime of violence under the common law and earlier tariff schemes, and under Annex B paragraph 2(1)(a) as 'a physical attack'. In this case, the two categories of criminal injury were, and continue to be, alternative grounds on which a claim might succeed: 'in appropriate circumstances resisting arrest would be capable of constituting a crime of violence for the purposes of paragraph 4 of the 2012 Scheme'.[156]

2.101 But if the injury was 'accidental' in the sense that the offender did not satisfy the relevant fault element of an offence against the person, there would, but for the law enforcement category, have been no criminal injury. Its history is the government's repeated efforts to limit the scheme's broad initial applicability to accidental law enforcement injuries sustained by the police and bystanders,[157] which are all now subject to the condition in paragraph 5(1) that they were at the time 'taking an exceptional and justified risk'.

B Law enforcement: the purposes

2.102 The earlier tariff schemes specified three law enforcement purposes for which an award might be payable. A fourth was provided in paragraph 12(b) by way of the application of the exceptional and justified risk requirement to accidental injuries arising, in addition to these three, from 'any other activity directed to containing, limiting or remedying the consequences of a crime.' There are some consequential changes in the 2012 Scheme. It provides that the risk the applicant takes is 'for the purpose' of one of the four named purposes; it is therefore unnecessary to specify, as did the earlier schemes, that this category applies to attempted law enforcement activity. That aside, their scope remains as it was under the earlier schemes.

1 Paragraph 5(1)(a): 'apprehending an offender or suspected offender'

2.103 Paragraph 5(1) of the 2012 Scheme provides that 'a person may be eligible for an award if they sustain a criminal injury which is directly attributable to their

[156] *CICA v First-tier Tribunal and LH*, JR/3330/2015 (AAC) [15] (Judge Levenson) (*CICA v LH*).

[157] For the history see David Miers, *State Compensation for Criminal Injuries* (Blackstone Press 1997) 92–101.

taking an exceptional and justified risk for the purpose, in a relevant place, of (a) apprehending an offender or suspected offender'. The phrase 'apprehension or attempted apprehension' had been substituted in the common law scheme for 'arrest or attempted arrest' following *R v Criminal Injuries Compensation Board, ex parte Carr*,[158] a claim that concerned an applicant injured when trying to detain an offender. That phrase has no meaning in law, but its substitution meant that a private citizen could qualify under this heading although, as in that case, he had no power of arrest.

The applicant may come within the law enforcement category even though the **2.104**
person apprehended could not have been convicted of any offence; it would be enough if in the circumstances as the applicant saw them that person had committed an offence. For example, where the person the applicant apprehended had run from a shop while being pursued by the shopkeeper shouting, 'Stop thief!', it would be irrelevant whether or not that person was a thief. This subjective approach was confirmed in *R v Criminal Injuries Compensation Board, ex parte Lawton*, where the Divisional Court held that where a police officer was injured when seeking to restrain a man who had initially been detained on suspicion of theft, but was at the time being held under the emergency provisions of the Mental Health Act 1959, it would introduce 'an unduly legalistic note into this essentially informal procedure' to expect the officer to pause to enquire in what capacity he was acting when injured.[159] This observation would no longer be appropriate to the statutory scheme, but the 2012 Guide suggests that there is no substantive change: 'You may be eligible for a payment if you were injured while trying to apprehend an offender or suspected offender'.

2 Paragraph 5(1)(b): 'preventing a crime'

The Court of Appeal took a similar approach in *R v Criminal Injuries Compensation* **2.105**
Board, ex parte Ince,[160] which concerned the interpretation of the phrase, 'the prevention or attempted prevention of an offence' in the earlier tariff schemes. In answer to a general alarm, the applicant's husband, a police driver, jumped a set of traffic lights and was killed by another police car answering the same alarm crossing on the green light. It transpired that the alarm was false, and for this reason the CICB found that the driver had not been engaged in the prevention of crime. Both the Divisional Court and the Court of Appeal held that this was in error. Preferring a subjective test of the police driver's belief, the Court of Appeal held that it was irrelevant whether there ever could or would have been an offence. The officer's actions were to be judged by his belief that he was engaged in the prevention of crime, even though he was mistaken.

---

158 [1981] RTR 122 (DC).
159 [1972] 1 WLR 1589, 1592 (DC).
160 [1973] 1 WLR 1334 (CA) (*ex parte Ince*).

3 Paragraph 5(1)(c): 'containing or remedying the consequences of a crime'

4 Paragraph 5(1)(d): 'assisting a constable who is acting for one or more of the purposes described in paragraphs (a) to (c)

2.106 With the omission of 'limiting', whose differentiation from 'containing' remained untested, paragraph 5(1)(c) restates paragraph 12(b) of the earlier schemes. It should be noted that this paragraph continues to apply to actions in respect of 'a crime', which will clearly cover a response to the victim of, for example, a physical attack, but is not limited in this way. Paragraph 5(1)(c) could extend to physical or mental injuries sustained by a rescuer who seeks to contain or remedy the consequences of, for example, an offence under section 1 of the CDA 1971, in which a person has been trapped by the damage to or destruction of the property. It could also extend to the rescuer's actions in going to the aid of a person who has been injured by 'the use of a vehicle', constituting an offence under the RTA 1988. This possibility raises an anomaly in the scheme. Annex B paragraph 4(1)(b) provides that a person injured by the use of a vehicle will not have been the victim of a crime of violence unless the vehicle was used 'with intent to cause injury to a person' (2.69–.77). If it were not so used, that victim would not sustain a criminal injury, whereas, provided that she had taken an exceptional and justified risk, the rescuer would.

C Law enforcement: 'An exceptional and justified risk'

1 Background

2.107 Because the common law scheme did not at first qualify the law enforcement gateway so as to exclude accidental injuries, their treatment caused problems in its application. To exert some control, the CICB sought to draw the line where a bystander was accidentally injured while an arrest was taking place, but who was not in any way engaged in assisting the police officer. In *R v Criminal Injuries Compensation Board, ex parte Schofield*, the Court of Appeal held that there was nothing in the scheme that warranted this restriction.[161] When coupled with its decision in *ex parte Ince* that the 'attempted prevention of an offence' included an instance in which an officer 'goes towards the place or supposed place of the supposed offence' in response to a police call,[162] the Home Office concluded that the scope of this gateway was too wide. It proposed that such injuries should only be compensable, in the words of paragraph 6(d) inserted into the common law scheme in 1980, 'if the applicant was at the time taking an exceptional risk which was justified in all the circumstances'.[163]

[161] [1971] 2 All ER 1011 (CA).
[162] *Ex parte Ince* (n 160) 1343 (Megaw LJ).
[163] Home Office (1978) para 5.23; (1986) para 6.9.

This condition was repeated in paragraph 12 of the earlier tariff schemes, providing that in any case where an injury was sustained accidentally by a person engaged in (a) any of the law-enforcement activities described in paragraph 8(c), or (b) any other activity directed to containing, limiting, or remedying the consequences of a crime, compensation would not be payable unless the person was, at the time that they sustained the injury, 'taking an exceptional risk which was justified in all the circumstances'. In a further concession to train drivers who suffered a mental injury as a result of attending a person injured on a railway line, paragraph 9(d) provided that this condition did not apply to 'a person employed in the business of a railway'. But a bystander, or a member of the fire and rescue service, who attended the scene would not be compensable unless he did meet that condition. **2.108**

These arguably anomalous outcomes are superseded by the 2012 Scheme, which treats all injuries that are directly attributable to the purposes listed in paragraph 5 equally. Its purpose is **2.109**

> to support the work of the police and those individual citizens who take action to prevent crime. We therefore propose to continue to make awards to those accidentally injured while taking an exceptional risk which in the circumstances was justified, either while trying to catch an offender or while helping the police to do so.[164]

2 Interpretation

Paragraph 5(1) of the 2012 Scheme presents the two primary conditions in slightly different terms, as 'an exceptional and justified risk', but their substantive scope remains. The conditions apply to any applicant who takes such a risk, but in a continuation of the intention behind paragraph 12(b), paragraph 5(2) provides that a risk taken in the course of a person's work will 'not be considered to be exceptional if it would normally be expected of them in the course of that work'. This will extend to private sector bodies that perform criminal justice functions, but it is of particular significance to public sector personnel, notably the police, and the fire and rescue service. **2.110**

Paragraph 5 invites separate consideration of its general application to any risk taken for the purpose of paragraph 5(1)(a)–(d), which includes the tests that should be applied when determining whether a risk is 'exceptional and justified', and its specific application to injuries sustained in the normal course of the claimant's work (paragraph 5(2)). Applications of paragraph 12 of the earlier schemes may be illustrative of these kinds of risk, but authoritative interpretation **2.111**

[164] Ministry of Justice (2012a) para 184. Compare the degree of statutory protection given by s 4 of the Social Action, Responsibility and Heroism Act 2015 where 'the alleged negligence or breach of statutory duty occurred when the person was acting heroically by intervening in an emergency to assist an individual in danger', and *Robinson v Chief Constable of West Yorkshire Police* [2018] UKSC 4, [2018] 2 WLR 595 [1]–[3], [75]–[80] (SC) (Lord Reed), where the police injured a bystander while they were struggling to arrest a suspected offender.

of paragraph 5, which should be read on its own terms, is found in two decisions of the Upper Tribunal, *Criminal Injuries Compensation Authority v First-tier Tribunal and KM*, and *CICA v LH*,[165] and in the Court of Appeal's decision in the subsequent joined appeals.[166]

2.112 In *CICA v KM*, a firefighter was called to a life-threatening fire at a block of flats that had been caused by arson; he was 'containing or remedying the consequences of a crime' within paragraph 5(1)(c). Believing that the seat of the fire was in an occupied first floor flat, the senior officer ordered the claimant and a colleague to put on the appropriate breathing equipment, enter the building in order to hose the flat, and enable the occupants to escape. When they arrived at what they believed to be the flat they discovered that it was in fact a storeroom, which contained a number of flammable cans of paint. At some stage, the claimant's hose became entangled and he tripped over debris, injuring his left ankle. The CICA dismissed the application on the ground that, as the claimant would be expected as part of his duties to go into a smoke-filled building in order to save life and was something for which he had been trained, the risk he took was not exceptional. This was so notwithstanding that this was not in fact the situation. On appeal, the FTT found that had the true situation been known at the outset, the claimant's actions would indeed have been exceptional, as the usual course of practice in such a case would be to fight the fire from outside the building. Whether or not he had been trained to deal with such a situation was irrelevant.

3 Paragraph 5(1): 'an exceptional risk': a subjective test

2.113 The Upper Tribunal confirmed, first, that both the CICA and the FTT were correct in applying a subjective test to the question of whether the claimant took an 'exceptional' risk; this turned on 'what was believed to be the position at [the] time the risk was taken. The concept of "taking" a risk in its very nature requires a subjective view of what that risk is'.[167] But in focusing exclusively on the time that the claimant entered the building, they both applied the test to the wrong point of time, which should have been when he entered what he believed was an occupied flat, but which turned out to be a storeroom. This was the 'point when the subjective view of the claimant' (that this was an occupied flat) 'and the objective reality' (that it was a storeroom full of flammable material) 'coincided'. In then (literally) taking steps to extinguish the fire in the storeroom, the claimant took a risk that *was* exceptional because this was not a risk that would normally be expected of him in the course of his work.[168]

[165] [2016] UKUT 338 (AAC), [2017] AACR 4 (*CICA v KM*), *CICA v LH* (n 156).

[166] *Criminal Injuries Compensation Authority and First-tier Tribunal (SEC)* and *Kenneth Mailer and Lewis Haigh* [2018] EWCA Civ 1175, 2018 WL 02338152 (*CICA v Mailer and Haigh*); (ch 6.172).

[167] *CICA v KM* (n 165) [18] (Judge Levenson).

[168] ibid [20].

In the CICA's appeal against this decision, the Court of Appeal held that in reaching this conclusion the Upper Tribunal had failed to comply with section 17 of the Tribunals and Courts Enforcement Act 2007, which governs its powers in judicial review proceedings. Having found that the FTT was in error, the tribunal could substitute its own decision if that were the only decision that was possible. This was not the case, since the FTT had never addressed the factual question of the claimant's perception of the risk when he entered the room. But the court also concluded that, had the claim been remitted (as it should have been), it was likely that the FTT would have found for the claimant.[169] **2.114**

The Upper Tribunal also approved the subjective test in *CICA v LH,* where a police officer was injured when trying to push an uncooperative and abusive offender he had just arrested into the small cage in a police van. The offender had a Police National Computer (PNC) 'extremely violent' marker against him but, applying a subjective test, the CICA dismissed his claim because the officer was at the time of arrest unaware of facts that might make the risk he took exceptional. Agreeing that the PNC marker was irrelevant, the Upper Tribunal did not, however, interfere with the FTT's finding on appeal that in trying to deal with the offender in circumstances in which the two other officers present throughout who, in contravention of the relevant police protocol, had failed to assist him, the claimant was taking an exceptional risk that would 'not normally be expected of him in the course of his work'.[170] **2.115**

As in the firefighter's claim, the Upper Tribunal found that the FTT had erred when it decided that the nature of the risk to the police officer could be assessed in the light of subsequently discovered facts. But because the FTT had clearly decided that the 'real and operable' cause of the claimant's injuries was the other officers' failure to assist him, the Court of Appeal held that the Upper Tribunal's conclusion, that no different decision was open to the FTT, was justified.[171] **2.116**

4 Paragraph 5(1): 'a justified risk': an objective test

The question of whether a risk is in any set of circumstances 'exceptional and justified' is therefore clearly fact sensitive. In determining whether a risk taken for the purpose of paragraph 5(1) is 'exceptional' depends first, on the claimant's understanding or perception of the risk, at the time that she takes it, that she might sustain a personal injury as result of her intervention. Secondly, the risk must be 'justified', which it is suggested, is an objective test, determined on the facts in any claim. This may include, as the 2012 Guide indicates, 'the seriousness of the situation, and whether there was an immediate threat to those involved', as **2.117**

[169] *CICA v Mailer and Haigh* (n 166) [17]–[21].
[170] *CICA v LH* (n 156) [21].
[171] *CICA v Mailer and Haigh* (n 166) [34] (CA).

was the case in *CICA v LH,* where the offender was threatening to harm himself and others, or as in *CICA v KM,* in an order or a direction given to the claimant by a superior.

5 Paragraph 5(2): the normal course of work and the relevance of training

2.118 In *CICA v KM,* the CICA's decision was also based on the ground that, as the claimant would be expected as part of his duties to go into a smoke-filled building which was on fire in order to save life, the risk he took was not exceptional. Paragraph 5(2) provides: '[A] risk taken for any purpose described in sub- paragraph (1) in the course of a person's work will not be considered to be exceptional if it would normally be expected of them in the course of that work.'

> The Upper Tribunal agreed with the FTT's finding that the fact that the applicant had been trained had no bearing on their claim, there being 'nothing in the 2012 Scheme itself which indicates that whether or not a person was trained to undertake a particular task was relevant to whether what they were doing was exceptional.[172]

2.119 When it decided the claim, the CICA's Guide to the 2012 Scheme then provided that: '[w]e will not compensate people who were doing something that would be expected of them in course of their normal employment'. This may well be read as fettering the CICA's discretion, and in light of the FTT's analysis the Upper Tribunal found that it was misleading, and recommended its revision.[173] The 2016 revision provides that 'a risk will not be considered exceptional if it was something that you might *reasonably* have been expected to do in the normal course of your work' (emphasis added), which raises the question, what does this objective element add to the terms of paragraph 5(2)? Injuries sustained when a police officer trips while walking or running towards an incident or going to apprehend an offender in broad daylight, or when climbing, or jumping over walls, fences, parapets, or other obstructions, might all be regarded as unexceptional risks; it might be otherwise where the officer cannot see what is on the other side of these obstructions, or the incident occurred at night. These were all instances under the common law scheme, and might be regarded as indicating some differentiation as to the reasonableness of what 'would normally be expected' of claimants in the course of their work as police officers.

2.120 One particular case may be noted. In *ex parte Ince,* the injured police officer succeeded in his claim because the Court of Appeal took the view that his actions were to be judged by his mistaken belief that he was engaged in the prevention of crime. Under the 2012 Scheme, it would need to be shown that in chasing or trying to intercept a car which had refused to stop after an accident,

---

[172] *CICA v KM* (n 165) [12].
[173] ibid [13].

the claimant met both the subjective and the objective conditions in paragraph 5(1), and that his actions were not what would normally be expected of him. But if the driver sought to evade capture by ramming the officer's car, there might be a claim under Annex B paragraph 4(1)(b).

The Guide continues to provide that 'in considering whether a risk is exceptional we will consider if the risk taken was unusual and was not something which you had been trained to deal with'. But training in a given risk cannot be a dispositive factor in the determination of whether the risk actually taken was exceptional. This in turn permits the CICA to apply, as the CICB did, different standards of risk-taking as between different claimants for the purposes of paragraph 5(1). An elderly, disabled, or physically weak person faced with circumstances in which a police officer is struggling to apprehend a violent offender, may well take an exceptional risk when she decides to assist 'a constable who is acting for one or more of the purposes described in paragraphs (a) to (c)' (paragraph 5(1)(d)). The CICA could, on the particular facts of such a claim, find that what is exceptional for a citizen, for example, tackling a man armed with a knife, may not be so for a police officer. **2.121**

IV Paragraph 6: Secondary Victims: 'Loved Ones'

A Introduction

In addition to those who are the 'direct victims' of violent crime, it has also been a core purpose of the scheme to compensate those who suffer (principally mental) injuries as a result of witnessing their 'loved ones' being criminally injured. Paragraph 6 of the 2012 Scheme provides: **2.122**

> A person may be eligible for an award if they sustain a criminal injury in a relevant place which is directly attributable to being present at and witnessing an incident, or the immediate aftermath of an incident, as a result of which a loved one sustained a criminal injury in circumstances falling within paragraph 4 or 5. For these purposes a "loved one" is a person with whom the applicant:
> (a) at the time of the incident had a close relationship of love and affection; and
> (b) if the loved one is alive at the date of the application, continues to have such a relationship.

This provision covers circumstances in which a person witnesses her spouse or child being attacked or killed as a result of a crime of violence, or being injured while taking an exceptional and justified risk to apprehend an offender or prevent a crime, although she is not herself in any danger, or being present and witnessing 'the immediate aftermath' of such incidents. This criminal injury was one of the four categories that were listed in paragraph 9 of the earlier tariff schemes as a case where compensation would be payable for mental injury alone. In common with that paragraph, paragraph 6 has clear echoes of the common law rules governing **2.123** damages for psychiatric injury for primary and secondary victims.[174] While the discussion will reflect those rules, they are not to be taken as dispositive for the interpretation of the scheme.[175]

2.124 This section deals in turn with the three principal conditions of paragraph 6: that both the primary and the secondary victims must sustain a criminal injury, and that there is 'relationship proximity', and 'event proximity' between them. The discussion draws on the Upper Tribunal's analysis, approved by the Court of Appeal in *Criminal Injuries Compensation Authority v RS*,[176] of the four stage task that was to be met in a case involving mental injury which engaged paragraph 9(b) of the earlier tariff schemes, adapted to the requirements of paragraph 6. While paragraph 9(b) was in almost the same terms as paragraph 6, the 2012 Scheme introduced some significant changes whose purpose is to limit the conditions of eligibility, but to which the Upper Tribunal's analysis remains relevant.

B The primary and the secondary victims' criminal injuries

2.125 'The first stage is to make findings of fact as to what physical and mental injury or injuries were sustained by the primary victim, as to how they were sustained, and as to the period during which they were sustained.'[177] Paragraph 6 extends, first, to 'incidents' in which the primary victim's injuries, which may be fatal, are (paragraph 4) directly attributable to a crime of violence as defined in Annex B paragraph 2(1). Secondly, it extends to personal injuries sustained by the primary victim while he was engaged in an act of law enforcement as defined in paragraph 5. Adapting the facts of *Chadwick v British Railways Board*, where the plaintiff recovered damages for the psychiatric illness caused to her deceased husband by the traumatic effects of his rescuing and comforting of the victims of the Lewisham railway disaster in 1957, to a train crash caused by a crime of violence, the husband would be a primary victim by virtue of paragraph 5(1)(c), and his wife, who was also present and witnessed her husband's actions, a secondary victim.[178]

2.126 It is not necessary, however, that the criminal injury which the primary victim sustains is itself sufficiently serious to qualify for an award under the scheme, although of course, it may. The primary victim's eligibility for an award is to be determined separately from any claim the secondary victim may have, which means that an award to the primary victim that would be withheld or reduced by virtue of any of the conditions in paragraphs 22–27 of the scheme does not affect the secondary victim's eligibility. The secondary victim's claim under paragraph 6 is

---

[174] Deakin, Johnston, and Markesinis (n 50) 125–35.

[175] *RS v First-tier Tribunal & Criminal Injuries Compensation Authority* [2012] UKUT 205 (AAC) [13], [2013] AACR 34 (Walker J) (*RS v CICA*); (ch 1.30).

[176] [2013] EWCA Civ 1040, [2014] 1 WLR 1313 (*CICA v RS*).

[177] ibid [10] (Laws LJ).

[178] [1967] 1 WLR 912 (CA).

also quite separate from any claim she might have independent of any claim she may have under paragraphs 57–84 of the scheme as a 'qualifying relative', should the primary victim subsequently die (paragraph 7). It may be noted that whereas the interpretation of a 'secondary victim' is a question of fact, that of a 'qualifying relative' is a matter of law (Chapter 3.88–3.95).

The 2012 Scheme does not specify what kind of injury the claimant sustains, save that it will be one which appears in Part A of the tariff in Annex E. This is what the Upper Tribunal identified as 'the threshold injury' that the secondary victim must satisfy; one that in the words of paragraph 6, 'is directly attributable' to the incident in which the primary victim was injured or to its immediate aftermath.[179] It may be that a secondary victim is unlikely to sustain a physical injury, but the 2012 Guide appears to confine the injury to mental injury: **2.127**

> If you are claiming a payment because you witnessed, or were involved in the immediate aftermath of the injury of a loved one, you must have suffered a mental injury as a result. We will need medical evidence from a psychiatrist or a clinical psychologist confirming that this is the case.

C Relational proximity

The second stage in the Upper Tribunal's analysis is to identify whether the physical or mental injury sustained by the primary victim was 'a compliant injury'; that is, whether at the time it was sustained, the secondary victim had, as required by paragraph 6(a), a 'close relationship of love and affection' with the primary victim. This requirement is based on the first of the two conditions established in *Alcock v Chief Constable of South Yorkshire Police* for the purpose of a claim by his relatives for the psychiatric injury they sustained a result of the injuries caused to the primary victim by the defendant's negligence.[180] The House of Lords did not prescribe a list of potential claimants, but held that there must be a close and intimate relationship between the plaintiff and the primary victim of the sort generally enjoyed by spouses, parents, and children. Whether there is a relationship such as that specified in paragraph 6(a) is a question of fact; a grandmother or an uncle who has lived with the primary victim's family, and looked after them in the absence of one of the natural parents, may well meet this requirement. **2.128**

By paragraph 6(b), if the loved one is alive at the date of the application, the secondary victim must continue to have such a relationship with him or her. If the primary victim's criminal injury was fatal, the relationship must have existed at the time of the incident (paragraph 6(a)). These circumstances were provided for in paragraph 9(b)(i) of the earlier tariff schemes; their sequence has been reordered in the 2012 Scheme, but they are substantively the same. **2.129**

---

179 *CICA v RS* (n 176) [10]. In the Upper Tribunal's analysis this was the third stage.
180 [1992] 1 AC 310 (HL) (*Alcock v CC*).

D Event proximity

2.130 28 The final stage is that in relation to each 'threshold injury', the CICA must decide whether the secondary victim's 'compliant injury' was directly attributable to one of the alternative limbs of paragraph 6;[181] that is, that the injury is the result of the victim '*being present at and witnessing an incident, or the immediate aftermath of an incident*' in which the primary victim sustained his criminal injury. The italicized words replace those in paragraph 9(b)(ii), that 'the applicant either witnessed *or was present on the occasion when the other person sustained the injury, or was closely involved in its immediate aftermath*'. This formulation gave rise to three particular issues of interpretation: the scope of the word 'occasion', the referent of the preposition 'its' in the alternative condition, and the scope of the word 'immediate'.

1 'Being present at and witnessing an incident' in which the primary victim is criminally injured

2.131 The second condition for common law liability to secondary victims is 'proximity to the accident', which 'must be close in both time and space' to the negligently caused injury to the primary victim.[182] This proximity will be clearly demonstrated where the secondary victim was physically 'present at' and 'witnessing' by sight 'the incident' when the criminal injury to the primary victim occurred. But a person may also 'witness' an incident where, for example, she *hears* an injury being caused to another; for example, where a parent or spouse is tied up and blindfolded in a room of the family home, in which the person can hear the child's or spouse's cries of pain from another part of the room, or, depending on the scope of the phrase 'present at', in another room. Less obvious is a case in which the applicant is present in time but not in space, in the sense that she can see the incident in which the primary victim is criminally injured but is not physically present at it; for example, where the applicant, driving away from a car park having left his spouse there, sees at an increasing distance the offender attack her.

2.132 A more striking example were the claims made by those secondary victims who had sustained mental injury in Great Britain when they were speaking to their spouses or other close relations by phone as the second plane struck the World Trade Centre in New York on 11 September 2001, or who saw the impact on television knowing that their spouses were there. The CICA found that, although they were not personally 'involved in its immediate aftermath', these secondary victims 'sustained an injury in Great Britain', and satisfied the alternative condition in paragraph 9(b)(ii) of the 2001 Scheme, by being, if not physically, then temporally 'present on the occasion' when the primary victim sustained physical

[181] *CICA v RS* (n 176) [10].
[182] *McLoughlin v O'Brian* [1983] 1 AC 410, 422 (HL) (Lord Wilberforce).

injury. This interpretation was closed by the additional requirement in the 2008 Scheme, that the injury must have been attributable to 'an act occurring in Great Britain', for which the 2012 Scheme has substituted in paragraph 4 the phrase 'committed in a relevant place' (Chapter 3.02).

The 2012 Scheme makes a further, and subtle, change in cases of this kind. An applicant who sustains mental injury while watching live on television a football match being played in 'a relevant place', where her loved one is attacked and injured by the other team's supporters, would now fall outside the scope of paragraph 6. This is because the 2012 Scheme requires the applicant to have 'been present *at* and witnessing *the incident*' (emphases added), in which the loved one sustained the criminal injury, which clearly means physical presence at the incident rather than remote, albeit contemporaneous, presence. Although the applicant is present in time, she is not present in space, 'at the incident'. Where, in the words of the 2012 Guide, 'someone is later told about the incident either by the victim or another person', or hears or reads the account in the following day's media broadcasts, the applicant is proximate neither in space nor in time. **2.133**

(a) The substitution of 'occasion' by 'incident' Paragraph 6 replaces 'occasion' in paragraph 9(b)(ii) of the earlier tariff scheme, which had been the subject of extensive analysis in *AP v First-tier Tribunal & Criminal Injuries Compensation Authority*,[183] with the word, 'incident'. The applicant's father had been attacked and hospitalized. Some three or four hours after he had been treated for his injuries, and was waiting to be discharged, his son visited him; this was some seven hours after his father had been admitted to the hospital. The following day, and in the presence of his son, the father died from his injuries. The CICA rejected the applicant's claim on the ground that he had neither witnessed, nor been present, 'on the occasion when the primary victim sustained the injury' of the attack. The Upper Tribunal considered whether that phrase could cover 'not simply the initial injury sustained by the deceased at the time of the attack, but the direct and very quickly occurring consequences of it' which led to his death and which his son witnessed, but on the natural meaning of the words, held that it could not. This interpretation was consistent with the underlying intention of paragraph 9(b)(ii), to reflect the law on the recoverability of damages in tort for psychiatric injury; it would be unusual if the scheme went beyond the common law on this point.[184] **2.134**

The Upper Tribunal's reasoning was approved in full by the Court of Appeal in *CICA v RS*. The applicant was the primary victim's husband. While he was away from home over a weekend, she had been attacked and raped at knife point by a man who lived next door, later convicted of that offence. During the weekend, **2.135**

[183] [2011] UKUT 368 (AAC) (*AP v CICA*).
[184] ibid [18]–[21] (JudgeTurnbull).

the rapist sent his victim text messages about the attack, but she did not tell her husband until his return on Monday. The wife would have had her own claim for the rape, and for any other physical and mental injuries, but the CICA refused the husband's claim for mental injury on the basis that he did not meet the conditions in paragraph 9(b)(ii). The FTT upheld the CICA's decision, but in the subsequent judicial review the Upper Tribunal found that a differently constituted FTT might arrive at a different conclusion 'as to the scope of the attack', a conclusion that the CICA appealed to the Court of Appeal.

2.136 The CICA argued that, in setting out its four stage approach, which the Court approved in general, the Upper Tribunal had in its particular articulation of stage 1 'confused two distinct concepts which the Scheme requires should be kept separate: (1) the occasion on which the primary victim sustained the relevant injury; and (2) the consequences of that injury'. In seeking to recognize that a series of events may amount to an 'occasion', so as to include injuries that 'may or may not coincide with the period during which an attack or other conduct', and thereby amount to a criminal injury, the Tribunal 'conflated the occasion of the injury with its consequences'. Allowing the CICA's appeal on this point, and following the Court's decision in *Taylor v A Novo UK Limited*,[185] Laws LJ held that the wording of paragraph 9(b)(ii) 'must refer to the event which constituted the infliction of the injury, in effect the commission of the crime'.[186]

2.137 The *Oxford English Dictionary* (OED), which defines an 'incident' as 'an instance of something happening; an event or occurrence', and an 'occasion' as 'a particular event, or the time at which it takes place', suggests that these words are very close in meaning. But it is clear that the government intended by the substitution of 'occasion' with 'incident', that paragraph 6 should be confined to a specific event of short and finite duration. The substitution also brings this paragraph's wording into line with the general use of 'incident' within this, and earlier tariff schemes, to signify the event that gives rise to the criminal injury.

2 'Being present at and witnessing . . . the immediate aftermath of an incident' in which the primary victim was criminally injured

2.138 **(a) The referent of the preposition 'its' in paragraph 9(b)(ii)** The interpretation of paragraph 9(b)(ii) in *CICA v RS* also disposed of an argument raised in *R (VG) v First-tier Tribunal (CIC)* concerning the ambiguity in the referent of the preposition 'its' in the phrase, 'or was closely involved in its immediate aftermath'.[187] The question was whether the preposition referred to 'the occasion' on which the

[185] [2013] EWCA Civ 194, [2014] QB 150 (CA), where a secondary victim was unable to claim in respect of her mother's death three weeks after an accident at work that the daughter had not witnessed.

[186] *CICA v RS* (n 176) [12]–[13].

[187] [2014] UKUT 247 (AAC) (*VG v FTT*).

primary victim was criminally injured, or to the 'injury' that was sustained. The applicant's mental health suffered badly following her discovery some eighteen years after the event that her son had been sexually abused on a number of occasions by a family friend. The CICA refused her claim on the ground that she had patently not been present on any of these occasions, nor had she been closely involved in their immediate aftermath, decisions that the FTT upheld on appeal. The Upper Tribunal concluded that 'in the context of this Scheme', the word 'its' 'refers to "the occasion when [the primary victim] sustained the injury", and not to the time of any subsequent mental reaction that [he] might sustain',[188] a conclusion that the Court of Appeal had 'readily' accepted in *CICA v RS*.[189] Paragraph 6 of the 2012 Scheme obviates any possible ambiguity in the referent of the preposition 'its' by substituting 'or the immediate aftermath of *an* incident' for the phrase 'or was closely involved in *its* immediate aftermath' (emphasis added).

(b) The scope of 'immediate' aftermath The phrase 'immediate aftermath' was coined by Lord Wilberforce in *McLoughlin v O'Brian* as a limited extension to the normal requirement that, to be compensable, a secondary victim must have been within sight or earshot of the event giving rise to the primary victim's injury. Together with the limitations to the category of persons who might be possible claimants—the 'compliant injuries' in the Upper Tribunal's analysis—that case concerned the limiting principles that the common law should adopt with regard to the liability of a negligent defendant. **2.139**

Under the earlier tariff schemes, a secondary victim could be eligible either when she was present at and witnessed the incident, or, without meeting those conditions, came upon its immediate aftermath in which she was then 'closely involved'. By omitting that phrase, and by paragraph 6, providing instead that the secondary victim must have been *present at and witnessed the immediate aftermath of the incident* the government's clear intention was to limit the scope of this alternative. **2.140**

This leaves the question, how immediate is 'immediate' in paragraph 6? There was no limit specified in the earlier tariff schemes, but it was clear that some periods of time between the incident and the onset of the secondary victim's criminal injury when she was 'closely involved in its immediate aftermath' would, even on the most generous interpretation of 'temporal and spatial flexibility',[190] be too remote. In *VG v FTT*, that period was eighteen years,[191] in *CICA v RS* a weekend, and in *AP v CICA*, where the claimant's father died some thirty-two hours after the **2.141**

188 ibid [12] (Judge Rowland).
189 *CICA v RS* (n 176) [16].
190 *CICA v RS* (n 176) [18]–[19].
191 *VG v FTT* (n 187) [15].

attack, the Upper Tribunal held that its consequences were 'not sufficiently proximate in either time or nature to the initial injury to be capable of falling within the "immediate aftermath" principle'.[192]

2.142 The 2012 Guide says: 'When we say "immediate" we are normally referring to the period of time immediately following the incident in which a loved one was injured'. Whether a secondary victim, not being present at or witnessing the incident, comes across the injured primary victim a very short time later, was present at and witnessed its 'immediate aftermath' is a question of fact. It may be that 'immediate' refers to the incident itself, and that 'aftermath' means events that happened straight after the incident, and not the events that might follow it, such as dealing with the police and medical authorities. In *CICA v RS* the Court of Appeal,[193] and in *VG v FTT* the Upper Tribunal,[194] adopted as being applicable to paragraph 6 the House of Lords' later comment that 'the concept of "the immediate aftermath" of the incident has to be assessed in the particular factual situation'.[195]

2.143 The 2012 Guide's comments cannot of course bind the tribunals, but they suggest that the CICA's position is that there should be very little 'temporal and spatial flexibility' in its application. Paragraph 6 may not extend the notion of the immediate aftermath of an incident beyond a point at which the victim is, for example, taken to hospital, as in *AP v CICA,* or on facts such as those in *McLoughlin v O'Brian.*[196] Nor would a secondary victim satisfy the terms of paragraph 6 where she sustained mental injury when she returned home from work to find that a 'loved one' had been murdered by an intruder,[197] or when she was later told of the incident by someone else, perhaps a police officer; in neither case would she have been present at, or witnessed, its immediate aftermath.

2.144 Underlying the interpretation of the phrase 'immediate aftermath' when establishing liability in negligence to secondary victims are the cautionary words of Lord Oliver in *Alcock v CC,* that liability should not be extended to cover injury 'for which there is no pressing policy need and in which there is no logical stopping point'.[198] In the case of the scheme, the policy implications are of a different and arguably more pressing order. The issue is not the liability of a privately insured defendant, but the extent of any claim on public funds. This

[192] *AP v CICA* (n 183) [22]–[23] (Judge Turnbull), discussing *Taylorson v Shieldness Produce Ltd* [1994] PIQR P329 (CA).
[193] *CICA v RS* (n 176) [11].
[194] *VG v FTT* (n 187) [14].
[195] *W v Essex County Council* [2001] 2 AC 592, 601 (HL) (Lord Slynn).
[196] *McLoughlin v O'Brian* (n 182).
[197] *R v Criminal Injuries Compensation Board, ex parte Johnston* (1994) 21 BMLR 48 (DC).
[198] *Alcock v CC* (n 180) 417; Deakin, Johnston, and Markesinis (n 50) 125–35.

qualitatively distinct consideration means, as Laws LJ cautioned, in terms that reinforced those of Walker J in the Upper Tribunal, that the test for the purposes of the scheme does not depend in the principles of civil liability in tort but on the ordinary meaning of its words, from which 'the decision-maker should not be distracted'.[199]

[199] *RS v CICA* (n 175) [13], *CICA v RS* (n 176) [19].

3

ELIGIBLE INJURIES AND ELIGIBLE PERSONS

I Introduction

All three eligible criminal injuries, that is, those caused by a crime of violence (paragraph 4), an act of law enforcement (paragraph 5), or being present at and witnessing one of these injuries to a loved one (paragraph 6), are defined by reference to their relationship to 'a relevant place'; that is, 'Great Britain or any other place specified in Annex C in such circumstances as may be described in that Annex' (paragraph 8). They also all require the criminal injury that the claimant sustains to be 'directly attributable' to the relevant incident. This chapter deals with the conditions of eligibility that apply to the injuries and the persons that are compensable under the 2012 Scheme. As elements of the earlier schemes, these conditions underwent only minor changes following the government's 2012 consultation;[1] but, in respect of the victim's eligibility, there are substantial new provisions concerning residence and status, and important decisions concerning injuries to unborn children, and to the interpretation of the 'same roof' rule, affecting victims of domestic violence. **3.01**

[1] Ministry of Justice (2012a).

II Eligible Injuries

A Extent

1 'A relevant place'

3.02 The 2012 Scheme's definition of 'a relevant place' is a further a refinement on the equivalent paragraph in the earlier schemes. In the 2001 Scheme, the phrase 'sustained in Great Britain' enabled the Criminal Injuries Compensation Authority (CICA) to conclude that the claims made by those secondary victims who had sustained mental injury in Great Britain when witnessing in real time via televised broadcasts the deaths of their relatives in the Twin Towers on 9 September 2001 were compensable. This possibility was closed in the 2008 Scheme by the requirement that the injury must have been attributable to 'an act occurring in Great Britain' (Chapter 2.132), which now reads 'committed in a relevant place'.

3.03 The scheme has always extended to the land borders of England, Scotland, and Wales and, with the specific extensions of jurisdiction mentioned below, also to British territorial waters.[2] Annex C paragraph 1 provides (as was the case under the earlier schemes) that British controlled aircraft, hovercraft, ships, or vessels used in navigation (or Her Majesty's aircraft, hovercraft, and ships), locations on, under, or above an installation in a designated area within the meaning of section 1(7) of the Continental Shelf Act 1964 or any waters within 500 metres of such an installation (for example, an oil rig), or in a lighthouse off the coast of Great Britain, are all 'relevant places'.

3.04 For example, injuries sustained as the result of a crime of violence committed on board a ship owned by a British company would be eligible, although it was at the time in Spanish waters,[3] as would injuries sustained by the taking of an exceptional and justifiable risk for the purpose of an act of law enforcement on a British-controlled aircraft or a Royal Navy submarine. By contrast, injuries sustained in a fight on a Danish North Sea ferry would be ineligible unless it was at the time in British territorial waters.[4] Neither did the British passengers taken prisoner by the Iraqi army after their plane landed in Kuwait in August 1990, and used as part of that army's 'human shield' at the beginning of the Gulf War, sustain a criminal injury, their injuries being sustained in Kuwait, not on 'a British controlled aircraft'.[5]

---

[2] Paragraph 1 does not apply in relation to an incident that occurs in Northern Ireland, including the sea adjacent to or the airspace above Northern Ireland, which has its own compensation scheme; Department of Justice for Northern Ireland, *The Northern Ireland Criminal Injuries Compensation Scheme* (2009).

[3] CICB, 26th Report (Cm 1365 1990) para 6.3.

[4] CICB, 29th Report (Cm 2421 1994) para 17.4.

[5] CICB, 30th Report (Cm 2849 1995) para 6.5.

Within Great Britain, the 2012 Scheme applies for the most part uniformly. To the extent that it is based, on the one hand, upon the common law governing criminal offences, or statutory provisions peculiar to England and Wales, and on the other hand to the criminal law of Scotland, there will continue to be differences in its application.[6] One area of obvious difference is the age of criminal responsibility, ten years in England and Wales and eight years in Scotland. That difference has, however, no practical significance, as the scheme has always provided that the fact that the 'assailant' cannot be convicted by reason of his age is no bar to a finding that the injury was attributable to the commission of an offence. **3.05**

2 Criminal injuries sustained abroad

A British citizen who sustains any of its three categories of criminal injury abroad has no recourse to the 2012 Scheme. This was true also of its predecessors, but in the three instances summarized below, compensation may be possible under other arrangements.[7] **3.06**

(a) **Injuries sustained in another Member State of the European Union** Under the arrangements giving effect to the Compensation Directive (2004),[8] whose purpose was to set up a system to facilitate cross-border access to compensation within the European Union (EU), British citizens criminally injured while in another Member State may, by Article 12.2, be eligible for compensation under that Member State's national rules. The victim's application is made to the designated 'assisting authority' in the Member State where they are resident. In the United Kingdom (UK) that is the CICA, which is responsible for its transmission to that Member State's 'relevant authority', being its CICA equivalent. The victim's eligibility under that scheme, and the kind and amount of compensation that is payable is entirely a matter for its 'deciding authority'. As there is considerable variation in what constitutes 'fair and appropriate' compensation between the twenty-seven schemes (Chapter 1.21), a successful British applicant may well find that any award is much less than would be payable under the 2012 Scheme. **3.07**

Section 2(1) of the European Union (Withdrawal) Act 2018 provides that 'EU-derived domestic legislation, as it has effect in domestic law immediately before exit day, continues to have effect in domestic law on and after exit day'. As the Compensation Directive was transposed into domestic law by one of the means specified in section 2(2),[9] the arrangements made under those regulations are to be preserved, at least in the short term. **3.08**

---

[6] [2013] UKSC 192, [2013] 2 AC 48 (HL) [17] (*Jones*).

[7] CICA, *Compensation if you're a victim of crime abroad.*

[8] *Council Directive (EC) 2004/ 80/ EC relating to compensation to crime victims* [2004] OJ L261/ 15.

[9] The Victims of Violent Intentional Crime (Arrangements for Compensation) (European Communities) Regulations 2005, 2005 No 3396.

3.09 (b) **'Designated' acts of terrorism abroad** Where they are sustained within Great Britain or another 'relevant place', injuries caused by an act of terrorism, such as at the Manchester Arena or on London Bridge in 2017, will, because they necessarily also constitute crimes of violence, fall within the 2012 Scheme. Following the Bali nightclub bombing in October 2002, the government introduced an *ex gratia* scheme to cover victims having an 'ongoing disability' directly caused by that or any other subsequent 'designated' terrorist incident occurring abroad. This was replaced by the Victims of Overseas Terrorism Compensation Scheme 2012 (VOTC 2012) made under sections 47 to 54 of the Crime and Security Act 2010. This scheme covers persons who sustain a relevant injury that is directly attributable to their being a direct victim of a 'designated' act of terrorism, and those who are present at and witness such act, or its immediate aftermath, where it directly causes a loved one to sustain a relevant injury. Administered by the CICA, the provisions in the VOTC 2012 concerning eligibility and the assessment of compensation are substantively the same as in the 2012 Scheme.

3.10 (c) **Criminal Injuries Compensation (Overseas) Scheme (CIC(O))** These two schemes apply to persons who were 'habitually resident' (the Compensation Directive) or, in the case of the VOTC 2012, a British citizen who was 'ordinarily resident' in the UK when he sustained the criminal injury abroad. The Ministry of Defence's Criminal Injuries Compensation (Overseas) Scheme (CIC(O)) is an *ex gratia* arrangement providing for the compensation of service personnel and their accompanying eligible dependants who, whilst serving overseas, are injured in circumstances that would fall within paragraphs 4–6 of the 2012 Scheme, and is designed to give comparable levels of award.[10] The analysis in this book will be of relevance to claimants under this scheme, and to their representatives.

B Proof of the criminal injury

1 The burden of proof

3.11 The previous tariff schemes were explicit as to the applicant's burden of proof. It applied generally to the application, to the specific matters of proving the injury, of an application to waive the time limit, and of satisfying the CICA that an award should not be reconsidered, withheld, or reduced under any of the scheme's provisions (2008 Scheme paragraph 19(1)). The burden of showing that a claim was not subject to the earlier equivalents of paragraphs 22–29 of the 2012 Scheme (Chapter 4) remained with the applicant; it was not for the CICA to show that it

[10] Ministry of Defence, Criminal Injuries Compensation (Overseas) (CIC(O)) Scheme Rules (Effective from 1 July 2017); see also the Armed Forces Compensation Scheme (AFCS), Andrew Bano, *War Pensions and Armed Forces Compensation: Law and Practice* (Simmonds and Hill Publishing 2016).

was. The 2012 Scheme itself makes no express reference to the applicant's burden of proof, but the government was clear that the applicant's obligation to make out her case would continue.[11] A number of particular obligations are specified in paragraph 92, which generally requires the applicant to 'provide such information in connection with their application as a claims officer may reasonably require' (Chapter 6.35).

2 The standard of proof

Section 3(2) of the Criminal Injuries Compensation Act 1995 (CICA 1995) provides: '[w]here, in accordance with any provisions of the scheme, it falls to one person to satisfy another as to any matter, the standard of proof required shall be that applicable in civil proceedings'. This was the case under the common law scheme and the previous tariff schemes, which made explicit provision to this effect in the case of the CICA. But it follows from the statutory wording that wherever the burden of proof falls on the applicant, she must satisfy the CICA on the balance of probabilities. **3.12**

C The relevance of convictions and acquittals

1 Conviction of an offence

For the purpose of establishing a criminal injury under paragraph 4 or its predecessors, a crime must have been committed that was a crime of violence, but neither the common law nor the tariff schemes required a conviction to be recorded against an assailant. This 'fundamental principle' is continued in paragraph 9 of the 2012 Scheme,[12] which provides that: 'a person may be eligible for an award under this Scheme whether or not the incident giving rise to the criminal injury to which their application relates has resulted in the conviction of an assailant in any part of the United Kingdom or elsewhere'. **3.13**

A conviction will be compelling evidence of a crime, but is not dispositive of the question of whether it was a crime of violence. Annex B paragraph 1 provides that: '[w]here a claims officer is satisfied that a crime has been committed it is still necessary for that crime to constitute a crime of violence in accordance with this Annex'. Formally separate from the question of whether there was a crime, this requires the CICA to determine whether, on the facts, the crime was, by its nature as opposed to its consequences, a crime of violence (Chapter 2.05–2.14). The nature of the sentence is not directly relevant, although it may assist in answering that question.[13] **3.14**

---

[11] Ministry of Justice (2012a) paras 259–60.

[12] *R (GI) v First-tier Tribunal and Criminal Injuries Compensation Authority* [2011] UKUT 83 (AAC) [30] (Judge Wikeley) (*GI v FTT*).

[13] *R (NJ) v First-tier Tribunal and Criminal Injuries Compensation Authority (CIC)* [2015] AACR 42 [25].

3.15 While it may be satisfied by the conviction, and by the facts surrounding the incident, that the injury was a criminal injury, the CICA's hands are not tied concerning its discretion to refuse or reduce an award because of the applicant's or, in fatal cases, the victim's conduct or character (Chapter 4). Notwithstanding that a jury has by its verdict rejected the assailant's evidence of self-defence, the CICA may reduce the award if it thinks that that is appropriate, in view of the victim's conduct in provoking the assailant into an unreasonable or disproportionate use of force.

3.16 A conviction for an offence other than a crime of violence, although obviously not directly in point, may nevertheless assist the claims officer to conclude that the conduct complained of falls within paragraph 4. Such was the case where some factory apprentices were convicted under section 7(a) of the Health and Safety at Work, etc Act 1974 when, as a practical joke, they pushed the applicant into a tank of caustic solution, causing him very severe burns.[14] Although the report is not explicit, the Criminal Injuries Compensation Board (CICB) would have been able to conclude that the apprentices had committed a crime of violence, such as section 47 of the Offences Against the Person Act 1861 (OAPA 1861). The burns would certainly have constituted actual bodily harm, and it would not be difficult to regard the factory apprentices' behaviour as being, on a civil standard of proof, reckless.

2 Absence of a conviction

3.17 As paragraph 9 of the 2012 Scheme makes clear,

> Payments under the revised Scheme may be made whether or not anyone has been convicted of the offence from which the injury arose. This reflects the current Scheme under which a claims officer will assess whether the facts are established on the balance of probabilities. But it will be a very rare case indeed where a payment is made in relation to circumstances which did not amount to a criminal offence for technical legal reasons.[15]

Failure to secure a conviction may be due to a number of factors; principal among these is that no prosecution was possible because the assailant was unknown, or though known was not proceeded against. An example of the latter is *R v Criminal Injuries Compensation Appeal Panel, ex parte Gravett*, in which the applicant nurse had been injured in what she described as an assault by the patient she was attending. There were widely differing accounts of the incident, as a result of which there was no prosecution. The Criminal Injuries Compensation Appeals Panel dismissed her appeal from the CICA's decision that she had not been injured by a crime of violence. Dismissing the claimant's application for judicial review, the High Court held that, while the scheme is clear that the conviction of

[14] CICB, 18th Report (Cmnd 8752 1982) para 28.
[15] Ministry of Justice (2102a) para 180.

the assailant is not a necessary precondition for a successful application, 'it does not follow that a decision not to prosecute is irrelevant'.[16] The fact that none was taken in this case was, nevertheless, a relevant factor in determining whether there was a crime of violence.

In the absence of a conviction, the question is whether the alleged assailant's conduct can be shown, or can be inferred from the facts, to comprise the requisite fault and external elements of a crime that is a crime of violence. It is for this reason that the scheme places an absolute obligation on the victim to report the circumstances to the police (Chapter 4.06–4.11). But applying the authoritative guidance in *Criminal Injuries Compensation Authority v RS*,[17] the Upper Tribunal held in *Criminal Injuries Compensation Authority v First-tier Tribunal and AS* that the FTT's assessment of any police report must exclude 'the subjective evidence of a police officer on a matter which it was for [the FTT] to decide'.[18] **3.18**

When determining whether the applicant's *own* account of the incident answers this question, the CICA is making a judgment about the applicant's credibility. This, as the Upper Tribunal made clear in *R (JG) v Criminal Injuries Compensation Appeal Panel*, 'is, of course, a classic "jury question", which means that [it] should not interfere with the FTT's finding unless it misdirected itself in some way', which in this case it had.[19] **3.19**

In sum, the CICA must be satisfied that there is sufficient evidence to warrant a finding, on the balance of probabilities, first, that a crime had been committed, and secondly, that it constituted 'a crime of violence' as defined by Annex B of the scheme. This exercise will necessarily exclude injuries that are accidentally sustained, disclose no offence, were the result of a crime against property, or are self-inflicted.[20] **3.20**

(a) **Immunity from conviction** Neither has it been an obstacle to a claim that the alleged assailant is immune from conviction. Although they were cast in somewhat different terms, the common law and the earlier tariff schemes both provided, in the words of paragraph 10 of the 2008 Scheme, that, 'It is not necessary for the assailant to have been convicted of a criminal offence in connection with the injury. Moreover, even where the injury is attributable to conduct within paragraph 8 in respect of which the assailant cannot be convicted of an offence by **3.21**

---

16 [2001] EWHC Admin 1193, (2002) 67 BMLR 21 [14] (QBD) Michael Supperstone QC, sitting as a deputy judge of the Queen's Bench Division).

17 [2012] UKUT 205 (AAC), [2013] AACR 34.

18 [2017] UKUT 43 (AAC) [10] and [81]–[88] (Judge Knowles QC); (ch 6.134–6.138).

19 [2012] UKUT 84 (AAC), [9] and [25].

20 The historical annual rate of rejection on this ground was around 10% of all applications. Of the 30,219 claims that were rejected in the last full year of the pre-2012 Scheme, 3,201 (11%) did not meet this condition; CICA (2012) 14. The equivalent figures in 2015–2016 were 2,322 of 16,772 rejections (14%), and in 2016–2017 1,818 of 13,175 (13%), CICA (2017) 9; in 2017–2018 the proportion was 15%, CICA (2018) Table 7.

reason of age, insanity or diplomatic immunity, the conduct may nevertheless be treated as constituting a criminal act'.

3.22 Diplomatic immunity and crimes of violence 'committed by an offender who is not criminally responsible by reason of mental abnormality' are two of those 'very rare cases' where a payment may be made 'in relation to circumstances which did not amount to a criminal offence for technical legal reasons'. The government was clear that 'innocent victims in these cases should not be denied payments simply because their assailant is deemed not capable of forming the intention to commit the crime. Similarly payment might be made in circumstances where the person responsible for the injury cannot be prosecuted due to their having diplomatic immunity'.[21] Unlike its predecessors, the 2012 Scheme makes no express reference to any of these excusing conditions, providing only by paragraph 9 that the conviction of an assailant is irrelevant.

3.23 The Crown Prosecution Service (CPS) has discretion not to prosecute where a person has been compelled to commit an offence as a direct consequence of their being subjected to acts of human trafficking.[22] A formal defence is provided by section 45 of the Modern Slavery Act 2015, applying with slightly different conditions to adult and to child offenders. Both of these may also be circumstances where the offender's immunity will not preclude a claim under the scheme.

3.24 **(b) Acquittal** Where an acquittal follows a successful defence, for example of alibi, it remains open to the CICA to conclude that there was nevertheless a crime: it was committed by someone else. This is no different from the conclusion that it might reach where the assailant was unknown. Nor need that conclusion be incompatible with an acquittal that follows the operation of the evidential or procedural rules peculiar to the criminal trial, or with the conclusion that, while guilt could not be proved beyond a reasonable doubt, the assailant could be said to be guilty on a balance of probabilities. Such a finding is analogous to the Court of Appeal's decision in *Gray v Barr*, where, notwithstanding the defendant's acquittal, he was said by Lord Denning to have committed manslaughter,[23] or in a civil claim for battery, where the CPS did not prosecute because it did not consider that it could disprove the defendant's account of the facts to the criminal standard of proof, Edis J holding that 'it was not necessary for a party to have been convicted of a crime before the civil court was able to act on the basis that he was in fact guilty of that crime'.[24]

3.25 The fact that no assailant was convicted of a crime, because there was no prosecution (whether or not a possible assailant had been identified), the CPS offered no

---

[21] Ministry of Justice (2012a) para 12.
[22] Crown Prosecution Service, *Human Trafficking, Smuggling and Slavery.*
[23] [1972] 2 QB 554, 568 (CA).
[24] *Flint v Tittensor and the MIB* [2015] EWHC 466, [2015] 1 WLR.4370 [43] (QB).

evidence, the assailant had immunity from prosecution, or there was an acquittal does not therefore present any definitional obstacle to a finding on the facts, and on the balance of probabilities, that there was a crime, and that it constituted a crime of violence. But it may be argued that there is such an obstacle where an assailant is acquitted because the facts do not show, on any standard of proof, that their conduct satisfies the fault and external elements of an offence; in this case the applicant falls at the first hurdle. A person who strikes and injures another while in a state of automatism might be acquitted because her involuntary action means that she cannot satisfy the external element of an offence under the OAPA 1861.

Proof of the fault element of the offence where there has been an acquittal may present more difficult questions. For example, where an assailant physically attacks the applicant in the mistaken belief that he is acting in public defence,[25] and the attack is entirely compatible with the requirements of the Criminal Law Act 2008 concerning the use of force, it would not be possible to establish the fault element of an offence under the OAPA 1861. Nor was the fault element in section 20 of the OAPA 1861 made out in *Jones*, where the Supreme Court held that the FTT had been entitled to find that there was no evidence as to the deceased's state of mind vis-à-vis any other road user, at the time that he ran in front of the lorry intending to commit suicide.[26] **3.26**

Where the claim is in respect of rape (or other sexual assault) under the Sexual Offences Act 2003, eligibility under paragraph 4 requires the CICA to find that there was a crime that was a crime of violence, as defined by Annex B paragraph 2(1)(d) (Chapter 2.46). It is therefore possible that despite a conviction—where the jury found beyond a reasonable doubt that the assailant did not reasonably believe that an adult victim had consented—the CICA may find on the balance of probabilities that the victim did in fact consent; that is, that there was a crime, but no crime of violence. Conversely, it may be that even where the victim did not consent in fact, but the assailant is acquitted on the basis of his reasonable belief that the victim had done so, should there be evidence available after the trial, for example a text message that shows on the civil standard that the assailant did not have that belief, the CICA could conclude that there was a crime, and a crime of violence. **3.27**

(c) **Child assailants and children's games** Previous schemes have expressly provided that the fact that the assailant 'cannot be convicted of an offence by reason of age' is no obstacle to a finding that a child's actions in causing injury to another person constituted a crime, and a crime of violence. The question for the CICA is typically not whether the child's actions constitute the external elements of an offence, but whether they permit the inference that the child could have **3.28**

[25] *Gladstone Williams* (1987) 78 Cr App Rep 276 (CA).
[26] *Jones* (n 6); (ch 2.66–2.67).

had the requisite fault element. In 2006, the CICA was faced with the question of whether it could pinpoint a crime of violence where a motor cyclist was seriously injured when he hit and killed a boy who, in playing 'chicken' on a motorway, ran in front of a van that he was overtaking. It seems that the CICA was satisfied that the boy's actions were reckless, and met the external elements of an offence under section 20 of the OAPA 1861. This analysis would now be conducted in accordance with the decision in *Jones,* where Lord Hope acknowledged that, notwithstanding the deceased's intention to commit suicide, there could be facts from which it could be inferred that they simultaneously met the fault element of section 20. So it might be that a child playing 'chicken' on a motorway could be found to have both desired his own safe passage to the central reservation, and been subjectively reckless as to death or injury to others being caused by his actions.

3.29 The question has more frequently arisen where the injuries are sustained during a children's game, for example firing air guns or playing with fireworks. In these cases, the offence that may be committed is likely to fall under sections 20 or 47 of the OAPA 1861, and the crime of violence within either paragraph 2(1)(a), where the child physically attacks the victim by throwing a firework at her, or paragraph 2(1)(b) as 'any other act or omission of a violent nature which causes physical injury to a person', where, without thinking, the child throws the firework over a wall, where it strikes and burns the victim. By Annex B paragraph 2(2), acts or omissions will not constitute crimes of violence unless they are done intentionally or recklessly. The difficulty in these cases frequently centres on the question of whether the child was subjectively reckless; if all that can be inferred is that the child was negligent, the injury is not a criminal injury.

3.30 As this determination is a question of fact, it is incumbent on the FTT to give adequate reasons for its conclusions. While accepting that reckless behaviour causing injury may constitute a crime of violence, the CICA rejected as an accident a claim where a child poured hot water over another child in a paddling pool, causing scalds that could readily constitute actual bodily harm under section 47 of the OAPA 1861. The FTT dismissed the appeal, but the Upper Tribunal found that, in assuming 'that *either* the act was a deliberate assault *or* it was an accident' (original emphasis), it had not addressed the proper question. Its binary choice precluded any consideration of 'the possibility that the act was reckless, in the sense of taking an unreasonable risk of which the risk-taker was aware'.[27]

3.31 Injuries caused by children comprise one instance of the 'exceptional cases' the government identified as leading to payments under the scheme, notwithstanding

[27] *GI v FTT* (n 12) [21] (Judge Wikeley).

that, as paragraph 181 of its consultation is headed, '[a] crime must normally have been committed'. But, it continued:

> [p]ayments will not normally be made, though, where injuries arise from risks against which those responsible for children should be expected to guard, for example, where injuries arise in controlled situations (in schools or clubs, or where there should be supervision) or from accidents caused by children. A payment will not normally be made in relation to anyone who suffers an injury resulting from willing participation in a dangerous game.[28]

This last comment also underpins the exclusion in Annex B paragraph 4(1)(d) of injuries 'sustained in the usual course of sporting or other activity to which a person consented by taking part in the activity' (Chapter 2.87–2.90). In the case of child participants, the question of consent will require a different approach to that relating to adults.

D Causation

1 *The test of causation under the pre-2012 Schemes*

Whether the claimant's injury was caused by one of the victimizing events in paragraphs 4–6 of the 2012 Scheme is plainly a question of fact.[29] The test of causation under the common law and the tariff scheme continues to be that the injury is 'directly attributable' to one of those events. The meaning of this phrase was considered in *R v Criminal Injuries Compensation Board, ex parte Schofield,* where the applicant was knocked down and injured either by a store detective or the man whom the store detective suspected of theft and was chasing (Chapter 2.107). On the question of whether the applicant's injuries were directly attributable to the law enforcement activity, Lord Parker CJ said that the phrase meant that the victimizing event must be a *causa causans* of the injury, that is, the effective or the immediate cause, or the last link in a chain of causation, and not merely a *causa sine qua non*, that is, a necessary or inevitable cause; a cause without which the effect in question could not have happened.[30] **3.32**

Of greater significance was the Court of Appeal's decision in *R v Criminal Injuries Compensation Board, ex parte Ince*. The Court held that 'directly attributable' did not mean 'solely attributable; but directly attributable in whole or in part to a state of affairs which existed or which the victim believed to exist, even where the intervening cause was the wrongful act of the injured person or of a third party'. The question was whether the circumstances described in paragraphs 4(a) and (b) of the common law scheme were, on the basis of all the relevant facts, a substantial cause of personal **3.33**

---

[28] Ministry of Justice (2012a) para 181.

[29] On causation in the criminal law Richard Card and Jill Molloy, *Card, Cross & Jones, Criminal Law* (22nd edn, Oxford University Press 2016) 56–74 (Card and Molloy, *Criminal Law*), and in the law of tort, Simon Deakin, Angus Johnston, and Basil Markesinis, *Markesinis and Deakin's Tort Law* (7th edn, Oxford University Press 2013) ch 5.

[30] [1971] 2 All ER 1011, 1013 (CA).

injury. By the word 'substantial', Megaw LJ meant 'that the relationship between the particular cause and the personal injury is such that a reasonable person, applying his common sense, would fairly and seriously regard it as being a cause'.[31]

3.34 The Upper Tribunal applied *ex parte Ince* in *BD v First-tier Tribunal and Criminal Injuries Compensation Authority*, where it held that the FTT had imposed too high a threshold when it decided that it was necessary for the applicant to establish that his mental illness was 'wholly attributable' to the incident in which he was injured. To be 'directly attributable' did not mean that the incident needed to be the sole cause of the injury; the correct approach was not the 'but for' test, which implied that the incident probably caused the injury, but whether there was a material increase in the risk of injury.[32] For example, in *Dawson*, the fatal heart attack suffered by the victim following an armed robbery in the petrol station where he worked[33] could be regarded as being 'directly attributable' to the crime of violence, and a fatal injury for the purpose of the scheme, notwithstanding that he had an underlying heart condition.

3.35 In both the law of torts and the criminal law, the causal significance of an intervening act raises the question of whether the chain of causation between the original cause in fact and the injury has been broken. The general answer is that this depends on whether the intervening act has extinguished the effects of the original act, but as both the civil and the criminal courts recognize, this judgment is determined in part by the policy that underlies the attribution of liability in those contexts. In *Pagett* the victim, who the defendant had used as a human shield, was shot and killed by the police officer at whom the defendant was firing. For the purpose of attributing criminal liability for manslaughter, the Court of Appeal held that, in instinctively returning the defendant's fire, the officer's intervening act did not break that chain.[34] Similarly, in the law of negligence an intervening cause will not necessarily extinguish a claimant's eligibility if the original cause continues to be regarded as operative.[35] Were a qualifying relative to apply on facts similar to *Pagett*, the CICA would be faced with the question of whether, for the purposes of the scheme, the chain of causation had been broken.

3.36 For the government, the decisions in *ex parte Schofield* and *ex parte Ince* drew too wide a boundary to the scope of the causal test. The 1986 Working Party took the view that Lord Denning MR's *dictum* in *ex parte Ince*, that an intervening cause would break the chain of causation only where it was 'so powerful a cause as to reduce the original offence to a piece of history',[36] went too far. It permitted the

---

[31] [1973] 1 WLR 1334, 1344 (CA) (*ex parte Ince*).

[32] [2016] UKUT 352 (AAC) [16] and [20] (Judge Turnbull), applying *Fairchild v Glenhaven Funeral Services* [2002] UKHL 22, [2003] 1 AC 32 (HL).

[33] (1985) 81 Cr App R 150 (CA).

[34] (1983) 76 Cr App R 279 (CA).

[35] Deakin, Johnston, and Markesinis (n 29) 242–44.

[36] *Ex parte Ince* (n 31) 1341.

scheme 'to cover injuries sustained in a much wider range of circumstances than was originally intended', and recommended 'that the statutory scheme should include a more stringent test of remoteness which clearly conveys the need for a very close and immediate link between the offence and the consequent injury'.[37]

Earlier *dicta* indicate some ambiguity concerning the application of a test of foreseeability for the scheme's purposes. In *R v Criminal Injuries Compensation Board, ex parte Johnson,* Kay J commented that while the CICB could have foreseeability in mind when determining whether the necessary causal link had been established, it 'is in no way the test for entitlement to compensation',[38] and in *R v Criminal Injuries Compensation Board, ex parte K,* Dyson J had concluded that foreseeability 'may not be relevant' to questions of causation in the scheme.[39] **3.37**

Much closer to the government's policy concerns was Laws LJ's reference, in *R v Criminal Injuries Compensation Board, ex parte Williams,* to Dyson J's comment in *ex parte K,* that 'one feature of paragraph 4 of the scheme is clear: the word "directly" is intended to impose a restrictive limitation on the causation contemplated by the word "attributable"'.[40] This, Laws LJ said, imports an approach 'somewhat narrower than is taken to the concept of causation in, for example, the common law of negligence'.[41] **3.38**

2 *The test of causation under the 2012 Scheme*

But no changes were made to the 1996 Scheme, or to its subsequent revisions. As 'there does not seem to be any direct authority' on the meaning of 'directly attributable',[42] the government may have either been unable to find a form of words that more 'clearly conveys' the causal link, or concluded that the retention of that phrase would in the majority of claims be sufficient. **3.39**

Under the 2012 Scheme, the criminal injury continues to be one that is 'directly attributable' to the circumstances specified in paragraphs 4–6. But in seeking to restrict the scope of 'a crime of violence' to 'a direct, hostile, physical attack, against a person rather than property, which *immediately* causes mental or physical injury',[43] paragraph 4 provides that the claimant's criminal injury must be 'directly attributable to her being *a direct victim* of a crime of violence' (emphases added). The consultation identified a number of cases that the government considered should, and in consequence of the additional (italicized) requirements would, fall outside the scheme. While some of these exclusions engaged issues **3.40**

---

[37] Home Office (1986) paras 4.9–4.10.
[38] [1994] PIQR P469 473 (DC) (*ex parte Johnson*).
[39] [1998] 1 WLR 1458, 1462E (QB).
[40] ibid.
[41] [2000] PIQR Q339 [39]–[40] (CA).
[42] ibid [28] (Ward LJ).
[43] Ministry of Justice (2012a) para 179.

of causation, others might also fail because the person causing the injury did not himself commit a crime of violence.

3.41 The first concerned third parties being 'injured inadvertently by an act the sole purpose of which is suicide (e.g. someone jumps off a building and someone below runs into another person, injuring them [the claimant], in an attempt to get out of the way of the suicide)'.[44] Here, the claimant will fail because the deceased's actions are specifically excluded by Annex B paragraph 4(1)(a) (Chapter 2.68). Secondly, the actions of the person running are unlikely to be consistent with the fault element of an offence under the OAPA 1861, and thirdly, if their actions are considered to be an intervening act between the suicide and the injury, the claimant is not a 'direct victim'.

3.42 The second case arises 'where a person is injured accidently as the result of an intervening event (e.g. a passing cyclist being knocked off his bike when impacted by a person who had been forcibly ejected [say, by the licensee] from a pub)'. For the question of causation to arise in this case, there would need to be a finding that the licensee's actions were accompanied by the fault element of an offence under the OAPA 1861, in respect either of the customer or of the cyclist. But here again the issue would be whether the cyclist was the direct victim of the licensee's actions. This is analogous to those cases in which a dog that is dangerously out of control runs into the road, causing a cyclist to serve away from it and into the path of an oncoming car (Chapter 2.82–2.84).

3.43 The intervening act may also be an act that the victim takes in response to the offender's use or threat of violence against him. Where, with the fault element of an offence under the OAPA 1861, the assailant unlawfully pushes the victim into the path of an oncoming vehicle, there is unlikely to be any difficulty in concluding that the injury was directly attributable to such an offence. The issue may be less clear where, being in fear of immediate physical or sexual violence, the victim takes evasive action, but in seeking to escape is injured,[45] perhaps when she runs into, or is hit by a vehicle,[46] or jumps from a vehicle in which she is travelling with the offender.[47]

3.44 The criminal law authorities indicate that, in determining whether the chain of causation has been broken, the issue is whether the victim's actions were the natural result of what the alleged assailant said and did, 'in the sense that [they were] something that could reasonably have been foreseen as the consequence of what

---

[44] ibid para 186.

[45] *Mackie* (1973) 57 Cr App R 453 (CA); CICB, 24th Report (Cm 536 1988) para 10.1 (to avoid the threat of rape).

[46] *Corbett* [1996] Crim LR 594 (CA); *Roberts* (1971) 56 Cr App R 95 (CA); *Lewis* [2010] EWCA Crim 151, 2010 WL 516948 (CA); CICB, 25th Report (Cm 900 1989) para 25.9.

[47] *Williams* [1992] 1 WLR 3802 (CA).

[the assailant] was saying or doing'.[48] This is an objective test; the reference to foreseeability does not mean that account has to be taken of the victim's own characteristics.[49] The question for the CICA in such cases is, to adapt in the interests of internal interpretive consistency the test in Annex B paragraph 2(1(c), whether the claimant's actions fell within the range of responses that a person of 'reasonable firmness' would take in the circumstances. Application of such a test would arguably exclude a case 'where a verbal (spoken) assault leads sometime later to a person doing physical harm to themselves', as the government considered is current policy.[50]

E Personal injuries: definition and scope

1 Introduction

The personal injuries that are compensable under the 2012 Scheme are those that are directly attributable to one of the criminal injuries defined in paragraphs 4–6, being 'an injury which appears in Part A or B of the tariff in Annex E'. Part A deals with 'physical and mental injuries', whose definition and scope are explained below; Part B, which deals with 'sexual and physical abuse and other payments', is discussed in Chapter 5. **3.45**

Under paragraph 9 of the previous tariff schemes, 'personal injury' was defined as including **3.46**

> [p]hysical injury (including fatal injury), mental injury (that is temporary mental anxiety, medically verified, or a disabling mental illness confirmed by psychiatric diagnosis) and disease (that is a medically recognised illness or condition). Mental injury or disease may either result directly from the physical injury or from a sexual offence or may occur without any physical injury.

These various descriptions have in the 2012 Scheme been unpacked in terms of Parts A and B of Annex E. The scheme no longer specifically includes 'disease' as a personal injury, but Part B of Annex E provides for 'additional payments' to be made for sexually transmitted infections, or 'infection with one or more of HIV, Hepatitis B or Hepatitis C' where the applicant was the victim of a sexual offence.

By paragraph 7 of the 2012 Scheme: 'An award may be made in accordance with paragraphs 57 to 84 where a person who has sustained an injury in circumstances falling within paragraph 4 or 5 subsequently dies'. Fatal injury payments are discussed in detail in Chapter 5.103–5.123. **3.47**

---

[48] *Roberts* (1971) 56 Cr App R 95, 102 (CA) (Stephenson LJ). See the Court of Appeal's analysis in *Wallace (Belinda)* [2018] EWCA Crim 690, 2018 WL 02337283 [46]–[85] (CA) (Sharpe LJ).
[49] *Marjoram* [2000] Crim L R 372.
[50] Ministry of Justice (2012a) para 186.

3.48 Where the criminal injury falls within paragraph 4 or 5 of the scheme, the claimant will typically have sustained one or more physical injuries. She may also have sustained a mental injury, for example, where a physical attack or an act of law enforcement has induced in her a morbid fear of being in a public place at night. Mental injury can also be a significant consequence of a sexual assault. The scheme makes specific provision for claims that are based on multiple physical injuries, or on a mix of physical and mental injuries, dealt with in Chapter 5.51–5.56.

3.49 Where the criminal injury caused mental but no physical injury, the superseded tariff schemes provided that compensation would be payable only if the claimant fell within one of the four categories specified in paragraph 9(a)–(d). One of those (mental injury sustained by train drivers) was omitted from the 2012 Scheme (Chapter 2.96–2.98). The three others have been recast as criminal injuries in their own right. They are: a sexual assault to which a person did not in fact consent (Annex B paragraph 2(1)(c), Chapter 2.41–2.58); a threat against a person, causing fear of immediate violence in circumstances which would cause a person of reasonable firmness to be put in such fear (Annex B paragraph 2(1)(d), Chapter 2.28–2.40); and, by paragraph 6 of the scheme, being present at and witnessing an incident, or the immediate aftermath of an incident, as a result of which a loved one sustained a criminal injury in circumstances falling within paragraph 4 or 5 (Chapter 2.122–2.144).

2 Annex E Part A: physical injury

3.50 As noted in Chapter 2.17–2.22, the majority of applications concern physical injury, and call for little further comment. Identification of the appropriate tariff band necessarily depends on the tribunal's findings of fact drawn from the medical evidence, the interpretation of the descriptors that qualify the impact and effects of the injury, that in turn place it in a higher or lower band, and the relevance of any of the scheme's other provisions. The categorical nature of the tariff is examined in Chapter 5.14–5.19 but, in order to illustrate some general matters concerning their relevance, it is useful to consider here the intimate relationship between the definition and scope of the injury for which the claim is made, and its corresponding tariff level. The following paragraphs focus on the award levels for injuries resulting in scarring, and on the interpretation of the phrases 'substantial recovery' and 'continuing significant disability', which are common qualifiers to the injury descriptors in Part A of the tariff.

3.51 (a) **Scarring** Scarring caused by acid attacks is an increasingly common consequence of injuries to the face, head, neck, torso, and the lower and upper limbs. Updated in 2001 and 2008, the scheme has differentiated its cosmetic effects as 'minor', 'serious', or 'significant' disfigurement. The 2012 tariff eliminates the awards for minor scarring, whether to the limbs or the face, but it continues to set awards for serious or significant disfigurement caused, for example, by facial scars, at higher levels (A4 and A8) than apply to scarring affecting parts of the body that are not normally publicly visible (levels A1 and A5).[51] It makes no distinctions, however, between scarring suffered by younger or older applicants, or by gender.[52]

The tariff has also made specific provision for the scarring that arises from an operation to correct the applicant's injury. Note 4 of the 2001 and 2008 Schemes provided that 'where the tariff compensates for an operation the award includes provision for the normal operation scarring', and those schemes specifically differentiated between 'no operation' and 'requiring operation', the latter being higher in the tariff levels for facial injuries. The 2012 Scheme deals with this matter generally in paragraph 35: 'Where a person is eligible for an injury payment in respect of an injury requiring an operation, no separate injury payment will be made in respect of scarring arising from that operation'. **3.52**

(b) 'Substantial recovery' and 'continuing significant disability' The question of whether the disfigurement caused by scarring was 'minor', 'serious', or 'significant' exemplifies the kind of judgment that claims officers have routinely made when determining the appropriate tariff level in any case. This is particularly so where they must choose between the descriptors 'substantial recovery' and 'continuing significant disability' in respect of injuries to the applicant's limbs. The implications of their choice for the allocation of the injury to a higher or lower tariff band were in issue in *PD v First-tier Tribunal and Criminal Injuries Compensation Authority.*[53] The applicant sustained a fractured wrist, of the 'Colles type or equivalent fracture/displacement of distal radius', which attracted a payment of £4,400 (level 9) if there was 'substantial recovery', or £8,200 (level 12) if there was 'continuing significant disability' under the 2008 Scheme (in the 2012 Scheme £2,400 (level A4) and £6,200 (level A7)). The FTT accepted that the applicant had some continuing disability, but on the medical evidence found there was no *significant* disability (emphasis added), and dismissed his appeal against the CICA's award of the lower amount. **3.53**

The Upper Tribunal held that this interpretation was in error, applying instead the court's analysis in *R v Criminal Injuries Compensation Appeals Panel, ex parte Embling*. In that case, Munby J had held that 'the phrase "full recovery" has to be contrasted not with "disability", but with "continuing disability". That carried with it the corollary that for this purpose the case can properly be treated **3.54**

[51] In 2016–2017 CICA dealt with nearly 3,000 claims involving scarring, *CICA statistics for 2016–17*.

[52] *Guidelines for the Assessment of General Damages in Personal Injury Cases* (14th edn, The Judicial College 2017) no longer distinguish between the impact of scarring on males and females.

[53] [2013] UKUT 371 (AAC) (*PD v CICA*).

as one of "full recovery" if the "disability" is merely temporary or short term'.[54] Applying that analysis in *PD v CICA*, the Upper Tribunal held that 'the descriptor "substantial recovery" must be read as meaning substantial recovery from what would otherwise be continuing significant disability, so that the existence of a significant continuing disability would preclude a finding that a claimant had made what would otherwise be regarded as a substantial recovery'.[55] Because the FTT had erred in not considering [w]hether there was any continuing observable or measurable loss of function in the claimant's wrist which could properly and sensibly be described as 'significant', the appeal was remitted to a fresh hearing. Should that hearing conclude that there was a continuing disability but one that was insignificant, the categorical nature of the tariff would mean that the injury would, by analogy with *ex parte Embling*, be treated as 'substantial recovery'.

3.55 The Upper Tribunal also cited with approval Munby J's comment in *ex parte Embling* that references in the 2001 Scheme to 'full recovery' and 'continuing disability' related to the condition of the relevant limb or organ, and not to the condition of the applicant as a person or worker: 'They are to be understood as carrying their ordinary dictionary meanings'. Adapting that understanding to the 2008 (and 2012) Schemes, 'proper emphasis is to be given to the word "substantial" in the phrase substantial recovery' and to the words 'continuing significant' in the phrase 'continuing significant disability'.[56]

3 Annex E Part A: mental injury

3.56 (a) **Scope** Compensation for nervous shock under the pre-tariff scheme did not extend to the grief, distress, or other emotional distress that any normal person would experience as the result of an injury to themselves or a loved one:[57] 'However unpleasant the experience', it had to be shown 'that the applicant suffered personal injury ... There must be some sort of injurious after-effects brought on by the shock'.[58]

3.57 In replacing common law damages, the 1996 tariff included an element of compensation for this normal reaction, but where a physical or sexual injury also caused a discrete 'mental injury', being, by paragraph 9, 'a medically recognized psychiatric or psychological illness', it provided tariff payments between levels 1 (a significantly disabling disorder where the symptoms or disability persisted for six to thirteen weeks from incident or date of onset) and seventeen weeks

---

[54] Unreported, *The Times*, 15 August 2000 (Munby J). Key elements of Munby J's decision are discussed in *PD v CICA* (n 53) [10].

[55] *PD v CICA* (n 53) [10]–[11] (Judge Bano).

[56] ibid [11].

[57] *McLoughlin v O'Brian* [1983] 1 AC 410, 431 (HL); Deakin, Johnston, and Markesinis (n 29) 124–40.

[58] *Ex parte Johnson* (n 38) 473.

(permanent disability). This injury was, confusingly, listed under Note 2 to the 1996 tariff as 'shock' or 'nervous shock', being 'conditions attributed to post-traumatic stress disorder, depression and similar generic terms covering (a) such psychological symptoms as anxiety, tension, insomnia, irritability, loss of confidence, agoraphobia and preoccupation with thoughts of guilt or self-harm; and (b) related physical symptoms such as alopecia, asthma, eczema, enuresis and psoriasis'.

In the 2001 and 2008 Schemes, the definition of 'mental injury' was broadened in paragraph 9 to mean a 'temporary mental anxiety, medically verified, or a disabling mental illness confirmed by psychiatric diagnosis'. Note 9 to the tariff required the mental anxiety to have been 'diagnosed by a registered medical practitioner', and by Note 10 that the disabling mental illness had been 'diagnosed or the prognosis made by a psychiatrist or clinical psychologist'. With minor grammatical changes, the conditions identified by Note 8 of the 2001 and 2008 Schemes as attributable to mental injury were substantively the same as in Note 2 of the 1996 Scheme. For both temporary mental anxiety and mental illness, the 2008 Scheme required their effect on the applicant to be 'disabling' or, where the diagnosis was permanent, either 'moderately' or 'seriously' disabling, with correspondingly increased tariff levels. **3.58**

Where it was medically verified, a 'disabling but temporary mental anxiety lasting more than six weeks' attracted the lowest tariff award (£1,000), but as a consequence of the government's decision to eliminate tariff bands for 'minor' injuries, this injury does not figure in the 2012 Scheme; nor have the specific conditions named in Note 8 been continued. The 2012 tariff heading is 'mental injury, and Note [2] explicitly provides that: ' "Mental injury" does not include temporary mental anxiety and similar temporary conditions'. Its payment levels comprise 'disabling mental injury', using the same periods of time as in the 2001 and 2008 Schemes. In all cases the injury must, as was the case under the previous schemes, be 'confirmed by diagnosis or prognosis of psychiatrist or clinical psychologist'. **3.59**

(b) The meaning of a 'disabling' mental injury Note 2 of the 1996 Scheme provided that: 'Disabling in this context will include impaired work (or school) performance, significant adverse effects on social relationships and sexual dysfunction'. Note 11 of the 2001 and 2008 Schemes made similar provision: '[m]ental anxiety or a mental illness is disabling if it significantly impairs a person's functioning in some important aspect of her/his life e.g. impaired work or school performance or significant adverse effects on social relationships or sexual dysfunction'. But in eliminating 'mental anxiety' from its scope, and in signalling by the use of 'mental injury' in place of 'mental illness' the greater seriousness (as reflected in the changes to the tariff) of the effect of the incident on the applicant, Note [2] to the 2012 tariff makes two substantive changes to this test. It **3.60**

reads: '[m]ental injury is disabling if it has a substantial adverse effect on a person's ability to carry out normal day-to-day activities for the time specified (e.g. impaired work or school performance or effects on social relationships or sexual dysfunction)'.

3.61 The first change is the substitution of 'significantly impairs' by the phrase '*has a substantial adverse effect*' (emphasis added) on a person's ability to carry out those activities. This phraseology is drawn from section 6(1) of the Equality Act 2010 (EA 2010), which provides that a person (P) has a disability if she has '(a) a physical or mental impairment, and (b) the impairment has a substantial and long-term adverse effect on P's ability to carry out normal day-to-day activities'. Section 212 provides that 'a substantial effect is one that is more than a minor or trivial effect', and is intended to reflect 'the general understanding of disability as a limitation going beyond the normal differences in ability which may exist among people'.[59]

3.62 The second change relates to the effects of the injury, which replaces 'in some important aspect of her/his life' with the phrase in section 6(1)(b) '*to carry out normal day-to-day activities for the time specified*' (emphasis added). The EA 2010 does not define what is to be regarded as 'normal day-to-day activity', although its guidance gives extensive illustrative examples of when it would, and would not, be reasonable to regard an impairment as having that effect.[60] 'For the time specified' is a reference to the periods of weeks or years over which the injury is disabling; as was the case in the 2008 Scheme, where the diagnosis was of permanent injury, being either 'moderately' or 'seriously' disabling, there are correspondingly increased tariff levels. The interpretation of the EA 2010 may therefore be of assistance in determining whether the injury satisfies the terms of Note [2]. Whatever the effect, it is a question of fact, to be 'confirmed by diagnosis or prognosis of psychiatrist or clinical psychologist', a requirement that continues from the 2008 Scheme.

3.63 It will be seen that this test is more demanding than was the case in the 2008 Scheme, but the definitional link between the injury and its impact on the applicant remains. In *R (VP) v First-tier Tribunal (CIC)*, the applicant had been sexually abused as a child, as a result of which he had developed an abnormal sexuality based on sado-masochism. The issue was whether this abnormality amounted to a 'disabling mental illness' within the 2008 Scheme. The psychiatric report failed to refer to Note 11, with the result that notwithstanding its finding that the applicant's sexual disorder did significantly impair his ability to form social relationships, the FTT concluded that it was not covered by the scheme. Acknowledging the complication created by the report's failure, the Upper Tribunal quashed the FTT's

59 Office for Disability Issues (2011) section B1.
60 ibid section D2.

decision, holding that the applicant's sexual disorder was by definition disabling and fell within the scheme.[61] In the case of the 2012 Scheme, the question would be whether the disorder had a substantial adverse effect on the claimant's ability to form social relationships; if so, it would be a 'disabling' mental injury.

4 Injuries not listed in the tariff

Section 2(6) of the CICA 1995 permits the government to add to or to remove from the tariff any description of injury. Where the applicant sustains an injury for which it makes no provision, section 2(3)(b) provides that the standard amount to be paid in respect of it shall be determined 'in accordance with such provisions of the Scheme as may be relevant'. In the 2012 Scheme, these provisions are paragraphs 38–41. By paragraphs 38 and 39 a claims officer may, having consulted the FTT, recommend that where the injury in a claim before him is of equivalent seriousness to an injury that is described in Annex A, the government should include a new description of injury. In the particular case, the CICA may make an injury payment of the recommended amount, applying any other relevant provisions of the 2012 Scheme. This means, for example, that all of the eligibility conditions in paragraphs 22–27 may apply to reduce or withhold that payment. Similar provisions existed in paragraphs 28 and 29 of the earlier schemes, but with the claims officer authorized only to make an interim award of not more than half of the recommended amount. By paragraph 53, the CICA could reconsider its decision at any time before actual payment of a final award, which similarly gave it power to reduce or withhold payment where the applicant's conduct or character fell within the disentitling conditions. **3.64**

Where the injury was not subsequently included in the tariff or, if included, qualified for less than the interim award paid, the earlier tariff schemes provided that 'No part of such an interim award will be recoverable'. They gave no power to the CICA to reconsider the interim award if there were eligibility issues that would have been relevant, had the recommended amount been included in the tariff. The 2012 Scheme in part remedies this gap. It provides by paragraph 40 that, where the injury is not subsequently included in the tariff, or if the injury is included in the tariff at a level lower than that recommended by the claims officer, 'no part of that injury payment is repayable by the applicant'. But paragraph 40 is subject to the conditions in paragraph 110, under which the CICA may require repayment of an award after final payment has been made (Chapter 6.73–6.75). None of paragraphs 38 to 40 applies in relation to any description of injury which is included in Bands 1 to 5 of the 2008 Scheme, but which is not included in the tariff at Annex E. Thus, they do not permit an applicant to resurrect the minor injuries that were included in that (or, by implication, any earlier) scheme. **3.65**

[61] [2015] UKUT 9 (AAC) [10].

III Eligible Persons

A Residence and status

3.66 It has always been the case that anyone criminally injured in Great Britain could make a claim under the scheme, irrespective of the duration or the status of his or her presence here. On the basis that the scheme exists to reflect some sense of social justice for injured *citizens* (Chapter 1.10), and in pursuit of the fiscal need to draw the conditions of eligibility more tightly than had been the case, the government's consultation proposed that applicants should have 'a defined connection to the UK'. That connection could be demonstrated where the applicant satisfies one of the three conditions set out in paragraphs 10–16 of the 2012 Scheme, paragraph 10 meaning that the claimant must have been lawfully present in the UK when the injury was sustained.[62] An applicant under the 1996 tariff scheme who had misrepresented her status was refused an award on the ground that her 'character', as shown by the available evidence, made it inappropriate to make any or a full award.[63] This discretion remains open in any analogous case (Chapter 4.88).

3.67 In common with all other aspects of the scheme, the 2012 Guide makes it clear that 'the responsibility for making a case for compensation lies with you'.[64] It summarizes the conditions in paragraphs 10–16 and sets out the evidence about the applicant's residency and nationality that the CICA will need to decide the claim. Where the injury resulted in the victim's death, a 'qualifying relative' who applies to the scheme for a payment under paragraphs 57–77 will need to meet the same residence requirements as any other applicant. However, the government indicated that the residence condition would not be applied in respect of the deceased, provided that the incident giving rise to the claim took place in Great Britain.[65]

1 Paragraph 10(a): 'ordinary residence'

3.68 The first alternative, set out in paragraph 10(a), is that the applicant 'was ordinarily resident in the United Kingdom on the date of the incident giving rise to the injury'.[66] Following the 2012 consultation, the government concluded that its

---

[62] Ministry of Justice (2012a) para 195, and (2012b) para 167.

[63] *R (on the application of R (on the application of Andronati)) v Criminal Injuries Compensation Appeals Panel* [2006] EWHC 1420 (Admin), [2007] PIQR P2.

[64] CICA, *Criminal injuries compensation: residency and nationality.*

[65] Ministry of Justice (2012a) para 194.

[66] There is extensive judicial and administrative guidance on the meaning of this phrase in social security law; *Arthur v HMRC* [2017] EWCA Civ 1756, [2018] AACR 10 [16] (CA); Home Office (2017), *Nationality policy: assessing ordinary residence Version 2.*

proposed condition, that the applicant should have been resident in the UK for at least six months at the time of the incident, was too stringent. For reasons of administrative simplicity, 'the date of the incident' is the relevant date for assessing whether the residence condition is met. A period of six months remains relevant, however, where the victim had been resident for that time at that date of the incident, but had since left the UK; in such a case, the victim's eligibility to make a claim would be unaffected.[67]

However, the government remained of the view that applicants 'should demonstrate at least an intention to develop and maintain a connection to the UK'.[68] Whether a person is ordinarily resident in the UK is a question of fact, depending on such factors as 'how often and for how long you are in the UK; the purpose and pattern of your presence; and your connections to the UK'; relevant factors include family, business, and property ties. The 2012 Guide adds **3.69**

> It is possible that you may have spent some time in another country but maintained strong ties to the UK, such as your job and house, which means that you remained ordinarily resident within the UK for the purposes of the Scheme. This may be the case if you were on holiday, studying abroad, or visiting a foreign country for some other reason.

2 Paragraph 10(b): British, EU, and EEA citizens, and the armed forces

The ordinary residence condition does not apply to the persons identified in paragraphs 10(b) and 11. These are British citizens and their close relatives, members of the armed forces and their close relatives, and nationals of EU and EEA Member States and their family members who are in the UK exercising their rights under EU law. As it is proposed that EU nationals living in the UK on 'exit day' will retain their existing rights, this condition will continue to apply to them. **3.70**

Paragraph 10(b) also applies to nationals of a state, not being an EU or an EEA Member State, that is party to the European Convention on the Compensation of Victims of Violent Crime (paragraph 11(e)).[69] This Convention applies to nationals of the member states of the Council of Europe who were injured in their own countries. It has not hitherto been engaged because such nationals injured in Great Britain would have been eligible under the earlier tariff schemes. But if they are not nationals of an EU or EEA Member State (paragraph 11(c) and (d)), they would but for paragraph 11(e) be caught by the residence test if they were to come within the 2012 Scheme. **3.71**

[67] Ministry of Justice (2012a) paras 188 and 192.
[68] Ministry of Justice (2012b) para 169.
[69] Council of Europe (1983). This Convention is not to be confused with the Compensation Directive (n 8).

3.72 Because existing international and EU obligations require the UK to pay awards to nationals of the countries specified in those obligations, 'we also propose that no British citizen will have to satisfy the residence test'.[70] By paragraph 11(a) and (b), British citizens and their accompanying close relatives are automatically eligible, regardless of where they normally reside. By paragraph 11(f) and (g), automatic eligibility also extends to 'serving members of the armed forces and their families, who would not otherwise be eligible and cannot satisfy the residence test due to their service'.[71] Paragraph 12 provides that the phrase 'close relative' for paragraph 11(b) and (g) means a person who was living with the victim on the date of the incident who was the victim's spouse or civil partner, or was living with the victim as a partner for two continuous years immediately before that date. A close relative may also be a child under 18, or the child's spouse, civil partner, or partner as defined, or a child 'who is financially or physically dependent on that person as a result of a physical or mental disability'. For the purposes of paragraph 11(g), paragraph 12(2) provides that 'a person is an accompanying close relative of a member of the armed forces if they were a close relative of that person and living with them outside the United Kingdom'.

3 Paragraph 10(c): victims of human trafficking and asylum-seekers

3.73 The residence test does not apply to applications by a person who has been referred to a competent authority as a potential victim of trafficking in human beings within the meaning of the Anti-Trafficking Directive,[72] or made an application for asylum under Immigration Rules made under section 3(2) of the Immigration Act 1971 (paragraph 13(a) and (b)). In both instances, the applicant may request that her application is deferred until a final decision has been taken in relation to her status under that Directive or those Rules (paragraph 14). However, the applicant will not be eligible for an award until, in the case of human trafficking she has been conclusively so identified by a competent authority (paragraph 15(a))[73] or, in the case of asylum, granted temporary protection, asylum, or humanitarian protection (paragraph 15(b)). Asylum-seekers who are not ultimately given leave to remain in the UK will have their claim rejected.

3.74 Article 17 of the Anti-Trafficking Directive imposes an obligation on EU Member States to ensure that victims of trafficking have access to existing schemes of compensation for victims of violent crimes. In *R (McNiece) v (1) Criminal Injuries Compensation Authority (2) The Lord Chancellor* and *Secretary of State for Justice*

[70] Ministry of Justice (2012a) para 190.

[71] Ministry of Justice (2012a) para 191; by Annex A, '"armed forces" means Her Majesty's United Kingdom armed forces'.

[72] *Directive 2011/ 36/ EU of the European Parliament and of the Council of 5 April 2011 on preventing and combating trafficking in human beings and protecting its victims, and replacing Council Framework Decision 2002/ 629/ JHA* [2011] OJ L101/ 1; Ministry of Justice (2012a) para 189(c).

[73] Paragraph 15(a), and para 16, and CICA, *Victims of human trafficking and the Criminal Injuries Compensation Scheme.*

and *R (1) A (2) B v (1) Criminal Injuries Compensation Authority (2) The Lord Chancellor and Secretary of State for Justice*, the Administrative Court considered the scope of Article 17 in the particular case of claims made under the 2012 Scheme by trafficked victims, but who themselves had been convicted of offences in the UK. On this point, the Court held that the provisions in the scheme limiting or excluding any award in such cases did not amount to a breach by the UK of its obligations under the Anti-Trafficking Directive. In the subsequent appeal by A and B, the Court of Appeal reached the same conclusion.[74] This, and other issues raised in this case concerning the lawfulness of paragraph 26 of the scheme are considered in Chapter 4.61–4.71.

B Adult victims

By Annex A of the scheme, an '"applicant" means the person for whose benefit an application for compensation is made'. In most cases this will be the victim of the criminal injury sustained under paragraphs 4–6. The previous tariff schemes explicitly provided that an 'applicant' could also mean a person (the victim) on whose behalf the application is made. The 2012 Scheme does not repeat this extension, but the CICA's online procedure indicates that an application can be made on behalf of someone 'you know has been hurt in a violent crime'.[75] The 2012 Guide provides advice in cases in which the claim is made on behalf of an adult who cannot apply themselves. The applicant will be required to demonstrate his right to act on the victim's behalf, which may require medical evidence that 'the person you are representing lacks capacity', or is 'incapable by reason of mental disorder', within the meaning of the Mental Capacity Act 2005. **3.75**

C Child victims and child abuse

In cases in which the victim is under 18 years of age, the application can be made by an adult with parental rights over the child; in such cases, the 2012 Guide advises that the adult will need to provide details and proof of her relationship to the child. As local authorities became aware of its enactment, applications by directors of Social Services in respect of the physical and sexual abuse of children in their care rose substantially, so that by the late 1990s they comprised some 13 per cent by volume, and 20 per cent by value, of the payments made under the statutory scheme. As 'the great majority of child victims of sexual abuse do not have claims for damages pursued through the civil courts',[76] the scheme continues to be a realistic source of compensation in such cases. **3.76**

---

[74] [2017] EWHC 2 (Admin), 2017 WL 11799 [131] (*McNiece v CICA*); *A and B v Criminal Injuries Compensation Authority and Secretary of State for Justice* [2018] EWCA Civ 1534, 2018 WL 03224139 [39]–[45] (Gross LJ).

[75] CICA, *Claim compensation for a criminal injury.*

[76] Home Office (1999) para 36. In 2016–2017 CICA dealt with nearly 4,500 claims arising from sexual offences, of which some 3000 concerned children, *CICA Statistics for 2016–2017.*

3.77 Claims of historic child sexual abuse arising within a children's home, a religious institution, a school, a media organization, a football club, or by sexual grooming within the local community pose a number of challenges. These include the need for a sympathetic understanding of its impact on victims who may have been traumatized by being abused in this way, in particular by family members, and possibly exacerbated by delay in the appearance of any mental injury subsequent to the incident and in obtaining a firm prognosis on the psychological impact of the abuse. These claims can also raise evidential issues concerning the verification of an incident or incidents that occurred some, or many, years earlier. It may be difficult to obtain corroborating evidence; the applicant might not have known, or cannot identify their alleged abuser, or the abuser might have died, or otherwise have become unavailable before any police investigation. These factors typically lead to delayed claims, which present the CICA with sensitive decisions concerning the exercise of its discretion to waive the two-year time limit (Chapter 6.26–6.30).

3.78 They can, in addition, raise questions concerning the possible relevance of the applicant's own conduct subsequent to the abuse (and possibly in consequence of it), in particular where they themselves have been convicted of offences. Finally, although it is of decreasing significance, claims made by children in respect of injuries arising from an incident that occurred before 1 October 1979 were subject to the mandatory operation of the 'same roof' rule. This rule continues to be controversial, and has been the subject of recent litigation (3.100–3.110).

1 Injuries sustained in the womb

3.79 In *Attorney-General's Reference (No 3 of 1994)* the House of Lords held that: '[i]t is established beyond doubt that a child in the womb does not have a distinct human personality, whose extinguishment gives rise to any penalties or liabilities at common law'.[77] Thus, where an offender, in physically attacking a pregnant woman, intends or is reckless as to the destruction of her unborn child, its death in the womb constitutes neither murder nor manslaughter (Chapter 2.91–2.92). It follows that a foetus cannot in these circumstances sustain a criminal injury in respect of which a qualifying relative (the mother) would have a claim on that basis. But the tariff scheme continues to provide a payment (£5,500) for loss of foetus as a result of the crime of violence that the mother sustained. Also, as she was herself criminally injured by that attack, the mother may be eligible for compensation in her own right under paragraph 4 of the 2012 Scheme.

3.80 Where the child is born alive but later dies from the antenatal injuries, there may then be an offence of murder or manslaughter, depending on the offender's intention when those injuries were inflicted.[78] The fact that there is an interval between the offender's actions and the child's death does not preclude liability, provided

[77] *Attorney-General's Reference (No 3 of 1994)* 245, 261F–G (HL) (Lord Mustill).
[78] ibid 254 (Lord Mustill).

that there was 'an unbroken chain of causation between those actions and the victim's death'.[79] In such a case the child would, upon its death, have been the victim of a crime of violence, and thus have sustained a criminal injury in respect of which a claim for a bereavement payment could be made by the mother as a qualifying relative.

A third possible outcome is that the child is born, and survives, with physical or mental disabilities that are directly attributable to the injuries it sustained while in the womb. The question of whether there are circumstances in which this constitutes a criminal injury was considered in two decisions of the Court of Appeal, *CP v First-tier Tribunal and Criminal Injuries Compensation Authority*[80] and *Criminal Injuries Compensation Authority and First-tier Tribunal (SEC) v Y*.[81] In *CP v CICA,* analysed in Chapter 2.93, the Court held that the injuries with which the child was born as a result of her mother's reckless consumption of alcohol could not amount to an offence under section 23 of the OAPA 1861, because the 'harm was done to the child when it was not a person, and the expert evidence showed that there was no further harm when it became one'.[82] **3.81**

In *CICA v Y* the claimant was conceived as a result of the incestuous rape of his mother, and was born with a genetic disorder. The claim was made under the 2008 Scheme, but rejected on the ground that he had not been injured by a crime of violence; his congenital condition was the result of the incestuous relationship between his parents. The FTT dismissed his appeal, relying on the decision in *Millar (Curator Bonis to AP) v Criminal Injuries Compensation Board* made under the common law scheme.[83] On similar facts, the Outer House of the Court of Session had held that such an injury 'could not be a personal injury within the scheme. There was no uninjured state in which Y could exist without the genetic disorder from which he suffers. There was no "pre-assault" Y'. *Millar* reflected the position at common law, where there was established authority for the proposition that there could be no liability for 'wrongful birth', and the Outer House was clear that, as it was applying a scheme requiring compensation to be assessed on the basis of common law damages, it was 'quite evident' that such an assessment would be impossible. **3.82**

The Upper Tribunal's hearing of the judicial review of the FTT's decision was stayed until the Court of Appeal had decided the appeal in *CICA v CP*. It approached the issue first by emphasizing that what fell to be interpreted was not the application of common law principles, but the terms of the statutory tariff scheme, which meant that position for which *Millar* was authority did not apply.[84] **3.83**

---

[79] ibid 268A–D (Lord Hope).

[80] [2014] EWCA Civ 1554, [2015] QB 45 (CA) (*CP v CICA*).

[81] [2017] EWCA Civ 139, [2017] 4 WLR 60 (CA) (*CICA v Y*).

[82] *CP v CICA* (n 80) [44] (Treacy LJ).

[83] 1997 SLT 1180, dated 13 November 1996.

[84] *Y v First-tier Tribunal and Criminal Injuries Compensation Authority* [2016] UKUT 202 (AAC) [9] and [17] (Judge Levenson).

The tribunal had sought to distinguish *CICA v CP* on the ground that, in that case, the claimant's mother had committed no offence under section 23 of the OAPA 1861, so there could be no crime of violence of which the claimant could be the victim. In *CICA v Y*, however, there had been a crime of violence against his mother (rape), and as there was nothing in its 'self-contained set of provisions' that the claimant must have been 'a person' at the time that it had been committed, his injuries fell within the scheme.[85]

3.84 The Court of Appeal also emphasized that, being a statutory scheme, its interpretation 'must now be governed by the rules of statutory construction which apply to all such instruments'.[86] Two linked questions arose. The first was whether the applicant was a victim who had sustained an injury directly attributable to the act of incestuous rape. This would involve a consideration of the necessity for a pre-existing state that had been altered by the rape. The second was whether compensation was being claimed in respect of a sexual offence covered by paragraph 9 of the 2008 Scheme, and whether that provision itself presupposed the applicant's existence at the time the offence: 'The link is the fundamental issue of whether it is sufficient that Y's condition is a consequence of the act of sexual violence which occurred prior to Y's existence'.[87]

3.85 The Court concluded that the scheme meant that the victim of the crime of violence in this case could only be the applicant's mother, who would herself be eligible for, and had received, an award for the personal consequences to her of the rape. But, allowing CICA's appeal,

> to suggest that Y, who had not been conceived at the time of the crime, was himself a victim of crime (the nature of the crime involved being difficult to discern) or that it is possible to assess compensation on the postulate that Y would otherwise have been born without disability and so should be compensated for the genetic disorder from which he suffers is to go beyond that which the Scheme was seeking to cover.[88]

3.86 On facts very similar to *CP v CICA,* it was argued in *CH v Criminal Injuries Compensation Authority* that the mother had, instead of a possible offence under section 23 of the OAPA 1861, committed an offence under section 20 in respect of her unborn child.[89] Applying the Court of Appeal's judgment in *CP* v *CICA*, the FTT dismissed her appeal against the CICA's rejection of the claim. The tribunal held that to establish a section 20 offence in such a case, (a) any grievous bodily harm inflicted by the mother's consumption of alcohol had to be inflicted on 'a person', (b) when she was injured while in the womb the claimant had not

---

[85] ibid [32]–[36].

[86] *CICA v Y* (n 81) [24]–[25] (Leveson P); (ch 1.27–1.28).

[87] ibid [8].

[88] ibid [26].

[89] Unreported 6 April 2016 (First-tier Tribunal), noted in Ben Collins QC and Katherine Fudakowski, 'Abuse Claims: Criminal Injuries Compensation: A Review of Some Relevant Case Law for Practitioners' [2016] *Journal of Personal Injury Law* 105.

acquired legal personality, and (c), her mother's drinking was not unlawful. At the time of writing, this case is the subject of an application to the Upper Tribunal for judicial review.

A slightly different but untested question is whether a child born disabled as a result of antenatal injuries caused by a third party's intentional or reckless 'physical attack' on its mother, constituting an offence against her under sections 18 or 20 of the OAPA 1861, sustains a criminal injury within the 2012 Scheme. Paragraph 4 requires the claimant to be 'a direct victim of a crime of violence', a new concept that could envisage an injury sustained by the foetus. Both Rules 3 and 5 in Lord Mustill's analysis in *AG's Ref 1994* contemplate circumstances in which a foetus may, by virtue of statute, be the victim of a crime of violence and, by Rule 4, of homicide where, following birth there is an unbroken causal connection between the act and the death. In the present case, what would be sought is an unbroken causal connection between the act, and the disability apparent when the child is born. By the Congenital Disabilities (Civil Liability) Act 1976 a child can recover damages for injury sustained *in utero* caused other than by its mother; applied to the scheme, this may be an analogy on which *CP v CICA* and *CH v CICA* could be distinguished from third party assaults. The question of whether a foetus injured *in utero* can ever be considered a victim of a crime of violence is therefore not necessarily clear-cut, notwithstanding *CP v CICA* and *CICA v Y.* **3.87**

D Fatal injuries: 'qualifying relatives'

The common law scheme provided that the CICB would entertain applications for *ex gratia* payments of compensation from a spouse or dependant of a person who sustained a criminal injury and who later died, 'dependant' having the same meaning as that in section 1(3) of the Fatal Accidents Act 1976 (FAA 1976). This included the deceased's spouse or former spouse, brothers, sisters, aunts and uncles, the deceased's children and parents, and a person who was living with the deceased immediately before his death, and who had been living with him in the same household for the past two years as husband and wife. In order to limit the range of eligible persons, and to dissociate it from the resonances of a fatal accident action, the tariff scheme replaced these categories (although there inevitably continues to be some overlap) with its own list of 'qualifying claimants'. This was amended over time, and simplified in the 2012 Scheme in what are now classed as 'qualifying relatives'. A qualifying relative is a person who 'at the time of the deceased's death' met one of the conditions in paragraph 59(a)–(f), a list that is formally exhaustive of this category of eligible persons. **3.88**

The exclusion of a deceased's sister was tested in *X v First-tier Tribunal and Criminal Injuries Compensation Authority and Secretary of State (Justice)*. The deceased had been murdered by her family when she sought to escape an arranged marriage. The applicant's claim, made in respect of her relationship with the deceased, was rejected by the CICA, and the FTT on appeal, on the ground that **3.89** she was not a 'qualifying relative'. Her application for judicial review argued that this decision was in breach of Article 14 of the European Convention on Human Rights (ECHR), in that it unlawfully discriminated against her on the ground of her sex. The Upper Tribunal concluded that, while it was true that she had been treated differently, it was not on the ground of her sex; a claim by a brother would have been treated in exactly the same way, as it would have been for anyone else who was neither a child nor a parent of the deceased.[90]

1 Spouses, civil partners, and cohabitants

3.90 By paragraph 59(a), a spouse or civil partner will be a qualifying relative where she was 'living with the deceased in the same household'. Partners in a homosexual relationship were initially excluded, but were included in the 2001 Scheme as 'a same sex partner' (paragraph 38(2)(a)(i) of the 2008 Scheme), now as a civil partnership, or as a spouse.[91] They will all be qualifying relatives within paragraph 59(a) although, as has always been the case, they were married to, or the civil partner of, the deceased only for a short time. But by paragraph 144, an award will not be made in relation to a person who was the same sex partner of the deceased on the date they sustained that injury, where the application relates to an injury sustained before 1 April 2001.

3.91 Although neither married nor in a civil partnership, a person who had been living together with the deceased as husband and wife in the same household for at least two years at the date of death was 'a qualifying claimant' under the previous schemes. In the 2012 Scheme, a cohabitant is included in paragraph 59(b) as 'the partner of the deceased (other than a spouse or civil partner), who was living with them in the same household and had done so for a continuous period of at least two years immediately before the date of the death'.

3.92 All three of these qualifying relatives must, at the time of death, have been living with the deceased 'in the same household'. In determining whether the applicant and the deceased were or were not, the Upper Tribunal held in *YA v First-tier Tribunal and Criminal Injuries Compensation Authority* that the tribunal of fact must consider the wider context of their relationship, together with judicial authority on the meaning of 'household, for example in the context of social security law'.[92] In coming to 'a common sense and realistic' conclusion on its scope, the Upper Tribunal held in *MA v Secretary of State for Work and Pensions* that the matters which should be considered commonly include: 'the circumstances in which

[90] JR2339/2011 (AAC), Tribunal case No X/07/241544 (31 May 2011) [31]–[33].

[91] Civil Partnership Act 2004, Marriage (Same Sex Couples) Act 2013.

[92] [2015] UKUT 399 AAC [46] (Judge Levenson). This case is reported as *Hutton v First-tier Tribunal (CIC) and Criminal Injuries Compensation Authority* [2012] EWCA Civ 806, [2013] 1 WLR 124 (CA), being a claim that initially concerned a decision on a late application; (ch 6.06–6.07).

the appellant and his wife came to be living in the same house; payment for the accommodation made by the appellant; arrangements for the storage and cooking of food; separate eating arrangements; domestic arrangements such as cooking, cleaning, gardening, and bits of household maintenance; the financial arrangements, and evidence of family life'.[93]

A spouse, civil partner, or cohabitant who, because of 'either person's ill-health or infirmity', was not living with the deceased in the same household at the time of death is, by paragraph 59(c) a qualifying relative, and in common with those who satisfy the conditions in paragraph 59(a) or (b), is eligible for both a bereavement and, if applicable, a dependency payment. By paragraph 59(d) a spouse or civil partner who does not meet any of the conditions in paragraphs 59(a)–(c), is nevertheless a qualifying relative, and provided she was not estranged from the deceased at the time of death, whether for example by divorce or separation, may be eligible for a bereavement payment (paragraph 61(b)). If she was also financially dependent on the deceased (paragraph 59(d)) she may be eligible for a dependency payment (paragraph 67), which 'may be made to a qualifying relative who at the time of the deceased's death was financially or physically dependent on the deceased. A qualifying relative was physically dependent on the deceased if the deceased was their main carer'. A former spouse or civil partner may also be eligible for an award under paragraph 67 where she was financially dependent on the deceased (paragraph 59(d)), but by paragraph 61(a) is not eligible for a bereavement payment. **3.93**

2 Parents and children

By paragraphs 59(e) and (f) respectively, a parent or a child of the deceased is a qualifying relative. A parent will be eligible for a bereavement payment, and if applicable, a dependency payment. A 'child', who is not limited to a person below the age of 18, includes adult children and a child of the deceased born after the incident, is eligible for a bereavement payment, and if the child was under 18 years of age at the time of death, a 'child's payment' (paragraph 63). A qualifying relative who was an adult child, that is, over 18 at the time of death and financially or physically dependent on the deceased, will be eligible for a dependency payment. Fatal injury payments are detailed in Chapter 5.103–5.122. **3.94**

3 The proviso in Annex A

An uncle, aunt, grandparent, or a sibling, being dependants under the FAA 1976, may be a qualifying relative where Annex A applies: 'a reference in this scheme to a child or parent of another person includes a reference to someone accepted as such by that other person'. **3.95**

[93] [2016] UKUT 262 (AAC) [12].

E Victims of domestic violence

1 The construction of the 'same roof' rule in the scheme

3.96 When first established the common law scheme entirely excluded applications arising from 'offences committed against a member of the offender's family living with him at the time'. This absolute bar included both adult and child family members. The factors that were then persuasive in the formulation of what became known as the 'same roof' rule—the difficulty of establishing the facts and of distributing blame, the possibility of fraud, and the administrative problem of ensuring that the assailant did not benefit—were reviewed by the 1978 Working Party. Acknowledging that these factors remained live, it recommended that it should be possible to compensate victims of intra-family violence where the applicant 'was innocent, serious injury was caused, and there was no prospect of the assailant benefiting from the award'.[94] This took effect in 1979, applying to all incidents occurring after 1 October 1979, subject to the conditions in paragraph 8(a). These were designed to assist the investigation of the facts and to prevent the offender from benefiting, and limited the exclusionary effect of the rule to adult family members (paragraph 8(c)). The continuation of the absolute bar in respect of incidents occurring before that date was challenged in *R v Criminal Injuries Compensation Board, ex parte P,* but the Divisional Court and the Court of Appeal both agreed that it was not unlawful that the changes had only a prospective, and not a retrospective, effect.[95]

3.97 These amendments were continued, with some modifications, in the first tariff scheme. They took effect as paragraph 7(b), which restated the absolute bar. In the case of injuries sustained before 1 October 1979, no compensation would be paid 'where the victim and the assailant were living together at the time as members of the same family'. The conditions that had been introduced in paragraph 8(a) and (c) of the common law scheme were restated, in the 2008 Scheme, as paragraphs 16 and 17. If the claim was not excluded under paragraph 7(b), 'but at the time when the injury was sustained, the victim and any assailant (whether or not that assailant actually inflicted the injury) were living in the same household as members of the same family, an award will be withheld unless (paragraph 17(1)):

(a) the assailant has been prosecuted in connection with the offence, or a claims officer considers that there are practical, technical, or other good reasons why a prosecution has not been brought; and

[94] Home Office (1978) para 7.

[95] [1993] PIQR P314 (DC), [1994] PIQR P400, 417 (CA). There is a comprehensive account of the legislative history of the same roof rule in *JT v First-tier Tribunal and Criminal Injuries Compensation Authority* [2015] UKUT 47 (ACC) [22]–[30] (*JT v CICA 1*), which discusses *ex parte P* in detail [44]–[46]; and in the Court of Appeal, *JT v First-tier Tribunal, Criminal Injuries Compensation Authority, and Equality and Human Rights Commission* [2018] EWCA Civ 1755, 2018 WL 03537078 [7]–[31] (*JT v CICA 2*).

(b) in the case of violence between adults in the family, a claims officer is satisfied that the applicant and the assailant stopped living in the same household before the application was made and are unlikely to share the same household again'.

These paragraphs therefore meant that a child victim, who under the absolute bar would, in common with adult members living in the same household, have been ineligible if the incident occurred before 1 October 1979, would in respect of injuries sustained on or after that date be eligible if the condition in paragraph 17(1)(a) was met. But adult victims would also need to comply with paragraph 17(1)(b).

The principal purpose of paragraph 16(a) was to prevent the assailant from benefiting from an award, both in relation to incidents before and after 1 October 1979.[96] In the case of the former, the government proposed no change to 'the historic rules relating to injuries prior to 1 October 1979. In these cases, awards will not be made where the victim and the assailant were living together as members of the same family'. Noting that the changes to this rule have always been prospective rather than retrospective, the government concluded that retention of the exclusion was justified on the basis that one of the aims of the reforms was to reduce the burden on the taxpayer, and to make the scheme sustainable in the long term. To act otherwise would increase its potential liability, and involve a significant administrative burden for the CICA, in particular in establishing the link between the offence and the injuries.[97] **3.98**

In the case of injuries sustained after 1 October 1979, the government proposed to remove the condition in paragraph 17(1)(a): **3.99**

> The reason for this is because we consider that the rules on cooperation with the criminal justice system and the requirement that the victim and assailant no longer live together should be sufficient to ensure that the offender does not benefit from the award, and, if possible, is brought to justice.[98]

While its substance reflects the government's 'retained policy', paragraph 17(1)(b) of the 2012 Scheme removes the condition that the adult members of the family live in 'the same household', in favour of the phraseology 'living together as members of the same family', a rephrasing that achieves consistency between the conditions relating to pre- and post-October 1979 injuries.

2 The 'same roof' rule in the 2012 Scheme

(a) **The scope of the rule** By paragraph 19 of the 2012 Scheme, 'an award will not be made in respect of a criminal injury sustained before 1 October 1979 if, at **3.100**

[96] CICA (2005) 7 (case summary 2: victim cohabiting with the offender with whom he had a long-term 'on and off' relationship).
[97] Ministry of Justice (2012c) paras 166–79.
[98] ibid para 176.

the time of the incident giving rise to that injury, the applicant and the assailant were living together as members of the same family'. This continues the absolute bar on injuries occurring before that date, including injuries sustained by the family's children. By paragraph 20:

> An award will not be made in respect of a criminal injury sustained on or after 1 October 1979 if, at the time of the incident giving rise to the injury, the applicant and the assailant were adults living together as members of the same family, unless the applicant and the assailant no longer live together and are unlikely to do so again.

The removal of the condition in paragraph 17(1)(a) of the 2008 Scheme means that a child victim will be eligible for an award in respect of injuries sustained after 1 October 1979, subject only to the generally applicable provisions concerning proof of the injury; the limitations imposed by paragraph 20 apply only to 'adult members' of the same family. But for both child and adult victims of intra-family violence, paragraph 21, which continues the substance of paragraph 16 of the 2008 Scheme, means that even where a claimant meets the conditions of paragraph 20, an award will not be made if the CICA considers that 'an assailant may benefit from the award'.

3.101 Where the application is made on behalf of a victim such as a child or an adult unable to manage her own affairs, the applicant's convictions will not be taken into account (although the victim's might). But the CICA would, applying paragraph 21, have to be satisfied that any award would not benefit anyone responsible for the injury, as might occur, for example, where a parent with a criminal record brings an application on behalf of his child, who has been injured by someone else living in the same household.

3.102 In the case of child victims, paragraph 16(b) of the 2008 Scheme provided that where the applicant was under 18 years of age when the claim is determined, the award would not be made if it would be against the applicant's interests to do so. In practice, this power has primarily been used in cases of sexual or physical injury to a very young child where there is no long-term effect. But so that the child victim should not be deprived of an award that might assist them later in life, paragraph 106(c) of the 2012 Scheme provides that a claims officer may make arrangements for 'retaining the award until the applicant's 18th birthday', for example by being placed in trust (Chapter 6.61–6.62). Given the circumstances in which the criminal injury was sustained, this option enables the family or carers of the child to 'explain the origin of the award, as they see fit at an appropriate time'.[99]

[99] Ministry of Justice (2012a) para 199; (2012b) para 173.

(b) 'Living together as members of the same family' The condition that the applicant and the assailant were not 'living together as members of the same family' is common to both paragraphs 19 and 20 of the 2012 Scheme. Neither the scheme nor the 2012 Guide provide any definition of what constitutes a 'family', although some guidance may be found in the list of those who constitute 'qualifying relatives' in paragraph 59(1). In *R v Criminal Injuries Compensation Board, ex parte Staten*, the Divisional Court held that the phrase 'living together' used in paragraph 8(c) of the common law scheme, which customarily referred to couples who lived together without being married, was to be given its 'ordinary sensible meaning', without reference to divorce law.[100] The husband had been convicted of cruelty to his wife, and returned home following his release from prison. They slept apart, had no sexual relations, and the applicant undertook no domestic activity for her husband. But as they were in other respects living together as a family, Lord Widgery CJ found that they were 'living together' for the purpose of the scheme. **3.103**

Whether two people were 'living together as members of the same family' is a question of fact.[101] The CICB's decisions on paragraph 8(c), being equivalent to the second condition in paragraph 20 of the 2012 Scheme that the applicant and the assailant 'no longer live together and are unlikely to do so again', are illustrative of this question. An award was not made where the victim indicated on her application form that she and her assailant might live together again 'if things work out', or having been raped or otherwise injured by him, she later married her assailant, resumed living with him, or attempted a reconciliation, or invited him to stay the night in breach of his bail condition.[102] An award was also withheld where the victim, being registered blind and partially disabled, continued to live with the assailant (her husband) upon whom she was wholly dependent.[103] In contrast, an award was made where the victim and the assailant had been living apart for fourteen days prior to the attack, and where, although the assailant lived in the same house as the applicant, this was at her mother's invitation and against the wishes of the applicant, who spent most of her spare time in the company of her fiancé and his family.[104] **3.104**

As is reflected in these decisions, the history of these provisions of the scheme largely concerns female victims of domestic violence and abuse. Since 1 February **3.105**

---

[100] [1972] 1 WLR 569 (DC).

[101] See the 'admirable signposts' (*PP v Basildon DC* [2013] UKUT 505 (AAC)) on the interpretation of 'living together as husband and wife' in *Crake v Supplementary Benefits Commission* (1981) 2 FLR 264 (QB).

[102] CICB, 27th Report (Cm 1782 1991) paras 25.2, 25.3, and 25.4–6; 30th Report (n 5) paras 24.2 and 24.3; and 31st Report (Cm 3169 1996) para 6.14.

[103] CICB, 26th Report (Cm 1365 1990) para 22.2.

[104] CICB, 25th Report (n 46) para 21.20.

2015, they have been required to indicate the nature of the assault(s) when making a claim; in 2016, 234 claimants were successful, averaging £7,500 per award.[105] Of more recent social concern are the injuries sustained by persons subject to conditions of modern slavery. Although it is a crime under section 1 of the Modern Slavery Act 2015 to subject 'another person to perform forced or compulsory labour', it is not of itself a crime of violence within the scheme, although it clearly will be where these persons are also subjected to physical or sexual abuse. While its legislative history has concerned intra-family violence, it should be stressed that paragraph 21 of the 2012 Scheme is of general application. Thus, where adult victims of modern slavery are housed by the offender, compensation may be withheld if an assailant may benefit from the award.

3.106 (c) **Interpretation of the 'same roof' rule in the 2012 Scheme** The impact of the absolute bar to pre-1979 injuries, restated in paragraph 19 of the 2012 Scheme, remains live, affecting current claims made by adults in respect of the physical and sexual injuries they sustained as children. Its application to these claims raises three principal issues, which have been the subject of decisions by the Upper Tribunal (*JT v CICA 1*), the Inner House of the Court of Session, the High Court of Northern Ireland, and the Court of Appeal (*JT v CICA 2*). The following paragraphs summarize the main issues in, and the Court's response to, JT's claim. Before the Upper Tribunal those issues were

- whether, when Article 1 of Protocol 1 (A1P1) to the ECHR[106] is read with Article 14,[107] the different treatment of 'same roof' victims injured before the revised date, compared with those injured on or after it, could, on the facts of the application, form the basis of a claim of discrimination under that Article,
- if so, whether the 'same roof' rule gives rise to less favourable treatment because of the claimant's age or sex within Article 14, and
- if there is relevant less favourable treatment, whether it is justified.

3.107 In *JT v CICA 1,* an application was made in December 2012 by a 47-year-old claimant in respect of the sexual abuse she sustained between 1968 and 1979 when she was a child, for which her stepfather was convicted of a number of sexual offences, including rape. It may be noted, first, that the CICA waived the two-year time limit for making an application, but it rejected the claim by reason of

---

[105] Hansard HC Debates, written answers 15 February 2017; https://www.parliament.uk/business/publications/written-questions-answers-statements/written-question/Commons/2017-02-07/63347/.

[106] 'Every natural or legal person is entitled to the peaceful enjoyment of his possessions. No one should be deprived of his possessions except in the public interest and subject to the conditions provided for by law and by the general principles of international law.'

[107] 'The enjoyment of the rights and freedoms set forth in this Convention shall be secured without discrimination on any ground such as sex, race, colour, language, religion, political or other opinion, national or social origin, association with a national minority, property, birth or other status.'

paragraph 19. As to the first issue, the Upper Tribunal held that, while the claimant would have had an entitlement if she came within the terms of the scheme, which entitlement would be a 'possession' under A1P1, there was in fact no such entitlement, and therefore no possession because the scheme's terms excluded her claim.[108] But the Upper Tribunal further held that, for the purposes of considering Article 14 read with A1P1, a claim under the scheme falls within the ambit of A1P1 such that it can form the basis of a discrimination claim under that Article, relying on *Stec v United Kingdom.*[109] The Court of Appeal agreed. The CICA 1995 legislation is to be regarded as establishing a proprietary interest falling within the ambit of A1P1. The terms 'welfare benefit' and 'social security' as used in the *Stec* case law are not terms of art; 'payments made by the state under the UK's criminal injuries compensation scheme are in my view to be regarded as welfare benefits'.[110]

As to the second issue, the claimant in *JT v CICA 1* argued that in setting 1 October 1979 as the cut-off date, paragraph 19 amounted to less favourable treatment of applicants in general, and her in particular, by reference either to her age or to her sex. As to age, the Upper Tribunal accepted the FTT's conclusion that the scheme did not discriminate against claimants born before October 1979; 'the defining factor is not age but rather *the date when the offence was committed*' (original emphasis).[111] **3.108**

The Court of Appeal disagreed. The claimant's 'other status' within Article 14, on which she had been discriminated against, was not her age, but was as a person who was 'living together as a member of the same family as her assailant'. The relevant comparator group was all of those whose situation was analogous to the claimant's, but who were not excluded by the rule; This was 'starkly illustrated by the award which has actually been made to her relative', who had also been abused by her stepfather, but did not live with them.[112] On this point the Northern Ireland High Court had found that '[I]t was [the claimant's] immutable family relationship [with the offender] which precluded her claim', observing that a non-family member staying in the same household would not have their claim excluded because of that status.[113] **3.109**

Finally, on the assumption that the 'same roof' rule amounted to less favourable treatment, the Upper Tribunal concluded that, taking account of their policy and **3.110**

---

[108] *Roche v UK* (2006) 42 EHRR 623 [129], cited in *JT v CICA 1* (n 95) [103]–[104] (Judge Turnbull).

[109] (2006) 43 EHRR 47.

[110] *JT v CICA 2* (n 95) [64]–[70] (Leggat LJ). The same conclusion was reached by the Inner House of the Court of Session in *MA v A Decision of the Criminal Injuries Compensation Board* [2017] CSIH 46 P243/ 15 [25] (*MA v CICB*) and the Northern Ireland High Court, where the 'same roof' provisions in the Northern Ireland Criminal Injuries Compensation Scheme are substantively similar to those that applied under the 2008 Scheme, but took effect after 1 July 1988, *In the Matter of an Application by F* [2018] NIQB 7 (*In re F*).

[111] *JT v CICA 1* (n 95) [41] and [55].

[112] *JT v CICA 2* [71]–[80], [114].

[113] *In re F* (n 110) [23].

legislative background, the schemes' retention of the absolute bar constituted a legitimate aim. The Court of Session had also taken the view that the 'same roof' rule was a 'prudent policy decision concerning the allocation of finite resources.' Allowing JT's appeal, the Court of Appeal did not agree. Whether there was 'an "objective and reasonable justification" for the difference in treatment, is to be judged by whether it has a legitimate aim and there is a "reasonable relationship of proportionality" between the aim and the means employed to realise it. The Court found that the rule 'appears flatly inconsistent' with [the government's] purposes for the 2012 Scheme, one of which is to compensate innocent victims of sexual offences. The justifications on which the government has traditionally relied for what the Court considered to be an arbitrary and unfair rule were no longer persuasive. Indeed, 'it might be thought that a victim in JT's position would have a greater claim to be treated as eligible for an award than a person who was assaulted by someone who was not living as a member of their family when the incident occurred.'[114]

3.111 At the time of writing, the claimant in *MA v CICB* has been granted permission to appeal to the Supreme Court. It remains to be seen what impact this decision will have on any similar outstanding claims, and whether the CICA will seek to join *JT v CICA 2* with that appeal. The Inner House of the Court of Session and the Court of Appeal agreed on two of the three central issues: that the claimants came 'within the ambit' of A1P1, and that they had 'other status' for the purpose of Article 14. They disagreed on whether the government's justifications for the 'same roof' rule could be sustained. Subject to particular differences in the law of England and Wales, and that of Scotland (3.05), the 2012 Scheme applies throughout Great Britain. As the Scottish Parliament has made no changes in the relevant primary or secondary legislation,[115] the Scheme should be interpreted uniformly as between courts of coordinate jurisdiction. The Supreme Court's decision on this point would clearly be desirable. But rather than pursuing an appeal in *JT v CICA 2*, an alternative for the government is to concede the appeal in *MA v CICB*, and then legislate in the light of these two decisions. In September 2018 the government announced that it would not appeal the decision in *JT v CICA 2*, and that it would abolish the 'same roof' rule as part of a wider review of the 2012 Scheme. Its recommendations will be published in 2019.'[116]

[114] *JT v CICA 2* (n 95) [92], [96] and [99]–[117].

[115] *R (MB) v First-tier Tribunal & Criminal Injuries Compensation Authority (CIC)* [2012] UKUT 286 (AAC)) [2013] AACR 10 [10].

[116] https://www.gov.uk/government/news/justice-secretary-announces-victim-compensation-scheme-review-scraps-unfair-rule.

4

ELIGIBILITY
Cooperation, Conduct, Convictions, and Character

I The Policy Context

4.01 When setting its underlying policy in 1964, the government considered that it would be inappropriate for those with significant criminal records, or whose own conduct before, during, or after the incident led to their being injured, to receive compensation from public funds.[1] In such cases, or where the victim's 'way of life' similarly made an award inappropriate, the common law scheme conferred on the Criminal Injuries Compensation Board (CICB) a wide power, which applied also in claims where the victim had died, to reduce, or to refuse an award entirely, and irrespective of whether the victim's injuries were attributable to these factors.

[1] Home Office (1961) paras 31 et seq.

4.02 There was considerable criticism of the scope that these provisions gave to the CICB to introduce moral judgments about the applicant. The provision concerning the applicant's 'way of life' was removed in the 1990 revision, but the Court of Appeal's confirmation in *R v Criminal Injuries Compensation Board, ex parte Thompstone and Crowe,* that the applicant's criminal record and conduct were not limited to matters relevant in some way to the particular incident, remained authoritative.[2] Apart from some amendments to its operative provisions, this discretion was unchanged in principle in the 1996 statutory Scheme, and in its 2001 and 2008 successors. The government's 2012 consultation was adamant that the revisions to the scheme should 'ensure that where payments are made they are to blameless victims of serious crimes'.[3] The scope of paragraphs 22–28 reflects the equivalent provisions in the earlier tariff schemes, but there are important differences, both in their definition and in their outcome, for the claimant.

4.03 The provision concerning the claimant's unspent convictions continues to be controversial,[4] and was challenged in *R (McNiece) v (1) Criminal Injuries Compensation Authority (2) The Lord Chancellor and Secretary of State for Justice,* and *R (1) A (2) B v (1) Criminal Injuries Compensation Authority (2) The Lord Chancellor and Secretary of State for Justice.* The Administrative Court held that the government's conception of the 2012 Scheme's purpose—to compensate only 'blameless' victims—constituted a legitimate aim (Chapter 1.02), for which the restrictions imposed by paragraph 26 were a proportionate application.[5] As a proportion of all resolved claims, the number rejected under paragraphs 22–28 is lower than was the case before the commencement of the 2012 Scheme,[6] but the underlying policy remains central to its purpose.

II Cooperation with the Criminal Justice Agencies and with the CICA

4.04 As it is unnecessary for an offender to have been convicted, and that many offenders are never identified, the scheme provided from the outset that the applicant

[2] [1984] 1 WLR 1234 (CA) (Lord Donaldson MR) (*ex parte Thompstone and Crowe*).

[3] Ministry of Justice (2012b) Foreword 4 (2012a) para 176.

[4] David Miers, 'Compensating Deserving Victims of Violent Crime: The Criminal Injuries Compensation Scheme 2012' (2014) 34 *Legal Studies* 242–78, 265–69.

[5] [2017] EWHC 2 (Admin), 2017 WL 11799 (QB) [131] (*McNiece v CICA*). The Court of Appeal upheld the Court's decision, dismissing the appeal by the claimants A and B; *A and B v Criminal Injuries Compensation Authority and Secretary of State for Justice* [2018] EWCA Civ 1534, 2018 WL 03224139 (*A and B v CICA*). These decisions are discussed below (4.61–4.72).

[6] Of the 57,480 claims resolved in 2011/2012, 15,342 (26%) were disallowed under one or more of these paragraphs; the equivalent figure in 2015/2016 and 2016/2017 were 28,152 and 7,214 (26%), and 32,021 and 5,582 (17%) respectively; CICA (2012) 11 and 14, (2017) Tables 2 and 17.

should have reported the incident to the police, and then to assist in bringing the offender to justice. These obligations serve two purposes. One is to enable the Criminal Injuries Compensation Authority (CICA) to investigate 'whether the incident in fact occurred or, indeed, whether the claimant ever suffered any injury'. The second 'implies that a person who seeks compensation from the State in respect of a criminal injury ought, as a quid pro quo, to assist the State to prosecute the offender insofar as that may be appropriate'.[7]

Under all of the earlier schemes, the applicant's failure to meet either of these two conditions could result in the refusal of, or a reduction in, an award. But in pursuit of its policy of ensuring that 'eligibility to claim under the Scheme should be tightly drawn so as to restrict awards to blameless victims of crime who fully co-operate with the criminal justice process',[8] the 2012 Scheme imposes the yet more stringent, single, consequence of refusal where the applicant fails to meet either of these obligations. In the case of the applicant's failure to meet their third obligation, to assist the CICA in the consideration of their application, the claims officer's discretion to reduce an award is retained. **4.05**

A Paragraph 22: reporting the incident to the police

Paragraph 22 of the 2012 Scheme provides: 'An award under this Scheme will be withheld unless the incident giving rise to the criminal injury has been reported to the police as soon as reasonably practicable'. This replaces paragraph 13(1)(a) of the 2008 Scheme, which required the applicant to 'take, without delay, all reasonable steps to inform the police, or other body or person considered by the Authority to be appropriate for the purpose, of the circumstances giving rise to the injury'. One important change is that, following the government's rejection of proposals that reporting in such workplaces as schools, prisons, and hospitals would be sufficient, the 2012 Scheme has removed the formal alternative that permitted the applicant to 'inform' another 'appropriate' body.[9] The CICA recognizes that some applicants will initially have reported the incident to 'someone else' but, as the 2012 Guide insists: **4.06**

> You should always report the incident to the police even if you have reported it somewhere else such as your place of work. If the incident took place while you were on duty, we will not penalise you for any minor delay in reporting to the police if you have complied with your employer's investigatory procedures.

Although the text of the Guides has changed over the years, the core message has remained constant. The 2012 Guide confirms that: 'If the crime for which you are seeking compensation has not been reported to the police we cannot make a payment'.

---

[7] *R (RW) v First-tier Tribunal (as successor of the Criminal Injuries Compensation Appeals Panel)* [2013] AACR 8 [24] (Judge Rowland) (*RW v FTT*).

[8] Ministry of Justice (2012b) (n 3) para 162.

[9] ibid paras 171 and 176.

1 Mitigating factors

4.07 The CICA (and before it the CICB) has long recognized that there may be 'some mitigating factor affecting the victim, such as age, mental capacity or the particular circumstances of the offence, which includes trauma arising from a sexual offence' that explains a failure to report.[10] A second important change in the 2012 Scheme replaces the phrase 'to take, without delay, all reasonable steps' with the requirement that the report should be made 'as soon as reasonably practicable'. This refocuses the reporting requirement on the victim's capacity to report, rather than on its timing, and in so doing aims to address the concerns raised in the Stern Review about the inhibitions that rape victims may feel about 'taking the legal route'.[11]

4.08 In deciding whether that requirement is met, paragraph 22 provides that 'particular account will be taken of: (a) the age and capacity of the applicant at the date of the incident; and (b) whether the effect of the incident on the applicant was such that it could not reasonably have been reported earlier'. These conditions reflect the Upper Tribunal's observations in *R (JC) v First-tier Tribunal (CIC): Reasons* that, in applying the terms of paragraph 13(1)(a) of the 2008 Scheme, the CICA and the First-tier Tribunal (FTT) 'are required to consider all material circumstances, having regard to the purpose of the paragraph'. These circumstances include the claimant's reasons for not having reported the incident, and that 'in considering whether the claimant took "all reasonable steps" to inform the police, regard must be had to the position as it would have appeared to him at the time'.[12] Allowing for the change in the terms of the reporting requirement, these considerations may be seen to underpin the advice contained in the 2012 Guide.

4.09 In the case of an injury to a child, it will normally be the parents who report the incident to the police, but it will be a local authority in the case of the physical or sexual abuse of a child in care. The victim's cooperation with the police has always assumed a particular significance, such that an adult victim's prevarication or reluctance to report the incident is likely to result in refusal, but in the case of a child victim who does not, or is not able to, report at the time the abuse he suffered, or until some years later, the CICA and the FTT may now have a greater sympathy (Chapter 6.26–6.30).

4.10 But in the case of an adult claimant, the CICA will surely look askance at a claim where the adult refused to confirm, when the police arrived at the scene or shortly thereafter, that any potentially criminal offence had occurred, refused to make

[10] Ministry of Justice (2012a) para 197; (2012b) para 172 CICA (2001) 13 (case summary one: victim not reporting until two weeks after being discharged from hospital).

[11] Government Equalities Office (2010) 16; Ministry of Justice (2012b) (n 3) para 175.

[12] [2010] UKUT 396 (AAC) [26]–[27] (Judge Rowland); *RW v FTT* (n 7) [25]–[26].

a formal complaint, offered an unacceptable or no explanation for their delay, thought they might themselves be suspected of having committed an offence, were vague about the date of the incident, had been drinking and did not want to go to the police station smelling of alcohol, were afraid of reprisals, or only reported the assault in order to make a claim. These factors were all instrumental in the CICB's decisions to refuse or reduce an award. It is also very unlikely that the CICA would accept as a good reason the victim's belief that the police would not believe him as was the case in *RW v FTT*.[13]

The third important change made by paragraph 22 concerns the consequence of the claimant's failure to comply with its requirements. Once the CICA has found that it was reasonably practicable for the applicant to have reported the incident to the police, and that his delay was inexcusable, there is no longer any discretion whether to withhold or reduce an award: by paragraph 22 it must be withheld.[14] **4.11**

B Paragraph 23: cooperating in bringing the assailant to justice

Paragraph 23 provides that: 'An award will be withheld unless the applicant has cooperated as far as reasonably practicable in bringing the assailant to justice'. This supersedes paragraph 13(1)(b) of the 2008 Scheme, which provided that an award could be withheld or reduced where the applicant 'failed to co-operate with the police or other authority in attempting to bring the offender to justice'. The CICB maintained an uncompromising approach towards this requirement; an application from someone who deliberately misled the police, either by refusing to give information or by giving false information, or refusing to cooperate with them, would be rejected unless there were strong reasons to explain such failure. The 2012 Guide is explicit: '[w]e expect you to have done everything reasonably possible to help the police catch your assailant, and bring them to justice'. **4.12**

Not all victims are cooperative; for some, cooperation may seem pointless, or it is not a choice that they would make. But in proposing that non-compliance with this obligation should no longer attract the alternative of a reduced award, the government commented: 'We believe that it is vital that victims engage with the criminal justice process in order to bring offenders to justice'.[15] A defining factor is that the scheme is publicly funded, as the Upper Tribunal noted in *R (CR) v First-tier Tribunal (CIC),* when it ruled that the word 'failure' in paragraph 13(1)(b) 'pre-supposed an obligation on the applicant to co-operate with the police to the extent and in the manner reasonably to be expected' of a person making a **4.13**

[13] *RW v FTT* (n 7) [22] and [29].

[14] Of the 16,772 claims disallowed in 2015/2016, 1,097 (6%) were disallowed because of a failure to report the incident to the police; in 2016/2017, the equivalent figures were 13,175 and 713 (5%); CICA (2017) Table 7; in 2017/2018 the proportion was 4%, CICA (2018) Table 7.

[15] Ministry of Justice (2012b) (n 3) para 174.

claim for a compensatory payment at public expense.[16] This means that the applicant should volunteer any information they have about the circumstances of the incident, and not wait until the police make a 'specific request' about some aspect of it. But it also means that the applicant does not fail to cooperate when, presented with a series of options, she does no more than 'express a preference' for one that later constitutes a reason why the police decided to take no further action.[17]

4.14 Whereas the obligation in paragraph 13(1)(b) was expressed in unqualified terms, in stipulating in paragraph 23 only refusal for failure to comply, the 2012 Scheme acknowledges that there may be a good reason why the applicant did not do so. Whether the applicant did cooperate 'as far as reasonably practicable' is, in common with paragraph 22, a question of fact. The CICA initially distinguished two sets of circumstances, based partly on CICB decisions. In the first of these, the obstacles to bringing the offender to justice could all be principally attributed to the applicant's action or inaction. This could include claims in which the applicant failed to supply a DNA sample, refused to view photographs of possible offenders, to attend an identity parade or to attend court, did not cooperate because he was known to the police, withdrew the complaint because of family pressure, refused to make a statement, or made a statement that he later withdrew or that was deliberately false. Under paragraph 13(1)(b), the CICA would normally make no award in such cases; so far as some resulted in a reduced award, that is, by virtue of paragraph 23, no longer an option.

4.15 Some victims may be afraid of reprisals or intimidation at trial, and may benefit from contact with such organizations as Victim Support. But, as in the case of non-reporting, the fact that the applicant has been threatened would not excuse a failure to cooperate. The 2012 Guide is explicit: 'While you may be reluctant to bring charges (for example, if you fear a revenge attack or reprisal) the Scheme is publicly funded and you will not be eligible for a payment unless you co-operate fully with the investigation into the crime and any prosecution that follows'.

4.16 The particular considerations in paragraph 22(a) and (b) to be taken into account in deciding whether it was 'reasonably practicable' for the victim to report the incident to the police do not apply to paragraph 23. But that phrase does imply that 'considerations which might be taken into account in determining what co-operation is reasonably practicable for the victim would include their age and mental or physical capacity'.[18] Notwithstanding the availability of 'special measures' in the case of vulnerable and intimidated witnesses,[19] it may not in all cases

16 [2010] UKUT 388 (AAC), [2011] AACR 19 [10] (Judge Bano) (*CR v FTT*).
17 ibid [11] and [14].
18 Ministry of Justice (2012a) (n 10) para 197.
19 Crown Prosecution Service, *Special Measures*.

be reasonably practicable to expect a child or adult victim of a sexual offence to agree to become a witness at trial.

The second set of circumstances that the CICB had identified were those in which the applicant did fully cooperate but the Crown Prosecution Service (CPS) decided to take no further action. In such a case, the CICA would, as *CR v FTT* suggests, normally make an award, assuming that no other issues of eligibility arose.[20] The same outcome could be expected where it is now impossible for any further action to be taken, for example, because the alleged offender has died. But if an award is made, paragraph 110(1) provides that the applicant may be required to repay all or part of it where a claims officer 'is satisfied that evidence received after final payment has been made shows that the applicant: (a) has not co-operated as far as reasonably practicable in bringing the assailant to justice' (Chapter 6.73–6.74). **4.17**

The greater focus on the police in paragraph 22 may have a negative impact for some victim groups, but of much greater potential impact is the removal of a claims officer's discretion to reduce an award where the victim fails to meet its or paragraph 23's requirements. Refusal, the only option, may result in harsh decisions in marginal cases. For example, should the victim of chronic sexual and physical abuse first withdraw and then restate her (truthful) allegations, leading to the conviction of her partner, but also to her own conviction for perverting the course of justice, a 'fair-minded person', sympathizing with the history of her abuse, might question a decision to make a reduced award.[21] Under the 2012 Scheme, there would be no option but to withhold any award.[22] **4.18**

C Paragraph 24: assistance in connection with the application

Paragraph 24 states that: 'An award may be withheld or reduced where the applicant fails to take all reasonable steps to assist a claims officer or other body or person in relation to consideration of their application'. This replaces paragraph 13(1)(c) of the 2008 Scheme, which provided that an award could be withheld or reduced where the CICA considered that the applicant had failed to give 'all reasonable assistance' to the authority or other body or person in connection with the application. The substitution of the words 'to take all reasonable steps' in the 2012 Scheme may imply a greater focus on the efforts that the victim made to comply with this obligation. The issue is not whether the applicant did give CICA any assistance, or whether he was willing to assist, but what practical steps, that were reasonable for him to take, he did in fact take. This obligation is restated **4.19**

---

20 *CR v FTT* (n 16) [14]; and CICA (Guide 2001) Pt 4 para 12.

21 *RT v First-tier Tribunal and CICA* [2016] UKUT 306 (AAC) [41] (*RT v FTT*).

22 Of the 16,772 claims disallowed in 2015/2016, 1,534 (9%) were rejected for a failure to co-operate in bringing the assailant to justice; in 2016/2017 the equivalent figures were 13,175 and 1,307 (10%); CICA (2017) Table 7 in 2017/2018 the proportion was 8%, CICA (2018) Table 7.

in similar terms in paragraph 91, which requires the applicant to '(d) assist the claims officer, and any other body or person, as far as reasonably practicable in relation to consideration of their application'.

4.20 An award may be withheld or reduced where the claimant failed to comply with CICA's requests for information, to attend a medical examination or inspection that the claims officer considered necessary to determine the application, or to take reasonable steps to assist such other authorities as their general practitioner (GP), a hospital out-patients' clinic, the Department for Work and Pensions (DWP), or their employer (all of whom the CICA may approach to verify these details). The 2012 Guide adds: 'We may refuse or reduce your claim if you don't tell us about something that could affect your claim, or give false or exaggerated details about your injuries'. Paragraph 24 will also apply to matters other than the immediate circumstances giving rise to the injury; a failure to disclose details of a prior conviction would be treated particularly seriously.

4.21 Paragraph 14(1) of the 2008 Scheme sought to address the chronic problem of non-responses from addresses from which the applicant had moved but not informed CICA. This is now included in paragraph 24. Failure to take all reasonable steps 'includes repeated failure to respond to communications sent to the address given by the applicant', and as indicated in the 2012 Guide, includes a failure to update the CICA of a change to the claimant's postal or email address, or to their circumstances. The obligation is restated in paragraph 91, which requires the applicant to '(e) provide the claims officer with any change in their correspondence address as soon as reasonably practicable'.[23]

III Paragraph 25: Conduct 'Before, During or After the Incident'

4.22 Paragraph 25 provides that: 'An award may be withheld or reduced where the conduct of the applicant before, during or after the incident giving rise to the criminal injury makes it inappropriate to make an award or a full award'. This maintains the claims officer's discretion in such cases that was provided by paragraph 6(c) of the common law, and by paragraph 13(1)(d) of the 2008, and earlier tariff schemes.

4.23 The 2012 Guide advises that 'before making a payment we have to consider if your behaviour before, during or after the incident caused or contributed to the

[23] Of the 16,772 claims disallowed in 2015/2016, 1,644 (9%) were rejected for a failure to assist CICA with the applicant's claim; in 2016/2017, the equivalent figures were 13,175 and 1,605 (12%); CICA (2017) Table 7; in 2017/2018 the proportion was 19%, CICA (2018) Table 7.

incident in which you were injured'. This formulation may allude to possible similarities between the application of the partial and the absolute defences in the law of tort, and the interpretation of the scheme. But the scheme is not intended to mimic the common law, and the reference to the applicant's 'contribution' should not be read as invoking the principles or the authorities governing contributory negligence. In *R v Criminal Injuries Compensation Board, ex parte Ince*, the Court of Appeal firmly rejected the analogy that the CICB drew between that defence and the terms of the common law scheme. In exercising its discretion, the CICB was 'unhampered by any concepts borrowed from another part of the law'.[24]

Where the source of funding for injuries sustained while serving in the armed **4.24** forces,[25] caused by industrial processes, medical accidents, or as the result of criminal activity, comes from the public purse, 'issues of public good versus private rights becomes more apparent'.[26] What is at issue for the scheme is not whether it is, in the terms of the Law Reform (Contributory Negligence) Act 1945, 'just and equitable' to apportion financial responsibility as between the taxpayer and a claimant who contributed in some way to the incident,[27] but whether the victim is a person whose moral worth, assessed according to strictly defined criteria, is such that their ensuing injuries should be compensated from public funds. In *Revill v Newberry*, the Court of Appeal agreed with the two-thirds reduction for the young burglar's contributory negligence, and with the rejection of *ex turpi causa*.[28] On similar facts, the Criminal Injuries Compensation Appeals Panel (CICAP) found that it would be 'inappropriate that someone who was injured in the course of illegal conduct burgling someone's home, and who struggled to escape [and was injured] when detained, should receive an award from public funds'.[29]

These points are well illustrated by reference to the CICB's and CICA's **4.25** longstanding approach to claims in which applicants themselves instigated the violence in which they were injured. As the vast majority of applications arise from a 'physical attack' (Annex B paragraph 2(1)(a)), paragraph 25 will frequently concern claims in which the applicant provoked or initiated a violent encounter with his assailant.

---

24 [1973] 1 WLR 1334, 1345 (CA) (Scarman LJ) (ch 2.105). Paragraph 21 of this scheme specifically provided that 'the Board will not be bound by any finding of contributory negligence by any court, but will be entirely bound by the terms of the Scheme'.

25 *Criminal Injuries Compensation (Overseas) Scheme*; (ch 3.10).

26 Sonia Macleod and Christopher Hodges, *Redress Schemes for Personal Injuries* (Hart Publishing 2017) 642.

27 See generally Simon Deakin, Angus Johnston, and Basil Markesinis, *Markesinis and Deakin's Tort Law* (7th edn, Oxford University Press 2013) 749–62, 776–806.

28 [1996] QB 567 (CA); Miers (n 4).

29 CICAP (1997) para 5.

A The claimant's own violent conduct

4.26 The 2012 Guide cautions: 'We will look at details from before the incident'. In a distillation of decisions taken by the CICB and the CICA,[30]

> [w]e will consider if you were acting in an aggressive or threatening way and provoked the incident in which you were injured; you intended to provoke an assault or fight; there was a history of violence between you and the assailant; or you were injured as a result of challenging someone over a previous incident.

CICA will also 'look at what happened at the time of the incident, such as whether you willingly took part in a fight' ... and 'consider your behaviour after the incident happened, such as whether you sought revenge against your assailant'.

1 Acting in an aggressive or threatening way/provoking the incident

4.27 The claimant's use of offensive, argumentative or insulting language,[31] and her threatening or obstructive behaviour towards others, are instances of conduct that could lead to a refusal of or reduction in an award. In *SB v FTT,* the CICA refused an application in which the claimant was assaulted after she had repeatedly blown a whistle in a cinema on each occasion that an audience member sitting next to her used a mobile phone. The FTT dismissed her appeal, finding that in the contested circumstances described by the police officer who attended, her behaviour was unjustified and provocative, and 'accordingly' it was not able to make any award. On its use of this adverb, the Upper Tribunal held that the FTT had fettered the discretion that paragraph 13(1)(d) required it to exercise. In treating its finding as to the applicant's conduct as conclusive, the FTT had asked the wrong question. Even if the claimant's behaviour was unjustified and provocative, the question remained: was it 'inappropriate that a full award or any award at all be made'?[32]

2 Intentional provocation of an assault or fight

4.28 Two particular issues arise in claims in which the applicant challenged or voluntarily agreed to fight their assailant, but emerged the loser.[33] The first is whether, where he had initiated a fight from which he had been able to run away, the injuries he sustained when his assailants chased and then attacked him were the result of a separate 'incident'. If so, it might be appropriate to make an award, but if it were a continuation of the incident that the applicant had initiated, it might not. This clearly depends on the facts, in respect of which the CICAP, in *R (on*

---

[30] See CICA (2001 Guide) Pt 4 para 16; and *R (SB) v First-tier Tribunal* [2010] UKUT 250 (AAC), [2011] AACR 11 [26] (*SB v FTT*).

[31] CICAP (2005) 18 (case study two: claimant repeatedly taunting his assailant having been asked to desist).

[32] *SB v FTT* (n 30) [9] and [17].

[33] CICA (2001) 10 (case summary three: claimant 'a willing participant' in a fight for which her alleged assailant was acquitted).

the application of Green) v Criminal Injuries Compensation Appeals Panel, did not make clear findings, nor give sufficiently full and clear reasons to indicate how and why it had refused the application.[34]

The second issue is whether an award should be withheld or refused where the applicant's injury is very much more serious than might have been expected by way of response. The 2001 Guide was clear that it should: 'If, without good cause, you struck the first blow, regardless of how seriously you were hurt when the person fought back'.[35] **4.29**

Its 'examples of situations where we may refuse or reduce an award' drew on decisions made by the CICB under paragraph 6(a) of the common law scheme, but were themselves indicative of a shift in its response to such applications. Its initial stance was that if a 'fair fight' ensued from the victim's conduct it was to be rejected, but where the offender's response was out of the ordinary, a reduced award was appropriate. But by the late 1970s the 'fair fight' approach had been replaced by one in which the actions of the victim became the determining factor; 'unless we adopt a realistic approach we could well end by making a full or reduced award to the one who comes out of the incident with injuries'.[36] **4.30**

The 'realistic approach' was exemplified by *R v Criminal Injuries Compensation Board, ex parte Comerford.* The victim, who had been annoying other customers in a public house, was head-butted by his assailant, causing him to fall and to fracture his skull, leaving him severely brain damaged. The Divisional Court confirmed the CICB's refusal of his application. Lord Donaldson observed that, in answering its colloquial question, 'did the applicant ask for it?', the CICB was entitled to find that he did ask to be hit, and to take that finding into account 'in either rejecting or reducing his claim, regardless of the unforeseeable and appalling circumstances which have in this case arisen'.[37] A similar outcome followed in *R (on the application of Mohammed) v Criminal Injuries Compensation Appeals Panel* where, following a serious argument with the offender in his home, the victim remained outside with a view to continuing the argument and to summoning reinforcements, but was in fact killed by the offender in the ensuing fight. Although the victim 'got very much more than he bargained for', the CICAP did not err when it rejected his widow's claim under paragraph 13(1)(d).[38] **4.31**

These decisions can be seen as a corollary of the well-established principle of both tort and criminal law, that a defendant must take his victim as he finds him: the **4.32**

[34] [2008] EWHC 3501 (Admin), 2008 WL 5758778 (QBD).

[35] CICA (2001 Guide) (n 30) Pt 4 para 16.

[36] CICB, 16th Report (Cmnd 8081 1980) para 26.

[37] CICB, 17th Report (Cmnd 8401 1981) para 20(a); unreported 19 June 1980 (*ex parte Comerford*). There is a close analysis of the Divisional Court's decision in *SB v FTT* (n 30) [20]–[21].

[38] [2008] EWHC 1733 (Admin), 2008 WL 3996451 [27]–[28] (QBD); there was no reference to *ex parte Comerford.*

victim must take his assailant as he finds him.[39] The question for the statutory scheme is whether this means that an award should be withheld or reduced, whatever the level of violence in the assailant's response to the provocation. In *SB v FTT,* the Upper Tribunal commented that '*Comerford* was obviously a very extreme case on the facts', but it did not assist in a proper understanding of the discretion to be applied under paragraph 13(1)(d). The paragraph did 'not allow any general balancing out of the nature of a claimant's conduct against the seriousness of the injury and other consequences'; rather, the nature of the assailant's response may be plotted against a continuum at one end of which is a line beyond which 'no reasonable person could have foreseen a reaction of violence of even the mildest degree or where no element of blame of any kind could be attached to the claimant'. But until that line is reached, when applying the criterion of inappropriateness of the award, the tribunal of fact is entitled to take into account, if that is the case, that 'some degree of violent reaction could have been anticipated, but the actual reaction (as opposed to the consequences of that reaction) was out of proportion to what was expected'.[40]

3 A history of violence with the assailant or challenging them over a previous incident

4.33 Refusal of or reduction in an award could also follow a claim where the incident in which the applicant was injured formed part of a pattern of violence in which they took part voluntarily; for example, if there was a history of assaults involving both sides and the applicant had previously been the assailant, or where the applicant was injured whilst attempting to obtain revenge against an earlier attack by the assailant.[41]

B The claimant's other conduct 'before, during or after the incident'

4.34 In some of the decisions noted above, the applicant's conduct before or during the incident may itself have been a criminal offence; for example, where he used 'threatening or abusive words' contrary to section 5 of the Public Order Act 1986, or his initial assault on the assailant constituted an offence under section 47 of the Offences Against the Person Act 1861 (OAPA 1861). Unlike the common law scheme there is no requirement in paragraph 25 (nor in the earlier tariff schemes) that her conduct was unlawful: it is sufficient that it is 'inappropriate'.

4.35 While the assailant's response may well be its direct result, it would be wrong to infer that paragraph 25 applies only when there is a *causal* link between the

[39] *R v Blaue* (1975) 61 Cr App R 271 (CA); *NHS Business Services Authority v Mrs Karen Young* [2017] EWCA Civ 8, [2017] ICR 599 (CA) [16] (Flaux LJ); Deakin, Johnston, and Markesinis (n 27) 760.

[40] *SB v FTT* (n 30) [27]–[31] (Judge Mesher).

[41] CICA (Guide 2001) (n 20) Pt 4 para 16.

victim's conduct and the criminal injury. There may be such a link but, as paragraph 25 makes clear, what is required is a *temporal* link: that the victim's conduct occurs 'before, during or after' the incident. As *SB v FTT* demonstrates, 'an approach purely in terms of causation of or contribution to the incident in question' does not necessarily assist in answering the question of whether it would be 'inappropriate' to make any award,[42] but depends on the policy to which paragraph 25 (together with paragraphs 26–28) gives effect. Whatever the causality, it would be inappropriate to allow a claim from an applicant injured in the course of committing a crime, for example, dealing in drugs, and some conduct may be inappropriate not because it is unlawful, but is of a questionable nature. The CICB refused an award to a 15-year-old boy who, having been asked to give a talk to his school class about a favourite pastime, described various ways of torturing cats, the result of which was that one of his classmates, who took objection to this, punched him in the face.[43]

The low social value exhibited in this application is present also in cases where children sustain injuries caused by playing dangerous games, in particular, by the use of air rifles and pistols. Annex B paragraph 4(1)(d) excludes injuries 'sustained in the usual course of sporting or other activity to which a person consented by taking part in the activity' (Chapter 2.87–2.90). But injuries sustained while playing a dangerous game, including those played by children, are likely to be caught by paragraph 25. Where the applicant was entirely innocent, the question will be whether the child who caused the injury could be regarded as having acted at least recklessly for the purpose (typically) of an offence under the OAPA 1861, and then whether that offence was a crime of violence.[44] CICA's approach, derived from the CICB's decisions, has been to make no award where there was nothing to choose between the conduct of the child who inflicted the injury, and that of the victim, in the context of their respective understanding of the risks involved: to compensate the victim merely compensates the loser. But 'where children are of different age groups or take unequal parts in the game, a full or reduced award may be made depending on the degree of participation and understanding of the risks involved'.[45] **4.36**

1 Temporal limits on the scope of paragraph 25

As the example discussed above illustrate, many of the claims that fall to be determined under paragraph 25 concern the claimant's conduct immediately 'before' the incident, which also raises the question of how far 'after' the incident her conduct might be relevant, on which there is no direct authority. As the scheme is a **4.37**

42 *SB v FTT* (n 30) [29]–[30] (Judge Mesher).

43 CICB, 24th Report (Cm 536 1988) para 36.1.

44 *R (GI) v First-tier Tribunal* [2011] UKUT 83 (AAC); (ch 3.30–3.31).

45 CICA (2001 Guide) (n 30) Pt 4 para 18; no reference to this issue is made in the 2008 or 2012 Guides.

form of subordinate legislation, to be interpreted according to the principles of statutory interpretation, the composite phrase in paragraph 25 is to be construed as a whole.[46] On the basis that the three prepositions that precede it denote some temporal relationship with 'the incident', in the absence of any provision in the scheme, the CICA and FTT are, as tribunals of fact and subject to their public law duty not to reach a conclusion that no reasonable tribunal could reach, entitled to decide how remote that relationship might be.

4.38 Giving effect to what Judge Rowland described in *R (SH) v First-tier Tribunal (CIC)* as the scheme's 'obviously intended principle that those who commit crimes themselves should not necessarily expect compensation for crimes committed against them',[47] there may be no 'bright line' beyond which the applicant's conduct *before* the incident will not be relevant, save in respect of convictions that have been rehabilitated (4.49). Other than those cases, the tribunal is required to determine whether the claimant's conduct makes it 'inappropriate' to make any award. Concerning the analogous issue, at what point does the assailant's response to the applicant's provocation become disproportionate, the Upper Tribunal in *SB v FTT* said: '[i]t may be dangerous to talk in terms of a crucial line beyond which it is not possible rationally to conclude that it is inappropriate even to reduce compensation, rather than of a continuum on which the case for refusal or reduction becomes weaker and weaker'.[48]

4.39 This reasoning will, it is suggested, similarly apply to the applicant's conduct 'after' the incident. Paragraph 25 of the 2012 Scheme would surely apply if, some months after the incident in which he sustained a criminal injury in an unprovoked assault, the applicant conducted a revenge attack on his assailant. In *R v Criminal Injuries Compensation Board, ex parte Moore*, the applicant was convicted of an offence subsequent to an interim award, which led to the rejection of his application when the CICB convened to consider its final award.[49] In *R v Criminal Injuries Compensation Board, ex parte Thomas* the applicant had, at the time of the incident, no convictions, but because he engaged in criminal activities in the period between its interim award and its final decision to take into account a final medical prognosis, the CICB made no further award.[50]

4.40 The question that then arises is for how long after the incident does the claimant's conduct remain relevant? In a simple claim where, following the application, the CICA's notification of an award and the applicant's acceptance of that determination, there will inevitably be a period of time between the incident, or the

46 Diggory Bailey and Luke Norbury, *Bennion on Statutory Interpretation* (LexisNexis 2017) s 22.3.

47 [2010] UKUT 186 (AAC) [8] (Judge Rowland) (*SH v FTT*).

48 *SB v FTT* (n 30) [30] (Judge Mesher).

49 [1999] 2 All ER 90 (QBD).

50 [1995] PIQR P99 (QBD) (*ex parte Thomas*).

application, and the final payment.[51] During this time, the applicant's conduct 'after' the incident continues to be relevant. If his conduct results in a conviction that remains unspent at the date of its final determination, the claim will be rejected (4.60). That period will vary, depending on the complexity of the facts surrounding the incident, the medical assessment of the applicant's injuries, and the delay between the application and CICA's first decision,. This has period has markedly reduced from 52% to 81% of claimants receiving a first decision within 12 months. Under its 'streamlined applicant journey', the CICA has reduced the time taken to reach a decision in sexual offence claims to between 8 and 12 weeks.[52]

C The relevance of the claimant's intoxication

It is a mundane fact that many incidents of violent crime are prefaced or accompanied by the excessive consumption of alcohol, or the use of illicit drugs, by both offenders and victims.[53] Whether it would be appropriate to compensate a claimant who sustained a criminal injury in such circumstances has long been a contentious question both of policy and practice. Neither the common law nor the 1996 tariff schemes specifically dealt with such claims but, following a review in 1999, the government concluded that simply being drunk at the time of the incident, and thus more likely to be the victim of a violent crime, should not of itself make an award inappropriate.[54] **4.41**

First introduced in 2001, paragraph 14(2) of the 2008 Scheme provided that when considering the issue of the claimant's conduct 'before, during or after the incident', 'a claims officer may refuse or reduce an award where he or she considers that excessive consumption of alcohol or use of illicit drugs by the applicant *contributed to the circumstances which gave rise to the injury* in such a way as to make it inappropriate that a full award, or any award at all, be made' (emphasis added). While the italicized words could extend to applicants who, because of their intoxication, were unable to make clear decisions concerning their own safety, the 2012 consultation was alive to the implications of its application to rape victims, a context in which public advice about any link between a woman's intoxication and her vulnerability to sexual violence continues to be highly controversial. Seeking to clarify its policy, the government took account of the recommendations of the Stern Review,[55] proposing that intoxication should be relevant only where it contributed to the injury or its effects, and not because it increased an applicant's vulnerability to attack.[56] **4.42**

---

[51] Activation of the scheme's procedures for reconsidering or reopening claims will interrupt and may alter their determination; (ch 6.65–6.72 and 6.76–6.95). In 2017/2018 7% of claims were refused on the ground of the claimant's conduct (5% in 2016/2017), CICA (2018) Table 7.

[52] CICA (2017); CICA (2018) 6 and Table 3.

[53] Office for National Statistics (2016) ch 1 s 15.

[54] Home Office (1999) para 50.

[55] Government Equalities Office (2010) (n 11) 15–16.

[56] Ministry of Justice (2012a) (n 10) para 202.

4.43 Paragraph 25 therefore provides that the applicant's conduct 'does not include intoxication through alcohol or drugs to the extent that such intoxication made the applicant more vulnerable to becoming a victim of a crime of violence'. Claims that fall to be considered under paragraph 25 will clearly be fact sensitive. For the purpose of the law governing non-consensual sexual offences, a woman does not consent to sexual activity where, through the voluntary consumption of drink or drugs she is so intoxicated that she has lost or severely impaired her 'freedom and capacity' to choose to consent. Where the claimants are adults, the question of whether there is an offence under sections 1–4 of the Sexual Offences Act 2003 (SOA 2003) depends on the reasonableness of the offender's belief as to consent. Where a belief in an intoxicated victim's consent is unreasonable, there will be an offence, but it does not follow that an award would not be withheld or reduced under paragraph 25. By Annex B paragraph 1, the claims officer would be required to find that the offence was a crime of violence, which in this case means that he would need to find on a balance of probabilities that the applicant was the victim of 'a sexual assault to which a person did not in fact consent' (Chapter 2.41–2.58).

4.44 Where the applicant became intoxicated *after* the incident, paragraph 25 might apply, as it could under paragraph 14(3) of the 2008 Scheme, where for that reason the applicant suffered worse injuries than might otherwise have been the case, or was unable to comply with medical or such other advice as would reduce the extent of injury. These are, arguably, cases where the applicant's 'conduct ... after the incident' has contributed in some causal way to his injuries, so that it is 'inappropriate to make an award or a full award'.

IV Paragraph 26: Convictions

4.45 The CICB would refuse or reduce an award where the applicant had convictions that it regarded as being qualitatively or quantitatively 'serious', whether they were, or as *ex parte Thompstone and Crowe* held, they were not causally related to the incident in which the applicant was injured.[57] This remained the case under the statutory scheme, but the terms under which an applicant's criminal convictions could be taken into account were substantially altered.

4.46 These alterations involved, first, the separation of the discretion in paragraph 6 of the common law scheme concerning the applicant's conduct (paragraph 13(1)(d) of the 2008 Scheme) from that relating to their 'character as shown by his criminal convictions or unlawful conduct' (paragraph 13(1)(e)). The government had been critical of the CICB's unforgiving response to an applicant's criminal record,

[57] *Ex parte Thomas* (n 50).

which could include a spent conviction,[58] a response that, 'in keeping with the spirit of the Rehabilitation of Offenders Act 1974' (ROA 1974), was removed from the statutory scheme.[59]

The alternative criterion in paragraph 6(c), that the applicant's character could be shown by his 'unlawful conduct', was replaced in paragraph 13(1)(e) by the phrase 'evidence available to the claims officer'. Otherwise the terms of this paragraph remained unchanged in the 2001 and 2008 Schemes, but concerned that it was not being applied with sufficient rigour, paragraph 14(3) was added in 2008. 'In considering the issue of character under paragraph 13(1)(e), a claims officer *must* refuse or reduce an award to reflect unspent criminal convictions unless he or she considers that there are exceptional reasons not to do so' (emphasis added). **4.47**

So far as unspent convictions are concerned, paragraph 26 and Annex D of the 2012 Scheme establish a regime that is both radical and highly restrictive. By Annex D paragraph 3, no award will be made where an unspent conviction resulted, broadly speaking, in either a custodial sentence or a community order. Unspent convictions not excluded by paragraph 3 will result in an award being withheld or reduced unless, by paragraph 4, in the exercise of a discretion essentially similar to that in paragraph 13(1)(e), 'there are exceptional reasons not to refuse or reduce it'. **4.48**

A Spent convictions under the tariff schemes

Section 4(1) of the ROA 1974 provides that 'a person who has become a rehabilitated person for the purposes of this Act in respect of a conviction shall be treated for all purposes in law as a person who has not committed or been charged with or prosecuted for or convicted of or sentenced for the offence or offences which were the subject of that conviction'. No evidence of a spent conviction is admissible in any judicial proceedings, or in 'proceedings before any tribunal' (s 4(6)), which, as the Upper Tribunal in *G v First-tier Tribunal* noted, 'must apply to the 2001 scheme', and by extension to all versions of the tariff scheme.[60] It follows that the first task is to determine whether the convictions in question were in law spent at the date of application. The answer depends on the current terms of the ROA 1974, most recently amended with effect in England and Wales from 10 March 2014.[61] This was the issue in *G v FTT*. By virtue of the retrospective effect of the amendments made to ROA 1974 by sections 139 and 141 of the Legal Aid, Sentencing and Punishment of Offenders Act 2012 (LASPOA 2012), all of the applicant's previous convictions, which were unspent at the date of the CICA's **4.49**

58 Home Office (1978) para 17.9.
59 Home Office (1993) para 27(iii).
60 [2016] UKUT 196 (AAC) [18] (*G v FTT*).
61 Ministry of Justice (2014a).

decision, had become spent before the FTT's hearing. The FTT erred when it reduced the applicant's award on the ground of those convictions.

4.49A In *G v FTT* the parties had agreed that had the amendments in LASPOA 2012 been force at the date of his application, all of his previous convictions would have been spent, and at the date of the FTT hearing, his post-application convictions. In *CICA v First-tier Tribunal and SN* the Upper Tribunal held that the correct approach under the 2008 Scheme was to treat, as the amended terms of ROA 1974 require, a claimant's pre-application convictions as spent, while any remaining convictions are to be dealt with in accordance with paragraphs 13(1)(e) and 14(3).[62]

B Unspent convictions under the earlier tariff schemes: 'penalty points'

4.50 Concerning the effect of the discretion in paragraph 13(1)(e), the Upper Tribunal observed in *AA v First-tier Tribunal* that it 'appears to be unfettered, but paragraph 14(3) restricts that freedom by saying that the decision maker must take into account unspent convictions. What paragraph 14(3) does *not* do is tell the decision maker *how* the unspent convictions are to be taken into account' (original emphasis)'.[63] This step, which therefore necessarily precedes the exercise of the discretion, the CICA calculated by reference to a system of 'penalty-points'. This was based in part on the rehabilitation periods in the ROA 1974, that is, the severity of the sentence or other disposal, and the period of time between the date on which it was ordered, and the date on which the CICA received the application; the longer that period, the fewer the resulting penalty points. Conversely, the more recent the conviction, and the more serious the sentence, the more penalty points the conviction would attract. Although the calculation of the applicable penalty points in any case might prove difficult, its purpose was 'intended to provide a readily understood guide to the relative significance of the claimant's criminal record'.

4.51 I do not reproduce here the entire penalty point system, which can be found in the Guide to the 2008 Scheme, or in the Upper Tribunal's decision in *AA v FTT*,[64] but give three examples drawn from it. At the lower end of the scale a conditional discharge attracted one point, and a compensation order unpaid at the date of application, two points. The calculations in the case of a sentence of imprisonment, which meant the sentence given by the court, whether suspended or not, and not the time spent in custody, were more complex. In the case of an applicant sentenced to a term of imprisonment between six and thirty months (say, twelve months):

- An application received within the period of that sentence would attract ten penalty points.

---

[62] [2018] UKUT 248 (AAC) [17], [24] and [31].
[63] [2014] UKUT 211 (AAC) [14] (Judge Lane) (*AA v FTT*).
[64] CICA (Guide 2008) paras 8.14–8.17; *AA v FTT* ibid [16].

- An application received on a date more than the period of sentence (say, two years later) but less than the period of sentence plus three years (that is, within four years of the date of sentence) would attract eight penalty points.
- An application received on a date more than the period of sentence (say, five years later) but less than the period of sentence plus seven years (that is, within eight years of the date of sentence) would attract six penalty points.
- An application received on a date more than the period of sentence plus seven years (that is, more than eight years from the date of sentence) would attract two penalty points.

Other sentences of imprisonment over thirty months or of less than six months, fines, and community orders attracted similarly structured penalty points. On the system's ten-point scale, the percentage reduction for ten penalty points would be 100 per cent, 90 per cent for nine points, and so on. In general terms, the penalty points system gave increasing credit as the period of time between the original sentence and the application to the CICA increased, formalizing the CICB's recognition of an applicant's efforts to be a good citizen. **4.52**

In the case of an application made within the period of a term of imprisonment of thirty months or more, the percentage was 100 per cent, and it could also be possible for a combination of penalty points in respect of a series of sentences to exceed that figure. This was the case in *AA v FTT*, where the FTT added the ten points for the claimant's suspended sentence of three months' imprisonment, to the three points for his requirement to attend a rehabilitation programme, dismissing his appeal against the CICA's refusal of his application. The Upper Tribunal held that this approach was wrong in law: 'the correct position is that there were only 10 penalty points'. The appropriate practice, which the CICA had followed, was to calculate the points on the basis of the element that attracted the highest number of points within the single sentence. Just to tot them all up 'could result in an accumulation of points disproportionate to the gravamen of the conviction and underlying offence'.[65] **4.53**

Nor could the fact that the penalties in any claim totalled or exceeded ten points absolve either the CICA or the FTT of the obligation to exercise their discretion under paragraphs 13(1)(e) and 14(3). For this purpose, the FTT was entitled to follow the CICA's Guide, 'if it thought that was the right thing to do in all of the circumstances', but it fell into error when it concluded that it would not be appropriate for the appellant to receive any award or any reduced award 'in accordance with the Scheme'. This result was *not* in accordance with the scheme; it was in accordance with the penalty point system which, as the CICA's Guide recognized,[66] may best be regarded as 'a starting point for claims officers'.[67] **4.54**

---

[65] *AA v FTT* (n 63) [20]–[21].

[66] CICA (2008 Guide) para 8.17.

[67] *AA v FTT* (n 63) [22]–[24] and [28]; *R (PB) v Criminal Injuries Compensation Appeals Panel* [2010] UKUT 124 (AAC) [6] (*PB v CICAP*). The error in the FTT's conclusion is similar to its inappropriate use of 'accordingly' in *SB v FTT* (n 30) [9] and [17].

4.55 The fundamental point is that CICA's Guides can only ever be advisory (Chapter 1.32). The FTT's error was to treat, or appear to treat, the penalty point system as dispositive, although the CICA was itself clear that the scale of penalty points is not binding at any stage, whether on itself or, as in *Cleary v Criminal Injuries Compensation Appeals Panel*, on a determination made by the appellate tribunal. In that case, the CICAP had very substantially reduced the applicant's award, although the two penalty points allocated to his convictions would not normally have had that result. Rejecting the application for judicial review, the Court of Appeal held that it was 'entirely open' to the CICAP to adopt a different approach from that of the CICA.[68] The Upper Tribunal reached the same conclusion in *PB v CICAP*: '[I]t was open to the Panel, as it is now open to the First-tier Tribunal, to reject the Guide altogether, provided it acted consistently with the Scheme and provided also that it gave a good reason for its approach'. In any event, the relevant paragraphs of the Guide 'do not provide for a rigid code', which in this case failed to supply any guidance concerning the starting point in respect of the claimant's record.[69]

4.56 It follows from the Guide's purely advisory status that the appellate body may also take a more lenient view of the applicant's criminal record. In *SH v FTT* the claimant had been convicted of a number of offences commencing three years after the rape that was the basis of her claim, and after the date on which she had applied for a review of the CICA's decision to reduce her award on those grounds. The Upper Tribunal held that it was open to the FTT to take a different view as to the impact of the penalty points. There was no reason in principle why the FTT should not be entitled to have regard to a very substantial period of time that had elapsed 'either between the relevant crime of violence and the commission of a subsequent offence or between the date on which an offence was committed and the date of a decision awarding compensation'.[70]

4.57 Indeed, in the exercise of its discretion the FTT might, as in *G v FTT*, choose not to apply the penalty points system at all.[71] Paragraph 8.17 of the 2008 Guide indicated that 'the convictions recorded in any individual case and the points attributable to them will be assessed within the context of the particular circumstances of the claim and other related factors ... there may be evidence of rehabilitation not otherwise indicated by the points system which may be taken into account'. But whether or not the CICA or the FTT applied the Guide, paragraphs 13(1)(e) and 14(3) required them either to refuse or reduce the award to reflect any unspent criminal convictions or, if they considered that there were exceptional reasons not

[68] [2003] EWCA Civ 1437, C1/2003/1 256 [8] (CA) (Buxton LJ); CICA (2003) 8 (case summary 1).

[69] *PB v CICAP* (n 67) [6] and [11].

[70] *SH v FTT* (n 47) [8] (Judge Rowland).

[71] *G v FTT* (n 60).

to do so, to do neither. In *AA v FTT*, Judge Lane summarized the joint effect of paragraphs 13(1)(e) and 14(3),[72] emphasizing in *NT v First-tier Tribunal (CIC)* that if there were no exceptional reasons, there *must* be *some* reduction from what would have been an award unaffected by any unspent convictions.[73]

C Unspent convictions under the 2012 Scheme

1 Paragraph 26 of the Scheme and Annex D paragraph 3: 'the exclusionary rule'

(a) **The scope of paragraph 3** In pursuit of its policy of controlling 'who is deemed "blameless" for the purpose of determining who should receive a share of its limited funds', the government's 2012 consultation concluded that applicants with unspent convictions 'should not generally benefit from an award under the Scheme'.[74] Accordingly, the 2012 Scheme introduced, with an exception in the case of fatal criminal injuries, yet stricter criteria for determining when an award would be appropriate in these cases. **4.58**

Paragraph 26 and paragraph 1 of Annex D set out the circumstances in which an award will be withheld or reduced 'because the applicant to whom an award would otherwise be made has unspent convictions'. The 2012 Guide confirms that this provision applies, as it did under the earlier schemes, to 'any convictions you have at the time of applying' and to 'any other convictions you receive before your claim is settled'. This follows from Annex D paragraph 7, which provides that '[p]aragraphs 2 to 6 also apply in relation to an applicant who after the date of application but before the date of its final determination is convicted of an offence which is not immediately spent'. The claimant must disclose all such convictions; it is then for CICA to determine the category into which they fall under Annex D. By paragraph 2 the operative provisions of Annex D (paragraphs 3–6) do not apply to a spent conviction. **4.59**

The central and radical change that the 2012 Scheme makes is set out in paragraph 3. This provides that 'an award *will not be made*' to an applicant who on the date of their application has an unspent conviction' (emphasis added) for an offence which resulted in (a) a sentence excluded from rehabilitation, (b) a custodial sentence, (c) a sentence of service detention, (d) removal from Her Majesty's service, (e) a community order, (f) a youth rehabilitation order, or (g) a sentence equivalent to a sentence in sub-paragraphs (a) to (f) imposed under the law of Northern Ireland or a member state of the European Union, or such a sentence properly imposed in a country outside the European Union'.[75] Paragraph 8 **4.60**

[72] *AA v FTT* (n 63) [17].

[73] [2014] UKUT 210 [8].

[74] Ministry of Justice (2012a) (n 10) para 207; (2012b) para 180.

[75] By para 6, para 3 does not apply in relation to a sentence under the law of a country outside the United Kingdom for conduct which on the date of conviction did not constitute a criminal offence under the law of any part of the United Kingdom.

provides definitions of a 'custodial sentence', 'community order', 'removal from Her Majesty's service', 'sentence of imprisonment', 'sentence of service detention', and 'youth rehabilitation order'.[76] To future-proof the scheme, paragraph 8 applies to any community or youth rehabilitation order, or any custodial sentence or sentence of service detention that is 'of a kind which, on the date this Scheme is made, has been superseded (whether directly or indirectly)' by an order or sentence specified in that paragraph. To reiterate: in none of these cases will an award be made. Refusal is mandatory.

4.61 The lawfulness of the exclusionary rule was challenged in the claims by McNiece, and by A and B, in *McNiece v CICA*. The following paragraphs summarize the Administrative Court's conclusions on the six grounds of their joined application,[77] and note the Court of Appeal's findings in the appeal brought by the claimants in *A and B v CICA*; the claimant McNiece did not appeal. A significant aspect of this decision concerns the application to the scheme of Article 1 of Protocol 1 (A1P1) to the European Convention on Human Rights (ECHR), an issue that has also been of significance in decisions concerning the 'same roof' rule (Chapter 3.106–3.111).

4.62 None of the applicants had sought either a review under the scheme's procedures, or an appeal to the FTT, as they had concluded that the absence of any discretion in Annex D paragraph 3 meant that such steps would inevitably fail. Before the Administrative Court, the first claimant (McNiece) argued that paragraph 26 constituted a disproportionate interference with his rights under A1P1, was unjustifiably discriminatory contrary to A1P1 read together with Article 14 of the Convention, was ultra vires the statutory powers pursuant to which the scheme was made, and was irrational.

4.63 The grounds in A and B's claims were identical to the first two grounds in McNiece's claim, but reflecting their history as victims of human trafficking, additionally argued that paragraph 26 was in breach of Article 17 of the Anti-Trafficking Directive (this formed Ground I of their appeal),[78] and of A1P1 read together with Article 4 of the ECHR. Ground II (Discrimination) of A and B's appeal was somewhat different to that argued before the Administrative Court, but in the following discussion, the Court of Appeal's judgment is linked to those original grounds.

4.64 *(i) Ground 1 in McNiece's claim,and Ground 2 in A and B's: a disproportionate interference with the claimant's rights under A1P1* This ground gave rise to three questions: did the claimants have a 'possession' for the purpose of A1P1; if so, was it interfered with and, if so, did that interference fall within the scope of the

[76] By para 2, 'conviction', 'service disciplinary proceedings', and 'sentence' have the same meaning as under the ROA 1974.

[77] *McNiece v CICA* (n 5). In *Tara Quigley v Criminal Injuries Compensation Authority, First tier Tribunal, Criminal Injuries Compensation*, X/13/72108 (16 November 2015), the FTT reached similar conclusions on the issues that were common.

[78] (ch 3.73–3.74).

public interest qualification in the article? The answer to the first question was 'no'. The 2012 Scheme created a single process in which all of the conditions of eligibility, including those in paragraph 26, were to be met before there could be a determination on whether the claimants were entitled to compensation:

> There was no moment in time when the claimants, by satisfying [those criteria] had an enforceable claim which was then withheld by reason of paragraph 26 of the Scheme. The reality was that there was a single determination on whether an award fell to be made which included both eligibility under paragraphs 4 to 21 and withholding an award under paragraphs 22 to 29 being considered.

As a consequence, 'this claim, insofar as it is based on A1P1, falls at the first hurdle'.[79]

(ii) Ground 2—the claim under Article 14: 'other status' in Article 14 and in Ground II of A and B's appeal, and 'justification' in both claims These grounds raised, first, **4.65**
the question of whether the claimants enjoyed any right or freedom within the Convention in respect of which the scheme had unlawfully discriminated against them. The Administrative Court had already concluded that their claim gave them no 'possession' within A1P1, but proceeded on the basis that the decision of the European Court of Human Rights (ECtHR) in *Stec v United Kingdom* could support the view that the scheme was sufficiently akin to rights arising under social security legislation,[80] that it too should be regarded as generating an interest sufficient to fall within the ambit of A1P1, so that the scheme must be compatible with Article 14.

The second question was whether the claimants' unspent convictions constituted **4.66**
'other status' as one of the grounds on which Article 14 prohibits discrimination. Here, because decisions of the House of Lords in *R (Clift) v Secretary of State for the Home Department*,[81] *Minter and Kay and Others v Lambeth Borough Council*,[82] and the subsequent decision of the ECtHR in *Clift v UK*[83] provided no clear answer, the Administrative Court concluded that the claimants did have 'other status' for this purpose, with which the Court of Appeal agreed.[84]

This conclusion raised, thirdly, the question of whether the discriminatory effect **4.67**
of paragraph 26 could be regarded as a justified and proportionate response to the government's policy with regard to the scheme's particular conditions concerning the use of public money. For this purpose, both courts applied the four-stage approach approved by the Supreme Court in *re Recovery of Medical Costs in Asbestos*

---

[79] *McNiece v CICA* (n 5) [62]–[63].

[80] [2006] ECHR 393. As did the Court of Appeal in *JT v First-tier Tribunal, Criminal Injuries Compensation Authority, and Equality and Human Rights Commission* [2018] EWCA Civ 1755, 2018 WL 03537078 [64]–[70]; (ch 3.107).

[81] [2006] UKHL 54, [2007] 1 WLR 1157 (HL).

[82] [2006] UKHL 10, [2006] 2 AC 465 (HL).

[83] [2010] ECHR 1106.

[84] *McNiece v CICA* (n 5) [80]; *A and B v CICA* (n 5) [68]–[74] (CA).

Cases (Wales) Bill,[85] being the approach that was apt both in respect of Article 14 and, had the court found that the claimants did enjoy a 'possession' that had been the subject of 'interference', of A1P1.

4.68 They concluded that the government's public statements on the scope of the scheme constituted a legitimate aim (4.03). The measure adopted was rationally connected to that aim, was not so intrusive as to extend to *any* unspent conviction (the exclusion applies only to custodial and community sentences (paragraph 3)), allows the exercise of discretion in exceptional cases concerning other unspent convictions (paragraph 4), and does not apply to the most minor convictions (paragraph 5). Paragraph 3 was a 'bright line of exclusion', but paragraphs 4 and 5 showed that Annex D did 'not represent a hard and fast, one-size fits all, approach'; it could not properly be described as a 'blanket rule'. Flexibility could be built in to Annex D by giving the decision-maker discretion to exclude or ameliorate the impact of paragraph 3 on grounds of exceptional circumstances or broader criteria, but neither court accepted that proposition. Given its nuanced nature, the measure struck a fair balance between the competing public interest in the allocation of public funds, and the private interest of those applying to the scheme. 'On no view' can the exclusionary rule be regarded as 'manifestly without reasonable foundation'. In reaching these conclusions the Court of Appeal emphasized that the rule 'operates in the realm of social policy and the Scheme has been reviewed and approved by Parliament; the matter cries out for judicial restraint'.[86]

4.69 *(iii) McNiece's claim—ground 3—ultra vires* Section 3(1)(a) of the Criminal Injuries Compensation Act 1995 provides that the scheme 'may, in particular, include provision—(a) as to the circumstances in which an award may be withheld or the amount of compensation reduced'. The use of the word 'may' did not, as the claimants argued, mean that that section can only provide for a scheme in which ultimate decision-taker has discretion whether or not to withhold or reduce the amount of compensation. It was not beyond the Secretary of State's powers to make a scheme in which the amount of the award was to be withheld or reduced wherever the terms of the scheme so provided.[87]

4.70 *(iv) The A and B claim—ground 1: breach of the Anti-Trafficking Directive: Ground I of their appeal* Among its other provisions, Article 17 of this Directive provides that 'Member States shall ensure that victims of trafficking in human beings have access to existing schemes of compensation to victims of violent crimes of intent'. The Administrative Court rejected the claimants' argument that if there is no prospect of them obtaining compensation via the scheme because of the operation of a mandatory exclusionary rule, they cannot be said to have access to an

[85] [2015] UKSC 3, [2015] 1 AC 1016 (HL).

[86] *McNiece v CICA* (n 5) [111]–[112]; *A and B v CICA* (n 5) [92]–[102] (CA) (Gross LJ) (ch 6.150 and 6.178).

[87] *McNiece v CICA* (n 5) [117].

existing compensation scheme in accordance with Article 17. It held that there was nothing in the terms of the Directive or in the guidance from the authorities on the interpretation of national law in the context of the EU Directives, which suggest that all victims of trafficking must receive awards of compensation under national schemes made or altered for the purpose, regardless of their circumstances and regardless of the terms of national schemes which are lawful under national law. These were similarly the conclusions reached by the Court of Appeal, which was clear that paragraph 26 did not give rise to a breach of Article 17.[88]

(v) The A & B claim ground 3—breach of Article 1 Protocol 1 read with Article 4 ECHR Article 4 of the ECHR provides that no-one shall be held in slavery or servitude, and no-one shall be required to perform forced or compulsory labour. The claimants argued that, in the same way as Article 14 can come into play when considering A1P1, when read with the Council of Europe Convention on Action against Trafficking in Human Beings,[89] there is a separate route whereby the scheme is to be regarded as unlawful, having regard to the United Kingdom's international obligations. The Administrative Court rejected this argument. This Convention is not incorporated into English law; nor did it and its associated documents indicate that all victims of trafficking must be entitled to compensation, regardless of having relevant unspent convictions.[90] **4.71**

(b) Annex D paragraphs 4 and 5: the exclusionary rule's 'nuanced nature' The terms of Annex D paragraph 3 necessarily mean that there can be no discretion to be exercised in respect of any of the unspent convictions that it lists.[91] Its effect, therefore, is that a large proportion of claims brought by those with unspent convictions resulting in custodial or community sentences will be barred altogether. And because paragraph 3(a) provides that an award will be withheld in the case of 'a sentence excluded from rehabilitation', adult victims who when young were convicted of offences that can never be spent will be ineligible, even where they have 'shown themselves to have fully reformed later in life'.[92] **4.72**

In respect of unspent convictions other than those listed in paragraph 3, paragraph 4 makes similar provision to that in paragraph 14(3) of the 2008 scheme: 'An award will be withheld or reduced where, on the date of their application, the applicant has a conviction for an offence in respect of which a sentence other than a sentence specified in paragraph 3 was imposed unless there are exceptional reasons not to refuse or reduce it'. **4.73**

---

[88] ibid [129]; *A and B v CICA* (n 5) [39]–[44].

[89] *Convention on Action against Trafficking in Human Beings, Council of Europe Treaty Series—No 197.*

[90] *McNiece v CICA* (n 5) [158]. The Court of Appeal's 'strong inclination' was that the appellants had failed to establish that their claim fell within the ambit of Article 4, but proceeded on the assumption that it did [53]–[67]. But as summarised above (4.65–4.68), while they had 'other status' within Article 14, the exclusionary rule's discriminatory effect was justifiable, *A and B v CICA* (n 5) [82].

[91] *McNiece v CICA* (n 5) [101].

[92] Ministry of Justice (2012a) (n 10) para 207.

4.74 By paragraph 5, paragraph 4 'does not apply to a conviction for which the only penalty imposed was one or more of an endorsement, penalty points or a fine under Schedule 2 to the Road Traffic Offenders Act 1988'; these unspent convictions have no bearing on the making or otherwise of an award.

2 The scope and implementation of Annex D paragraph 4

4.75 (a) **The scope of paragraph** 4 For the purpose of calculating the reduction under paragraph 4 of Annex D, the CICA employs the same penalty point system that it applied to an unspent conviction under the earlier tariff schemes. Its application is to the same effect—the more recent the conviction and the more serious the sentence, the more penalty points the conviction will attract—and is subject to the same principles. Neither the CICA nor the FTT is bound by the system, but each has the same obligations as applied in the case of the joint effect of paragraphs 13(1)(e) and 14(3) of the 2008 Scheme (4.57). Depending on the facts, they may make a greater or lesser reduction than the points total indicates, although the 2012 Guide indicates that a low point score 'is no guarantee that [the CICA] will make an award if your record includes violent or sexual offences', or ignore the penalty points altogether. But whatever they do, they must make a decision to withhold or reduce an award unless there are exceptional reasons not to do so.

4.76 Annex D paragraph 4 applies to sentences other than those specified in paragraph 3, but does not specify those to which it does. Appendix 2 to the paper 2012 Guide lists absolute or conditional discharge, fines, and compensation orders; these may attract between one point for a fine of £250 or less, or a conditional discharge over two years from date of sentence, and three points for a fine over £250 less than two years from date of sentence. In the case of fines, this Guide adds: 'Payment may be withheld if the fine was imposed for a crime of violence or sexual offence'.

4.77 Appendix 2 also lists a 'contract made as a penalty by the court' as a sentence, the nature of which 'determines that no payment will be made'. By Annex D paragraph 3(f), this determination specifically applies to a youth rehabilitation order, which is a 'second tier' sentence for young offenders. A referral order is a 'first tier' mandatory response to a first time young offender who pleads guilty, resulting in a 'youth offender contract'.[93] The court determines its duration and formally oversees the young person's compliance with his 'contact', but its exclusion from Annex D paragraph 3, and lower punitive level, suggests that a referral order may fall within paragraph 4. It may be noted that none of these guidelines in the paper 2012 Guide is repeated in the later digital version.

4.78 If, in the circumstances of the sentence, the CICA considered that it, or any other 'contract made as a penalty by the court' should not be included in paragraph 4, it would, in common with the full range of other orders that the court may make upon conviction, fall to be considered together with those that may be made in

[93] Powers of Criminal Courts (Sentencing) Act 2000 ss 16–31; (ch 10.29–10.34).

civil proceedings, as evidence of the applicant's 'character' under paragraph 27. Given its terms, it is likely that the cases to which Annex D paragraph 4 applies will be limited.

(b) Exceptional reasons under paragraph 4 Following its review of the implementation of paragraph 6(c) of the common law scheme, the government recommended that regard should be had of cases in which the claimant was at the time of the incident engaged in some meritorious conduct.[94] This was reflected in the Guide to the 2008 Scheme,[95] and in the 2012 Guide: '[w]e may make a smaller reduction or no reduction at all, if you were injured while helping the police uphold the law, or while helping someone who was being attacked'. **4.79**

'Exceptional reasons' could also include cases in which the seriousness of the claimant's criminal injury significantly outweighed that of his unspent convictions, an unspent but minor conviction predates a serious sexual or violent assault on the applicant,[96] or conversely, where the unspent conviction postdates by some years a criminal injury in which the applicant was sexually or physically abused when a child. This was the case in *Muir v Criminal Injuries Compensation Appeals Panel*, where the applicant had been subject to sexual abuse as a child and was later convicted of a number of serious offences, both before and after her application. The Court of Appeal held that 'the discretion to be exercised was a broad one', by which the CICAP could 'on a common sense basis' properly take account of the abuse as a contributory factor in the post-abuse convictions, but offered less scope where the convictions were subsequent to making the application'.[97] **4.80**

The claim in *Muir v CICAP* was made under the 1996 Scheme, which did not include the 'exceptional reasons' provision. It was in issue in *RT v First-tier Tribunal and Criminal Injuries Compensation Authority*, where the applicant, who had been the victim of chronic sexual and physical abuse, later committed a number of motoring offences. Because it did not consider them to be wholly attributable to that historic abuse, the FTT dismissed her appeal against the CICA's refusal of an award. Being a matter for the FTT's discretion, and in the absence of an error of law in its exercise, the Upper Tribunal could not interfere, although its conclusion, that '[I]t is certainly reasonably arguable that in the present case there were exceptional reasons' not to reduce the award might suggest a different outcome.[98] **4.81**

As the FTT's decision implicitly indicates, claims of this kind raise the question of whether there must be a causal link between the applicant's criminal injuries and their subsequent convictions. In *MC v First-tier Tribunal and Criminal Injuries* **4.82**

94 Home Office (1978) para 17.9.

95 CICA (2008 Guide) para 8.17, CICA (2004) 12 (case summary 3: victim otherwise with a 25% reduction made a full award when protecting a woman from an assault by two armed men).

96 Ministry of Justice (2012b) (n 3) para 181.

97 [2004] EWCA Civ 1382, 2004 WL 2678562 [21]–[23] (CA) (Potter LJ) (*Muir v CICAP*).

98 *RT v FTT* (n 21) [47] (Judge Levenson).

Compensation Authority, the applicant had been the victim of extremely serious sexual abuse as a child. As an adult, he himself committed a number of sexual offences, first a few years after the abuse and ten years later, which shortly predated his application under the 2008 Scheme. These later convictions attracted twenty-one penalty points, the only issue being whether the criminal injuries he sustained constituted exceptional reasons justifying a different outcome. The FTT heard extensive psychiatric evidence on the impact of such offences and, on the basis of the ten-year gap between the first set of offences, the absence of offending during that period, and the value of the therapy the applicant had undergone, concluded that 'there was *a* link, but not a *significant* link, between Mr C's childhood experiences of abuse and his recent sexual offences' (original emphasis). The Upper Tribunal did not disturb the FTT's findings, being 'ultimately factual issues which fall squarely within the province of the Tribunal's decision-making expertise'.[99]

V Paragraph 27: Character

4.83 A victim's bad character is paradigmatically evidenced by her unspent convictions. The government was clear that the CICA would retain the alternative power in paragraph 13(1)(e) permitting claims officers to take account of 'evidence available' to them;[100] for this purpose, paragraph 27 provides that: 'An award may be withheld or reduced because the applicant's character, other than in relation to an unspent conviction referred to in paragraph 3 or 4 of Annex D, makes it inappropriate to make an award or a full award'.

4.84 By comparison with the penalty point provisions relating to Annex D paragraph 4 and the extensive guidance on the scope of the phrase 'conduct before, during or after the incident' in paragraph 25, paragraph 27 confers on the CICA and FTT a wide discretionary power constrained only by their obligation to act in accordance with the scheme, and with public law principles. Under the earlier schemes, this other evidence would typically emanate from the police, enabling the CICA to consider matters relevant to the applicant's character in cases in which the CPS had decided not to prosecute, or to take into account findings of guilt following proceedings in a youth court, or admissions of guilt, as typically in a caution.

4.85 The word 'character' in paragraph 27 is unqualified, which could permit the tribunals to take account of evidence of the applicant's good character. But it is clear from the scheme's purpose, and the heading to paragraphs 22–29, 'Grounds for refusing or reducing an award', that paragraph 27's focus is on what sections 98 and 112 of the Criminal Justice Act 2003 (CJA 2003) describe as evidence of 'bad

[99] [2014] UKUT 544 (AAC) [24] (Judge Wikeley).

[100] Ministry of Justice (2012a) (n 10) para 203 n 35. In 2017–2018 10% (as in 2016–2017) of claims were refused on the grounds of the claimant's convictions or character, CICA (2018) Table 7.

character', that is, 'a disposition towards misconduct' that includes 'reprehensible behaviour'. The scheme does not in terms specify what particular aspects of the victim's character might be relevant. The 2012 Guide indicates that: 'We will consider any evidence available about your character, other than in relation to unspent convictions, which makes it inappropriate for us to make a full or reduced payment'; this includes involvement or association in illegal drugs or crime, tax evasion,[101] benefit fraud,[102] any simple cautions,[103] or reprimands.[104] Evidence as to character may also include 'cases involving conduct of questionable dishonesty', where, being a question of fact, people, including CICA and the FTT, 'might differ as to whether the conduct in issue was dishonest'.[105] Dishonesty may indicate a criminal offence, but it is not necessary for paragraph 27 that the applicant should be guilty of one.

In addition to the principal sentences that might fall within Annex D paragraph 4, both criminal and civil courts can impose a range of ancillary orders that potentially stand as evidence of the applicant's character for the purpose of paragraph 27. There are many such orders, which cannot all be reviewed here, not least because they are subject to frequent change both of name and content. It is against that possibility that, in the case of unspent convictions, Annex D paragraph 8 provides for future direct or indirect replacement. Some, such as a restitution, deprivation, or confiscation order may be made only upon conviction for an offence. Others, such as what were antisocial behaviour orders (ASBOs), which the 2012 Guide specifically includes,[106] may be made in civil proceedings; and some, such as a football banning order,[107] or a sexual harm prevention order,[108] on **4.86**

---

[101] *PM v First-tier Tribunal (SEC)* [2015] UKUT 174 (AAC) (applicant's failure to declare his earnings to HMRC).

[102] *MK v First-tier Tribunal and Criminal Injuries Compensation Authority* [2013] UKUT 345 (AAC) (applicant had dishonestly claimed disability living allowance) (*MK v CICA*); CICAP (2006) 50 (case study 3, applicant guilty of social security fraud).

[103] A simple caution is a formal warning that is given by the police to a person who has admitted the offence. It is not technically classed as a conviction; under ROA 1974 it becomes spent immediately.

[104] Reprimands replaced cautions as a police response to a young offender arrested for committing a minor first offence; Crime and Disorder Act 1998 s 65 (CDA 1998), and were themselves replaced in s 66Z by youth cautions and youth conditional cautions; (ch 10.26–10.27).

[105] *MK v CICA* (n 102) [22] (Judge Lane).

[106] An ASBO could be ordered against anyone over the age of 10 years in civil proceedings under CDA 1998 s 1 (a 'stand-alone ASBO'), breach of which constituted an offence. ASBOs were replaced by the Injunction to Prevent Nuisance and Annoyance (IPNA) by Pt 1 of the Anti-Social Behaviour, Crime and Policing Act 2014 (ASBCPA 2014). Where an ASBO could be ordered on conviction for an offence, the court can now order a Criminal Behaviour Order (CBO) under CDA 1998 s 1C, where the offender has acted in an anti-social manner.

[107] Football Spectators Act 1989 ss 14A and 14B.

[108] ASBCPA 2014 Sch 5, replacing sexual offences prevention orders (s 104), foreign travel orders (s 114), and risk of sexual harm orders (s 123) in the SOA 2003. See also the notification requirements, ss 80 and 81, relating to the former Sex Offenders Register.

application to the court. Any of these could be regarded as indicative of misconduct that makes it inappropriate to make any award.

4.87 But, as the Upper Tribunal made clear in *MK v CICA*:

> Not every type or instance of misconduct which affects the view the F-tT takes of a person's character will necessarily lead to a reduction or refusing of compensation. In exercising its discretion, the F-tT must behave proportionately. It would be disproportionate for a decision maker to refuse to make an award of compensation on the basis, for example, of mere distaste for a claimant's behaviour and lifestyle, in the absence of notable misconduct.[109]

4.88 Even so, paragraph 13(1)(e) of the earlier tariff schemes did not require that the aspect of the applicant's character that made it inappropriate that he should receive any award should be in any way connected with the incident giving rise to the application. In an echo of the Court of Appeal's judgment in *ex parte Thompstone and Crowe*,[110] in *Andronati v Criminal Injuries Compensation Appeals Panel*, the High Court held that the paragraph did 'not place any limitations on the type of conduct which might justify the conclusion that an applicant's character renders an award of compensation inappropriate'.[111] The applicant was a Ukrainian woman who was unlawfully in the UK, having overstayed her leave to remain. She was raped by five men and applied for compensation. The CICA refused her application on the ground of her unlawful status, which the CICAP upheld. The court held that, while the scheme made no reference to an applicant's immigration status, it was open to the Panel to consider it. What her 'notable misconduct' demonstrated was that the applicant was not the sort of person who would 'merit an award from public funds'.[112]

VI Paragraph 28: Fatal Cases

4.89 The provisions in the common law and earlier tariff schemes described above equally applied to claims in which the victim died following an initial criminal injury, whether or not in consequence of it. If the victim's conduct, convictions, or character were such as would have resulted in a reduced or nil award had they survived the injury, or if the qualifying relatives themselves presented such features, or had failed to cooperate with the police, the criminal justice authorities or the CICA, an award could be withheld or reduced. For example, a qualifying claimant's claim arising from a homicide could be reduced or refused because the claimant had failed to assist the police in finding the deceased's killer. In *R (on the*

109 *MK v CICA* (n 102) [16] (Judge Lane).
110 *Ex parte Thompstone and Crowe* (n 2).
111 [2006] EWHC 1420 (Admin), [2007] PIQR P2 [9] (QB) (Keith J).
112 *MK v CICA* (n 102) [4].

application of Hudson) v Criminal Injuries Compensation Appeals Panel, the court held that there was no error when the CICAP upheld the CICA's decision in a claim in which the applicant's 'common law' husband was the victim of homicide to make a one-third reduction for his conduct, and then to make no award because of the applicant's failure to cooperate with the police.[113]

The discretion applied whether or not the qualifying relatives were themselves of good character. In *R v Criminal Injuries Compensation Board, ex parte Cook*, the applicant, who was wholly innocent of her husband's criminal activities, applied under the common law scheme when he was shot and killed in a contract killing. The CICB rejected her application, the Court of Appeal holding that it had no duty to take her good character into account.[114] **4.90**

Substantively similar provisions apply to those claimants now designated as 'qualifying relatives' in the 2012 Scheme (Chapter 3.88–3.95). By paragraph 28, **4.91**

> In addition to paragraphs 22 to 27, an award made in respect of a fatal criminal injury may be withheld or reduced if: (a) the deceased's conduct before, during or after the incident giving rise to their death, makes it inappropriate to make an award or a full award. Conduct does not include the deceased's intoxication through alcohol or drugs to the extent that it made the deceased more vulnerable to becoming a victim of a crime of violence.

Paragraph 28 makes it clear, first, that a claim by a qualifying relative may fail in whole or part because of her own failure under any of paragraphs 22–24 or conduct under paragraph 25. Secondly, in its application to a deceased victim, paragraph 28(a) reflects the exact terms of paragraph 25 as they apply to a victim's conduct who survives the incident, including the qualification on the relevance of intoxication. The 2012 Guide says: **4.92**

> We may also reduce or refuse a payment if the conduct of either you or the deceased, before, during or after the incident makes it inappropriate to make an award or a full award. An example might be where the conduct of the deceased led or contributed to the incident in which they were fatally injured.

But in one respect the 2012 Scheme is less stringent. The consultation proposed to discontinue the unqualified application of paragraph 15 of the 2008 Scheme in respect of the deceased's character, as 'being unfair to blameless applicants who were dependent on the deceased'. By paragraph 28(b), an award made in respect of a fatal criminal injury may be withheld or reduced if: 'for exceptional reasons, the deceased's character on the date of their death, whether due to their unspent convictions or otherwise, makes it inappropriate to make an award or a full award'. Unlike the 'exceptional reasons' that apply to Annex D paragraph 4, where a **4.93**

[113] [2002] EWHC 463 (Admin), 2002 WL 31173439 (QBD); a similar outcome followed in *Mohammed v CICAP* [2008] EWHC 1733 (Admin).

[114] [1996] 1 WLR 1037, 1043 (CA).

claims officer may invoke them in favour of an applicant whose claim would otherwise be withheld or reduced, in the case of paragraph 28(b) the claimant will receive an award unless the exceptional reasons apply to refuse or reduce it. These 'exceptional reasons' could include a deceased victim who was 'subject to a life sentence themselves or had unspent convictions for serious sexual offences against children'.[115] In these circumstances, the victim's bad character survives him to the detriment of his estate or dependants.

4.94 The 2012 Guide concludes:

> The character of the deceased, as shown by their criminal convictions or otherwise, will not ordinarily be taken into account. However, we will refuse to make a payment where the deceased's convictions or behaviour was so serious that to pay for their funeral, or to make other payments, would be an inappropriate use of public funds.

[115] Ministry of Justice (2012a) (n 100) paras 209–10.

5

ASSESSMENT OF COMPENSATION

I Introduction

The assessment of compensation under the common law scheme was based on the principles applicable to a civil personal injury action or to an action under the Fatal Accidents Act 1976 (FAA 1976). This was subject to three principal qualifications: the exclusion of the survival of a deceased victim's action and of compensation for loss of expectation of life, and a maximum global payment of £500,000, when awards for loss of earnings, earning capacity, or dependency were included. These qualifications were primarily attributable to the fundamental distinction in their sources of funding: the taxpayer on the one hand and the (insured) wrongdoer on the other. It was a model of assessment about whose costs the government became increasingly concerned, and was fundamentally changed by the 2012 Scheme (Chapter 1.19–1.22). **5.01**

5.02 Section 1(1) provided for the making of arrangements 'for the payment of compensation to, or in respect of, persons who have sustained one or more criminal injuries'. By section 2(2):

> provision shall be made for (a) a standard amount of compensation, determined by reference to the nature of the injury, (b) in such cases as may be specified an additional amount of compensation calculated with respect to loss of earnings, (c) in such cases as may be specified an additional amount of compensation calculated with respect to special expenses, and (d) in cases of fatal injury, such additional amounts as may be specified or otherwise determined in accordance with the Scheme.

5.03 The 'standard amount' was, by section 2(3), to be determined in accordance with a table (the Tariff), prepared by the Secretary of State. This comprised 310 injuries that attracted one or, depending on the injury, more of twenty-five levels of awards of increasing value from £1,000 to a maximum of £250,000, intended to reflect their severity.

5.04 A primary consequence of the substitution of the tariff for common law general damages was that no reduction was to be made to the 'standard amount' because of the applicant's receipt (or eligibility to receive) any payment of state benefits, insurance, or pension payments for the same contingency. Tariff payments were, and continue to be, ring-fenced. A claimant who, in an unprovoked assault, sustains a dislocated jaw with continuing significant disability will receive a tariff award of £3,950 (level A5) under the 2012 Scheme, unaffected by any payments he receives by way of collateral benefits, with the exception of payments by the offender.

5.05 In many other respects, the statutory scheme continued on the same basis as its common law predecessor. However, in order to bring further control over its expenditure the 2012 Scheme made substantial reductions in the levels of award for loss of earnings and earning capacity and, in fatal cases, of dependency, where statutory sick pay (SSP) became the basis for their assessment. The revised tariff eliminated the lowest levels of awards in the 2008 Scheme (bands 1–5: £1,000–£2,000), and reduced those that fell within bands 6–12 (£2,500–£8,200). Injuries that were set at level 6 (£2,500) were reset to £1,000 (level A1), and those between levels 7 and 12 were reduced by set proportions between 40 per cent and 75 per cent of the initial figure. The 550 injury descriptions in the 2008 Scheme were reduced to 352.

5.06 The government's ambition 'to strike a balance between protecting the most seriously injured and making reductions to the overall cost to the Scheme'[1] proceeded from two assumptions about the impact of crime on its victims, and on the role of public funds to its amelioration. The first was that small compensation payments after the event are not the most effective way to help victims recover

1 Ministry of Justice (2012a) para 212.

from the effects of minor injuries; rather, they are better served by support services offering immediate emotional and practical help.[2]

The second assumption was that the long-lasting and often physically or mentally disabling impact on their victims of injuries that are severe or are caused by sexual violence or persistent physical abuse, whether as a child or adult, warranted the continuation of the 2008 levels of award. Those for the most serious injuries (bands 13–25: £11,000–£250,000) were unchanged, as were awards for the 'protected' injuries in Part B of Annex E, that is, sexual offences and physical abuse of adults and children. Given greater prominence in the 2012 tariff, awards in respect of 'a pattern of abuse', whether physical or sexual, associated with domestic violence, or with the abuse of children and adults, are similarly 'protected'. **5.07**

The 2012 Scheme provides for eight 'types of payment' (paragraph 30). They are: (a) injury payments, (b) loss of earnings payments, (c) special expenses payments, (d) bereavement payments, (e) child's payments, (f) dependency payments, (g) funeral payments, and (h) certain other payments in fatal cases. The awards that comprise 'injury payments' are those that are payable under the tariff, and it is only where an applicant is eligible for such a payment that she is also eligible for a payment under paragraph 30(b) or (c). However substantial the loss of earnings, or the level of special expenses, neither of these payments may be made if there is no injury payment. This continues the position under the earlier tariff schemes. **5.08**

The primary focus of this chapter is the arrangements for the assessment of these eight types of payment. It does not deal directly with the equivalent provisions in the earlier statutory schemes, save where they provide relevant context for the analysis of the 2012 Scheme. **5.09**

A Minimum and maximum awards under the 2012 Scheme

1 The minimum award

Paragraph 5 of the common law scheme provided that compensation was not payable unless, after the deduction of social security benefits but before any other deductions, the total payable would be not less than the minimum amount, which was £1,000 at the time when it was replaced by the statutory scheme. The 2012 Scheme has no equivalents to paragraphs 25 and 26 of the earlier tariff schemes, which provided that the 'minimum amount' payable for any injury was 'Level 1', but that is implicit in the fact that £1,000 remains the lowest tariff award in Annex E. This remains the most common reason for a claim being disallowed.[3] **5.10**

---

[2] Home Office (2005);.

[3] Of 16,772 claims disallowed in 2015–2016, 5,451 (32%) did not meet the minimum award; in 2016–2017, the figures were 13,175 and 4,282 (32%), respectively; CICA (2017) Table 7; in 2017–2018 the proportion was 25%, CICA (2018) Table 7.

5.11 The 2012 Scheme continues to permit an award of less than the minimum in the three cases that the earlier schemes specified. The first are claims in which an award in excess of £1,000 has been reduced to a 'lesser amount' by the operation of the eligibility criteria relating conduct or character in paragraphs 24–28 (Chapter 4). This outcome cannot apply, however, where the incident was not reported to the police or the applicant did not co-operate with the authorities, as paragraphs 22 and 23 provide that in such cases an award will be withheld; in this respect the 2012 Scheme differs from the earlier schemes (Chapter 4.05). The two other instances concern payments made by way of damages or a compensation order (5.130), and funeral expenses incurred by a person who is not a 'qualifying relative' (5.105–5.106).

2 The maximum award

5.12 Being based on the common law, there was no maximum award for general damages under the pre-statutory scheme or, subject to the cap on loss of earnings, on the combined total of pecuniary and non-pecuniary loss, but the statutory scheme introduced a maximum global award of £500,000, covering both the tariff and all payments for pecuniary loss. By paragraph 31 of the 2012 Scheme, this is the maximum that is payable 'in respect of 'one or more criminal injuries directly attributable to an incident'; that is to all of the injuries that are the result of the same incident in which they were sustained. By paragraph 60, this maximum figure also applies in the case of a claim 'in relation to a fatal criminal injury'; that is, irrespective of the number of qualifying relatives, or of their level of financial or physical dependency.

5.13 Both paragraphs 31 and 60 provide that the assessment is to be made before any reductions under paragraphs 24–28, as was the case under paragraph 24 of the earlier tariff schemes. A claimant whose award, absent paragraphs 24–28 would, but for the maximum exceed £500,000 (say £500,500) will receive just the maximum. Where paragraphs 24–28 apply, any reduction (say £500) will leave an award of £499,500, not £500,000.

II Paragraphs 32–41: Injury Payments

A The categorical nature of the tariff

5.14 By section 2(4) of the Criminal Injuries Compensation Act 1995 (CICA 1995): 'The Tariff shall show, in respect of each description of injury mentioned in the Tariff, the standard amount of compensation payable in respect of that description of injury', and by section 2(5) gives discretion to describe an injury in the tariff 'in such a way, including by reference to the nature of the injury, its nature, severity or the circumstances in which it was sustained, as the Secretary of State considers appropriate'.

When introduced, the scheme was criticized for containing no explicit award for pain and suffering. The government's response was that as the payment level for each tariff band had been calculated on the basis of the median award for each named injury drawn from a sample of some 20,000 awards under the common law scheme, every award would reflect an element of pain and suffering. But its exact contribution to each band was unclear. Because that scheme's awards were paid as a global lump sum, they could also have included some elements of special damages, thus inflating (to an unspecified degree) each tariff band to a level greater than would have been the case if the median award could have been based solely on a disaggregated general damages award.[4] **5.15**

The tariff's categorical nature was also criticized for its inflexibility in making no distinctions that could reflect the different impact of their injuries on different claimants. This criticism was to an extent misplaced, as it did make some such distinctions, but the government resisted amendments designed to give claims officers discretion to increase the standard amount of compensation to reflect special factors affecting the claimant. Such discretion 'would undermine the whole rationale of the tariff scheme. In effect it would introduce a common law damages scheme ... with the associated delays and complexity. The whole point of a tariff system is that it provides a quicker, simpler and more transparent arrangement'.[5] This was also the government's response when the same criticisms were made of the 2012 Scheme. Anybody who thinks that its aim is 'to provide individually tailored compensation packages covering each and every type of damage' misunderstands the scheme's nature and purpose.[6] **5.16**

The government's resistance was also founded on section 2(6) of the CICA 1995, which gives the Secretary of State power 'to add to or to remove from the tariff any description of injury, to increase or reduce the amount shown as the standard amount of compensation for any given injury, or to alter the Tariff in such other way as he considers appropriate'. It had resisted attempts to introduce an annual review of the tariff, but agreed to a three-year review which took place in 1999,[7] which was followed by the first set of revisions in the 2001 Scheme. **5.17**

The implications of the tariff's categorical nature are illustrated by *Criminal Injuries Compensation Authority v First-tier Tribunal and ML (CIC)*.[8] The applicant had been subjected to a number of sexual assaults committed on separate occasions by two separate assailants, causing her to develop an emotionally unstable personality disorder. One question that arose was whether the applicant's claim should be treated as a single claim in respect of 'one or more criminal injuries', as **5.18**

---

[4] Home Office (1993) paras 14–15.
[5] Hansard HL vol 556 cols 337 (19 July 1995), and 619 and 637 (16 October 1995).
[6] First Delegated Legislation Committee HC Session 2007–08 col 13 (14 July 2008).
[7] Home Office (1999) para 51.
[8] [2017] UKUT 206 (AAC), [2017] AACR 36 (*CICA v ML*).

provided by section 1(1) of the CICA 1995, or as two separate claims, one in respect of each assailant. Referring to section 2(5), the Upper Tribunal said:

> where a descriptor is expressed in terms of the circumstances in which injury occurred, as in the case of the indecent assault descriptors, there seems to me to be no reason not to apply the descriptor as often as the terms of the descriptor are satisfied, unless the injury then falls within the terms of another descriptor. On the other hand, if a descriptor is expressed in terms of the nature or severity of an injury, it seems to me that there is no basis for holding that a single injury can satisfy the terms of the descriptor more than once.[9]

In this case the two assailants had each committed one of the four 'indecent assault descriptors', that is 'two or more isolated incidents of non-penile penetrative acts' and 'non-penetrative frequent assaults over clothing', but in respect of both of these there was only a single mental injury. The First-tier Tribunal (FTT) had erred in making two separate level 16 awards of £19,000 for the 'moderately disabling permanent mental illness' in respect of the assaults by the two different assailants.

5.19 Similarly, *R v Criminal Injuries Compensation Appeals Panel, ex parte Embling* illustrates the binary choice between two injury descriptors that can be presented by the tariff's categorical nature. The applicant had sustained a broken index finger in her right hand in an assault. Her claim under the 1996 Scheme turned on whether her injury fell within the descriptor 'fractured finger(s) or thumb—one hand (full recovery) £1,500' or 'fractured finger(s) or thumb—one hand (with continuing disability) £3,500'. As a preliminary to its decision on the meaning of the alternative descriptors, the court held that the nature of the tariff meant that the applicant's injury had to fall into one or the other category. Each descriptor had to be given such a meaning that if the injury fell outside of the scope of one, it could nevertheless be sensibly described as within the scope of the other (Chapter 3.53–3.55).

B Annex E Part B: sexual and physical abuse

5.20 Chapters 3.50–3.55 and 3.56–3.63 respectively discussed the definition and scope of 'physical injury' and of 'mental injury' in Part A of Annex E. In the earlier schemes payments for the physical abuse of and sexual offences against children and adults were listed in the single tariff of injuries. In the 2012 Scheme these payments fall under Part B. The 2008 Scheme required amendment to align its terminology with the offences specified in the Sexual Offences Act 2003 (SOA 2003), but in general terms the injury descriptors, their place in the payment structure, and because they are 'protected' payments, their respective award levels, have remained constant since the 2001 Scheme.

---

[9] ibid [12] (Judge Bano).

As elements in their 'protected' status, payments in Part B incorporate factors that were recognized in the 2001 and 2008 tariffs as significant contributors to the physical and mental injuries that arise in such cases. In the case of sexual offences, payments for some incidents have always been set at a higher level where they were committed by more than one 'attacker', distinguish non-penetrative from penetrative assaults, and provide for higher payment levels where these offences result in permanently disabling mental illness. **5.21**

In the case of both physical and sexual abuse, an important factor in their assessment has been that the injuries were sustained as a result of 'a pattern of abuse', as may occur in private or local authority care homes and other accommodation. These injuries were dealt with as a coda to Notes 13 and 14 of the 2001 and 2008 tariff (there was no equivalent in the 1996 Scheme). They are replaced by Notes [5] and [6] in Annex E Part B of the 2012 Scheme, in which 'a pattern of abuse' is a defining element in the identification of the appropriate tariff level. **5.22**

1 'A pattern of abuse'

Note [5] concerns the injury payments that may be made where there has been a pattern of physical abuse of adults and children. Note [6] applies to cases in which there has been a pattern of sexual abuse where 'the victim is any age (if not already compensated as a child)' ('victims of any age'), or is 'a child (under age of 18 at time of, or commencement of, the offence), or an adult who by reason of mental incapacity is incapable of giving consent ('a child or an adult victim unable to give consent'). **5.23**

Notes [5] and [6] are similar in their purpose. They provide, first, that payments in respect of a pattern of abuse apply in respect of all physical injuries or sexual assaults to both adults and children. Secondly, they provide, as did Notes 13 and 14 of the 2001 and 2008 Schemes, that payment would normally be made to reflect the pattern of abuse rather than each separate injury or incident. But Notes [5] and [6] go further, providing that 'an exception may be made' where a single injury or incident sustained as part of the pattern of abuse would give rise to a higher tariff payment than that for the abuse, 'in which case the higher payment may be made instead of the award for the pattern of abuse'. **5.24**

For example, a 'persistent pattern of repetitive violence resulting in moderate multiple injuries (e.g. bruising and minor fractures) or minor disfigurement' to a child is set at £5,500 (level B6); but if one of those fractures caused 'continuing significant disability' to its heel bone in one foot (£6,200 (level A7), the higher award would apply. Similarly, a pattern of 'repetitive frequent severe sexual abuse (whether by one or more attackers)' over a period of more than three years is set at £8,200 (level B8), but the level for one incident of 'non-consensual penile penetration of one or more of vagina, anus or mouth' by two or more attackers is **5.25**

£13,500 (level B14). If this was an 'exceptional' case, the claimant would receive the higher amount.

5.26 Notes [5] and [6] may also be seen as being restrictive in that those single higher awards are to be made '*instead of* the award for the pattern of abuse' (emphasis added). This phraseology is more specific than that in Note 13, which provided that in such cases the claimant would qualify for an award as the victim of a pattern of abuse, *rather than* for a separate award for each incident' (emphasis added).

5.27 *R (LM) v First-tier Tribunal (CIC)* concerned the relationship between this coda to Note 13 and paragraph 27 of the 2001 Scheme, which set out the 'multiple injury formula' to be used when the claim relates to two or more injuries arising from the same incident (5.45–5.62). The question was whether the FTT had, given the terms of Note 13, erred when making three separate awards for three separate offences of sexual abuse, when a single award should have been made on the basis that the applicant was a victim of a pattern of abuse. As the matter was not fully argued before it, the Upper Tribunal made no ruling, but did contemplate that in such a case there could be one higher award for the single most serious injury, and a second award subject to the multiple injury formula for the pattern of abuse. It is suggested that that option is foreclosed by the clear words of Notes [5] and [6].

5.28 The Upper Tribunal also noted that, although the scheme refers in several places to the word 'pattern', whether in the phrase 'a pattern of abuse' or a 'pattern of incidents', there was no clear indication as to what amounts to a 'pattern' either in the tariff or in paragraph 27.[10] Neither did Note 13 nor Note 14 throw any light on the issue. Whether a sequence of assaults amounts to a 'pattern' of abuse or of incidents (whether or not that they were carried out by different people), is a question both of law (what constitutes a 'pattern' for the purposes of the scheme), and of fact. So far as the question of fact is concerned, Notes [5] and [6] provide that: 'Whether injuries have arisen as part of a pattern of abuse will be assessed by reference to all the circumstances, including whether there was one or more assailants (and whether they acted together), the nature of the injuries and incidents, and the period in which they occurred'.[11] It is suggested that the question of whether a single injury, for the purpose of awarding a tariff payment higher than the level for the pattern of abuse is exceptional, is also a question of fact.

---

[10] [2011] UKUT 179 (AAC) [38]–[43] (*LM v FTT*).

[11] See eg *R (M) v Criminal Injuries Compensation Appeals Panel* [2001] EWHC Admin 720, 2001 WL 1476332 (QB). The claimant had been subject to serious sexual abuse between the ages of 5 and 11 by her stepfather. The CICA identified this as constituting a 'pattern of serious abuse: repetitive, frequent non-penetrative indecent acts' at level 5 in the 2001 Scheme (£2,000).

In common with Notes 13 and 14 of the earlier schemes, Notes [5] and [6] to the 2012 tariff use the word 'incident' to describe the occasion giving rise to the criminal injury to which the claim relates, but unlike them, the 2012 Scheme provides a qualification to its application. By Annex A, 'Other than in the tariff in Annex E, and unless otherwise stated, a reference in this Scheme to an incident includes a series of incidents and, in the case of a series of incidents, a reference to the date of the incident means the date of the first incident in the series'. As is clear, Notes [5] and [6] do otherwise apply when determining whether or not there has been a pattern of abuse, and in identifying the appropriate tariff level where there has been more than one 'incident' of sexual abuse. **5.29**

2 Physical abuse of children and adults, including domestic abuse

The 1996 Scheme did not single out physical abuse of adults as comprising separate categories of injury, but did so in respect of children, specifying three levels of abuse. 'Minor abuse' comprised 'isolated or intermittent assault(s) resulting in weals, hair pulled from scalp etc' (£1,000: level 1); 'serious abuse', being 'intermittent physical assaults resulting in an accumulation of healed wounds, burns or scalds, but with no appreciable disfigurement' (£2,000: level 5), and 'severe abuse', a 'persistent pattern of repetitive violence resulting in: moderate multiple injuries (e.g. bruising and minor fractures) and/or minor disfigurement' (£5,500: level 10), 'significant' (£8,200 level 12) or 'severe' multiple injuries (£10,500: level 14). The 2001 and 2008 Schemes maintained this scale of injuries and their descriptors in respect of children, and introduced a similar scale in the case of adults. This differentiated 'serious' (level 5) and 'severe' (level 10) injuries, and those caused by a 'persistent pattern of severe abuse over a period exceeding 3 years' (level 12). The 2012 Scheme has not amended these categories, and being 'protected' injuries under Part B, their values are unchanged. **5.30**

3 Sexual offences against children and adults

The two categories of victims of sexual abuse and assault, that is, victims of any age, and a child or an adult victim unable to give consent, were introduced in the 2001 Scheme, replacing the single category in the 1996 Scheme. It also introduced further differentiation between the injury descriptors in each category, in particular in respect of the most serious injuries, attracting the highest awards. The descriptors, but not their corresponding tariff levels, were in turn all amended in the 2008 Scheme to align with the major changes in the SOA 2003. The structure of the tariff remained; with minor adjustments, Part B of the 2012 tariff maintains the descriptors and tariff values of the 2008 Scheme. **5.31**

The question posed in *Criminal Injuries Compensation Authority v First Tier Tribunal & JC (CIC)* concerned the impact on the 2001 tariff of the changes made to the definition of rape in section 1 of the SOA 2003. The claimant had sustained a criminal injury when her ex-husband forcibly penetrated her mouth with his **5.32** penis. She was made an award under the 2001 Scheme at level 7 (£3,300) for an indecent assault comprising 'severe non-penile penetrative and/or oral-genital act or acts'. The claimant's appeal was that, following the change in the definition of rape and the prospective complementary change made in the 2008 Scheme as 'non-consensual penile penetration of the vagina and/or anus and/or mouth', the FTT should interpret the closest 2001 descriptor, 'non-consensual vaginal and/ or anal intercourse' by one attacker (£11,000: level 13), as being equivalent to the new definition of rape.

5.33 The FTT allowed the appeal,[12] but the Upper Tribunal quashed its decision, substituting the original award level. It accepted that there was some lack of clarity as to the scope of the level 7 descriptor, but rejected the claimant's argument that, as the government had agreed the changes to be made in section 1, and that the scheme should be amended accordingly, it should adopt a purposive approach to the interpretation of the 2001 tariff. The scheme was to be interpreted by reference to the essential ingredients of the offence of rape, *as then statutorily defined* (original emphasis).[13]

C Annex E Part B: other tariff payments

5.34 This category covers four separate conditions in which an additional payment will be made, none of which is subject to the multiple injury formula.

5.35 The first two comprise awards for pregnancy, or for a sexually transmitted infection (STI), other than HIV, Hepatitis B, or Hepatitis C, being in all cases a direct result of a sexual offence; as in the case of the mother in *Criminal Injuries Compensation Authority and First-tier Tribunal (SEC) (CIC) v Y,* who had become pregnant with the claimant following the incestuous rape of which she was the victim.[14] The award for pregnancy remains £5,500. In the case of an STI, the 2001 and 2008 Schemes differentiated between the effect on the victim of a 'substantial recovery' (£5,500: level 10) and of 'permanent disability' (£11,000, level 13), levels that continue in the 2012 Scheme.

5.36 The two other 'additional payments' comprise, first, an award for an infection with one or more of HIV, Hepatitis B, or Hepatitis C 'sustained as a result of any crime of violence'. Under the broad heading of 'sexual offences', the 2001 Scheme included an 'additional award' for 'Infection with HIV/AIDS', and in 2008 for 'HIV/Hepatitis B/Hepatitis C', at level 17 (£22,000). As 'a crime of violence' may, by Annex B paragraph 2(1)(d), include 'a sexual assault to which a person did not in fact consent', the specifications made in this category mean that any

[12] [2011] UKUT 77 (AAC) [4].
[13] ibid [9]–[10].
[14] [2017] EWCA Civ 139, [2017] 4 WLR 60 (CA); (ch 3.81–3.85).

of these infections caused by a 'sexual assault' within the SOA 2003 will attract this award.

The final award under this heading is for loss of foetus. A foetus has no legal personality, and if killed while in the womb no claim on its behalf can be brought under the 2012 Scheme (Chapter 2.91–2.92). But where a pregnant woman sustains a criminal injury as a result of which the foetus is killed, all the tariff schemes have since 2001 set a similar payment for its loss: £5,500. **5.37**

D Acceleration or exacerbation of an existing injury

Where the criminal injury exacerbates or accelerates an existing condition, paragraph 25 of the 1996 tariff scheme provided that the compensation to be awarded would reflect only the degree of exacerbation or acceleration. In this respect, it followed the common law, which would now ask whether the negligent defendant's conduct amounted to a 'material contribution' to the claimant's condition.[15] This paragraph made no reference to the amount to be awarded, but subsequent schemes sought to limit it to cases where the acceleration or exacerbation was sufficiently serious to qualify for compensation 'equal at least to the minimum award'. **5.38**

Elements of this approach continue in the 2012 Scheme. By paragraph 36: **5.39**

> Where an applicant's criminal injury as described in the tariff includes the acceleration or exacerbation of an existing condition, an injury payment: (a) will be paid only in relation to the degree of exacerbation or acceleration; (b) will be calculated by reference to such criminal injuries described in the tariff as a claims officer considers appropriate; and (c) will be reduced to zero, unless the amount calculated under sub-paragraph (b) is £1,000 or more.

There is no equivalent to the saving clause in paragraph 25 of the 2008 Scheme, which provided that 'lesser compensation may be paid' if an award were to be reduced under the scheme's eligibility criteria in paragraphs 22–29. The 2012 Guide is emphatic: where the exacerbation 'is valued at less than £1,000, no payment will be made'.

In *BD v First tier Tribunal and Criminal Injuries Compensation Authority* the applicant had been attacked while driving his bus, sustaining a cut under his eye. Subsequently, he developed a mental illness, in which the attack was only one of a substantial number of possible contributing causes. On the question of whether there had been 'an exacerbation of a pre-existing condition', the Upper Tribunal held that if a mental illness has a number of effective causes, one of which is the commission of a criminal offence, 'the applicant is entitled to an unreduced award **5.40**

[15] *Jobling v Associated Dairies Ltd* [1982] AC 794 (HL); *Bailey v Ministry of Defence* [2008] EWCA Civ 883, [2009] 1 WLR 1052 (CA).

in respect of that illness unless (possibly) it can be identified that the criminal offence merely exacerbated a pre-existing mental injury'.[16]

5.41 As the 2012 Guide indicates, that exercise involves a calculation of what award the pre-existing condition would attract if it were a criminal injury, and then of what degree of exacerbation was caused by the actual criminal injury. In *BD v FTT*, the FTT had concluded that the applicant's mental illness amounted to no more than 10 per cent of the tariff award of £13,500 for 'a non-permanent disabling mental illness lasting over 5 years', but that owing to the operation of the scheme's rules on awards for multiple physical and mental injuries, there could be no payment.

E Multiple injury payments

1 Multiple minor injuries

5.42 The 1996 Scheme maintained the Criminal Injuries Compensation Board's (CICB) approach to 'minor injuries such as scratches or bruises', which alone would not qualify for an award. But, by paragraph 26, they could do so if the applicant had sustained at least three separate injuries of the type listed in Note 1 to the tariff. These were (a) grazing, cuts, lacerations (no permanent scarring); (b) severe and widespread bruising; (c) severe soft tissue injury (no permanent disability); (d) black eye(s); (e) bloody nose; (f) hair pulled from scalp; and (g) loss of fingernail.

5.43 It will be noted that these were all physical injuries. *R (SB) v First-tier Tribunal* confirmed that it was not open to an applicant to argue that she should be compensated where she sustained two of the exemplified injuries, together with a mental injury.[17] These conditions were continued in the 2001 and 2008 Schemes as Note 12 to the tariff, amended to read minor 'physical' multiple injuries. At least one of them must have had significant residual effects six weeks after the incident, and all injuries must have necessitated at least two visits to or by a medical practitioner within that six-week period. In *Criminal Injuries Compensation Authority v First-tier Tribunal* the Court of Appeal held that: '"Necessitates" in this context means "makes necessary"; it naturally connotes some element of compulsion, and not simply whether attendance on a doctor can be said simply to be appropriate'.[18]

5.44 If these conditions were met, the minimum award of £1,000 would be made. But the elimination of tariff bands 1–5 in the 2012 Scheme necessarily cut any payments for minor injuries, however many were caused, as it did for all other injuries set at between £1,000 and £2,000.

---

[16] [2016] UKUT 352 AAC [18]–[19] (Judge Turnbull) (*BD v FTT*); on the question of causation; (ch 3.32–3.44).

[17] [2010] UKUT 133 (AAC) [14]–[17].

[18] [2015] EWCA Civ 1329, 2015 WL 5949401 [26] (CA) (Davis LJ).

2 The multiple injury formula

5.45 Many applications will be founded on more than one injury being sustained in the incident. Paragraph 26(a)–(c) of the 1996 Scheme provided that, where the applicant sustained two or more injuries, each of which would each attract at least a level 1 award, the applicant would receive the full tariff amount for the highest-rated description of injury, plus 10 per cent of the second highest-rated and 5 per cent of the third highest-rated. Following the 1999 review,[19] these proportions were increased in the 2001 Scheme to 30 per cent and 15 per cent, which continue to apply in paragraph 37 of the 2012 tariff.[20]

5.46 Where there are separate injuries that meet the descriptors in Part A, up to three separate payments may be made. It is necessary initially to determine what those separate injuries are, and not, as in *C v Home Office and Criminal Injuries Compensation Authority*, to treat the individual consequences of a single injury as separate injuries to which the multiple injury formula would apply.[21] In this case, the applicant had, when 10 years old, been viciously assaulted, resulting in severe brain damage, blindness, and hemiplegia. As the Upper Tribunal later observed in *CICA v ML,* the claimant in *C v Home Office* described her injuries on the claim form as being 'sexually and physically abused', and did not seek to differentiate between the harm caused to her by each of her assailants.[22] Her claim was therefore in respect of this single tariff descriptor for her brain injury, and the CICA's assessment, which treated these separate sequelae of that injury as three separate multiple injuries was 'plainly wrong'. It was therefore in error to apply the discounts under paragraph 27.[23]

5.47 When calculating the injury payment for which an applicant may be eligible, the formula set out in paragraph 37(1) is to be applied after any calculations made under paragraphs 34–36. The formula provides that:

> [w]here an application relates to more than one criminal injury each of which would qualify for an injury payment under paragraph 32, the amount of the injury payment for which the applicant will be eligible is:
>
> (a) the full tariff amount for the criminal injury which gives rise to the highest payment;
> (b) 30 per cent of the tariff amount for the criminal injury with an equal or second highest payment; and

[19] Home Office (1999) para 64(i).

[20] By way of comparison, art 22 of the Armed Forces and Reserve Forces (Compensation Scheme) Order 2011 No 517 provides that, where an injury or injuries are described by more than one descriptor, the amount payable is to be calculated for the first descriptor at 100%, and for the second to the fifth and any subsequent descriptors, at 80%, 60%, 40%, and 20% of the relevant amount.

[21] [2004] EWCA Civ 234, [2004] UKHRR 813 (CA) (*C v Home Office*).

[22] *CICA v ML* (n 8) (Judge Bano).

[23] *C v Home Office* (n 21) [20] (Sedley LJ).

(c) where there are three or more criminal injuries, 15 per cent of the tariff amount for the criminal injury with an equal or third highest payment.

5.48 Two issues arise where there are two or more injuries. The first concerns the formula's application where those injuries are set at the same tariff level. In *R (HD) v First-tier Tribunal (CIC)*, the applicant had sustained three head injuries as the result of a serious assault. These were brain damage, for which the FTT considered 'moderate' was the appropriate descriptor under the 2001 Scheme, total deafness in one ear, and very severe tinnitus in the other ear, all three attracting awards at level 15 (£16,500). The FTT applied paragraph 27, giving 100 per cent for the brain damage, 30 per cent as the second award (£4,950), and 15 per cent as the third award (£2,475), a total tariff award of £23,925. The claimant argued that paragraph 27 did not apply, as it was concerned only with 'minor' multiple injuries. The Upper Tribunal rejected this, finding that the FTT had not erred in its application of the provision.[24]

5.49 The formula set out in paragraph 37 of the 2012 Scheme differs slightly from its predecessors. It provides that once the injury giving rise to the highest payment is identified, the second and third payments will be 30 per cent and 15 per cent respectively 'of the tariff amount for the criminal injury *with an equal or* second (or third) highest payment' (added emphasis). Apart from the obvious case where the second and third injury payments are progressively lower, the italicized phrase means that where those injuries are of an 'equal' amount to the highest injury, the formula will apply to them in the order in which they are chosen. This is an explicit confirmation of the interpretation reached in *HD v FTT* as to the effect of paragraph 27. There is therefore a choice as to which of these equal injury payments is to be preferred for the purpose of identifying the level of discount. This choice is likely to turn, primarily, on the strength of the medical evidence in each case.

5.50 The second issue concerns the application of paragraph 37 where there are more injuries than the two that attract awards at the lower levels. This was also the case in *HD v FTT*, where the claimant had suffered a fourth injury at a lower tariff level, permanent vestibular damage (causing giddiness) at level 12 (£8,200). It followed from the Upper Tribunal's rejection of the claimant's argument concerning paragraph 27 that as the FTT had accepted that the claimant had three injuries that would, taken by themselves, give rise to tariff awards at level 15, 'no lesser injury could have affected the total tariff award'.[25] The following paragraphs illustrate the application of the multiple injury formula where there are multiple physical, sexual, and mental injuries.

5.51 (a) **Multiple physical injuries** Suppose the applicant was struck in the face with a bottle containing acid, which was then thrown at her, causing a fractured jaw

---

[24] [2014] UKUT 243 (AAC) [19], [21]–[22] (*HD v FTT*).
[25] ibid [23].

bone requiring an operation from which she made a substantial recovery (£1,500: A2), scarring of her neck with serious disfigurement (£4,600: A6), and fractures to one or more teeth requiring surgery (£1,800: A3). The applicant would receive 100 per cent of the payment for scarring, 30 per cent of the injury to the teeth (£540), and 15 per cent of the injury to the jaw bone (£225), totalling £5,365. Where there are multiple injuries it is clearly important that the most accurate medical evidence should be obtained. 'Continuing significant disability' to the fractured jaw bone following an operation would become the highest payment (£6,200: A7), while the payment for scarring would be £1,380 (30% x £4,600) and the payment for the injury to the teeth would become the third highest, £270 (15% x £1,800), totalling £7,850.

(b) Multiple physical and mental injuries Suppose that in an incident similar to that in the preceding paragraph the applicant also sustains a disabling mental injury lasting two years or more up to five years (£6,200: A7), caused by the serious disfigurement to her neck. The mental injury would be the highest payment, the payment for the scarring and for the injury to the applicant's teeth would be the second and third payments, and there would be no payment for the injury to the jaw bone at level A2. Conversely, where the tariff level for the mental injury is less than that for any physical injury, the paragraph 37 multiple injury formula will also apply, as the 2012 Scheme has removed the limitation in Note 5 of the earlier schemes. This provided that where the applicant sustained a physical and a mental injury, he would not be eligible for a separate award for the mental injury if its tariff level was lower than that for the physical injury; this was because when it was first set the tariff included an element in respect of pain and suffering (5.15). Under the 2012 Scheme, if the mental injury were less disabling (lasting twenty-eight weeks or more up to two years: £2,400: A4), the applicant would receive the full amount for the disfigurement (£4,600), £720 (30% x £2,400) for the mental injury, and £270 for the injury to her teeth (15% x £1,800), totalling £5,590. There would again be no payment for the injury to the jaw bone. **5.52**

(c) Multiple physical and mental injuries caused by brain damage The implications of Note 5 to the earlier tariff schemes in these cases were illustrated in *HD v FTT.* The issue turned on the severity of the brain damage the applicant sustained, which, in addition to the physical injury, also caused 'permanent mental illness, confirmed by psychiatric diagnosis—seriously disabling'. If the brain damage was classed as 'serious' (£44,000: level 20), Note 5 would preclude an award for the mental injury as it attracted an award at level 18 (£27,000). But if the brain damage was 'moderate' (£16,500: level 15), payment for the mental injury could, being higher, be made, while that for the brain damage would attract a payment of £4,950 (30% x £16,500) under the multiple injury formula.[26] **5.53**

[26] *HD v FTT* (n 24) [25]–[27].

5.54 There is an important qualification concerning multiple physical and mental injuries to the brain, introduced as Note 15 to the 2008 tariff. Its purpose, with some substantive amendment, is repeated in Note [3] to the 2012 tariff. This provides:

> A brain injury can cause physical or mental damage, resulting in, for example, loss of muscle or nerve control, loss of balance, incontinence, or impairment of concentration, memory, motivation or personality. It can also commonly cause epilepsy, to a greater or lesser extent. Where the cause of any injury is brain damage there will not be additional awards for separate injuries but the seriousness of the combined effects will be measured together.

5.55 The implications of Note [3] can be seen *HD v FTT.* The claim for brain damage was decided under the 2001 Scheme, which permitted separate awards to be made for its effects.[27] The CICA had made a payment for 'serious' impairment of social/intellectual functions (£44,000: level 20), but had done so erroneously, believing that Note 15 to the 2008 tariff applied, which would have excluded payment for these effects.[28] Had the claim indeed been decided under the 2008 Scheme, which made substantial changes to the tariff levels for brain damage, a possible descriptor was 'moderately severe brain damage' (£110,000: level 23 of the 2008 tariff (level A18 in 2012)); but by Note [3] there will in such a case be no separate award for any mental injury under the 2012 Scheme. This case also illustrates the binary effect of the tariff's categorical structure.

5.56 To summarize, the limitation in Note 5 to the 2008 Scheme was removed in 2012, 'so as to apply the multiple injury formula in cases where both the physical and mental injury are sufficiently serious to be listed in the tariff'.[29] Awards for both injuries are payable under that scheme, subject to the multiple injury formula in paragraph 37, and in the case of multiple injuries causing both brain damage and mental injury, to Note [3] to the 2012 tariff.

5.57 **(d) Multiple sexual and physical injuries** The category of sexual offences against victims of any age specify tariff levels for 'serious internal bodily injuries' arising from sexual assault and for non-consensual penile penetration of one or more of vagina, anus, or mouth (£22,000: B12), and where these injuries are accompanied by permanent disabling mental illness (£33,000: B14). Similar provision is made for the category of children under 18 and adults unable to consent, with the addition of a descriptor where these injuries are the result of sexual assault comprising one or more of non-penile penetrative or oral genital act(s) (B12).

---

27 See further *Colefax v First Tier Tribunal (SEC)* [2014] EWCA Civ 945, [2015] 1 WLR 35 (CA), where the Court of Appeal confirmed that an applicant should make a single application in respect of all his qualifying personal injuries, rather than separate applications in relation to each; (ch 6.33).

28 ibid [18].

29 Ministry of Justice (2012a) para 225.

But separate awards subject to paragraph 37 may be made where the physical injury the applicant sustains is external in nature, for example, as she tries to fight off her attacker. Suppose the applicant is raped by two or more attackers, and in trying to protect herself she sustained 'a permanently and seriously impaired grip in one hand' (£6,200: A7) and 'continuing significant disability' in both wrists (£11,000: A8). She would receive the full award of £13,500 (B10 non-consensual penile penetration of one or more of vagina, anus, or mouth), £3,300 (30% x £11,000) for the injury to her wrists, and £930 (15% x £6,200) for the hand injury, totalling £17,730. **5.58**

These three injuries may be distinguished from a case in which the rape constitutes 'a single incident in a pattern of abuse' (5.23–5.29). A 'pattern of repetitive frequent severe abuse (whether by one or more attackers) over a period of 3 years or more' is set at £8,200 (B8), but if the rape had occurred as part of the pattern of abuse, Note [6] to the 2012 tariff means that the applicant would instead receive the higher tariff payment at £13,500. However, this does not mean that an award is precluded where the applicant sustains other injuries that do not form part of the pattern of abuse, nor constitute a single incident within it, such as the injuries to the applicant's hand and wrists. In *LM v FTT* the Upper Tribunal commented: '[t]he mere fact that a person has suffered two injuries is not sufficient to bring paragraph 27 into play if the assaults are completely unrelated to each other'.[30] While the injuries in the hypothetical case are related to each other in the sense that they occurred as part of the incident in which the applicant sustained a criminal injury (rape), they are otherwise not indicative of a pattern of abuse. The payments indicated above would therefore be applicable. **5.59**

(e) **Multiple sexual and mental injuries** As in the case with physical injuries that fall within Part A of the tariff, injuries arising from the sexual abuse of children or adults falling within Part B may also cause mental injury. Note 5 of the earlier tariff schemes provided that 'when a person is a victim of a sexual offence and also suffers a mental injury, the applicant will be entitled only to whichever is the higher of the two tariff amounts'. The justification for this limitation is, as the 2012 Guide puts it, 'because the tariff for a sexual assault [under Part B] takes account of the mental trauma'. The implications of this element of Note 5 were illustrated in *CICA v ML.* In addition to the awards for the applicant's mental illness, the FTT made a 30 per cent tariff award amounting to £1,320, for 'two or more isolated incidents of non-penile penetrative acts' committed by one of her assailants (£4,400: B5), and a further 30 per cent tariff award, amounting to £450, for 'non penetrative frequent assaults over clothing', in respect of assaults committed by the other. Even one award for the mental illness would attract £19,000, far in excess of the awards for the sexual injuries, meaning that, in the **5.60**

[30] *LM v FTT* (n 10) [43] (Judge Rowland).

absence of Note 5, there would be an appropriate application of the multiple injury formula. But, as the Upper Tribunal confirmed, these decisions directly contradicted Note 5.[31]

5.61 Paragraph 34 of the 2012 Scheme maintains the effect of Note 5 of the earlier schemes: 'Where a person has sustained a mental injury as a result of a sexual assault, they will be entitled to an injury payment for whichever of the sexual assault or the mental injury would give rise to the highest payment under the tariff'. For example, a child of 10 who is a victim of a sexual assault comprising 'a pattern of repetitive, frequent incidents, one or more of non-penile penetrative or oral genital act(s) over a period up to 3 years' (£6,600: B7), which also causes a disabling mental injury 'lasting 2 years or more up to 5 years' (£6,700: A7), will receive the award for the mental injury. But if the pattern of abuse were over a period of three years (£8,200: B8), the child would receive that award, but none for the mental injury.

5.62 In short, there will be no payment for a mental injury if its tariff level is less than that for the sexual assault. But if a sexual assault results in pregnancy or the applicant is infected by a sexually transmitted infection, an additional award may be made that is not subject to paragraph 37.

III Paragraphs 42–49: Loss of Earnings Payments

A Introduction

5.63 The common law scheme entitled an eligible applicant to compensation for past and future loss of earnings from the date of the criminal injury, and for as long as the evidence showed a relevant connection between the injury and those losses. The period of loss was significantly reduced in the 1996 statutory scheme by the exclusion of the first twenty-eight weeks of the applicant's incapacity for work. This period was chosen because it coincided with the entitlement to statutory sick pay (SSP), and it remained the threshold for eligibility for these payments under the 2001 and 2008 Schemes.[32]

5.64 The calculation of past loss was based on a comparison of the claimant's earnings or other income before and after the injury (paragraph 31(1)). In the case of future loss, the function of paragraphs 31(2) and 32 was to determine how much the applicant would lose every year as a result of the injury from the date of assessment (the multiplicand), and for how long that loss would last (the multiplier), the exercise being intended to produce a net annual rate of loss, much like the

[31] *CICA v ML* (n 8) [13].

[32] Courts and Tribunals Judiciary, *Criminal Injuries Compensation Tribunal—Rules and Legislation*, Practice Guidance CI-1.

position at common law.[33] Reflecting common law practice, compensation was paid as a lump sum, whose purpose was to ensure that the applicant was neither over- nor under-compensated.[34]

No criminal injury compensation scheme provides full compensation for loss of earnings or earning capacity, chiefly because it has been held to be politically indefensible as a matter of principle for public money to support high earners.[35] Both the common law and the previous tariff schemes provided for awards for these losses to be made on the basis of the victim's income, but capped at 1.5 times the median gross weekly earnings at the time of assessment (paragraph 34 of the 2008 Scheme); that is, earnings before deductions for income tax and National Insurance Contributions (NIC).[36] Amounting at the time of the 2012 consultation to a net annual salary of around £39,000, the limit gave some effect to this principle, but since 'as a rule of thumb, an applicant's gross income will have to be more than £54,900 per annum before the cap will be relevant',[37] it could hardly be said to vindicate its emphatic assertion that 'it has never been the Government's intention that the Scheme should pay *actual* lost earnings'.[38] At the time of writing, average regular weekly pay (excluding bonuses) for employees in Great Britain was £509 per week or £26,468 a year before tax and other deductions. **5.65**

Similar criticisms were made of the 2012 restructuring as had been made in 1996.[39] Victims who were likely to experience financial hardship included the low paid, and workers on short-term contracts, or who were not making NICs, employees with no contractual right to sick pay, or having occupational sick pay arrangements but whose years of service were incomplete, the self-employed, and employees of small businesses. At the time of writing, it would exclude applicants on zero hours contracts, some of those working in the 'gig' economy,[40] and employees earning less than £113 a week. As was the case in 1996, the government resisted its critics' efforts to make it both more flexible and more generous.[41] **5.66**

---

33 See James Edelman, James Varuhas, and Simon Colton, *McGregor on Damages* (20th edn, Sweet & Maxwell 2017) ch 39.

34 In *LHS, JBO and SJB v First-tier Tribunal (CIC) and Criminal Injuries Compensation Authority payment* [2017] EWCA Civ 2138, 2017 WL 06502241 [24] (CA) (Sales LJ), the Court of Appeal held that, in calculating the lump sum payable under the common law Scheme, the appropriate discount was to be based on the discount rate (2.5%) made under the Damages Act 1996 s 1(1).

35 Home Office (1961) para 49.

36 *R v Criminal Injuries Compensation Board, ex parte Richardson* [1974] Crim LR 99 (DC).

37 Courts and Tribunals Judiciary, *Criminal Injuries Compensation Tribunal—Rules and Legislation, Practice Guidance CI-4*. The 2011 Annual Survey of Hours and Earnings gave £501 as the median weekly pay for full-time employees.

38 Ministry of Justice (2012a) para 230 (original emphasis).

39 Hansard HL vol 566 cols 678–79 (17 October 1995).

40 Department for Business, Energy & Industrial Strategy (2018), *Gig Economy Research*.

41 Ministry of Justice (2012b) para 195.

5.67 Introduced alongside the 2012 Scheme, the CICA's Hardship Fund is a discretionary £500,000 fund that 'provides temporary relief from financial hardship to very low paid workers who are temporarily unable to work because they have been a victim of a violent crime'. It only applies to injuries sustained in England and Wales and where the victim earns less than £111 per week, has not received SSP or an equivalent sick pay scheme run by the employer, could not work for at least seven consecutive days as a result of the crime, and had no unspent convictions that resulted in a custodial sentence or community order (Chapter 4.60).

B Loss of earnings payments under the 2012 Scheme

5.68 By paragraph 42, 'an applicant who is eligible for an injury payment will be eligible for a loss of earnings payment if the conditions in paragraph 43 are met'. The calculation of the claimant's loss of earnings payments in the 2012 Scheme is fundamentally different to its predecessors. There is no reference to his actual or potential losses, which will be limited in all cases to 'the weekly rate, at the date of determination, of statutory sick pay under s 157 of the Social Security Contributions and Benefits Act 1992' (SSCBA 1992) (paragraphs 47(a) and 48(a)), currently £89.35 a week.[42] The government's purpose in choosing SSP was both to cut expenditure and to make the scheme 'administratively simple both for applicants and claims officers'.[43] Calculation of the actual annual loss figure is indeed much simpler, most notably by virtue of the elimination of the need to take account of work-related pensions, insurance payments, or social security benefits relating to the applicant's unemployment or capacity for work.

5.69 The corresponding provisions of the 2008 and earlier tariff schemes therefore no longer apply. However, the claimant should be as clear as possible about his potential eligibility for a loss of earnings payment. The Upper Tribunal's admonition that the FTT should, in a case decided under the superseded arrangements, have itself raised the matter, although it had not been the subject of the appeal, remains live, in particular where the claimant is unrepresented.[44]

5.70 By paragraph 44, 'the period to which a loss of earnings payment will relate begins on the first day of the 29th week in which the applicant satisfies the condition in paragraph 43(1)'. This 'first day' may, as was the case, fall at some time after the effects of the injury on the applicant's capacity for work become apparent, but it will not be triggered until the more stringent eligibility conditions are met. By

[42] Social Security Benefits Up-rating Order 2017 (SI 2017/260) art 9.

[43] Ministry of Justice (2012a) paras 235–38; (2012b) para 194.

[44] *R (SH) v First-tier Tribunal (CIC)* [2010] UKUT 186 (AAC) [11]–[12]; *LM v FTT* (n 10) [26]–[27] and [36]–[37].

paragraph 46, where they are met, 'a loss of earnings payment may relate to earnings lost before an application is determined (past loss of earnings) and such loss after the determination (future loss of earnings)'. Threshold eligibility for a loss of earnings payment is that the applicant must be eligible for an 'injury payment' (paragraph 42), which by definition excludes all those who would have fallen within tariff bands 1–5 under the earlier schemes to which the same threshold applied. At this point, the conditions governing eligibility for these payments radically diverge.

Applicants must meet the two conditions in paragraph 43. The first significantly raises the bar in respect of the impact of the injury: that as a direct result the applicant must have 'no or very limited capacity for paid work' (paragraph 43(1)). There is no definition in the scheme of what constitutes this condition, but the 2012 Guide indicates **5.71**

> Your criminal injury must be serious enough to have resulted in a total inability to undertake paid work, or a very limited capacity to do so. By very limited capacity we mean that the extent of your injuries means that you are not capable of undertaking more than a few hours of paid work per week.

Decisions about what constitutes 'very limited capacity for paid work' will depend on such factors as the nature of the injury, the number of hours that the applicant is capable of working, the salary that a person with residual earning capacity might earn, and the medical evidence.[45]

Unlike the position under paragraph 30 of the earlier schemes, where an applicant who lost earnings or earning capacity after the twenty-ninth week would have been eligible for an award, none will be payable under the 2012 Scheme if the applicant's capacity for work is no more serious than 'limited'. The 2012 Guide continues: 'If you have capacity for paid work, but the type of work is restricted because of your injuries, you will not qualify for a loss of earnings payment'. It remains to be seen how the CICA will interpret the scope of the phrase 'the type of work' to which the applicant is restricted; for example, a teacher whose injuries mean he can no longer attend his school but can conduct private tutoring from home might not qualify for this payment. But he might if all he could do was to perform a physically menial task requiring little mental application. **5.72**

Secondly, the applicant must be able to 'show a work history at the time of the incident'.[46] As was the case under the earlier schemes, the applicant will need to provide documentary evidence of her work history. Blameless victims are deserving of compensation for loss of earnings only where they were in paid work at the date of the incident, and had contributed to civil society through **5.73**

[45] Compare Department for Work and Pensions, *Capability for work questionnaire.*
[46] Ministry of Justice (2012a) para 234.

their prior employment. This condition provides (paragraph 43(2)) that the applicant:

> (a) was in paid work on the date of the incident giving rise to the injury, or, in the case of a series of incidents, at any time during the series; (b) had been in regular paid work for a period of at least three years immediately before the date of the incident giving rise to the injury; or (c) had a good reason for not having been in regular paid work for the period mentioned in paragraph (b).

There is no guidance on the scope of 'regular' in paragraph 43(2)(b) but, in respect of paragraph 43(2)(c), by paragraph 43(3) 'a person will be considered to have a good reason for not having been in regular paid work if, for example, they were unable to work because they were in full-time education, or by reason of their age or caring responsibilities'.

5.74 By paragraph 47, payment for past loss of earnings is calculated by multiplying the weekly rate of SSP at the date on which the claim is determined by the number of weeks, treating part weeks as full weeks, during the period beginning on the first day of the twenty-ninth week in which the applicant satisfies the condition in paragraph 43(1), and ending on the day the application is determined. It may be that before that day the applicant had ceased to satisfy paragraph 43(1), in which case the payment would end on that day.

5.75 By paragraph 48, a payment for future loss of earnings is calculated by multiplying the weekly rate of SSP at the date on which the claim is determined by the number of weeks, treating part weeks as full weeks, during the period beginning on the day after the day on which the application is determined. This period ends on whichever is the earliest of the day on which the applicant no longer satisfies the condition in paragraph 43(1), reaches state pension age, or, where the criminal injury has resulted in a life expectancy below the state pension age, the expected end of the applicant's life. Being restricted to payment based on a benefit currently generating around £4,650 for each year of loss, all that is required is a multiplication of the weekly rate by the applicable period of loss (the multiplicand), to which the 2012 Scheme applies the multipliers and discount factors in Annex F. These differ from Tables A–C of the earlier schemes, being instead based on the Ogden Tables.[47]

IV Paragraphs 50–56: Special Expenses Payments

A Introduction

5.76 Although the numbers affected by the changes to loss of earnings payments—some 1,100 applicants a year—will be considerably fewer than those affected by

[47] Government Actuary's Department, *Ogden tables: actuarial compensation tables for injury and death*.

the changes to the tariff, they will bear particularly heavily upon the two-thirds of severely injured victims who are disabled by their injuries. In its effort to balance savings with its ambition that these victims should 'be able to rely on CICS for the long-term, which means giving it financial stability by focusing resources on the most compelling cases',[48] the government retained, with some amendment, the scheme's provisions for special expenses.

By paragraph 50, an 'applicant who is eligible for an injury payment will be eligible for a special expenses payment if, as a direct result of an injury for which they are eligible for an injury payment, they have lost earnings or earning capacity, or been incapacitated to a similar extent, for more than 28 weeks', where that incapacity is in relation to an expense of the type listed in paragraph 52. Unlike the provisions governing loss of earnings, once the twenty-eight-week threshold has been met, an award for special expenses is payable from the date of the actual injury, as was the case under the earlier schemes. There is no definition of 'incapacitated' in the 2012 Scheme, which in the 1996 Scheme 'included injuries that prevented the applicant from working, attending school or, if retired, from following his normal lifestyle to a significant extent'.[49] **5.77**

B Paragraph 51: special expenses: prior conditions

Paragraph 51 specifies three prior conditions that all special expenses payments must meet. They will 'only be made in relation to expenses of the types listed in paragraph 52' where they are necessary, not free of charge from another source, and reasonable. This represents both a clarification and a tightening of the conditions under which these payments may be made. **5.78**

1 A necessary expense

To be compensable the special expenses must, first, be 'necessarily incurred by the applicant on or after the date of the injury as a direct result of the criminal injury giving rise to the injury payment'. In the earlier schemes, the test of necessity expressly applied only in the case of 'care' in paragraph 35(d)(iii), and to 'supervision' in the 2008 revision, but by paragraph 51(a) they must all now explicitly meet this condition. Whether they are necessary depends on the medical and other evidence as to the costs associated with such of the applicant's present and future needs as are permitted by paragraph 52. In reaching that decision the FTT must, as the Upper Tribunal held in *HD v FTT,* adequately explain the conclusions it reached on that evidence, in particular where it concludes that the care sought to be paid for was unnecessary in its amount.[50] **5.79**

---

[48] Ministry of Justice (2012a) Foreword p 3.
[49] CICA (1996 Guide) para 11.
[50] *HD v FTT* (n 24) [32].

2 An expense not free of charge from another source

5.80 A special expenses payment will only be made in relation to expenses 'for which provision, or similar provision, is not available free of charge from another source' (paragraph 51(b)). This was a condition specified in the earlier schemes only in the particular case of 'care', and in the 2008 Scheme, of 'supervision' of the applicant, and only in respect of costs 'not provided or available free of charge from the National Health Service, local authorities or any other agency'. The 2012 Scheme retains this condition in paragraph 52(b), but by paragraph 51(b) the principle applies to all special expenses.

3 A reasonable expense

5.81 Lastly, all expenses must be 'reasonable' (paragraph 51(c)). Here, again, the earlier schemes only specified this condition in respect of those costs falling under paragraph 35(d) (special equipment, home adaptation, and care), but it was clear from the CICA's approach that other costs (for example for private medical treatment) were also required to be reasonable. Under the 2012 Scheme, this condition is of general application.

C The types of special expenses

5.82 A number of the expenses listed under paragraph 52 closely resemble those for which damages may be paid at common law. Claims officers may refer to equivalent personal injury awards, but it is important to stress that they 'are not automatically or directly transferable' to claims under the scheme, upon which they may take a stricter view, for example, of what is 'necessarily incurred' under a care regime.[51] A claimant's choice of privately run rather than local authority funded residential care may not be unreasonable in a civil claim, but it would surely fail under the scheme. In short, these expenses must always be both necessary and reasonable: it is the taxpayer, not an insurance company, that is footing the bill.

1 Paragraph 52(a): property or equipment on which the applicant relies

5.83 Paragraph 52(a) provides that a payment may be made in respect of 'the applicant's property or equipment which was relied on by the applicant as a physical aid and which was lost of or damaged as a result of the incident giving rise to the injury'. The earlier schemes all made similar provision (paragraph 35(1)(a)); it was the sole exception to the general exclusion of compensation for loss of or damage to property. This expense will cover smaller items such as spectacles, dentures, hearing aids and walking sticks; as well as, in more serious cases, more substantial aids such as wheelchairs and orthopaedic beds.

[51] *R (DB) v Criminal Injuries Compensation Appeals Panel* [2002] EWHC 698 (Admin), 2002 WL 31050280 (QB) (*DB v CICAP*).

The applicant will be required to produce receipts for these items, although that may be impossible where they were purchased some years earlier. In these cases, an estimate of their replacement from a reputable source may be sufficient. Paragraph 52(a) might also cover a house alarm or a mobile phone for a disabled applicant, but compensation has not been payable for items such as jewellery, watches (other than talking watches), or rings that were lost or damaged at the time of or after the incident, or in the course of medical or other treatment. Neither is lost or damaged clothing a compensable item. **5.84**

2 Paragraph 52(b): medical expenses

By paragraph 52(b), a special expenses payment may be made in respect of **5.85**

> costs (other than in respect of loss of earnings) arising from treatment for the injury under the National Health Service or a state health service other than the National Health Service where those costs would also have arisen if the applicant were being treated under the National Health Service in England and Wales.[52]

This continues the position under the earlier schemes covering such expenses as NHS prescriptions, dentists' and opticians' charges, travel to and from, and car parking at, a hospital (paragraph 35(1)(b)). These costs will be met only if the applicant paid for them, for which the CICA will need proof.

A significant change is the omission from the 2012 Scheme of the provision in paragraph 35(1)(c) of the earlier schemes that permitted an award to be made for 'the cost of private health treatment for the injury, but only where a claims officer considers that, in all the circumstances, both the private treatment and its cost are reasonable'. Private treatment, for example plastic surgery to correct facial scarring, or other cosmetic or dental work, might be compensable where it was not routinely available on the NHS in the applicant's area, but the burden was on the applicant to show that this was a reasonable option. These payments will no longer be made. Respondents to the government's consultation commented that private medical care should be retained in these cases, and for therapies such as counselling, psychological therapy, and physiotherapy, but the government was unmoved. The presumption in favour of the NHS continues to be emphatic: 'If applicants wish to purchase health care beyond that which the NHS provides they can use some of their tariff award for this purpose'.[53] **5.86**

3 Paragraphs 52(c) and 53: special equipment

By paragraph 52(c), a special expenses payment may be made in respect of 'special equipment', as was the case in all of the earlier schemes (paragraph 35(d)(i)). The 2012 Guide lists physical aids, which include specially adapted vehicles, wheelchairs and walking aids, and kitchen implements to help people whose grip has weakened. **5.87**

[52] That is, the costs associated with the devolved health services in Wales.
[53] Ministry of Justice (2012a) para 241.

Where the applicant has bought them, she must provide receipts or an estimate. But, underlining the conditions in paragraph 51, the CICA will consider an award for these costs only where the equipment is necessary (rather than desirable), and that something similar is not available free of charge from another source.

5.88 The schemes have always provided for the cost of replacements of special equipment to be included in the award. By paragraph 53 of the 2012 Scheme, which reproduces the substance of paragraph 36(2) of the earlier schemes,

> where the need for special equipment [within paragraph 52(c)] is likely to continue, a claims officer will: (a) assess the cost of replacement, taking into account the number of likely replacements; (b) deduct the amount for which the applicant's existing equipment could be sold on each occasion; and (c) apply an appropriate discount factor in accordance with Table B of Annex F.

Where at some future date there has been so material a change in her medical condition that allowing the original determination to stand would give rise to an injustice, the applicant may, by paragraph 115(b), seek a further payment on a reopening of her application (Chapter 6.76–6.95).

4 Paragraph 52(d): adaptation of the applicant's accommodation

5.89 By paragraph 52(d), a special expenses payment may be made in respect of 'adaptation of the applicant's accommodation', as was the case in all of the earlier schemes (paragraph 35(d)(ii)). The 2012 Guide indicates that the CICA may pay for adaptations that include changes both inside and outside the claimant's home (such as a ramp or a stair lift), or other alterations to improve the applicant's ability to get around, which might include the installation of a hoist for use in a bathroom, or the widening of doorways to accommodate a wheelchair.

5 Paragraph 52(e): the cost of care in connection with the applicant's bodily functions or meal preparation

5.90 Past losses arising from the care of the applicant should be a relatively straightforward matter based on the applicant's payment records and receipts. The calculation of the future costs of care is more complex, in part because the claimant's future condition, and thus his need for long-term care, may be very uncertain. There have been some important changes in the schemes' provisions in these cases. The 1996 and 2001 Schemes provided by paragraph 35(d)(iii) for additional amounts of compensation for 'care, whether in a residential establishment or at home, which are not provided or available free of charge from the National Health Service, local authorities or any other agency, provided that a claims officer considers such expense to be necessary as a direct consequence of the injury'. Following the key decision in *Criminal Injuries Compensation Authority and First-tier Tribunal v IM*,[54] the words '(in connection with the applicant's bodily

[54] [2011] UKUT 70 [4] and [20] (*CICA v IM*).

functions or the preparation of meals) and supervision (to avoid substantial danger to the applicant or others)' were inserted after the word 'care' in the 2008 Scheme. These two conditions, which substantially restricted the scope of 'care' within the scheme, were in turn divided in the 2012 Scheme between paragraphs 52(e) and 52(f).

(a) **The scope of the word 'care'** In *CICA v IM,* the claimant sustained severe brain damage in a violent assault that substantially affected all aspects of his life. The issue was whether, as recommended by its social services department, he required care over and above that which it was agreed would be provided by the local authority; if he did, the total cost would far exceed £500,000. The FTT allowed the claimant's appeal from the CICA's decision that there was no case for future loss beyond what could be provided by the NHS and the local authority, or met by what it might reasonably pay under the terms of paragraph 35(d)(iii). **5.91**

Before the Upper Tribunal, the CICA accepted that, while the applicant would benefit from the regime that was set out, that was not the test to be applied under paragraph 35(d)(iii), which was far more restrictive. It had relied on the government's statements during the debates on the CICA 1995,[55] which, it argued, required recognition only of 'the core considerations of the tariff for the injury, loss of earnings, care and aftercare for an injury'. The tribunal accepted that it was necessary to identify the scope of the 'care' that the scheme would cover, and acknowledged that it is capable of a variety of narrower and wider meanings. The government's statements offered 'very little assistance'; but what was absolutely clear was that there was no warrant for some test based on 'core losses' or 'core compensation' over and above the express conditions in paragraph 35.[56] **5.92**

Following *CICA v IM,* paragraph 35(d)(iii) was, as noted, amended in the case of 'care' to costs 'in connection with the applicant's bodily functions or the preparation of meals'. This phraseology, which is in substance maintained in paragraph 52(e) of the 2012 Scheme, stems in part from what Judge Mesher noted as being similar to 'many of the conditions of entitlement' for different rates of the care component of disability living allowance (DLA) and attendance allowance (AA). A claimant may be so severely disabled physically or mentally that they require frequent attention throughout the day in connection with bodily functions, or help with such other tasks as cooking meals.[57] **5.93**

---

55 Hansard HL vol 566 cols 627–28 (16 October 1995).

56 *CICA v IM* (n 54) [25]. Judge Mesher's analysis of the scope of 'care' for the purposes of para 35(d)(iii) was applied in *CG v First-tier Tribunal and Criminal Injuries Compensation Authority* [2011] UKUT 225 [74]–[75].

57 *CICA v IM* (n 54) [34]; GOV.UK, *Carers and disability benefits.*

5.94 (b) **A 'necessary' expense** Paragraph 35(d)(iii) of the 2001 and 2008 Schemes provided that a special expenses award in respect of 'care' (and as the scope of that word had been narrowed in 2008) could be made 'at reasonable cost', if it was 'necessary as a direct consequence of the injury'. One of the central questions addressed in *CICA v IM* concerned the scope of that phrase. The Upper Tribunal rejected the CICA's suggestion that the test of necessity restricted any award to care directed only towards the injuries, excluding care directed towards enabling the applicant to lead a more independent life. Judge Mesher concluded: 'The 2001 Scheme cannot have been intended to include only the barest minimum for physical survival, but must have been intended to cover the care that is necessary to enable the injured person, as far as practicable in the particular circumstances, to live a reasonably normal life'.[58]

5.95 The scope of 'care' is now limited by the terms of paragraphs 53(e) and 52(f), which substantially reduce the impact of *CICA v IM* on the interpretation of these paragraphs. Where the costs of care are not otherwise provided, and have been met by or on behalf of the applicant, the 2012 Guide indicates that the CICA 'may pay the cost of care relating to your bodily functions (including toileting, bathing, and continence management), or to the preparation of meals (when you are physically unable to cook)'. Whether such associated costs as dressing, laundry, sleeping arrangements, housework, and shopping are recoverable is pre-eminently a question of fact for the tribunal: was the expense both 'necessarily incurred' (paragraph 51(a)) and 'reasonable' (paragraph 51(c)).

5.96 (c) **Whether in a residential establishment or at home'** The final question that arose in *CICA v IM* was whether the 'care' to be provided was literally to be restricted to these two venues. The Upper Tribunal held that it was not. A 'reasonably normal life includes not only the narrowly physical benefits of fresh air and exercise outside the home but the mental and emotional benefits of mixing with others, taking part in the life of the community and undertaking recreational and cultural activities'.[59] This phraseology in paragraph 35(d)(iii) of the 2008 Scheme is omitted from the 2012 Scheme. Whether these or similar elements of a care package are compensable will depend on their compliance with the conditions in paragraphs 51 and 52, but it is not obvious, for example, that access to leisure, social, and community activities would meet any of the conditions in paragraph 52.

6 Paragraph 52(f): supervision to avoid substantial danger to the applicant or another person

5.97 This special expense was added to paragraph 35(d)(iii) of the 2008 Scheme, and was severed from it in the 2012 Scheme. As in the case of the cost of care in

[58] *CICA v IM* (n 54) [28] and [32]–[33].

[59] ibid [27].

connection with the applicant's bodily functions or meal preparation, the need for the applicant to be supervised in order 'to avoid putting yourself or others in danger' derives from the conditions relating to the DLA.

Where it is not otherwise provided, paragraph 52(f) will cover the supervision of an applicant who cannot, for example, cross a road or travel on public transport safely, or is prone to violent physical (or possibly verbal) interactions with other people, but only where the danger presented in these cases is 'substantial'. This is a high bar, which is likely to exclude simply accompanying the applicant to a community or leisure centre, or otherwise supervising the applicant's everyday mobility. In its implied reference to paragraph 52(e), the 2012 Guide includes costs relating to the preparation of meals where 'it would be dangerous for [the claimant] to do so'. This, too, would have to be a 'substantial' danger under paragraph 52(f), but the Guide otherwise gives no indication of the kind of expense that the CICA will meet, but it must be both 'necessarily incurred' and 'reasonable'. **5.98**

7 Gratuitous care and supervision

Paragraph 52(b) of the 2012 Scheme effectively requires the applicant to rely upon the NHS or his local authority in respect of its statutory obligations, or those imposed on any other statutory agency. Beyond these services, expenses and losses incurred by a spouse or parent who gives up a job to nurse or care for the victim were recoverable under the common law scheme,[60] and the earlier tariff schemes. Their exact terms varied, but all three gave claims officers a wide discretion when applying paragraph 35 to make these calculations on such basis as they considered appropriate in all the circumstances, which could include any allowances that the friend or relative received or could receive, for example as a 'carer's allowance'.[61] **5.99**

Such an award presupposed that it was possible to identify the nature of the applicant's future care needs, and the level of care that the relative or friend could bring, when the relative or friend herself was older and possibly less able. This was the case in *DB v CICAP*, where CICAP awarded the cost of the mother's care of her disabled son only for seven years from the date of assessment, as it could not accurately determine whether, when, and for how long the cost of care would be incurred.[62] This is a determination that the Upper Tribunal held in *CICA v IM* must be based on sufficient findings of fact on which a proper basis for the predictions could be formed.[63] **5.100**

60 *Donnelly v Joyce* [1974] QB 454 (CA); *Roberts v Johnstone* [1989] QB 878 (CA); *Housecroft v Burnett* [1986] 1 All ER 332 (CA).
61 *Carers and disability benefits* (n 57).
62 *DB v CICAP* (n 51).
63 *CICA v IM* (n 54) [43].

5.101 The 2012 Scheme makes no specific provision for gratuitous care, which, by virtue of the restricted definition of 'care' and of 'supervision' in the 2008 and 2012 Schemes, is likely to impose more extensive burdens on a friend or relative than could have been met in the earlier schemes. The 2012 Guide indicates those expenses associated with the applicant's bodily functions that the CICA will meet, but given the absence of a provision equivalent to paragraph 35 of the earlier schemes, and that those listed in paragraph 52 are the only compensable special expenses, it is not obvious whether or how the costs of gratuitous care might be recoverable. In any event, they must be necessary and reasonable.

8 Paragraphs 52(g), (h), and (i): costs relating to the administration of the award

5.102 The 2012 Scheme continues to make provision for special expenses payable by way of fees payable to the Court of Protection or the Public Guardian, costs arising from the administration of the applicant's affairs owing to their lack of mental capacity, and the cost of setting up a trust following a claims officer's direction under paragraph 106. By paragraph 29, none of these payments is subject to reduction under the conditions concerning the applicant's or victim's conduct, convictions, or character, unless the whole award for which that person is otherwise eligible is withheld under those paragraphs.

V Paragraphs 57–84: Payments in Fatal Cases

A Introduction

5.103 In making provision for awards in respect of fatal injuries the 2012 Scheme continues to distinguish between claims in respect of victims who died as a direct result of the criminal injury, and those who died from unrelated causes. In both cases, the applicant's eligibility for an award depends upon him being a 'qualifying relative' of the deceased (Chapter 3.88–3.95). In the former case there was and is no survival under either the common law, or paragraph 37 of the earlier tariff schemes, of what would have been the deceased's eligibility akin to the cause of action that that survives under section 1 of the Law Reform (Miscellaneous Provisions) Act 1934 for the benefit of the estate, save for payments for funeral expenses.

5.104 The following sections analyse the provisions in the 2012 Scheme, noting any significant changes to the earlier schemes. Before doing so, it is convenient to deal briefly with the schemes' provision for funeral expenses, whose eligibility conditions differ from the main provisions. The reader may also be reminded that the CICA may also reduce or withhold a payment if the deceased's or the applicant's unspent convictions, conduct, or character make it inappropriate that a full or any award should be made (Chapter 4.89–4.94).

B Funeral payments under all schemes

Paragraph 37 of the earlier tariff schemes provided that the reasonable costs of a funeral would be paid even where the person bearing those costs was otherwise ineligible to claim; that is, where she was not a 'qualifying claimant'. Neither did the possibility of refusal apply to an applicant who, if she was making a claim for her own criminal injury, would be met by the conditions relating to her unspent convictions, etc.[64] This payment could also be made notwithstanding that the expense was less than the minimum financial limit. **5.105**

In the 2012 Scheme, 'funeral payments' are governed by paragraphs 75–77. By paragraph 75, 'where a person has died as a direct result of sustaining a criminal injury in circumstances falling within para 4 or 5 of the Scheme a funeral payment may be made in respect of their funeral expenses for the benefit of their estate'. This continues the exception in favour of the deceased's estate, and also that eligibility for an award does not depend on the person incurring the expense being a 'qualifying relative'. By paragraph 76, the amount of a funeral payment is £2,500, and by paragraph 77 a payment up to a further £2,500 may be made in respect of funeral expenses reasonably incurred; both are 'protected' payments. In addition to the cost of the funeral itself, the 2012 Guide lists payable expenses as including a tombstone, flowers, newspaper announcements, funeral breakfasts/non-alcoholic refreshments, memorials, and transporting the deceased back to his country of origin. **5.106**

The 2012 Scheme continues to apply the eligibility provisions where the deceased's conduct and character was, as the 2012 Guide makes clear in respect of paragraph 28, 'so serious that to pay for their funeral, or to make other payments, would be an inappropriate use of public funds'. In pursuit of its policy of tightening the scheme's eligibility conditions in favour of innocent victims, a claim made by the person who paid for the funeral may now fail in whole or part because of the application to him or her of paragraphs 22 to 27.[65] **5.107**

C Death as a direct result of sustaining a criminal injury

The 2012 Scheme provides that a 'qualifying relative' of a person who has died as a direct result of sustaining an injury in circumstances falling within paragraphs 4 or 5 may, depending on her relationship with the deceased, be eligible for one or more of three payment types. These closely resemble the categories specified in paragraphs 38–42 of the earlier tariff schemes in the case of 'qualifying claimants'. They are: **5.108**

---

64 CICA (1998 Guide) Appendix 3 para 6.
65 Ministry of Justice (2012a) para 254.

- a 'bereavement payment' (a 'standard amount of compensation' under paragraph 39 of the earlier schemes, the equivalent of damages in respect of bereavement under section 1A of the FAA 1976)
- a 'child's payment' (an 'additional' amount for the loss of parental services under paragraph 42 of the earlier schemes)
- a 'dependency payment' where the claimant was at the time of death financially or physically dependent on the deceased (an 'additional' amount to reflect loss of financial or physical dependency under paragraph 40 of the earlier schemes). Under the earlier schemes, claims for dependency were largely treated in the same way as the assessment of loss of earnings where the victim survived the criminal injury. This was fundamentally changed in the 2012 Scheme, which sets dependency payments in fatal cases in line with the government's proposals for loss of earnings; that is, based on SSP.

1 Paragraphs 61–63: bereavement payments

5.109 By paragraph 61, a bereavement payment may be made to anyone who is a qualifying relative of the deceased within paragraph 59 of the 2012 Scheme, with the exception of a former spouse or former civil partner, or a person who is estranged from the deceased at the time of the death (Chapter 3.93). The payment is £11,000 where there is only one qualifying relative, and £5,500 each where there is more than one (paragraph 62), and they are 'protected' payments. The categories of 'qualifying relatives' are more numerous than those dependants who may benefit from the conventional award of £12,980 under section 1A(2) of the FAA 1976, which is to be divided between the deceased's parents where they are both eligible.

2 Paragraphs 64–66: child's payments

5.110 By paragraph 64, 'A child's payment may be made to a person who is a qualifying relative under paragraph 59(f) if that person was at the time of the death of the deceased under 18 years old and dependent on the deceased for parental services'. This payment does not require the child claimant to show either financial or physical dependence on the deceased parent; nor does it depend on the making of a bereavement payment.

5.111 The child's payment replaces, but to the same effect, the award for 'the loss of parental services' in paragraph 42 of the earlier schemes, itself based in part on the award for loss of society under the Damages (Scotland) Act 1976. The scheme differs from Scots law in that paragraph 42, and paragraph 65 of the 2012 Scheme, comprise elements both of conventional and assessed compensation.

5.112 The purpose of the conventional sum, set by paragraph 65(a) of the 2012 Scheme at £2,000 for each year (pro rata for each part year) of the period to which the payment relates is, in the words of the 2012 Guide, 'to provide some small recognition of what a child loses as the result of the death of a parent, such as: love and affection; care and supervision; being taken to and from clubs and activities; and treats'. Being a conventional sum it is unnecessary to gauge whether the parent's services were of good or poor quality, as in the FAA 1976 dependency cases.[66] But neither does it, nor can it, reflect the particular nature of the child's relationship with or routine personal dependence on the parent; in these respects, the multiplicand is fixed, but the multiplier will reflect the child's age at the date of the parent's death. However, the loss of the child's personal dependence on the parent might give him or her a claim under paragraph 65(b), or where it constitutes 'physical dependence' under paragraph 67.

Paragraph 65(b) provides for assessed compensation: 'such additional amount in relation to any expenses suffered by the child as a direct result of the loss of parental services as a claims officer considers reasonable', which broadly reflects paragraph 42(b) of the earlier schemes: 'such other payments as a claims officer considers reasonable to meet other resultant losses'. This 'additional amount' might be apt to cover reasonable expenses that the child incurs because she is now looked after by someone else,[67] or requires a higher level of care as a consequence the parent's homicide. The CICA will, normally, initially retain the full value of any payment, but by paragraph 106 can make annual advances to the person with parental responsibility for the child, or for the child's advancement, education, or long-term benefit (Chapter 6.63–6.64). These payments should be distinguished from an award to a child who, having witnessed that homicide, qualifies as a secondary victim under paragraph 6 of the 2012 Scheme. **5.113**

By paragraph 64 of the 2012 Scheme 'the period to which a child's payment will relate begins on the day of the death and ends on the day before the child's 18th birthday', and is payable to any of the deceased's children. A child's payment is made as a lump sum, the multiplicand being the conventional sum (£2,000) plus any additional amount in relation to any expenses, applying the relevant Tables in Annex F (multiplier and life expectancy tables), to such part of the payment as relates to losses arising after the day on which the application is determined' (paragraph 66). **5.114**

3 Dependency payments

By paragraph 67 of the 2012 Scheme, a dependency payment 'may be made to a qualifying relative who at the time of the deceased's death was financially or physically dependent on the deceased. A qualifying relative was physically dependent on the deceased if the deceased was their main carer'. The 2012 Guide provides that 'physical dependency' includes getting help with 'personal hygiene (toileting/bathing); continence management; food preparation and eating; medication and simple treatments; or keeping you safe from harm'. **5.115**

66 *Spittle v Bunney* [1988] 1 WLR 847 (CA); *Stanley v Siddique* [1992] 2 QB 1 (CA).
67 *R v Criminal Injuries Compensation Board, ex parte McGuffe and Smith* [1978] Crim LR 160.

5.116 As was the case under the earlier schemes, there can be no payment if the deceased's main source of income was from social security benefits (paragraph 70). Nor will financial dependency be established where the deceased's income derived from a life of crime.[68] The 2012 Scheme also retains the provision that 'when calculating the amount of a dependency payment, no account will be taken of a qualifying relative's remarriage or new civil partnership, or their prospects of remarrying or entering into another civil partnership' (paragraph 69(2)). Under the superseded schemes, the claims officer could take account of the quality and continuity of the services that the deceased provided for any children, or the possibility that he might have left the marriage, as these factors would affect the level of the dependency.[69] But in respect both of the calculation of the dependency and of the level of the payment, the 2012 Scheme significantly reduces the scope of its predecessors.

5.117 First, the qualifying claimant's financial dependency is not based on her loss as it was previously calculated, but, by paragraph 70, on the deceased's compliance during his lifetime with the conditions in paragraph 43(2); that is, that he had been in regular paid work for a period of at least three years immediately before the date of the incident. Secondly, a dependency payment is based on SSP, 'calculated by reference to each week in which one or more qualifying relatives is eligible', and that weekly amount will be divided in equal shares between each qualifying relative who is eligible in any week (paragraph 71). The total amount of a payment for financial dependency will be the aggregate of the amounts allocated to the qualifying relative under paragraph 71 for the whole period of the dependency (paragraph 72), and will 'be made in a lump sum, applying the relevant Tables in Annex F to such part of the period to which the payment relates as occurs after the day on which the application is determined' (paragraph 73).

5.118 The period to which the payment relates begins on the day of the death (paragraph 68), and ends on whichever is the earliest of (paragraph 69):

> (a) in the case of a qualifying relative who is a child under the age of 18, the day before their 18th birthday; (b) the day upon which the deceased would have reached state pension age; (c) the date on which, before the incident giving rise to their criminal injury, the deceased's life would have been expected to end in accordance with Table C of Annex F or other available medical evidence; (d) the expected end of the qualifying relative's life; or (e) the 50th anniversary of the day referred to in paragraph 68'.

These limits are important: apart from the fifty-year cut-off, there is, for example, no financial dependency payment once a child turns 18, although if the child was physically dependent on the deceased a payment in respect of physical dependency may be made.

[68] *Burns v Edman* [1970] 2 QB 541 (CA).
[69] *Stanley v Siddique* (n 67).

Consistent with its revisions in respect of special expenses, the 2012 scheme provides that a payment in respect of physical dependency 'will be calculated as if it were a special expenses payment to the dependant for the cost of that dependant's care and supervision under paragraph 52(e) and (f)' (paragraph 74). This therefore brings to these payments the same restrictions as apply where the victim survives the injury (5.80–5.98). Paragraph 74 also extends to physical dependency payments the scheme's provisions concerning the replacement of special equipment (paragraph 53). **5.119**

There may be cases in which the deceased had survived for some time before dying as a result of the criminal injury, during which time he had successfully applied in his own right. This did not preclude the dependants from making a claim under paragraphs 37–42 of the earlier schemes, but by paragraph 43 those claims were subject to the conditions set out in paragraphs 56–57 for the reopening of cases (Chapter 6.76). Apart from any award in respect of funeral expenses or bereavement, any compensation for dependency payable to a qualifying claimant would be reduced by the amount paid to the victim. The 2012 Scheme makes similar provision to offset that award against the dependency payment as it does against a child's payment (paragraphs 78–79). By implication, there is no reduction from a tariff award or a funeral payment. **5.120**

D Death as a result of an unrelated cause

It is also possible that the deceased may have survived for some time before dying as a result of an unrelated cause. In these cases, paragraph 38(1)(b) of the 2008 Scheme provided that where death had occurred before title to the award had been vested in the victim, 'supplementary compensation' could be payable to a qualifying claimant (paragraph 44), provided that the deceased had himself been eligible for 'additional compensation'. This did not include any 'standard amount' or other compensation, and 'dependency' meant only financial dependency. **5.121**

The 2012 Scheme makes similar provision for 'payments resulting from a criminal injury where the victim dies of an unrelated cause before an award is made to them' (paragraph 58). The conditions under which a payment may be made are set out in paragraphs 80–84. A qualifying relative's eligibility for an award is limited to financial dependency, thus excluding, as under the earlier tariff schemes, a bereavement payment or a child's payment. A payment may be made to a qualifying relative of a person who has sustained a criminal injury and who has died otherwise than as a direct result of that injury 'if on the date the deceased died: (a) the deceased was eligible for, but had not received, a final award under this Scheme; and (b) the qualifying relative was financially dependent on the deceased.' If the deceased had received a final award, paragraph 83 provides that that any payment made under paragraph 80 will be reduced by the amount of that award. **5.122**

5.123 The qualifying relative's application must be made (a) within two years after the date of the deceased's death, or (b) if later, with supporting evidence which means that the application can be determined without further extensive enquiries by a claims officer (paragraph 81). The phraseology in paragraph 81(b) is used in the scheme's provisions for the extension of time limits for applications (Chapter 6.19–6.25). Payment may be made for the deceased's loss of earnings, and for any special expenses they incurred, in each case arising as a direct result of the criminal injury and to the date of death. A payment for loss of earnings is calculated in accordance with paragraphs 42–47, and for special expenses, in accordance with paragraphs 50 to 52 and 54 to 56 (paragraph 82). The total of any awards paid to the deceased and their qualifying relatives shall not exceed £500,000 (paragraph 84).

VI Deductions and Other Payments

A Introduction

5.124 A distinguishing feature of the common law scheme was that almost all collateral benefits were to be deducted from any compensation that was payable, that is, including any award for pain and suffering. So far as the scheme sought to substitute for the offender, it was thought right that where he could be pursued to judgment, the taxpayer's burden should be correspondingly reduced. Deduction of social security benefits was 'based on the sound principle that there should be no duplication of payments from public funds'.[70] The deduction of any benefits payable by an employer by way of insurance, gratuity or pension was justified on the basis that state compensation should not provide an income that was in effect higher than the victim, or those financially dependent on them, enjoyed before the injury.

5.125 This reasoning also underpinned the statutory scheme, but the separate provision of tariff payments restricted any deduction to the equivalent head of pecuniary loss. By paragraph 45, an award would be reduced to take account of any social security benefits or insurance payments made by way of compensation for the same contingency,[71] 'irrespective of the period in respect of which the benefit had been or would be paid, and whether or not any actual loss occurred or would occur in that period'.[72] The benefits that fell to be deducted

[70] Home Office (1986) para 19.1.

[71] It was of particular importance in fatal cases where the applicant was claiming, on her own behalf and that of her children, that these benefits and other payments should be properly allocated to the applicant who receives them; *R v Criminal Injuries Compensation Board, ex parte Barrett* [1994] PIQR Q44 46–47 (QBD) (Latham J); *HD v FTT* (n 24) [42].

[72] This qualification was included in the 2008 Scheme in response to the decision in *R (Vick) v Criminal Injuries Compensation Appeals Panel* [2005] EWHC 1575 (Admin), 2005 WL 1902441.

comprised those that were current at the date of assessment, and which were payable for loss of earnings, care costs, or loss of mobility. They included those benefits listed in section 4.2 of the Department of Work and Pensions' guidance on the recovery regime in the Social Security (Recovery of Benefits) Act 1997 (SSRBA 1997),[73] or their Universal Credit or Personal Independence Payments (PIP) equivalents under the Welfare Reform Act 2012. Amendments made in 2017 provide an exception to the general exclusion from Universal Credit of claims in respect of more than two children, where a child has been born as a result of a sexual act to which the claimant mother did not or could not have consented and, among other possibilities, there had been an award under the Criminal Injuries Compensation Scheme in respect of a relevant criminal injury sustained by C, 'an award under the Criminal Injuries Compensation Scheme in respect of a relevant criminal injury' that she had sustained.[74]

Paragraph 46 made virtually identical provision to that in paragraph 45 for the deduction of any payments made under an occupational pension in respect of loss of earnings, or, where the victim died as a result of the injury, dependency. The full deduction of any 'pension benefits' could have a particular impact on public sector employees, who might well find that, following this exercise, their awards would be substantially reduced. This was the outcome in *Cantwell v Criminal Injuries Compensation Board*, a claim decided under the similar provision in the common law scheme. The applicant policeman had been injured while on duty and consequently forced to retire on medical grounds. Having deducted the value of his annual ill-health pension and other benefits from the retirement pension to which he would have become entitled had he remained in service, the balance was less than £1,000; accordingly, the CICB made no award. The claim was ultimately heard by the House of Lords, which held that the scheme required that the assessment of the loss of the applicant's retirement pension had to take account of the ill-health pension he was receiving in consequence of the injury.[75] **5.126**

Under the 2012 Scheme it is no longer necessary, when dealing with loss of earnings or financial dependency, to take account of any occupational pensions, insurance, or social security benefits relating to the applicant's unemployment or incapacity for work. But the scheme continues to prevent double recovery for the applicant at the taxpayer's expense. It requires, first, the full deduction of social security benefits and insurance payments from special expenses payments. Secondly, it requires full deduction from any award, including a tariff award, **5.127**

[73] Department for Work and Pensions (2017), *Recovery of benefits and lump sum payments and NHS charges: technical guidance*.

[74] The Social Security (Restrictions on Amounts for Children and Qualifying Young Persons) Amendment Regulations 2017, SI 2013/376, inserting Schedule 12 (availability of the child element where maximum exceeded—exceptions para 5) into the Universal Credit Regulations 2013.

[75] [2001] UKHL 36, 2002 SC 1 (HL).

where the applicant receives payment by way of compensation from the offender, or other similar compensation scheme. As the 2012 Guide puts the matter: 'the Scheme is intended to be one of last resort'.

B Paragraphs 54–56: deductions from special expenses payments

5.128 With the exception of those payable in respect of the first twenty-eight weeks (paragraph 50), 'a special expenses payment will be withheld or reduced to take account of the receipt of, or entitlement to, social security benefits in respect of the applicant's special expenses' (paragraph 54). By Annex A, the 2012 Scheme defines 'social security benefits' as including 'all state and local authority benefits or assistance, whether paid in whole or in part from the funds of any part of the United Kingdom or elsewhere'. Depending on the date of assessment and the age of the applicant, this provision could include benefits relating to the DLA and its mobility components, or their PIP equivalents, and those relating to the carer's costs (attendance allowance and carer's payments).

5.129 By paragraph 55(1), 'a special expenses payment will be withheld or reduced to take account of the receipt of, or entitlement to, an insurance payment in respect of the applicant's special expenses'. This deduction proceeds on the same principles as apply to social security benefits (paragraphs 50 and 56). The refusal or reduction is therefore made in respect of an 'entitlement' to that benefit, irrespective of the period to which it relates, and whether or not any actual loss occurred or will occur in that period. By paragraph 56, if the benefits are to be paid in the future, the amount of the reduction will be calculated as a lump sum, applying the relevant Tables in Annex F, and the reduction under paragraph 54 will be the total amount of the benefits, net of income tax.

5.130 In the case of payments made under insurance policies, the 2012 Scheme maintains the distinction made in the earlier schemes between those that were paid for by the applicant and those paid for by a third party. By paragraph 55(2) payments made in relation to paragraphs 52(a), (b), and (i), or to their future losses under paragraph 53, will be disregarded where the policy was 'paid for entirely: (a) by the applicant; or (b) in relation to an applicant who was a child on the date when they sustained the criminal injury, by their parent or guardian'. Thus, payments in respect of loss of or damage to property or replacement of equipment relied on by the applicant (paragraphs 52(a) and 53)), costs associated with NHS treatment for the injury (paragraph 52(b)), or the cost of setting up a trust following a claims officer's direction under paragraph 106 (paragraph 52(i)) will be disregarded. But in the case of payments for special equipment (paragraph 52(c)), adaptation of the applicant's accommodation (paragraph 52(d)), the cost of care in connection with the applicant's bodily functions or meal preparation (paragraph 52(e)), or of supervising the applicant in order to avoid substantial danger to the applicant or another person (paragraph 52(f)), a reduction will be made 'regardless of who paid the premium if you are claiming for things like adaptations to your home or personal care'.[76] Where these payments are made under a policy for which the applicant (or her parents) had paid, these outcomes are in striking contrast with the position at common law.[77]

C Paragraph 85: payments by the offender and under other state compensation

By paragraph 85(2), the award is to be reduced by the amount of any of the listed payments, net of any benefits recoverable under the SSRBA 1997 or equivalent legislation (whether in any part of the United Kingdom or elsewhere). This continues the substance of paragraph 48(2) of the 2008 Scheme. Assuming that the applicant's injury qualifies for a tariff award, the sum remaining after the 'full value' of any payment made by way of a compensation order or damages has been deducted, may leave an amount to be paid under the scheme that, as in *VG v First-tier Tribunal and Criminal Injuries Compensation Authority*,[78] is less than the minimum payment (5.135). Paragraph 85(1) provides: **5.131**

> (1) An award under this Scheme will be withheld or reduced if in respect of the criminal injury to which the award relates the applicant, whether in any part of the United Kingdom or elsewhere: (a) receives or is awarded criminal injuries compensation or a similar payment; (b) receives an order for damages from a civil court; (c) agrees the settlement of a damages claim; or (d) receives a compensation order or offer made during criminal proceedings.

1 Paragraph 85(1)(a): Criminal injuries compensation or a similar payment

This heading supersedes paragraph 48(1)(a) and (b) of the 2008 Scheme, which provided for the full reduction of any criminal injury compensation award made under the arrangements in force at the relevant time in Northern Ireland, or from the funds of a country or other territory outside the United Kingdom. Such arrangements are now captured by the phrase 'whether in any part of the United Kingdom or elsewhere'. It is possible, although unlikely, that an applicant could be eligible under both the Northern Ireland compensation arrangements and the 2012 Scheme. Similarly, it is possible but unlikely that where the injury was sustained in another Member State, a person resident in Great Britain might, in addition to seeking compensation from that state's own scheme under the arrangements giving effect to the Compensation Directive (Chapter 3.07–3.08), also apply under the 2012 Scheme. Many other jurisdictions have criminal injury or similar arrangements; awards made under these would similarly be deducted.[79] **5.132**

[76] Paper Guide to the 2012 Scheme, Appendix 4 para 26.

[77] *Parry v Cleaver* [1970] AC 1 (HL); *Hussain v New Taplow Paper Mills Ltd* [1988] AC 514 (HL) (*Hussain v New Taplow*).

[78] [2017] UKUT 49 (AAC) (*VG v CICA*).

[79] CICA, *Compensation if you're a victim of crime abroad.*

5.133 It is an open question whether the applicant's receipt of money from the benevolence of third parties is to be deducted. At common law the position is clear: it is to be disregarded,[80] being the second exception to the general rule that in a civil action for personal injury the claimant should not be left in a better position than if the injury had not occurred. In *Hussein v New Taplow* Lord Bridge acknowledged that 'there is in one sense double recovery', but in justifying the exception posed the rhetorical question, why should the tortfeasor derive any benefit from the money provided by the third party with the sole intention of benefiting the injured plaintiff?[81] The difference is that under the scheme it is not the tortfeasor but the taxpayer who foots the bill. This argues for deduction, but there is no specific provision to this effect in the 2012 Scheme.

2 Paragraph 85(1)(b): an order for damages from a civil court

5.134 This paragraph supersedes paragraph 48(1)(c) of the 2008 Scheme, which related to an order by a civil court, whether in the United Kingdom or elsewhere, for the payment of damages. It is rare that civil proceedings can be successfully pursued against an offender. But the claimants in *AT, NT, ML, and AK v Dulghieru,* who had been trafficked from Moldova and effectively imprisoned by the defendants in order to provide sexual services on their behalf, were awarded substantial sums for general and aggravated damages. Three of the claimants had also been made awards under the scheme, in respect of which the court observed that because of paragraph 49, 'there will be no risk of double recovery'.[82]

3 Paragraph 85(1)(c): an agreed settlement of a damages claim

5.135 This supersedes paragraph 48(1)(d) of the 2008 Scheme: 'a settlement of a claim for damages, compensation or both on terms providing for the payment of money'. The application of paragraph 85(1)(c) to the settlement of an action for damages was considered in *VG v CICA.* The claimant's son had been killed by a paranoid schizophrenic who had been released from his NHS care home. The offender was convicted of murder; the claimant's action against the NHS trust was based on a breach of the Human Rights Act 1998 and for negligence in respect of its duty to protect life under Article 2 of the European Convention on Human Rights. The trust denied liability but offered a sum of £10,000 'in settlement of the whole of her claim'. The claimant accepted this, and from her subsequent claim under the 2012 Scheme for a bereavement payment, the CICA deducted this sum, leaving £500. On appeal, the FTT 'concluded that the cause of the claim that was settled was a crime of violence and that the "unvarnished reading" of paragraph 85(1)(c) includes article 2 compensation'. Dismissing the application for judicial review,

---

[80] *Redpath v Belfast and County Down Railway* [1967] NI 147 (CA).
[81] *Hussein v New Taplow* [1988] AC 514, 528 (HL).
[82] [2009] EWHC 225, 2009 WL 364337[53] (QB) (Treacy J).

the Upper Tribunal agreed that the FTT's decision gave paragraph 85 'its plain and proper meaning'.[83]

4 Paragraph 85(1)(d): a compensation order or offer made during criminal proceedings

This supersedes paragraph 48(1)(d) of the 2008 Scheme: 'an order by a criminal court whether in the United Kingdom or elsewhere for payment of compensation in respect of personal injuries or a compensation offer under section 302A of the Criminal Procedure (Scotland) Act 1995'.[84] The court's responsibilities under sections 130–34 of the Powers of Criminal Courts (Sentencing) Act 2000 concerning the making of compensation orders are dealt with in Chapters 7–9. But a payment made by a court in recognition of a victim's attempts to enforce the law arguably escapes deduction. Although it is paid out of public funds, it does not fall within the terms of paragraph 85(1)(d). **5.136**

The vast majority of compensation orders made in respect of offences of violence against the person are for amounts less than £1,000. It may be that, in these cases, such an amount accurately reflects the severity of the injury, in which case there would be no possible claim under the scheme. Where the injury does exceed the Scheme's minimum, any compensation order, even it is itself less than £1,000, will be deducted. This was the case in *R (JA) v First-tier Tribunal and Criminal Injuries Compensation Authority*, where a reduction of £50 was made under paragraph 48 of the 2008 Scheme, being the amount of the compensation order made against the applicant's assailant.[85] Equally, there may be instances where an applicant does receive exactly the compensation that the CICA would award, which would therefore be deducted in full to prevent double recovery at the taxpayer's expense. As the compensation order will also reflect the impact of the duty on the court to take the offender's means into account, the victim may well receive an amount less than an 'ideal assessment' of their injury. If that assessment exceeds the scheme's minimum, there will nevertheless be a deduction to reflect the compensation order, as was the case in *YT v First-tier Tribunal (SEC).* In that case, there was a reduction of £3,000 under paragraph 48 of the 2001 Scheme, being the amount of the compensation order made against the applicant's assailant, the scheme award being £5,225.[86] **5.137**

Where the victim does not in fact receive his full award under a compensation order, the CICB made arrangements by which its award would be for the full sum less only so much of the compensation order as the victim had received, the **5.138**

[83] *VG v CICA* (n 78) [20] and 23] (Judge Levenson).

[84] For compensation orders in Scotland see the Criminal Procedure (Scotland) Act 1995 ss 227 and 249–53.

[85] [2015] UKUT 457 (AAC) [2].

[86] [2013] UKUT 201 (AAC) [13]. On the sentencing court's duty to take the offender's means into account, see ch 8.35–8.52.

outstanding instalments paid by the offender being forwarded to the CICB by the magistrates' court responsible for their enforcement. The slightly different wording in the 2012 Scheme may mean that the CICA will deduct the compensation to which the claimant is entitled under the order.

5 Notification and recovery of payments

5.139 By paragraph 91(c) of the 2012 Scheme, the applicant must inform the claims officer of any claim or other proceedings that may give rise to an award or payment mentioned in paragraph 85, and of the progress of the claim or proceedings. This is a particular element of the more general power in paragraph 98(b) of the 2012 Scheme, which permits the claims officer to defer determination of the application until he is 'satisfied that the applicant has taken all reasonable steps to obtain any social security benefits, insurance payments, damages or compensation to which the applicant may be entitled in respect of the same injury'.

5.140 The CICA has always treated compliance with this obligation seriously. It is clearly in the applicant's best interests that she has as complete and accurate an account as possible of what she has received and is entitled to receive. By paragraph 110(c), repayment may be required where the claims officer is satisfied that evidence received after final payment has been made shows that the applicant has received a payment in respect of which a reduction could have been made under paragraph 85. By section 3(1)(c) of the CICA 1995, these repayments are debts due to the Crown (section 3(3)).

5.141 The CICA 1995 made no provision for the recovery of any compensation from a person convicted in respect of the injury. Section 57 of the Domestic Violence, Crime and Victims Act 2004 inserted sections 7A–7D in the CICA 1995, giving the Secretary of State powers to make provision for the recovery from an appropriate person of an amount equal to all or part of the compensation paid in respect of a criminal injury. An 'appropriate person' is a person who has been convicted of an offence in respect of the criminal injury, and the amount recoverable must be determined by reference only to the extent to which the criminal injury is directly attributable to an offence of which he has been convicted. No regulations have been made as these sections were not in force at the time of writing.

6

APPLICATIONS, AWARDS, REVIEW, APPEALS, AND JUDICIAL REVIEW

I Introduction

This chapter deals with the procedural aspects of claims under the 2012 Scheme. In many respects the equivalent provisions under the earlier statutory schemes have been continued. Where relevant the text summarizes these, noting their interpretation and any substantive changes, but the principal focus is the procedures that now apply. **6.01**

II Applications (Paragraphs 86–97)

A Time limits

6.02 By section 3(1) of the Criminal Injuries Compensation Act 1995 (CICA 1995) the scheme may include provision '(e) requiring claims under the Scheme to be made within such periods as may be specified by the Scheme'. By section 1(f), provision may be made 'imposing other time limits'. These other limits affect such matters as the applicant's acceptance or otherwise of a determination in his case, or his request for it to be reviewed, and are dealt with in the relevant paragraphs below.

1 The standard time limit

6.03 Repeating in substance the requirements of the earlier tariff schemes, paragraph 87 of the 2012 Scheme requires the applicant to submit her application 'so that it is received by the Authority as soon as reasonably practicable after the incident giving rise to the criminal injury to which it relates, and in any event within two years after the date of that incident'; by paragraph 86, the application 'will be determined by a claims officer in the Authority in accordance with this Scheme'.

6.04 Section 3(4) of the CICA 1995 provides for the appointment of claims officers for the purpose of determining claims and making awards and payments of compensation. They are pivotal to the scheme's implementation, enjoying extensive powers over all aspects of the making and determination of an application. The use of the indefinite article in the phrase 'a claims officer' means that unless otherwise provided (as in paragraph 117(g)), there may be a succession of claims officers dealing with different aspects of an application and its determination.

6.05 Under the common law scheme an application had to be made within three years, the limitation period applicable to civil actions for personal injury.[1] While a majority of victims did apply well within the time limit, the proposed reduction to two years in the statutory scheme, prompted in part to encourage timely application, was controversial. There was particular concern that applicants would be disadvantaged where their claims, when made as an adult, arose from sexual offences committed against them in childhood. While alert to the practical difficulties involved in investigating and substantiating late claims (Chapter 3.76–3.78), the 1996 Scheme continued the discretion previously operated by the Criminal Injuries Compensation Board (CICB) to waive the time limit. The following sections summarize the criteria for its initial and subsequent exercise under their stricter formulations in the 2001 and 2008 Schemes. This history both demonstrates the continuing relevance of these difficulties, and the reasons why the 2012 Scheme makes those criteria yet more stringent.

[1] Home Office (1978) ch 9; (1986) para 4.14.

2 Extending the standard time limit under the earlier schemes

Paragraph 17 of the 1996 Scheme and paragraph 18 of the 2001 Scheme permitted a claims officer to waive the time limit where she considered that 'by reason of the particular circumstances of the case, it is reasonable and in the interests of justice to do so'. The application of these criteria was extensively reviewed in two decisions of the Court of Appeal arising from the same set of claims. **6.06**

In the first of its decisions, *Hutton and Others v First-tier Tribunal and Criminal Injuries Compensation Authority*,[2] the Court held that the FTT had erred in its interpretation of the phrase 'the particular circumstances of the case'. It did not imply some 'special' circumstances 'in the sense of there being unusual or extraordinary circumstances', but meant 'the actual or distinct circumstances of the individual case'.[3] In its rehearing of the three connected claims, the FTT again refused to waive the time limit. In its second decision *Criminal Injuries Compensation Authority v Hutton and Others and First-tier Tribunal (CIC)*, the Court held that as the FTT had taken full account of the test the Court had formulated in its earlier decision, it was entitled to reach that conclusion.[4] **6.07**

In order to control the administrative and resource burdens implicit in dealing with late applications, the criteria for extending the time limit were tightened in the 2008 Scheme. Replacing the earlier, single, test, paragraph 18 provided that an extension depended on whether it was (a) 'practicable for the application to be considered' and (b) 'in the particular circumstances of the case, it would not have been reasonable to expect the applicant to have made an application within the two-year period'. **6.08**

(a) Paragraph 18(a) of the 2008 Scheme: practicability In *R (MM) v First-tier Tribunal and Criminal Injuries Compensation Authority*, the applicant had been raped when he was a child of 8. The offence was not reported at the time, nor before his application some forty years later. Refusing to extend the time limit, the Criminal Injuries Compensation Authority (CICA) found that he could have made a report to the police within two years of reaching the age of 18, a decision the FTT upheld, finding that in its absence there was no evidence to corroborate his claim, and that to investigate the circumstances would take time, and be expensive. While the FTT was correct in requiring verification of the offence, the Upper Tribunal held that it had relied too closely on the scheme Guides (Chapter 1.32),[5] **6.09**

---

[2] [2012] EWCA Civ 806, [2013] 1 WLR 124 (CA) (*Hutton v CICA*).

[3] ibid [41]–[42].

[4] [2016] EWCA Civ 1305, [2017] ACD 20 [59] (CA) [76]–[80] (*CICA v Hutton*). The facts, and the decisions in the three claims that were reached by the CICA, the FTT, and the Upper Tribunal, are summarized at [15]–[31].

[5] CICA (1996 Guide) paras 7.3 and 7.5; (2001 Guide) Part 5 para 4; (2008 Guide) section 2 para 1.

which focused on the practicability 'of *investigating* a claim, whereas paragraph 18 of the scheme refers to *considering* an application' (original emphasis).[6]

6.10 **(b) Paragraph 18(b) of the 2008 Scheme: reasonableness** One of the issues that arose in *Colefax v First Tier Tribunal and Criminal Injuries Compensation Authority* was whether it was reasonable to expect the applicant to have made an application for an injury (epilepsy) that was diagnosed more than two years after the incident, where there were other injuries for which an application within the time limit could have been made. The Court of Appeal's decision turned, first, on 'the evident distinction' between paragraph 18(a), which speaks of 'the application', and paragraph 18(b), which speaks of 'an application', a distinction that focused the question on whether, in his particular circumstances, the applicant 'both *could* and *should*' have applied within the time limit. As this was precisely the formulation that the CICA adopted in its review of its decision to refuse the late claim, and was upheld by the FTT, the appeal failed.[7]

6.11 Referring to the Court's judgment in *Hutton v CICA,* that the phrase 'in the particular circumstances of the case' was a reference to the specific facts of the specific case, Briggs LJ observed that it would be open to an applicant to show that even if he had suffered some immediately apparent relatively minor injury, 'it was reasonable for him, in his particular circumstances, not to make it the subject of a compensation claim, even if another person in the same circumstances might reasonably have done so'.[8]

6.12 This possibility was consistent with the Upper Tribunal's decision in *TG v First-tier Tribunal and Criminal Injuries Compensation Authority*, but which imported a more explicit element of subjectivity: 'the concept of "the particular circumstances of the case" must include circumstances relating to the state of the claimant's knowledge'.[9] In this case FTT erred in not fully examining the reasons for the applicant's conscious delay in making a claim pending the outcome of the police's investigations.

6.13 The Upper Tribunal also explicitly endorsed the CICA's submission that ignorance of the scheme is no reason for extending the limitation period; neither did the Criminal Injuries Compensation Authority Panel (CICAP) accept ignorance as an excuse. It is difficult to envisage circumstances in which ignorance of the scheme alone and of itself, might justify a late application, but the implication of *TG v CICA* was, as the tribunal held in *YA v First-tier Tribunal and Criminal*

---

[6] [2013] UKUT 402 (AAC) [21] (Judge Jacobs) (*MM v FTT and CICA*).

[7] [2014] EWCA Civ 945, [2015] 1 WLR 35 (CA) [27], [29], [31]–[32] (Briggs LJ) (*Colefax v CICA*). The Court had earlier given leave to appeal the Upper Tribunal's decision not disturb this finding; [2014] EWCA Civ 60, 2014 WL 287758 (CA).

[8] *Colefax v CICA* (n 7) [30].

[9] [2013] UKUT 366 (AAC) [24]–[28] (Judge Levenson) (*TG v CICA*).

Injuries Compensation Authority, that it was not sufficient for the FTT to rule out waiving the time limit simply because the applicant was unaware of the scheme. It had erred in not properly considering the particular circumstances relating to the state of the claimant's knowledge.[10]

The question of whether the applicant's lack of knowledge of the scheme, or tardiness in applying, was attributable to a third party's (poor) advice, was considered in *GS v First-tier Tribunal (SEC)*, and in *R (AM) v First-tier Tribunal (CIC)*. In the former the Upper Tribunal again found that the FTT had made no real effort to investigate the factual basis on which the applicant had come to the decisions he did; 'it simply *excluded* from consideration circumstances which the applicant put forward to show why it was reasonable to extend time in his favour'.[11] In the latter, it found that it was reasonable for an elderly disabled man with poor English to rely on the promise by a victim liaison officer provided by the National Probation Service to deal with his claim, but that he had not acted reasonably when he failed to check whether she had submitted the application.[12] **6.14**

(c) **The extent of the discretion** The question of whether the conditions in paragraph 18(a) and (b) were exhaustive of the claims officer's discretion was the subject of conflicting interpretations by different judges of the Upper Tribunal, which led to a three-judge panel being convened to hear the application for judicial review of the FTT's decision in *R (MJ) v First-tier Tribunal and Criminal Injuries Compensation Authority*.[13] Between the ages of 6 and 13 the applicant had been repeatedly sexually abused, but the CICA only received his application under the 2008 Scheme in 2010, some twenty years after the last of the incidents in 1990. Notwithstanding a conviction, there was considerable uncertainty about the facts surrounding the abuse. The CICA and the FTT refused to waive the time limit, deciding that neither paragraph 18(a) nor (b) was satisfied. The Upper Tribunal allowed his application in respect of what the three judge panel called *MJ (No 1)*, but in the subsequent fresh hearing (*MJ (No 2)*), the FTT again refused to waive the limit.[14] **6.15**

When giving permission in *MJ (No 1)* because of errors in the FTT's disposal of the appeal, Judge Ward interpreted paragraph 18 to mean that once paragraphs **6.16**

[10] [2015] UKUT 399 (AAC) [48] (*YA v CICA*). This was the mother's application that followed the judicial review permission granted in *Hutton v CICA* (n 2). It failed because she was not a 'qualifying claimant': ibid [39]; *CICA v Hutton* (n 4) [30]–[31], [60]–[63], [79(ii)]. See also *MM v Criminal Injuries Compensation Authority* [2018] CSOH 63, 2018 WL 02942739 [45]: 'much will depend on the underlying circumstances and the reasons for the ignorance' (CSOH) (Lord Glennie) (*MM v CICA*).

[11] [2013] UKUT 628 (AAC).

[12] [2012] UKUT 55 (AAC) [19] (*AM v FTT*).

[13] [2014] UKUT 279 (AAC), [2015] AACR 3 (Charles J, Judges Levenson and Wikeley) (*MJ (No 3)*).

[14] *MJ (No 2)* [2014] UKUT 76 (AAC).

18(a) and (b) were satisfied, no further general discretion arose.[15] But in *MM v FTT and CICA* Judge Jacobs held that paragraph 18 did leave a residual discretion, so that the claims officer could decide, although its terms were met, that it was not appropriate to waive the limit. The terms of paragraph 18 denoted a power, 'may', but not a duty to waive the limit.[16]

6.17 In *MJ (No 3)* the three judge panel preferred Judge Jacobs' analysis: 'If both conditions (a) and (b) are satisfied, then the claims officer (and, on appeal) the tribunal) must consider whether to exercise the discretion to admit the late claim', but there would have to be good reasons to justify not exercising the discretion in the applicant's favour'.[17] This was the outcome for which the CICA had argued. The Upper Tribunal accepted the linguistic argument that the use of 'may' in paragraph 18, immediately following the obligation on the applicant who 'must' submit his application within two years, was being used 'in its normal discretionary sense, so vesting the claims officer with a power to waive the time limit'.[18]

6.18 A central element of the panel's reasoning was its reliance on the political and policy choices concerning its scope as justification for the integrity of the scheme's time limits. The applicant had argued that a residual discretion was inconsistent with the scheme's purpose, to ensure that victims of crimes of violence obtained proper compensation. The panel acknowledged this, but it was 'not an absolute or open-ended goal'. In a very clear recognition of its history (Chapter 1.05–1.10), it continued:

> The goal of protecting victims' rights must also be traded off against other considerations, one such being that the making of timely applications is a legitimate objective of the scheme, as stale claims are more likely to consume scarce administrative resources. Time limits thus serve the purposes of good public administration.[19]

3 Extending the standard time limit under the 2012 Scheme

6.19 In order to control further the costs associated with the scheme's administration, the criteria by which by which the standard time limit may be extended have become more demanding. Paragraph 89 of the 2012 Scheme permits a claims officer to extend the limit where they are 'satisfied that: (a) due to exceptional circumstances the applicant could not have applied earlier; and (b) the evidence presented in support of the application means that it can be determined without further extensive enquiries by a claims officer'. Paragraph 89 also reverses the order in which these revised conditions are to be considered. This suggests that

---

15 *MJ (No 1)* [2011] UKUT 402 (AAC) [3] (*MJ (No 1)*).

16 *MM v FTT and CICA* (n 6) [30]–[31].

17 *MJ (No 3)* (n 13) [31]. The panel observed that the right of appeal and full rehearing on the merits, and the role of the Tribunal on judicial review, are sufficient to guard against 'the spectre of arbitrary and inconsistent decisions', paras [21], [29], and [34].

18 ibid [27].

19 ibid [21] and [28]; *Colefax v CICA* (n 7) [31]–[32].

from an administrative standpoint it may be more efficient to consider the reasons for the applicant's failure to apply in time, before the claims officer considers what enquiries need to be made.

It follows from these revisions that the authorities decided under the earlier tariff schemes are not directly applicable, but the principles concerning the FTT's disposal of an appeal remain relevant, as illustrated by the Upper Tribunal's decision in *BC v First-tier Tribunal and Criminal Injuries Compensation Authority*. The applicant had been sexually abused in the mid-1980s when he was a child, but did not report the abuse until 2010, making his application in 2013. In his teens he had developed a drug habit from which he was recovering, but to which he relapsed upon hearing of the sudden death of his father in 2012. The FTT dismissed his appeal against the CICA's refusal to waive the time limit, finding that while his father's death 'was clearly a distressing period' the circumstances were not 'exceptional'.[20] **6.20**

The Upper Tribunal addressed two aspects of the interpretation of paragraph 89(a). The first was whether the comparative adjective 'earlier' refers to a date within the two year period specified in paragraph 88(1)(b), or to any date prior to the date on which the claim was actually made. The tribunal was clear that the plain meaning of paragraph 89(a) is the latter.[21] **6.21**

The second, and more important aspect, is its analysis of what it termed the 'two subsidiary questions that need to be asked' when applying paragraph 89(a). These are, (i) were there exceptional circumstances, and (ii) did any of them mean that the applicant could not have applied earlier than he did apply? Whether anything is exceptional is primarily a question of fact for the CICA or the FTT, as to which the 2012 Guide advises that the applicant will need to provide the CICA with medical, psychiatric or other relevant evidence 'that shows why this application could not have been made earlier'. **6.22**

Given their purpose, these subsidiary questions are to be determined objectively. But, 'in answering question (ii) 'those bodies [the CICA and the FTT] must be reasonable in reaching a conclusion'.[22] Whether circumstances are 'exceptional' must, it is suggested, relate to whether they are exceptional for the claimant. Circumstances are not 'exceptional' in the abstract: 'circumstances' may be normal for one claimant, in which case delay will not be excused, but exceptional for another who is differently placed. The test is whether the exceptional circumstances (reasonably) explain why *this* (possibly vulnerable) claimant did not apply earlier: 'the question of exceptionality must be considered in relation to the whole package of circumstances relied on'.[23] **6.23**

---

20 [2016] UKUT 155 (AAC) (*BC v CICA*).
21 ibid [16].
22 *BC v CICA* (n 20) [15] (Judge Levenson).
23 *MM v CICA* (n 10) [37], [45].

6.24 Assuming that the CICA accepts that the applicant could not have applied earlier than she did, it is no longer a question of whether 'it is practicable for the application to be considered', but whether it meets the more demanding test in paragraph 89(b). This requires clear and available evidence that there was a crime of violence, and that the applicant was the victim, as to which the 2012 Guide firmly emphasizes the obligation on the applicant: 'We will make basic enquiries of the police, but you will need to be able to provide evidence that you were a victim of a crime of violence and that you suffered an injury as a result'.

6.25 Finally, it may be noted that there is no specified limit to the length of the extension that is granted under paragraph 89. In *MJ (No 3)* the panel expressly approved Judge Rowland's observation in *AM v FTT,* that once the limit had been waived, 'it cannot be right that a person who could not be expected to submit an application within two years has an unlimited time thereafter in which to do so',[24] but disagreed with the suggestion that this imposed a 'third test'. The 'possibility or practicability of submitting the claim earlier was simply one consideration that may be relevant to the exercise of the residual discretion under paragraph 18'.[25] In the case of the 2012 Scheme, as the claims officer would, when granting the extension, have been satisfied that the condition in paragraph 89(b) was met, the question is whether, at the time when it is made, there were no 'exceptional circumstances' to explain why the applicant could not have applied earlier than they did (paragraph 89(a)).

4 Applications by or on behalf of children

6.26 As the facts in *MM v FTT and CICA, MJ (No 3),* and *BC v CICA* illustrate, claims arising from historic child abuse have always proved difficult. Although it was not authorized by the statutory scheme,[26] both the 2001 and 2008 Guides expressly continued the CICB's approach, which had been to take a sympathetic approach where the victim had made an application 'within a reasonable time of reaching maturity'. On the particular issue in *MJ (No 3),* the panel held that in such claims 'it is not enough simply to rule the application as being irredeemably out of time because it was made 20 years after the last of the incidents in question'. In reaching this decision it relied on the powerful observations of Lord Boyd in *JM v Advocate General for Scotland,* that as a child's silence is a recognized and direct consequence of her sexual abuse, 'to suggest that this effect disappears once the child has reached adulthood is to misunderstand the pervasive nature of the trauma which victims of childhood sexual abuse invariably suffer'.[27]

---

[24] *AM v FTT* (n 12) [14].
[25] *MJ No 3)* (n 13) [32].
[26] *MJ (No 1)* (n 15) [10].
[27] [2013] CSOH 169, 2014 SLT 475 [20]. In a sensitive analysis of the impact of sexual offences on victims, Lord Glennie singled out as 'important' this last point in Lord Boyd's opinion; *MM v CICA* (n 10) [1]–[3].

Holding that the present case was not one where there had obviously been inexcusable delay in making the application,[28] the panel specified a number of Directions that the FTT should follow in the rehearing in *MJ (No 1)*. Three are of particular relevance: **6.27**

- as a general principle, the longer the period of delay in making the claim, the stronger the reasons for waiver will need to be
- however, the simple fact that there has been a lengthy delay in making an application does not of itself mean that a case for waiver cannot be made out, especially in cases of historic sexual abuse [and]
- in exercising the residual discretion under paragraph 18 [of the 2008 Scheme], all the relevant circumstances must be taken into account and the reasoning for the decision must be appropriately explained.

The 2012 consultation confirmed that the scheme would expressly include the established discretion 'where the applicant could not reasonably have made an application within the two year period (for example in cases of historic sexual abuse), and it is still practicable for the application to the considered'.[29] Covering both physical and sexual abuse, paragraph 88(1) of the 2012 Scheme provides that: **6.28**

> where the applicant was a child under the age of 18 on the date of the incident giving rise to the criminal injury, the application must be sent by the applicant so that it is received by the Authority: (a) in the case of an incident reported to the police before the applicant's 18th birthday, within the period ending on their 20th birthday; or (b) in the case of an incident reported to the police on or after the applicant's 18th birthday, within two years after the date of the first report to the police in respect of the incident.

The leeway that the scheme allows in these cases is qualified by paragraph 88(2), which, repeating the test in paragraph 89(b), provides that an application under paragraph 88(1) will not be accepted unless the evidence presented in support of the application 'means that it can be determined without further extensive enquiries by a claims officer'. The time limits in paragraphs 88(1)(a) and (b) may, however, by paragraph 89 be extended where 'due to exceptional circumstances' the applicant could not have applied within the specified periods. For example: **6.29**

- The CICA could, subject to paragraph 88(2), accept an application under paragraph 88(1)(a) where, the claimant being 10 at the time, the incident was not reported until she was 17, the application being made when she was 19 (that is, 'within the period ending on her 20th birthday'); but if it were not made until after her 20th birthday it would be accepted only if paragraph 89 applied.
- The CICA could, subject to paragraph 88(2), accept an application under paragraph 88(1)(b) where, the claimant being 10 at the time, the incident was not

[28] *MJ (No 3)* (n 13) [35].
[29] Ministry of Justice (2012a) para 258.

reported until she was 21, but if the application was not made 'within two years after the date of the first report to the police', it will be rejected unless paragraph 89 applies.

6.30 This second example may be illustrated by the facts of *BC v CICA*. The sexual assaults sustained by the applicant between the ages of 9 and 12 were not reported until he was 33, his application being made 3 years later. That case turned on the application of paragraph 89(a), but as there was a relatively recent conviction the FTT had decided that the late claim could be considered without the need for 'further extensive enquiries' (paragraph 89(b)). The 2012 Guide advises that it 'is best if you apply as soon as possible', but arguably a prompt claim is essential. It would be unwise to rely on the claims officer exercising his discretion in the applicant's favour unless the conditions in paragraph 88(2) and 89(a) are clearly met. It is, for example, very unlikely to be a good idea to await the outcome of a prosecution—a conviction is not necessary and delay can be fatal, as *TG v CICA*, decided under the 2008 Scheme, illustrates.[30]

5 Applications on behalf of an adult who cannot apply himself

6.31 There are no additional provisions governing the application of the standard time limit in the case of adult applicants who, because they lack capacity or are 'incapable by reason of mental disorder', are unable to apply themselves (Chapter 3.75).

6 Challenging a refusal to waive the time limit

6.32 By paragraph 117(e) an applicant may seek a review of a claims officer's decision not to extend the time limit under paragraph 89, and by paragraph 125 'if dissatisfied with a decision on a review' may appeal that decision. If the FTT allows an appeal against a decision under paragraph 117(e), the CICA will arrange for the application to be treated as if the time limit had been extended by a claims officer in accordance with the 2012 Scheme.

B Paragraphs 90–92: completing the application

6.33 By paragraph 91, an applicant must '(a) make their application on the form available from the Authority', that is, online or by writing to the CICA. The online application form asks first whether the application is in respect of a single injury, a period of abuse, or because someone has died. In *Colefax v CICA*, the Court of Appeal confirmed that in all cases the applicant should make a single application in respect of all his qualifying injuries, rather than separate applications in relation to each.[31] By paragraph 97, an applicant may withdraw his application at any time before a payment is made.

[30] *TG v CICA* (n 9).
[31] *Colefax v* CICA (n 7)); CICA, *Claim compensation for a criminal injury.*

Paragraph 18 of the 2012 Scheme continues the restrictions that existed under paragraph 7(a) of the earlier schemes. Subject to the transitional arrangements in paragraphs 141–144: **6.34**

> An award will not be made to a person in respect of a criminal injury where that person has previously made an application in respect of the same injury under this Scheme or any Criminal Injuries Compensation Scheme mentioned in paragraph 141, irrespective of whether or how that application was finally disposed of.

This is relevant where, for example, that application had been rejected or an award reduced.[32] Paragraph 141 provides, in essence, that any application received before 27 November 2012 (the day the 2012 Scheme came into force) will be determined according to the date that it was received, being a date falling between the termination of a previous scheme and the commencement of its successor.

By paragraph 92, 'the applicant must provide such information in connection with their application as a claims officer may reasonably require'. The fact that, in the exercise of its inquisitorial role the CICA can examine documents and witnesses, does not relieve the applicant of her burden to prove, on the balance of probabilities (Chapter 3.11–3.12), that she is eligible for a payment. The applicant is required to make a consent declaration authorizing the CICA to contact those agencies and authorities that may have information relevant to her application. It is clearly vital that the answers that the applicant gives to the questions and choices asked by the online application form are as complete and accurate as possible. **6.35**

There was nothing in the earlier schemes that indicated the kind of information that the CICA required, but following the government's consultation paragraphs 91 and 92 list a number of particular requirements.[33] The following paragraphs refer to the questions asked under the first of the options in the online form, 'personal injury'; with appropriate adjustments these requirements equally apply to 'a period of abuse' and 'fatal injury'. **6.36**

Where the injury was caused by a crime of violence or a sexual offence, the CICA will seek confirmation that the incident in which the claimant was injured was reported to the police within the terms of paragraph 22 (Chapter 4.06–4.11). Its Customer Charter indicates that it will 'check some of the facts by getting a report from the police', and asks that the applicant declares all unspent criminal convictions and cautions on his application form, adding that: 'we will however, conduct a criminal records check on all claims'.[34] The CICA will also seek confirmation from the police or any witnesses that the applicant's behaviour did not contribute to the incident in which the injuries were sustained. **6.37**

32 *CJ v First-tier Tribunal (CIC)* [2016] UKUT 7 (AAC) [5] and [9] (*CJ v FTT*).
33 Ministry of Justice (2012a) para 260.
34 CICA, *About our services*.

6.38 By paragraph 91(b) the applicant must 'comply with any direction made or condition imposed by a claims officer in relation to their application' made under paragraph 90. This gives the claims officer a general power to 'give directions, impose conditions, and make such other investigations and arrangements in connection with an application as the claims officer considers appropriate'. By paragraph 91(c) the 2012 Scheme requires the applicant to 'inform the claims officer of any claim or other proceedings which may give rise to an award or payment mentioned in paragraph 85 in respect of the criminal injury giving rise to the application, and the progress of the claim or proceedings' (Chapter 5.130–5.139), by paragraph 91((d) to 'assist the claims officer, and any other body or person, as far as reasonably practicable in relation to consideration of their application', and by paragraph 91(e) 'to provide the claims officer with any change in their correspondence address as soon as reasonably practicable' (Chapter 4.19–4.21). Failure to comply with any of these three conditions may lead to refusal or reduction of an award.

6.39 By paragraph 92(a), the evidence that the applicant must supply comprises in particular, first, 'that the applicant satisfies the requirements of paragraph 10 in relation to eligibility' (Chapter 3.68–3.74); that is, proof that he meets the residency or status requirements, along with his identity and personal details. Secondly, by paragraph 92(b) he must supply any 'medical evidence in relation to the injury giving rise to the application', which in a simple case may comprise notes made by a general practitioner or an Accident & Emergency discharge note. The medical, and any psychiatric, evidence will be the basis for a tariff award. Where the application includes a claim for a payment 'other than an injury payment', for example for loss of earnings or special expenses, the applicant must supply evidence in support of that part of the application (paragraph 92(c)).

6.40 Paragraph 92(d) provides, finally, that the applicant must provide 'such information as the applicant has, or which is reasonably available to them, in relation to their eligibility for a payment from any other source in relation to the injury or other losses to which their application under this Scheme relates'. If a criminal injury defined in paragraph 5 of the scheme was sustained in the course of the applicant's employment, the CICA might seek confirmation that there was no liability on the employer's part, or that there were no injury-based workplace schemes available. Although it is not explicit, this requirement includes the applicant's eligibility for social security benefits and insurance payments, in particular as they apply to any claim for a special expenses payment (Chapter 5.78–5.81).

C Paragraphs 93–96: costs associated with the application

1 Costs of representation

6.41 Subject to the provisions concerning medical evidence outlined below, paragraph 93 continues the position under the earlier schemes: 'The Authority will not normally meet any costs incurred by the applicant in connection with an application.

In particular, it will not meet the costs of legal or other representation incurred by the applicant'. The 2012 Guide advises: 'You do not need a paid representative such as a solicitor or claims management company to apply for compensation ... You can check what is available in your local area by visiting the *Victims' Information Service* website. If you belong to a trade union, they may be able to help'. The 'ease of access' section of its Customer Charter indicates that the CICA will assist the applicant via its telephone helpline service, but it can of course do no more. The applicant may also ask a friend or a relative to represent her and help with the claim; in this case, the CICA requires confirmation from the applicant that she is 'happy for them to deal with the case'.

Legal aid is not available for claims under the scheme; the cost of paid legal representation therefore falls on the applicant. The state's failure to provide funds for persons who might otherwise be incapable of pursuing their right to compensation under the CICA 1995 was challenged in *C v Home Office and Criminal Injuries Compensation Authority* as being incompatible with the applicant's Article 6(1) right under the European Convention on Human Rights. The Court of Appeal held that, while it was true that her award would be diminished by the fact that the scheme did not reimburse her solicitors' costs, she was not deprived of the possibility of a fair hearing.[35] Where they do instruct solicitors, applicants must notify the CICA of any changes or discontinuance of that representation; it will hold back any outstanding fees owed to that representative if an award is made. The amount will be released when the applicant and the representative have confirmed that any disagreement as to costs between them has been resolved. **6.42**

C v Home Office raised a second issue. Contrary to paragraph 20 of the 1996 Scheme, the CICA initially refused to reimburse the 'reasonable expenses' the applicant incurred in complying with the arrangements made by the claims officer for a medical examination of her injuries. Following a judicial review it accepted that it was not lawful for it 'to displace' those costs.[36] **6.43**

2 Medical costs

The reimbursement of the applicant's medical costs is dealt with in paragraphs 94–96, whose purpose is also to reduce the scheme's expenditure. Responsibility for them should, 'within reason, lie with the applicant to provide the necessary medical evidence to make their claim'.[37] By paragraph 92(b) the applicant must provide 'medical evidence in relation to the injury', and by paragraph 94(a) the CICA will meet the reasonable costs incurred in obtaining this evidence, if the claims officer is satisfied that the applicant could not reasonably obtain it herself, cannot afford it, or it exceeds £50. The 2012 Guide indicates that, in the second **6.44**

[35] [2004] EWCA Civ 234, [2004] UKHRR 813 [49]–[51] (CA).
[36] ibid [18] and [47].
[37] Ministry of Justice (2012a) paras 261–65.

case, the applicant should provide evidence that she relies solely on social security benefits, are in receipt of tax credits, or earn less than the minimum amount needed to qualify for statutory sick pay. There is no guarantee that medical expenses will be reimbursed.

6.45 If an award is made, the CICA may deduct from it the cost of that evidence, again up to an overall maximum of £50 (paragraph 96(a)). Where more costly expert evidence is required, such as a full psychiatric report where the claim is for a mental injury, or the applicant suffered from any pre-existing conditions that the criminal injury nay have accelerated or exacerbated (Chapter 5.38–5.41), the CICA will continue to pay for those reports if they are necessary for the proper consideration of the application, and it would be reasonable to do so (paragraph 94(b)). It will also meet any ancillary costs in connection with those reports (paragraph 95).

6.46 Finally, the CICA will meet the reasonable costs that the applicant, and where necessary a carer, have incurred travelling to and from a 'medical or other appointment' that it requires. By paragraph 96(b), it may deduct those costs from the award if the applicant has, without reasonable excuse, failed to attend any required appointment. Any deductions from an award under paragraphs 94(a) or 96 are subject to review (paragraph 117(f)); if the FTT allows an appeal against a decision on review under this paragraph 'it may make such direction as it considers appropriate for the determination of the application by a claims officer in accordance with this Scheme'.

D False and fraudulent applications

6.47 Occasionally, applications are revealed as being false or fraudulent. In some instances, applicants may simply invent an injury for the purpose of applying for compensation, imagine that they were the victim of an offence,[38] are injured as the result of an accident, or falsify receipts or records of their income or expenses. Under section 2 of the Fraud Act 2006, the 'dishonest making of a false representation' may readily be construed as 'a material aspect' of the application, in respect of which the applicant has 'deliberately misled a claims officer', being grounds for the repayment of the award (paragraph 110(b)). The CICA will report incidents of fraud or suspected fraud to the police, and support any prosecution.

E Paragraph 98: deferring the determination of an application

6.48 By paragraph 98 there are three circumstances in which a claims officer may defer the determination of the application. They are, first, by paragraph 98(a) 'in

[38] David Brown, 'Paedophile trial collapses over lurid claims of "serial fantasist"' (The Times, London, 19 January 2018) 10, reported that the alleged victim had succeeded in a claim to the CICA of £20,000.

exceptional cases, until the end of any criminal proceedings relating to the incident giving rise to the criminal injury which the claims officer is satisfied are material to the determination'. This is likely only where the CICA considers that the proceedings may have a bearing on the outcome of the application; for example if the applicant's assailant's defence is one of self-defence.

Secondly, determination may be deferred (paragraph 98(b)) 'until the claims officer is satisfied that the applicant has taken all reasonable steps to obtain any social security benefits, insurance payments, damages or compensation to which the applicant may be entitled in respect of the same injury'. Finally, it may be deferred where the applicant has made a request under paragraph 14; that is, is a potential victim of human trafficking or an applicant for asylum, whose status in either case has yet to be determined (Chapter 3.73). **6.49**

F Paragraphs 99–108: determination and payment

1 The CICA's approach to the determination of the application

In *R (SB) and others v First-tier Tribunal and Criminal Injuries Compensation Authority*, the three judge panel of the Upper Tribunal that was convened to determine the scope of the FTT's jurisdiction over appeals (6.143–6.148),[39] drew attention to what it considered to be the alternative approaches that the CICA brought to the determination of an application. Its choice is of particular importance to the applicant, as the comprehensiveness with which it records the reasons for its decisions can affect the applicant's request for a review or, if that is unsuccessful or the applicant wishes to challenge its decision, an appeal to the FTT. **6.50**

In the 'first approach' the claims officer considers 'each and every criterion under the scheme along the way to an award being made or not being made'. In a simple claim the claims officer will determine whether the applicant was injured in a crime of violence, whether he reported the incident to the police as soon as reasonably practicable, and what the tariff award should be. This means that the CICA must spell out 'clearly, intelligibly and comprehensively the basis on which all the criteria have been determined', at both the initial decision and on review. If a claimant has been found not eligible for an award only because he failed to meet the reporting conditions in paragraph 22, the decision would also need to address all the other eligibility criteria, for example, that there was no likelihood the assailant would benefit if an award was made (paragraph 21). **6.51**

In the 'second approach', which the panel considered likely to be the one that the CICA currently operates, decision making is taken 'in stages (whether in terms of the stages suggested by the paragraph numbering in the scheme or the evidence) **6.52**

[39] [2014] UKUT 497 (AAC), [2015] AACR 16 [97]–[99], [102] (Charles J, Judges Bano and Wright) (*SB v CICA*).

and stop at the first criterion where it is considered a (full) award cannot be made'. So if the claimant did not meet the conditions in paragraph 22, a claims officer pursuing the second approach would stop at that point, without considering what tariff might be applicable if the claim were to succeed. It follows from this approach that some issues may remain undetermined. In this case any review, and subsequent appeal would, following *SB v CICA*, only be in respect of the question of compliance with paragraph 22. This would be because it is that paragraph 'against' which that the claimant is appealing, and is that part of the review decision with which they are 'dissatisfied'.[40]

G Paragraphs 99–104: notice, acceptance, or review of the determination

6.53 By paragraph 99 'a claims officer will notify the applicant in writing of the determination of the application'. This may meet the applicant's claim in full, withhold, or reduce the amount of his claim. If he does wish to accept it, he must send written notice of his acceptance within those fifty-six days (paragraph 100). This time limit is a reduction from ninety days under the earlier schemes, primarily intended to expedite the settlement of claims. Alternatively, the applicant may seek to review the determination (paragraph 117(a)); if so, he must notify the CICA so that it receives the application for a review within those same fifty-six days (paragraph 101).

6.54 The time limit in paragraphs 100 and 101 may be extended for up to one further period of fifty-six days where there is an application for an extension within that time (paragraph 102(a)), or, if made later, only if there are 'exceptional circumstances' which meant that the applicant could not have requested an extension within that period (paragraph 102(b)).

6.55 If the applicant is dissatisfied with the review decision, or with a decision not to extend a time limit under paragraph 102, she may appeal (paragraph 125). In the former case the FTT may, while considering that appeal, by paragraph 133 direct that an interim payment is made to the applicant. If in the latter case it is allowed, the applicant must, by paragraph 131, notify the CICA within fifty-six days after the date of the appeal decision, that she either accepts the determination that it then reaches, or seeks to review it under paragraph 117(a).

6.56 If the applicant gives no time compliant notice under paragraphs 100, 101 or, having been granted an extension, under paragraph 102, 'a claims officer may withdraw the determination, and no award will be made' (paragraph 103(1)). By paragraph 103(2), this withdrawal cannot be made before the end of the period of two years starting on the day after the day on which the relevant time limit

[40] ibid [97]–[99], [102].

expires, that is, the fifty-six-day time limit in paragraphs 100 and 101, or the limit not exceeding a further fifty-six days granted under paragraph 102. A written notice of withdrawal must be sent to the applicant (paragraph 104). The applicant may seek a review of a paragraph 130 decision (paragraph 117(b)), which, if refused, may be appealed. If that is allowed the applicant must, by paragraph 130, notify the CICA within fifty-six days after the date of the appeal decision that she either accepts the determination that it then reaches, or seeks to review it under paragraph 117(a).

III Awards (Paragraphs 105–108)

A Paragraph 108: entitlement

By paragraph 108, 'subject to a direction, condition or arrangement in connection with the award under paragraph 106, the entitlement to an award only arises on the date on which the Authority receives written notice of acceptance of the determination'. This continues the position that obtained under paragraph 50 of the earlier tariff schemes. It follows, first, that no title to the award vests in an applicant until she has complied with the notification requirements in paragraph 100. Neither, secondly, does it vest if she has responded to the paragraph 99 notification by making a paragraph 101 application for a review. By section 7 of the CICA 1995, an award cannot be assigned or be made subject to a charge, or pass to the benefit of the applicant's creditors should she be declared bankrupt. **6.57**

B Paragraphs 105–107: payment

Wherever possible the CICA will, as authorized by paragraph 105, make a single lump sum payment, but in practice only where the applicant's medical condition and any entitlement to special expenses have been established. Section 3(1)(b) of the CICA 1995 provides that the scheme may make provision 'for an award to be made subject to conditions'. Maintaining the wide discretion in paragraphs 50–52 of the earlier schemes, a claims officer may, by section 106, 'give directions, impose conditions and make such other arrangements as the claims officer considers appropriate in connection with the acceptance, payment or administration of an award, including for the purpose of' the matters listed in paragraph 106(a)–(f). **6.58**

Two of these require little comment. Where the CICA considers that it is not in the applicant's best interest to make a payment as a lump sum it may provide that an award is to consist in whole or in part of an annuity (paragraph 106(d)), but which does not cover any of its associated costs. Where an adult is legally defined as not capable of managing her own affairs, it may require the appointment of a deputy or guardian (paragraph 106(e)). In the case of the three other purposes, the sections below draw on the 2012 Guide. **6.59**

1 Paragraph 106(a): interim awards

6.60 Where it is clear that the applicant is eligible for an award that is likely to be substantial, but in respect of which the long-term impact of the injury has yet to be fully understood, the CICA may by paragraph 106(a) make 'one or more interim payment'. This option has been available from the scheme's inception, and has been regularly used in such cases. However, this does not mean that a final award will inevitably follow. Under paragraph 109, a claims officer can reconsider a determination before final payment is made, which may lead to its refusal or reduction, whether or not an interim payment has been made.

2 Paragraph 106(b) and (f): establishing a trust to administer the award

6.61 By section 3(1)(d) of the CICA 1995 provision may be made 'for compensation to be held subject to trusts, in such cases as may be determined in accordance with the Scheme'. By paragraph 106(b) a claims officer may establish a trust to administer the award, 'on such terms or in accordance with such arrangements as [they] may specify'. This is likely where, having concluded that the applicant is not capable of managing his own finances, the claims officer considers that a trust will prevent an assailant benefiting from a payment, or does not think it would be in the applicant's best interests for the payment to be made as a lump sum.[41] If the value of a payment is significant, the CICA may, by paragraph 106(f), consider arrangements that will provide for 'the repayment of the award in full or in part in the event that it is no longer required by the applicant, including by means of a trust on terms which provide for unused funds to revert to the Authority'.

6.62 Paragraph 107 provides that with the exception of the cost of setting up a trust to administer an award in respect of a special expenses payment under paragraph 52(i), the CICA will not meet any costs arising 'as a result of a direction, condition or arrangement under paragraph 106'. Nor will it meet any costs where the applicant sets up a trust that the CICA has not directed, or those associated with the administration of her affairs. The only exception is where, owing to the injuries she sustained in the incident that led to the claim, the applicant does not have the capacity to manage her own affairs.

3 Paragraph 106(c): retaining the award until the applicant's 18th birthday

6.63 Where the applicant is under 18 years of age when she accepts a tariff award, a bereavement payment or a child's payment, the CICA will normally retain the full value and arrange for it to be retained in an interest-earning deposit account until the applicant's 18th birthday. If there is evidence suggesting that it would

[41] Putting the award into a trust whose funds are derived from a payment made in consequence of any personal injury to the claimant has major advantages in terms of access to means-tested benefits, as such funds are disregarded as capital; Income Support (General) Regulations 1987/ No 1967 Sched 10 para 12 and 12A.

not be in the applicant's best interests to be given a lump sum payment at that point, it may consider the use of an annuity or setting up a trust. It will also consider making a full payment if the applicant is 16 or 17 years of age and living independently.

The CICA can make payments for loss of parental services and dependency through annual advances, but only to the person with parental responsibility for the applicant. It can consider a request from that person to make the payment to a Child Trust Fund, a Junior ISA or another type of account, where the full value of the payment is protected until the applicant is 18 years old. The CICA will not meet any additional costs should the parent or guardian choose one of these options. If it continues to hold the payment, it will allow advances for the applicant's advancement, education, or long-term benefit. Failure to provide evidence that they have been used for the intended purposes will preclude any further advances. **6.64**

C Paragraphs 109–113: reconsideration and repayment

1 Reconsideration

Paragraph 53 of the earlier statutory schemes provided for the reconsideration of a decision before payment of a final award where there was new evidence or a change in the applicant's circumstances. This power is contained in paragraph 109 of the 2012 Scheme, which retains the substance of the earlier provision. It provides that 'a claims officer may reconsider a determination before final payment of an award, whether or not an interim payment has been made, where the claims officer becomes aware of evidence or a change in circumstances which, if known prior to the determination, would have affected whether an award was made or its amount'.[42] **6.65**

It is clear that reconsideration may result in the refusal of, or reduction in, the award. As the Upper Tribunal observed in *CJ v FTT*,[43] issues of eligibility may arise where the claims officer 'becomes aware of evidence' concerning, for example, the applicant's conduct, convictions or character. But the neutral terms in which the trigger conditions are (and were) expressed prompt a consideration of the question of whether paragraph 109 can result in an increase in the award, as well as a decrease or refusal. Paragraph 117(c), which provides for the circumstances in which a decision may be reviewed, refers to 'a final decision notified under paragraph 113 on reconsideration of an award', neutral terms that are consistent with either outcome. **6.66**

---

[42] In *SB v CICA* (n 39) [112] the Upper Tribunal held that the powers conferred by paras 53 and 55 were unaffected by the making of an interim payment. This also appears to be the case under para 109 of the 2012 Scheme.

[43] *CJ v FTT* (n 32) [20].

6.67 Under the earlier tariff schemes, it appeared to be the case that a reconsidered decision would have been one that was adverse to the applicant. Paragraph 58 provided that there could be a review of a claims officer's decision '(c) to withhold an award, including such decision made on reconsideration of an award under paragraphs 53–54; or (d) to make an award, including a decision to make a reduced award whether or not on reconsideration of an award under paragraphs 53–54'.

6.68 The 2012 Scheme also offers the possibility of 'an additional payment' in cases that are reopened under paragraphs 114–116. This may support the view that paragraph 109 is, in contrast, concerned only with cases in which an award would have been reduced or withheld. Headings in legislation may have some interpretive weight,[44] and it may be noted that paragraph 109 is coupled with paragraph 110 ('reconsideration and repayment'), which deals with repayment of awards where the applicant has been at fault when making the application. But there are two obvious points of difference between the terms of the relevant paragraphs.

6.69 First, paragraph 115 deals only with changes in the victim's medical condition, or where they have since died in consequence of the injury, whereas paragraph 109 does not qualify the wider scope of its trigger condition. There is, secondly, a clear difference in their temporal application. Paragraphs 114 and 115 only permit the additional payment to be made '*after a final award has been made*' (emphasis added), which may suggest that where the claims officer becomes aware of 'evidence or a change in [the applicant's] circumstance', as paragraph 109 provides, '*before final payment of an award*' (emphasis added) an increased award, including an award in respect of a change in the applicant's medical condition, could be made.

6.70 By paragraph 111 the claims officer must notify the applicant of his decision to reconsider the determination (which may be to take no further action). This suggests that it is only the claims officer who can take the initiative, the claimant's role being confined by paragraph 112 to making representations within thirty days of receiving that notification. But there is nothing in the scheme that precludes the claimant from drawing to the claims officer's attention evidence of a change in circumstances that arise after the fifty-six-day time limits in which the claimant could have sought a review (paragraphs 101 and 102), but before final payment. The earlier schemes were also silent on the question of whether the applicant had a right to request that her claim be reconsidered, and in *CJ v CICA* the Upper Tribunal observed that the equivalent provision in the earlier schemes 'can operate with or without a request for re-opening from the claimant'.[45]

[44] Diggory Bailey and Luke Norbury, *Bennion on Statutory Interpretation* (LexisNexis 2017) 16.7. Whether they are of help is entirely a matter for the tribunal; *SB v CICA* (n 39) [84].

[45] *CJ v FTT* (n 32) [11] (Judge Lane).

In summary, there appears to be no procedural obstacle to a claimant requesting a reconsideration of his claim where, following its determination, but beyond the time limits for a review, there are changes in his circumstances, of which the claims officer thereby becomes aware. These changes, or other evidence, could concern deterioration in the claimant's medical condition, a loss of employment by reason of a disability, or an element of a special expenses payment. In *R (SS) v First-tier Tribunal (CIC)*, the Upper Tribunal noted that a claimant might become alerted to an issue, not previously considered by the claims officer dealing with the tariff award, for example, concerning loss of earnings, and if the claimant wished, could raise the matter by way of 'a request for reconsideration' under the equivalent provision in the 2001 Scheme.[46] The distinction between reconsideration and reopening may therefore be a matter of timetabling. It is a reconsideration before a decision on an award is made, but a reopening afterwards. **6.71**

Finally, it may be noted that there is no equivalent in the 2012 Scheme to paragraph 55 of the earlier schemes. That paragraph provided that once the FTT had decided an appeal and under paragraph 77 had directed the claims officer make an award, any reconsideration that the officer then thought appropriate in the light of new evidence had to be referred back to the FTT. This was an exception to paragraph 53, which otherwise vested the power to reconsider a decision in the claims officer alone.[47] By paragraph 109 of the 2012 Scheme, reconsideration is now for the claims officer in all cases. **6.72**

2 Repayment

Paragraph 110(1) gives effect to section 3(1)(c) of the CICA 1995, by which provision may be made 'for the whole or any part of any compensation to be repayable in specified circumstances'. On the basis of evidence received after final payment, a claims officer may require repayment where the applicant: **6.73**

> (a) has not cooperated as far as reasonably practicable in bringing the assailant to justice; (b) has deliberately misled a claims officer in relation to a material aspect of their application; or (c) that they have received a payment in respect of which a reduction could have been made under paras 54 or 55 (receipt of social security benefits or insurance payments in respect of special expenses), or para 85 (receipt of other criminal injury compensation payments or damages).

Giving effect to the government's proposals,[48] this paragraph goes further than its equivalent under the earlier schemes, which authorized repayment of an award only in this third case.

[46] [2015] UKUT 374 (AAC) [17] (*SS v FTT*); *Colefax v FTT* (n 7) [8].

[47] *SB v CICA* (n 39) [111].

[48] Ministry of Justice (2012a) para 268, (2012b) para 215.

6.74 The application of paragraph 110(1)(b) may be illustrated by one of the issues that arose in *CJ v FTT*. One of the grounds on which the CICA had refused to reopen the case under paragraph 56 of the 1996 Scheme was that the applicant had deliberately given false or misleading information in his application.[49] Had the case concerned paragraph 53 (or paragraph 109), the CICA would have had the discretion to reconsider its decision in the light of this new evidence, but could only do this 'before actual payment of a final award' (paragraph 53) or 'before final payment of an award' (paragraph 109). If final payment has been made, paragraph 110(1)(b) provides the ground on which, in such circumstances (non-disclosure of previous convictions) a claims officer may require repayment of some or all of the award.

6.75 The amount to be repaid is, by paragraph 110(2)(a) in the case of the payments relating to the applicant's special expenses, the full amount of the award, and (b) in the case of payments under paragraph 85, the amount she has received which could have been deducted from her award. As in the case of the reconsideration of a determination, paragraph 111 requires the claims officer to notify the claimant of his decision to require repayment, paragraph 112 gives the claimant thirty days in which to give the reasons for any disagreement she may have, and by paragraph 113 the final decision on repayment must be issued to the claimant in writing. This decision may be reviewed (paragraph 117(d)), and the review decision appealed. In that case, the FTT may direct that an interim payment is made (paragraph 133), and if it allows the appeal, may by paragraph 129 'make such direction as it considers appropriate for the determination of the application by a claims officer in accordance with this Scheme'.

D Paragraphs 114–116: reopening an application

6.76 A distinguishing feature of all of the schemes has been the power to reopen final awards in narrowly defined circumstances. In paragraph 56 of the earlier tariff schemes, this discretion applied 'where there has been such a material change in the victim's medical condition that injustice would occur if the original assessment of compensation were allowed to stand, or where he has since died in consequence of the injury'. In the latter case, reopening the award would permit the CICA to make a bereavement payment, or a child's or a dependency payment to a 'qualifying claimant', in the 2012 scheme to a 'qualifying relative'. This power is retained in this case by virtue of paragraphs 114 and 115(a): a claims officer may reopen an application after a final award has been made, including when the award followed a direction by the tribunal, in order to make 'an additional payment' where the condition in paragraph 115(a) is satisfied, that is, 'a person who has accepted an award subsequently dies as a result of the criminal injury giving rise to the award'.

[49] *CJ v FTT* (n 32) [23].

The former case is governed by paragraphs 114 and 115(b) of the 2012 Scheme, where 'there has been so material a change in the medical condition of the applicant that allowing the original determination to stand would give rise to an injustice to the applicant'. The slightly different phraseology of paragraph 56 gave rise to three key questions: what constitutes a 'material' change in the applicant's medical condition, for whom would it be 'unjust' for the determination to stand, and whether, irrespective of that change, it would be 'unjust' to the applicant to take account of new evidence relating to his eligibility. The second question has been answered in paragraph 115(b) by its reference to an 'injustice *to the applicant*' (emphasis added), but both that and the third question were considered by the Upper Tribunal in *CJ v FTT,* a complex case whose reasoning continues to have relevance for the interpretation of paragraphs 114 and 115(b). **6.77**

1 A 'material' change

In *Criminal Injuries Compensation Authority v (1) Criminal Injuries Compensation Appeals Panel (Now First-Tier Tribunal (Criminal Injuries Compensation)) (2) Irene Lamb,* the Court of Appeal held that in determining whether the alleged subsequent deterioration in the applicant's (mental) health was directly attributable to the injury, the tribunal (CICAP) had failed to answer the three questions of fact required of it. These were: (1) what is the applicant's current psychiatric condition? (2) Is that condition directly attributable to the assault? and (3) has there been a material change in the applicant's psychiatric condition since the hearing in which she was made an award in respect of that assault?[50] This case was decided under paragraph 56 of the 1996 Scheme, but it is suggested that the same analysis applies to the interpretation of paragraph 115(b) of the 2012 Scheme. These questions are, in essence, questions of medical fact.[51] **6.78**

The Court's approach was very similar to its earlier interpretation of a 'serious' change in *R v Criminal Injuries Compensation Board, ex parte Williams,*[52] which, being decided under the common law scheme was not directly applicable, and to which it did not refer. That decision did, however, concern a question that may well arise under the statutory scheme, where the 'material' change in the applicant's medical condition might alternatively be attributable to a subsequent unconnected injury. **6.79**

In 1985, the applicant received an award for an injury sustained in an assault. Ten years later, following police training in self-defence, he suffered a very severe injury to his back that the medical evidence concluded was a 'summation' of his 1985 injury. The Court of Appeal held that the questions of whether there was **6.80**

[50] [2010] EWCA Civ 1433, 2010 WL 5059109 [32] (CA) (Hooper LJ).

[51] *BN v First-tier Tribunal and Criminal Injuries Compensation Authority (JR)* [2017] UKUT 175 (AAC) [9]–[11] (*BN v CICA*).

[52] [2000] PIQR Q339 (CA) (*ex parte Williams*).

a change in his medical condition, and whether it was a 'serious' change, were questions of fact. But whether that change should itself be directly attributable to the crime of violence was a question of law; in the classic formulation, was there 'an unbroken line of causation, unbroken that is by some new and intervening or supervening event which of itself is so powerful or dominant as to render the initial operating cause to be wholly nugatory'. Whether or not the line was unbroken 'must be a matter of fact and degree in every case'.[53]

6.81 *Ex parte Williams* also considered the question of how to determine whether there had been a 'serious', or under the statutory scheme, a 'material' change, where there had allegedly been an initial mis-prognosis of the applicant's medical condition. This was in issue in *R (SS) v First-tier Tribunal and Criminal Injuries Compensation Authority*.[54] In 2002, the applicant had been made an award in respect of an injury to his hand, which was increased following a review in 2007. The 2002 medical report noted that he displayed symptoms of anxiety and depression, but that these were unchanged since the incident, and concluded that he was likely to recover fully in a year's time. In accordance with the tariff, there was no separate award in 2002 for the anxiety the incident caused. In 2008, he applied to reopen his case on the ground that his mental health had deteriorated. The question of law was whether, if there had been a material change in his medical condition, the period of time to which the 'original assessment' in his case referred was the 2002 award, or the increased award in 2007.

6.82 In *ex parte Williams* the Court of Appeal had said that whether there had been a 'material change' in the applicant's medical condition was 'a matter for pure comparison between the condition of the applicant at the date of the original award, and his condition at the date when he is seeking reconsideration [reopening under paragraph 56] of the 'original award'.[55] This would suggest that the comparator is the 2002 award, but the Upper Tribunal held that this phrase must refer to the finally accepted review decision in 2007: 'Then there must be a "pure comparison" between the applicant's medical condition at that date and at the date when re-opening is being considered'.[56]

2 The 'injustice' caused by the material change

6.83 That comparison may show a change in the applicant's medical condition, but that does not mean that it was 'material' for the purpose of paragraph 115(b). It was not the CICA's practice to reopen a case where there was no chance of the result being a higher award, or where it had taken specific account of the possibility of deterioration in the applicant's medical condition. The 2001 Guide gave three examples of what, for the purpose of paragraph 56, could constitute 'such

[53] ibid [25]–[29] and [35]–[36].
[54] [2010] UKUT 410 (AAC), [2011] (AACR 21) (*SS v CICA*).
[55] *Ex parte Williams* (n 52) [26].
[56] *SS v CICA* (n 54) [27].

a material change that injustice would occur if the original assessment of compensation were allowed to stand'. These were 'injuries that seemed to be minor at the time but are now serious enough to qualify for an award, or that would now qualify for an award from a higher tariff band', or the applicant's medical condition had become so much worse that he could no longer work.[57]

But the phraseology of paragraph 56 was ambiguous. The impact of the change may well worsen the applicant's medical condition, but it could equally be 'material' in the sense that his condition had 'unexpectedly or substantially improved'. In this case, as the Upper Tribunal found, paragraph 56 'can plainly work in favour of, or against, an applicant'. Where the change worsened the applicant's condition, a further payment could be made, and where there was no such change, the assessment would stand. But where his condition had improved, the implication of the Upper Tribunal's analysis is that paragraph 56 permitted the claims officer to reopen the case, with the possibility of a reduced assessment where the original award 'would no longer be appropriate'.[58] **6.84**

There is no ambiguity as to the injustice that is addressed by paragraphs 114–116, which are headed, 'Further payment on re-opening of an application'. Paragraph 114's purpose is to make 'an additional payment' where, in the case of paragraph 115(b), the change is such that to allow the original determination to stand 'would give rise to an *injustice to the applicant*' (emphasis added). Where there has been no material change in the applicant's medical condition, whether for good or ill, the original determination will stand: there is no injustice to the applicant. **6.85**

3 Injustice and the applicant's eligibility

The third question that the Upper Tribunal considered in *CJ v FTT* was whether there would be an 'injustice' if the application to reopen the decision was refused on the grounds that it would be inappropriate to make an award because of the applicant's conduct or character, or because he had deliberately given false or misleading information in his application. The applicant had made two applications, in 1999 and 2011, in respect of the same incident in 1998. The 1999 application did not disclose either his convictions, or that he had been successful in an unrelated application in 1992. The CICA decided that his injuries did not meet the minimum award, and refused both a review and an extension to its time limit on the ground that it was well out of time. The 2011 application was also refused, and confirmed on review under paragraph 7(a) of the 2008 Scheme, the applicant having lied about his criminal record and his previous applications. **6.86**

The applicant then sought to reopen the 1999 decision. The CICA refused the application, deciding '(i) that the applicant's character was such that he was not **6.87**

---

[57] CICA (2001 Guide) Pt 2 para 16; these examples were not repeated in subsequent Guides.
[58] *CJ v FTT* (n 32) [11] and [49].

eligible for an award and (ii) that that the medical evidence did not show a material change directly attributable to the injuries sustained in the assault'. To simplify a complex chronology, the CICA maintained on review the claims officer's decision on (i), which the FTT upheld in part on appeal.[59]

6.88 Applying the ruling of the three judge panel in *SB v CICA* concerning the scope of the FTT's jurisdiction, the Upper Tribunal held that the FTT was in error. Once it had decided the issue (or issues) which was the subject of the review decision under appeal (not to reopen the refusal decision), it had fully discharged its functions, and had no power to decide any matters that had not been the subject of that decision (the matters as to eligibility). So far as the decision under review was concerned, paragraph 60 of the statutory scheme did not 'give a claims officer *carte blanche* to change *any* decision regarding *any* matter regardless of the scope of the particular provision' which they are asked to review'; it asks the claims officer to answer a specific question from a specific perspective: would there be injustice, in the changed medical circumstances, if the earlier decision remained in place.[60]

6.89 In reaching this conclusion, the Upper Tribunal rejected the CICA's submission that 'injustice' encompassed issues of bad character or convictions. The core issue in *CJ v FTT* therefore turned on the CICA's position, which was that there is a single question for the claims officer conducting the review, namely, whether it is appropriate to reopen the application, of which the change in the medical condition is only one part. The CICA has been given permission to appeal *CJ v FTT* to the Court of Appeal.

6.90 The FTT had been persuaded that to permit the claim to be reopened, with the possibility of a further award, would constitute an injustice *to the taxpayer* (emphasis added).[61] Given its explicit terms, 'injustice to the applicant', this issue cannot arise in the application of paragraph 115(b) of the 2012 Scheme. But in such a case a claims officer could, if final payment has not been made, reconsider the determination before it is made (paragraph 109), or, if it has been, require repayment (paragraph 119(1)(b)).

4 The time limit to reopen an application

6.91 The desire to do justice in these cases has always been tempered by strong bureaucratic considerations; as Briggs LJ commented in *Colefax v CICA,* 'the principles of finality and economy ... underlie those provisions of the scheme dealing with reconsideration of decisions and re-opening of cases'.[62] While limited in number,

59 ibid [24] and [30].
60 ibid [17], [22]–[23], [28] (Judge Lane).
61 ibid [37].
62 *Colefax v CICA* (n 7) [31].

reopened awards involve a substantial amount of staff time. They typically concern complex medical conditions posing difficulty in establishing both the link between the incident and the subsequent 'change', and the materiality of that change. There may in fact be no causal connection but an applicant may come to believe that her subsequent ill-health is necessarily connected to the criminal injury. Reopened awards also likely to be procedurally complex.[63]

In response to these considerations, the initial three-year limit on reopening a case was reduced to two years in the statutory scheme. By paragraph 116 of the 2012 Scheme, an application may be reopened **6.92**

> (a) within two years after the date on which the Authority received the notice of acceptance of the determination, or the date of the Tribunal's direction to make an award; or (b) if later, with supporting evidence which means that the application can be determined without further extensive enquiries by a claims officer.

These conditions are substantially the same as under paragraph 57 of the earlier schemes, and the condition in paragraph 116(b) is the same as that in paragraphs 88 and 89.

As under paragraph 56, paragraph 114 gives claims officers discretion to reopen a case with or without a request for reopening from the claimant. Where the applicant does so request, it is clearly essential that she supplies persuasive medical evidence of what could constitute the material change to her condition, and where she applies out of time, supply such other supporting evidence that will satisfy paragraph 116(b). On receipt of the request, whether in or out of time, the claims officer must first decide whether the terms of paragraph 115(b) are met. In *JY v First-tier Tribunal and Criminal Injuries Compensation Authority*, the Upper Tribunal held that paragraph 56 contains an overarching condition for all applications for medical reopening. The CICA may reject an application for reopening, even in an older case, on the basis that the paragraph 56 condition is not met. In that case, it follows that the claims officer does not have to rely on, or address the conditions in, paragraph 57 for extending the time limit.[64] **6.93**

Although the tribunal did not have to deal with paragraph 57, it noted that there was a potential ambiguity in the dual reference to 'the application', and where it is out of time, 'the renewed application'. It held that the 'need for extensive enquiries' could only refer to the applicant's substantive case for compensation, and not to any enquiries in connection with the application to reopen the case.[65] **6.94**

---

63 *R (Criminal Injuries Compensation Authority) v First-tier Tribunal and Harris* [2016] EWHC 2463 (Admin); *R (Criminal Injuries Compensation Authority) v First-tier Tribunal and MB* [2016] EWHC 2745 (Admin), [2016] ACD [26]–[27] (*CICA v MB*).

64 [2016] UKUT 101 (AAC) [28].

65 ibid [29].

6.95 By paragraph 117(g) the applicant may seek a review of a decision not to reopen his application. If a claims officer does decide to reopen it, paragraph 124 provides that in this case it will be the same officer who will determine the application; an applicant who is dissatisfied with that determination may appeal it (paragraph 125). Should the claims officer decide not to reopen the application, the applicant may appeal to the FTT, which, before allowing it, must apply the same test as in paragraph 114(b), that is, be satisfied that the application can be determined without further extensive enquiries by a claims officer. If it does allow the appeal, 'the Authority will re-open the case' (paragraph 132).

IV Review (Paragraphs 117–124)

A Introduction

6.96 By section 4 of the CICA 1995, the scheme 'shall include provision for the review, in such circumstances as may be specified, of any decision taken in respect of a claim for compensation'. The possibility of a review of the claims officer's determination was introduced in the statutory scheme with a view to delivering decisions more quickly, cutting out unnecessary appeals, and, by requiring applicants to have been through the review process before formally appealing, relieving some of the pressure on the appeals process. It was also thought that reviews would assist quality control.

B Paragraphs 117–118: grounds for a review

6.97 The seven grounds provided by paragraph 117 upon which an applicant may seek a review are listed below. These supersede, reorder, rephrase and add to the six grounds set out in part 58(1) of the earlier tariff schemes, included in parentheses by way of comparison. An applicant may seek a review of:

(a) a decision as to the determination of an award or its amount, including on reopening under paragraph 114; (paragraph 58(1)(d): to make an award, including a decision to make a reduced award)
(b) a decision under paragraph 103 to withdraw a determination; (paragraph 58(1)(f): to withdraw an award under paragraph 50(1))
(c) a final decision notified under paragraph 113 on reconsideration of an award; (paragraph 58(1)(f): to make an award, including a decision to make a reduced award on reconsideration of an award under paragraphs 53–54, and paragraph 58(1)(c): to withhold an award, including such decision made on reconsideration of an award under paragraphs 53–54)
(d) a final decision notified under paragraph 113 to require repayment or partial repayment of an award; (paragraph 58(1)(e): to require repayment of an award under paragraph 49)

(e) a decision not to extend a time limit under paragraph 89, 102 or 120; (paragraph 58(1)(a): not to waive or extend the time limit in paragraph 18 (application for compensation) or paragraph 59 (application for review))
(f) a decision in respect of medical evidence under paragraph 94(a) or a deduction under paragraph 96, and
(g) a decision not to reopen an application under paragraph 114; (paragraph 58(1)(b): not to reopen a case under paragraphs 56–57).

By paragraph 118, there are two categories of decision that may not be the subject of review: 'an applicant may not seek a review of a decision made on review or appeal'. An applicant who is dissatisfied with the CICA's decision made on review may appeal to the tribunal, but cannot seek a review of that decision. Neither may the decision that the CICA has made following a successful appeal be reviewed, since that decision was itself the outcome of the applicant's successful appeal. **6.98**

C Paragraphs 119–120: time limits to apply for a review

Within fifty-six days of the date of notification of the determination of her application, the applicant may, by paragraph 101, notify the CICA that she wishes to seek a review.[66] The application for review itself must, by paragraph 119, be sent so that the CICA receives it within those fifty-six days; it 'must be made in writing and be accompanied by the grounds on which review is sought and any supporting evidence'. By paragraph 120, that time limit may be extended for one further period of up to fifty-six days on the same terms as apply in paragraph 102, for which the applicant will need to enclose any additional evidence that she wishes the CICA to consider. By paragraph 121, any extension of time will be decided by a claims officer 'other than the claims officer who made the decision to which that application relates'. **6.99**

D Paragraphs 121–124: conducting the review

Paragraph 121 gives effect to section 4(2) of the CICA 1995, which provides that 'any such review must be conducted by a person other than the person who made the decision under review'. The claim is considered afresh on the basis of the original application, together with the reasons for requesting the review, and any additional information provided by the applicant, or that the claims officer has sought. It is important to stress that an applicant who 'wishes to seek a review' (paragraph 101), has thereby not accepted the CICA's determination of his application. Paragraph 121 then provides: 'the claims officer who conducts the **6.100**

[66] In 2017/2018 the proportion of first decisions proceeding to review increased, to 23% in consequence of the late 2016/2017 decisions; CICA (2018) Table 5.

review will not be bound by any previous decision made in connection with the application'.

6.101 It therefore continues to be the case that an application for review carries the risk that the claims officer may come to a wholly different conclusion on the particular matters that were dealt with in the decision being reviewed. The original decision may be unchanged, or may be more favourable to the applicant, but as the 2012 Guide cautions, 'it is also possible that you will get a lower payment or no payment at all'. An applicant who has been made an award reduced by 25 per cent because of his conduct at the time of the incident, runs the risk that the claims officer will take a more serious view.

6.102 Irrespective of the particular ground on which the applicant requested a review, the broad terms of paragraph 121 also imply that the claims officer may consider any other matters as to eligibility or amount than those directly engaged by that decision, as was expressly provided by paragraph 60 of the earlier schemes. This possibility raises the same issue that was considered in *CJ v FTT* where, following *SB v CICA*, the Upper Tribunal held that the FTT has no jurisdiction to consider any matter beyond that which is the subject of the appeal. As summarized earlier (6.88–6.89), the CICA's position is that its decision on review remains part of a claims process that is yet to reach the single decision, whether or not the claimant is eligible for an award. That decision is, in its turn, subject to an appeal to the FTT.

6.103 By paragraph 122, unless paragraph 124 applies, that is, where they decide on a review to reopen an application, the claims officer conducting the review must send the applicant written notice of the review decision; the applicant may accept the review decision, or appeal it. But an applicant cannot 'both accept an award and appeal it'. The Court of Appeal commented:

> The reasons for the clear demarcation between acceptance of the determination and the payment of an award on one hand, and the rejection of the determination and review/appeal on the other, were obvious: the need for finality and certainty in awards made and administered by CICA. Good public administration required finality because public authorities needed to have certainty as to the legal validity of their decisions and actions, and third parties needed to be able to rely on those decisions and actions.[67]

If the CICA does not receive a notice of appeal in respect of it, paragraph 123 provides that a claims officer will proceed to determine the application in accordance with the review decision.

[67] *R (on the application of Mongson) v Upper Tribunal* (AAC), Court of Appeal (Civil Division), Unreported 8 March 2018 (*Mongson v Upper Tribunal*).

V Appeals (Paragraphs 125–134)

A Introduction

By section 5(1) of the CICA 1995 the scheme 'shall include provision for rights of appeal to the First-tier Tribunal against decisions taken on reviews under provisions of the Scheme made by virtue of section 4'.[68] Appeals are heard under arrangements that were introduced by the Tribunals, Courts and Enforcement Act 2007 (TCEA 2007), transferring the CICAP to the Tribunals Service with effect from 3 November 2008.[69] The Social Entitlement Chamber of the FTT, established by section 3(1) of the TCEA 2007, is assigned all functions relating to 'proceedings concerning the payment of compensation under a scheme made under the Criminal Injuries Compensation Act 1995';[70] its procedures are set out in the Tribunal Procedure (First-Tier Tribunal) (Social Entitlement Chamber) Rules (FTT Rules).[71] **6.104**

By section 5(9) of the CICA 1995 Act the power conferred by section 3(1)(a) to provide for the reduction of an amount of compensation, includes power to provide for a reduction where the appeal is frivolous or vexatious. Maintaining the position under the earlier schemes, paragraph 134 provides that it may do so in three cases. These are: where it is hearing an appeal concerning the determination of an award or its amount, including on reopening under paragraph 114 (paragraph 117(a)), a final decision under paragraph 113 on reconsideration of an award (paragraph 117(c)), or a final decision notified under paragraph 113 to require repayment or partial repayment of an award (paragraph 117(d)). **6.105**

Two further points may be noted. The members and staff of the FTT are entirely independent of the CICA, and subject to the limits in *SB v CICA*, will consider the whole claim afresh. As is the case with a review, the CICA's decision may be upheld, or be more or be less favourable than its decision. For example, in *SS v FTT* the FTT increased from 25 per cent to 50 per cent the reduction imposed by the CICA on account of the applicant's conduct at the time of the incident.[72] **6.106**

Secondly, the FTT has no power to award costs (FTT rule 10), but by FTT rule 16(2)(b) may make provision for the necessary expenses incurred by a person, not being a party to the proceedings, who has been summonsed to attend a hearing, to be paid, and state who is to pay that person. In addition, by FTT rule 20 the **6.107**

[68] Section 5(1) was substituted for s 5(1)–(7) by the Transfer of Tribunal Functions Order SI 2008/2833. In 2017/2018 the overall appeal rate was 3.5% (2.4% in 2016/2017); that is, 96.5% of decisions on review are final; CICA (2018) Table 5.

[69] ibid Sch 3 para 124(a).

[70] The First-tier Tribunal and Upper Tribunal (Chambers) Order 2008, SI 2008/2684 art 3(b).

[71] 2008 SI 2008/2685 (L13), in force on 21 August 2015; generally, GOV.UK, *Criminal injuries compensation tribunal.*

[72] *SS v FTT* (n 46) [7].

FTT may meet reasonable expenses '(a) incurred by the appellant, or any person who attends a hearing to give evidence, in attending the hearing; or (b) incurred by the appellant in connection with any arrangements made by the Tribunal for the inspection of the appellant's injury'. The tribunal will also pay a reasonable fee where the CICA has agreed with the appellant that a specialist report is necessary; save in exceptional circumstances, it will not normally direct the CICA to reimburse the appellant for such a report where there was no agreement to commission it.[73]

B Paragraphs 125–128: notice and formalities of appeal

6.108 The 2012 Guide outlines the main steps for initiating an appeal, whose conditions are set out in Chapter 1 (Before the hearing) of Part 3 (Proceedings before the Tribunal) of the FTT Rules. When it sends the applicant its review decision the CICA also sends the form to use to ask for an appeal. This may relate to a decision on a review, or a determination on reopening under paragraph 124 (paragraph 125). The appellant is required to complete the form explaining why she thinks the decision was wrong, enclosing a copy of the CICA's decision, and providing any extra material which supports her reasons for an appeal, such as medical records or evidence of loss of earnings (FTT rules 22(3) and (4)). This notice of appeal must be sent so that the tribunal receives it within ninety days of the decision being challenged (FTT rule 22(2)(b)), a time limit that the tribunal may, by rule 5(3)(a), extend. When it receives a copy of this notice the CICA (i.e. 'the decision-maker') has forty-two days within which to respond to the tribunal, providing any written record of the decision under challenge, any statement of reasons for that decision if not sent with the notice, and copies of all documents relevant to the case. This response and its accompanying documents must be sent to the appellant, who has one month within which to respond to the tribunal (FTT rule 24).

6.109 Where, following the CICA's response to the notice of appeal, the FTT is satisfied that an oral hearing is required to determine whether or not the applicant is eligible for an award under the relevant scheme, the appeal will be listed for a hearing on eligibility on the first available date after one month from the date of its response. The tribunal will hear only the issues that were raised in the response, refusing any that the CICA has not raised, unless it shows good cause for the delay, 'or there is new evidence or a change in circumstances', evidence that could relate to the disentitling conditions in paragraphs 25–27. If the tribunal decides in the appellant's favour, it will proceed to assess compensation at that hearing, but only if there is sufficient evidence fairly so to do.[74]

---

[73] Courts and Tribunals Judiciary, *Criminal Injuries Compensation Tribunal—Rules and Legislation, Practice Statement CI-3* para 2.

[74] Courts and Tribunals Judiciary, *Criminal Injuries Compensation Tribunal—Rules and Legislation, Practice Statement CI-2*.

It may be that when they receive a copy of the notice of appeal, the CICA decides, under paragraph 126(a), that the review decision under appeal was made in error, in which case it will (para 126(b)) send written notice of a revised review decision to the applicant. On receipt of a revised review decision the applicant must, by paragraph 27, 'send written notice to the Authority and the Tribunal of: (a) acceptance of the revised review decision; or (b) rejection of that decision'. If the CICA receives a paragraph 127(a) notice and a claims officer is satisfied that the applicant has withdrawn his appeal in accordance with the FTT Rules, 'the application will be determined in accordance with the revised review decision' (paragraph 128). FTT rules 17(2) and (3) provide that a notice of withdrawal will not take effect unless the tribunal consents to it. **6.110**

C Extending the time limit for giving notice of appeal

FTT rule 5(1) of its case management powers provides that 'subject to the provisions of [TCEA 2001] and any other enactment, the Tribunal may regulate its own procedure', and by rule 5(3) 'in particular, and without restricting the general powers in paragraphs (1) and (2), the Tribunal may—(a) extend or shorten the time for complying with any rule, practice direction or direction'. Inevitably, there have been a number of cases in which the notice has been late, which has raised the questions, what factors should the FTT take into account when determining whether to extend the time limit under rule 5(3)(a), and, if it does extend it, whether there is any limit to the exercise of its discretion. These questions were considered in a sequence of judicial review applications heard by the Upper Tribunal, comprehensively reviewed by Judge Wikeley in *YT v First-tier Tribunal (SEC)*.[75] This section draws extensively and in particular on Appendix 2 to his judgment in that case. **6.111**

The first of the 'key principles in the Upper Tribunal's case law'[76] is that its 'power to extend time is unfettered and the circumstances which will be relevant in exercising it will vary from case to case'. In reaching this conclusion in *R (CD) v First-tier Tribunal (Criminal Injuries Compensation Authority)*,[77] Judge Turnbull relied in particular on *Information Commissioner v PS*[78] and *OFSTED v AF*,[79] two decisions dealing with other areas of the FTT's jurisdiction to which a close variant of rule 5(3)(a) applies.[80] **6.112**

That power must, secondly, 'be exercised judicially and in accordance with the overriding objective in rule 2' of the FTT Rules; in essence, 'fairly and justly'. In **6.113**

[75] [2013] UKUT] 201 (AAC) (*YT v CICA*).
[76] ibid Appendix 2 [2.5].
[77] [2010] UKUT 181 (AAC), [2011] AACR 1 [26].
[78] [2011] UKUT 94 (AAC).
[79] [2011] UKUT 72 (AAC), [2011] AACR 32 [21].
[80] *YT v CICA* (n 75) Appendix 2 [1.1]–[1.2].

R (KS) v First-tier Tribunal the Upper Tribunal held that this in turn means that the FTT must 'take account of any factor that is rationally related to the proper judicial exercise of the power to extend time'. This includes the length of and reasons for the delay, the chances of the appeal succeeding if the application is granted, and the degree of administrative prejudice to the CICA if the application is granted. Its sole concentration in this case on the reasons for the delay excluded any consideration of these other factors.[81]

6.114 The decision in *KS v FTT* also raised the question of whether it was appropriate for the Upper Tribunal to give guidance to the FTT on how it should exercise its power under rule 5(3)(a). The CICA argued in *CD v FTT* that it should, where they apply,[82] have regard to the matters listed in rule 3.9 of the Civil Procedure Rules (relief from sanctions), such as the interests of the administration of justice, whether the application for relief has been made promptly, whether the failure to comply was intentional, and whether there is a good explanation for the failure.[83] In *R (JA) v First-tier Tribunal and Criminal Injuries Compensation Authority* Judge Jacobs agreed with the Upper Tribunal's clear view in *CD v FTT*, repeated in *OFSTED v AF* and *KS v FTT*,[84] that while it was in order draw attention to 'the range of information' that the FTT had to take into account, 'it is something altogether different to tell a tribunal how to exercise its discretion in relation to that information'.[85]

6.115 This caution was firmly endorsed by Judge Wikeley in *YT v CICA*. Provided that the FTT had correctly met its public law responsibilities when engaged in what is a 'classic discretionary decision' under rule 5(3)(a), the Upper Tribunal held that it is not its role to question *how* relevant the FTT found them to be when applied to the facts of the case, but it is its role to identify *what* those factors might be.[86] In the present case, which concerned delays brought about by the tardiness of the applicant's solicitor to proceed with her claim, those factors included but were not limited to (i) the length of the delay:, (ii) the reasons for the delay, (iii) the consequences of the delay, (iv) the merits of the case, (v) the fact that the applicant appeared to have an alternative remedy in negligence against her solicitor's firm, and (vi) the applicant's health and personal circumstances.[87]

6.116 One of the 'wider' issues raised in *YT v CICA* was whether it was appropriate for the FTT to consider the merits of an applicant's claim when exercising its

[81] [2012] UKUT 281 (AAC), [2013] AACR 9 [11] (*KS v CICA*).
[82] *BPP Holdings Ltd v Revenue and Customs Commissioners* [2017] UKSC 55, [2017] 1 WLR 2945 [23]–[26].
[83] Civil Procedure Rules 1998, SI 1998/3132 (CPR 1998).
[84] This sequence is summarized in *YT v CICA* (n 75) Appendix 2 [2.1]–[2.7].
[85] [2013] 457 (AAC) [8] (*JA v CICA*).
[86] *YT v CICA* (n 75) [40]–[41] and Appendix 2 [3.4]–[3.11].
[87] ibid [34] and [42]–[43].

discretion under rule 5(3)(a). Their significance will vary, but the key point is that to exclude them as a matter of course would be inconsistent with the fundamental point confirmed in *CD v FTT*, that the power to extend time is unfettered, and that rule 5(3)(a) 'is left wholly unqualified'.[88]

The FTT's refusal to extend the time limit in *JA v CICA* was therefore defective because it did not enquire into or consider the potential merits of the applicant's appeal.[89] The 'narrow' issue in *YT v CICA* concerned the lawfulness of the FTT's rejection of the applicant's late notice of appeal on the ground that she had 'an open and shut case' against her solicitor's firm for their professional negligence in handling her claim. In treating that as a more or less conclusive reason for its decision, the FTT had fettered its discretion.[90] **6.117**

D The First-tier Tribunal's procedures

The FTT's procedures are necessarily extensive and cannot be fully examined here;[91] but the tribunal will explain its procedures when it receives the applicant's request for an appeal. **6.118**

When implementing them the FTT is, as CPR 1998 and the Criminal Procedure Rules 2015 also provide,[92] under an obligation to give effect to the FTT Rules' overriding objective, and to the parties' obligation to cooperate with the tribunal. The overriding objective is to enable the tribunal to deal with cases fairly and justly (rule 2(1)). This includes: **6.119**

> (a) dealing with the case in ways which are proportionate to the importance of the case, the complexity of the issues, the anticipated costs and the resources of the parties; (b) avoiding unnecessary formality and seeking flexibility in the proceedings; (c) ensuring, so far as practicable, that the parties are able to participate fully in the proceedings; (d) using any special expertise of the Tribunal effectively; and (e) avoiding delay, so far as compatible with proper consideration of the issues.

Compliance with the overriding objective has particular significance where the FTT is minded to reach a decision that is adverse to an applicant, and in such cases the Upper Tribunal will scrutinize its decision closely.

By FTT rule 2.3, the CICA must seek to give effect to the overriding objective when it '(a) exercises any power under these Rules', or '(b) interprets any rule or practice direction'. This may mean that when reviewing the circumstances that led to the very lengthy delay in the application, the interests of justice may 'demand' that the applicant be given the opportunity to challenge the (CICB's) refusal to **6.120**

---

[88] ibid Appendix 2 [3.12]–[3.17], [26]–[27].
[89] *JA v CICA* (n 85) [7].
[90] *YT v CICA* (n 75) [6] and Appendix 2 (n N) [5.1]–[5.3].
[91] Edward Jacobs, *Tribunal Practice and Procedure* (4th edn, Legal Action Group 2016).
[92] Ministry of Justice (2015b), *Rules and Practice Directions*.

allow it.[93] Finally, the parties must, by rule 2(4) '(a) help the Tribunal to further the overriding objective; and (b) co-operate with the Tribunal generally'.

1 Hearings

6.121 (a) **Preliminaries** Given the scope of paragraph 117, it is possible that the review decision will have dealt with both an issue of eligibility and of an award. The claims officer may have decided that the claimant did not cooperate with the CICA, and applied, for example, a 50 per cent reduction to the assessment that she then made in respect of the injury. In *SB v CICA* the Upper Tribunal observed that in such a case it may be sensible for the FTT to hold separate hearings on the two issues under appeal. If so, rule 5(3)(e) provides that the FTT 'may deal with an issue in the proceedings as a preliminary issue', and if invoked and the preliminary issue were decided, 'the time limit for judicial review of that decision would run from the date of the decision or written reasons being given for it.[94] In short, 'care may therefore need to be taken by [the FTT] when faced with deciding more than one issue on an appeal'.[95]

6.122 The provisions governing hearings are contained in Chapter 2 (Hearings) of Part 3 of the FTT Rules. By rule 28 each party to the proceedings is entitled to attend a hearing. In a criminal injuries compensation case this must be held in private unless the appellant has consented to its being held in public, and the FTT considers that it is in the interests of justice to do so (rule 30(2)). Where it is held in public, the FTT has power to exclude persons who might be disruptive, likely to prevent a witness from giving evidence or making submissions freely, whose attendance would defeat the purpose of the hearing, or to give effect to a direction under rule 14(2) prohibiting the disclosure of evidence (FTT rule 30(5)). Witnesses may be excluded until they have given evidence (rule 30(6)), after which they may be permitted to remain 'as moral support' for the appellant.[96]

6.123 The tribunal's procedures for listing a hearing are set out in Practice Statement CI-5. In short, it aims to list a case for an oral hearing as soon as possible after the appellant and the CICA have provided all the required documents, or following a request made by either party giving notice that the appeal should be listed. It must give the CICA and the appellant 'reasonable notice of the time and place of the hearing', that is, at least fourteen days, and of any adjourned or postponed hearing, or of changes to the time and place of the hearing. There must be 'compellingly good reasons' to displace 'the presumption' that the tribunal will refuse the postponement of an agreed hearing date;[97] any request on the day to postpone

---

93 *CICA v MB* (n 63) [23].

94 The Tribunal Procedure (Upper Tribunal) Rules 2008, SI 2008/2698 (L 15) r 28(2) and (3)(a).

95 *SB v CICA* (n 39) [104].

96 *SS v FTT* (n 46) [6].

97 Courts and Tribunals Judiciary, *Criminal Injuries Compensation Tribunal—Rules and Legislation, Practice Statement CI-5* para 8.

it will be considered by the panel. If the appellant (or, which is unlikely, the CICA) fails to attend, the tribunal may proceed with the hearing if it is satisfied that they have been notified or that reasonable steps have been taken to notify them of the hearing, and it considers that it is in the interests of justice to proceed (FTT rule 31)).

Assuming the preceding provisions are met, rule 27(1) provides that the tribunal 'must hold a hearing before making a decision which disposes of proceedings unless (a) each party has consented to, or has not objected to, the matter being decided without a hearing; and (b) the Tribunal considers that it is able to decide the matter without a hearing'. But FTT rule 27(4) specifically provides that 'in a criminal injuries compensation case—(a) the Tribunal may make a decision which disposes of proceedings without a hearing'. The obligation to hold a hearing does not extend to 'correcting, setting aside, reviewing and appealing Tribunal decisions' dealt with under Part 4 of the Rules. Nor does it have to hold a hearing if the case has been struck out (rules 8 and 27(3)). **6.124**

(b) Striking out and the refusal of a hearing FTT rule 8(3)(c) provides that a claim may be struck out if 'the Tribunal considers there is no reasonable prospect of the appellant's case, or part of it, succeeding'. This power is, as the Upper Tribunal stressed in *NT v First-tier Tribunal (CIC),* permissive, not mandatory. The FTT was wrong in law when it concluded that '*it had no alternative* but to strike out the appeal (as having no reasonable prospect of success)' (original emphasis).[98] But where the appellant had accepted the CICA's decision on review, the FTT was right to strike out the appeal under rule 8.2 because it had no jurisdiction to hear it, and the Upper Tribunal was wrong to hold otherwise.[99] **6.125**

Given that striking out inevitably deprives the appellant of a hearing, it 'is a drastic step', or as Judge Lane put it in *CJ v FTT,* 'a draconian power of last resort'.[100] Its exercise may be largely unobjectionable where, as in *AM v FTT* 'the issue is a straightforward point of law arising on uncontentious facts, since an appeal on a point of law or judicial review provides an adequate remedy in the event of a Tribunal being wrong',[101] or by reason of a provision in the scheme the appeal 'cannot possibly succeed'.[102] But it is not appropriate to strike out a case where as in *NT v FTT, CJ v FTT,* and *AM v FTT,* 'there are unresolved issues of fact requiring the hearing of evidence', or as in *MM v FTT and CICA*, where the very limited evidence of a historic sexual offence 'might not be remedied otherwise than by an oral hearing'.[103] **6.126**

98 [2014] UKUT 210 (AAC) [17] (*NT v FTT*).
99 *Mongson v Upper Tribunal* (n 67).
100 *CJ v FTT* (n 32) [44].
101 *AM v FTT* (n 12) [19] (Judge Rowland).
102 *FL v First-tier Tribunal and Criminal Injuries Compensation Authority* [2010] UKUT 158 (AAC) [8].
103 *MM v FTT and CICA* (n 6) [14]–[15] (Judge Jacobs).

6.127 Moreover, the choice of oral argument is particularly acute where the claimant is representing himself, the issue being one that is to be determined as a matter of discretion. Given that different tribunals may reasonably take different views as to the facts, which might in turn comprise the difference between a successful and an unsuccessful appeal, 'it is in principle inappropriate to pre-empt a Tribunal from hearing the substantive appeal by striking out proceedings under rule 8(3)(c), at least without an oral hearing'.[104]

6.128 Similarly, the Upper Tribunal will scrutinize closely the use of FTT rule 27(4) to deprive the claimant of an oral hearing, and will not hesitate to quash the FTT's decision where it should not have been so used.[105] There may be disputed or limited evidence of the incident, or of the injury and its impact on the claimant that needs to be resolved for the appeal to be properly determined. The bungled police investigation into the applicant's claim that she had been raped was one of the many factors in *AG v CICA* that required a hearing. And in *TG v First-tier Tribunal and Criminal Injuries Compensation Authority* the FTT gave no reasons at all for not offering the applicant the opportunity of an oral hearing, given the complexity of the factual background to the claim, and her 'obvious difficulties in keeping to the most relevant matters when expressing herself in writing'.[106]

6.129 A common theme in the Upper Tribunal's criticism of the FTT's decisions in these cases was to question its compliance with the overriding objective in rule 2(1) to deal with cases 'fairly and justly', and to exercise its discretion judicially when striking out a case,[107] or refusing a hearing.[108] One particular aspect of 'fair' treatment of the appellant, is that the FTT should not challenge the appellant's honesty or integrity where there has been no hearing and no chance to respond to the matters leading to such a challenge.[109]

6.130 A second issue that fell to be decided in *NT v FTT* was the nature of the appellant's remedy. By rule 27(4)(a), the FTT may make a decision which disposes of proceedings without a hearing and, if it does so, (b) either side may, within a month of receiving its decision (rule 27(6)) apply in writing for the decision to be reconsidered at a hearing. This application may not be made in relation to a decision (a) not to extend a time limit, (b) not to set aside a previous decision, (c) not to allow an appeal against a decision not to extend a time limit, or (d) not to allow an appeal against a decision not to reopen a case (FTT rule 27(5)). The question was

[104] *AM v FTT* (n 12) [19] (Judge Rowland).

[105] *AG v First-tier Tribunal and Criminal Injuries Compensation Authority* [2013] UKUT 357 (AAC) [32] (*AG v CICA*).

[106] [2013] UKUT 399 (AAC) [28] (Judge Levenson).

[107] *NT v FTT* (n 98) [23].

[108] *AG v CICA* (n 107) [28].

[109] ibid [30]–[31].

whether an application not to strike out the claim was similarly excluded when rule 27(4) was read subject to rules 27(1) and (3).

The Upper Tribunal held that FTT rule 27(4) created 'a free-standing regime for criminal injuries compensation cases', which, as rule 27(5) does not list striking out leaves the way open for its reconsideration. In having limited rights of appeal, criminal injury compensation cases 'are unique'. Unlike other SEC cases there is, as section 11 of the TCEA 2007 provides, no appeal against any decision of the FTT made in compliance with section 5(1)(a) of the CICA 1995.[110] **6.131**

2 The conduct of a hearing

Under its case management rules the FTT may regulate its own procedures for the conduct of a hearing: deciding its form, requiring a party to produce a bundle for, and adjourning or postponing, the hearing (rule 5(3)(g)–(i)). Rule 14 concerns the use and disclosure of documents. The hearing will usually be held in the area covered by the police force which investigated the crime, and be attended by two or three tribunal judges or members, a clerk, a representative from the CICA and any witnesses. **6.132**

The FTT may, on its own initiative or on the parties' application **6.133**

> require any person to attend as a witness at a hearing at the time and place specified in the summons or citation and order them to answer any questions or produce any documents they possess or control which relate to any issue in the proceedings (rule 16(1)). The summons or citation must give 14 days' notice of the hearing or such shorter period as the Tribunal may direct, but by rule 16(3) 'no person may be compelled to give any evidence or produce any document that the person could not be compelled to give or produce on a trial of an action in a court of law in the part of the United Kingdom where the proceedings are due to be determined.

These documents, and the issues to which they give rise, and upon which the tribunal may seek clarification or explanation, are necessary precursors to the performance of its inquisitorial function. Its role, in particular in claims such as that in *MJ (No 1)*, is to examine and to seek to verify the facts upon which the claim is based where they are contested or unclear.[111]

It is unlikely that the offender will be called as one of the witnesses, who are most likely to be a police officer familiar with the case, and in medically complex case, a medical expert. Where the circumstances surrounding the incident are unclear or in dispute, the role of the police will be relevant, but the FTT must not accept their evidence as being determinative of any questions of fact to which it gave rise. In appearing in *Criminal Injuries Compensation Authority v RS*,[112] a case that turned on whether the claimant had been closely involved in the 'immediate **6.134**

[110] *NT v FTT* (n 98) [34]–[36].
[111] *MJ (No 1)* (n 15) [18]–[33].
[112] [2012] UKUT 205 (AAC), [2013] AACR 34 (Walker J, Judges Levenson and Bano).

aftermath' of his wife's criminal injury (Chapter 2.135), 'to have sought, and accepted, the subjective evidence of a police officer on a matter which it was for it to decide', the FTT had abrogated its duty as a tribunal of fact.

6.135 Noting that this was not the first time that the FTT had accepted the evidence of the police officer who attended the incident as determinative of any questions of fact to which it gave rise, the three judge panel set down authoritative guidance on the proper role of the police when giving evidence. The principles it described 'are of fundamental importance and are of general application', and a failure to respect them 'runs the risk of undermining confidence in the judicial independence which is the cornerstone of the modern tribunal system'. They are summarized here.

6.136 As with any other witness, a police officer can give evidence on what she perceived through her five senses. The tribunal may also hear the officer's evidence of what other witnesses said or heard (hearsay evidence is admissible) and, taken in sum, may be minded to accept these accounts as true. In making a finding of that kind, the tribunal is not relying on the opinion of the police officer but on the police officer's evidence of fact as to what was said, and done; and before accepting this account of events will consider any relevant evidence going to credibility and accuracy as regards both the officer, and those who gave their accounts to the officer.

6.137 But in this case, in its acceptance of the officer's opinion as to the duration of the attack upon the claimant's wife,

> the tribunal appears to have misconceived – and perhaps abrogated—its duty. Acceptance of what the officer had said ... involved having regard to the officer's personal opinion. That opinion was irrelevant to the functions that the tribunal needed to perform. Moreover, those functions are judicial functions which are to be performed without interference by the executive arm of the state.

The panel concluded:

> When deciding factual matters, in the absence of some special need for expert assistance, it is in principle wrong for tribunals to ask police officers for their opinions as to what happened, as opposed to receiving (1) the officer's evidence about what the officer perceived and what others have told the officer about what they perceived, and (2) any evidence the officer can properly give on matters which go to the credibility and accuracy of the officer's evidence and the account of events given by others.[113]

6.138 These strictures, which the CICA accepted,[114] apply equally to any misplaced reliance on the evidence of a police officer who offers his understanding of provisions of the criminal law:

> The Upper Tribunal has said often enough that it is for the First-tier Tribunal itself to establish what the law is and how to apply it, and that police officers are not

---

[113] ibid [22]–[26], applied in *Criminal Injuries Compensation Authority v First-tier Tribunal and AS* [2017] UKUT 43 (AAC) [81]–[88].

[114] *CICA v RS* [2013] EWCA Civ 1040, [2014] 1 WLR 1313 [7]–[9] (CA).

expert witnesses in relation to legal provisions, although they are often expert witnesses as to procedure, and clearly can be witnesses as to fact.[115]

Where the application relates to the physical or sexual abuse of adults or children, the parties may wish to call as a witness a child, a vulnerable adult within the meaning of section 60 of the Safeguarding Vulnerable Groups Act 2006,[116] or a 'sensitive witness' within the meaning of the 2008 Tribunals Practice Direction.[117] In these cases, the witness will only be required to attend and give evidence where the tribunal determines that the evidence is necessary to enable a fair hearing of the case, and the witness's welfare would not be prejudiced by doing so. Should the witness be called, the FTT may direct that the evidence be given by telephone, video link, or other means, or otherwise consider how to facilitate the giving of evidence. **6.139**

In cases involving (historic) sexual abuse of children and adults, the applicant or the CICA may wish to call expert psychiatric or medical evidence. This expert opinion evidence may be relevant, but it is still for the FTT to make its own findings of fact as to the impact of the injury, as it is in such other cases as the acceleration or exacerbation of a pre-existing injury (Chapter 5.38–5.41), or of the impact of 'a material change' in the applicant's medical condition where an application has been reopened (6.76–6.95). **6.140**

By rule 15(1), the FTT may give directions as to the issues on which, and the nature of, evidence or submissions it requires, on the number of witnesses, or expert witnesses required or permitted. It may admit evidence whether or not it would be admissible in a civil trial in the United Kingdom, thus including hearsay, or was available to a previous decision-maker. It may exclude otherwise admissible evidence where it was not provided within the time allowed by, or in a manner compliant with, a direction or a practice direction, or 'it would otherwise be unfair to admit the evidence' (rule 15(2)). **6.141**

If it is the applicant who is appealing, the hearing typically proceeds with the presentation of his case, calling his witnesses. A representative from the CICA will usually attend in order to explain its decision (a 'presenting officer'). The FTT will ask the presenting officer and the applicant about the crime and resulting injuries, which may disclose inconsistencies in their evidence. Where this suggests that the applicant is seeking to mislead the tribunal, it should warn the applicant of the possible consequences and, if satisfied that that was the applicant's intention, **6.142**

---

115 *Criminal Injuries Compensation Authority v First-tier Tribunal and BW* [2017] UKUT 97 (AAC) [17] (Judge Levenson).

116 'Any adult to whom an activity which is a regulated activity relating to vulnerable adults by virtue of any paragraph of paragraph 7(1) of Schedule 4 is provided.'

117 Courts and Tribunals Judiciary, *Practice Direction, First Tier and Upper Tribunal Child, Vulnerable Adult and Sensitive Witnesses* para 1 (Tribunals Judiciary, Sensitive Witnesses).

refuse any award, no matter that one was made by the CICA.[118] Otherwise the applicant may ask the CICA's witnesses questions during the hearing, and can make points at its conclusion.

E Decisions

1 The permissible limits of the First-tier Tribunal's decisions

6.143 It was for many years the FTT's practice, and that of its predecessor the CICAP, when deciding an appeal on a question of eligibility, to adjourn to itself issues of compensation where its answer was in the applicant's favour. In SB v CICA the Upper Tribunal's short, and defining ruling was that it was not so permitted. Once it has decided the issues that arose in the appeal the FTT's jurisdiction ends, and any remaining issues that arise in order to determine whether any award of compensation should be made, including its amount, is for the CICA to decide. Its further decisions will attract a further right of appeal to the FTT, which its earlier practice could bypass.[119]

6.144 The following paragraphs summarize the main points of the Upper Tribunal's analysis of this principal issue; aspects of the subsidiary issues have been noted in earlier sections. While they specifically concerned the 2001 Scheme, the tribunal's conclusions constitute 'an authoritative statement as to the correct legal position' on the scope of the FTT's jurisdiction under the 2008 and 2012 Schemes.[120]

6.145 The Upper Tribunal's starting point was that the claimant's right of review under paragraph 58 of the 2001 Scheme applied to all decisions relating to his eligibility under paragraphs 6–17, albeit that paragraphs 58(c) and (d) specified reviews only in respect of decisions to withhold or reduce an award. It followed that, as paragraph 61 conferred a right of appeal against 'a decision taken on a review' under paragraph 60, that right 'exists in respect of any type of decision which is adverse to a claimant made under paragraphs 6 to 17 of the 2001 Scheme'.[121]

6.146 Whether the FTT's jurisdiction extended to issues not raised in the appeal turned first on the distinction in the functions performed respectively by claims officers, and, as they are termed under section 5(1)(b) of the CICA 1995, the scheme's 'adjudicators'. These were the persons appointed to the CICAP to hear appeals, and now comprise its successor's judges of the FTT. Claims officers' functions include determining whether an award should be made, and if so, in what amount, and giving effect to FTT decisions in line with any 'necessary' directions it gives on

---

118 *SS v FTT* (n 46) [11].

119 *SB v CICA* (n 39) [5].

120 *Criminal Injuries Compensation Authority v First-tier Tribunal and CB* [2015] UKUT 371 (AAC) [28] (Judge Wikeley) (*CICA v CB*).

121 *SB v CICA* (n 39) [74]–[75].

determining the appeal (2001 Scheme, paragraph 77). They also enjoy investigative powers, notably in respect of medical evidence. By contrast, there is nothing in the CICA 1995 or in the 2001 Scheme to suggest that either adjudicators or the FTT judges 'were intended to have powers of investigation and determination extending beyond the issue or issues covered by the actual review decision which is the subject of the appeal'.[122] Their functions are, by section 5 of the CICA 1995, limited to the hearing of appeals from review decisions.

An obvious practical objection is that the 'investigation and determination' of the incident and of the injury that the claims officer would undertake would be bypassed. In *SS v FTT* Judge Rowland held that notwithstanding that the CICA had made a tariff award, the FTT had no jurisdiction to consider a claim for loss of earnings without a claims officer having first considered that issue.[123] **6.147**

But the key point is that a construction that permitted the FTT to determine issues other than those that had been the subject of the review decision would seriously disadvantage claimants. It would deny the claimant of the rights of reconsideration and review which, had those determinations been made by a claims officer, would have been available to them.[124] Before the Upper Tribunal in *SS v FTT*, the CICA agreed that the FTT decision should be set aside on the ground that it had improperly considered whether any award should be withheld under paragraph 13(e) of the 2001 Scheme, a matter that it had not considered at any point.[125] **6.148**

2 The correctness and adequacy of the First-tier Tribunal's reasons

The FTT is required to give reasons for its decision, which it may give orally at the hearing or in a written statement of reasons to each party. If given orally, either party may apply within one month of the decision notice for this written statement (rule 34). Its decision is final, subject to the correction of clerical mistakes and accidental slips or omissions under FTT rule 36, or to it being set it aside under FTT rule 37 if it considers that it is in the interests of justice to do so, and there was, broadly speaking, a procedural irregularity. That decision must not itself be procedurally defective.[126] **6.149**

It goes without saying that the FTT's reasons for its decision must demonstrate that it has not erred in law in its interpretation and application, either of the scheme under appeal, or of any relevant legislative or judicial authority. Its obligation is to give 'proper, sufficient and intelligible reasons' concerning the issues **6.150**

---

[122] ibid [76]–[80].
[123] *SS v FTT* (n 46) [15]–[17].
[124] *SB v CICA* (n 39) [81].
[125] *CJ v FTT* (n 32) [34].
[126] *R (SB) v First Tier Tribunal and Criminal Injuries Compensation Authority* [2010] UKUT 133 (AAC) [4]–[6].

addressed before it,[127] in particular where a claim is rejected or the compensation payable is reduced. This does not mean, as Kerr J held in *CICA v MB*, that the decision-maker must 'mention expressly, and elaborately, each and every material consideration she takes into account'.[128] This caution is, as the Supreme Court emphasized in *R (Jones) v First-tier Tribunal (SEC)*, of general and well-established application to tribunal law and practice: 'Judicial restraint should be exercised when the reasons that a tribunal gives for its decision are being examined. The appellate court should not assume too readily that the tribunal misdirected itself just because not every step in its reasoning is fully set out in it'.[129]

6.151 It must, however, be clear from the context and the manner in which the decision was given that 'the judge may be taken to have read and absorbed the written materials that were presented'.[130] Clarity may be assisted by the FTT's use of a template or a standard form in which its reasons are recorded, but as Judge Jacobs commented in *MM v FTT and CICA*, there is a danger that 'off the shelf' reasons that might have been sufficient in an earlier appeal are insufficient in the one now being decided. What was lacking in this case 'was any consideration of what points the tribunal considered in favour of holding a hearing'.[131] Similarly, a decision notice that comprised a series of unnumbered bullet points, with no further discussion of the FTT's reasons, was an unsatisfactory approach to 'a document which may need to be analysed by others'.[132]

6.152 Conversely, as *SB v CICA* makes very clear, neither may the FTT include reasons relating to a decision that it had no jurisdiction to make. In *YA v CICA* the Upper Tribunal found (as in *MM v FTT and CICA*) that the FTT's reasons for not allowing an appeal concerning the CICA's discretion to waive the time limit for the submission of an application were not 'as crisply and clearly [stated] or as free from error' as they should be, and that it had improperly taken into account factors that had not previously been considered.

6.153 The tribunal also observed that, if it were in order for it to do so, should the FTT propose to take account of matters not canvassed before it, or in the CICA review decision, the rules of natural justice and fair procedure might require that all parties be given proper warning of those issues, and a proper opportunity to present evidence and argument.[133] This passage was closely relied upon by the claimants in *CICA v Hutton,* but the Court of Appeal held that given the detail and the

---

[127] *R v Criminal Injuries Compensation Authority, ex parte Leatherland, Bramall and Kay* [2001] ACD 13 (QBD). CICA's approach to its public law obligations is now very different to the procedures that Turner J criticized in this this case.

[128] *CICA v MB* (n 63) [35].

[129] [2013] UKSC 192, [2013] 2 AC 48 [25] (SC) (Lord Hope) (*Jones*).

[130] *CICA v MB* (n 63) [35].

[131] *MM v FTT and CICA* (n 6) [15].

[132] *VAA v First-tier Tribunal* [2010] UKUT 36 (AAC) [9].

[133] *YA v CICA* (n 10) [45].

clarity of the terms of the FTT's decision in that case, there could be no objection on the ground of procedural unfairness.[134]

3 Notification of decision

With the parties' consent, but only if it considers it appropriate, the FTT may by rule 32 make a consent order disposing of the proceedings, making such other appropriate provision as the parties have agreed. In this case it does not need to hold a hearing or to provide reasons for the order. Where there has been a hearing, it may give its decision orally at the hearing (rule 33(1)); this may be to uphold the CICA's decision, to increase or reduce the award, to refuse an award altogether, or to require the CICA to make its decision again. In any event the FTT must, as soon as reasonably practicable after making a final decision issue the parties with **6.154**

> (a) a decision notice stating the Tribunal's decision, (b) where appropriate, notification of the right to apply for a written statement of reasons under rule 34(3), and (c) notification of any right of appeal against the decision and the time within which, and the manner in which, such right of appeal may be exercised (rule 33(2)).

With the exception of the five specific matters listed in Practice and Guidance Statement (CI-6),[135] there is no general right of review under the FTT Rules (FTT rule 40), or of appeal (TCEA 2007 section 11), but the applicant (or the CICA) may, 'somewhat paradoxically',[136] bring a claim for judicial review of the decision to be heard by the Upper Tribunal.[137] **6.155**

VI Judicial Review

A Introduction

The Upper Tribunal was established as a superior court of record by section 3(2) and (5) of the TCEA 2007. By section 15, it is vested with a judicial review jurisdiction over the FTT's decisions, performed by the Administrative Appeals Chamber of the Upper Tribunal,[138] and governed by the Tribunal Procedure (Upper Tribunal) Rules 2008 (UT Rules).[139] There is no formal difference between the judicial review jurisdiction in the Upper Tribunal and that of the **6.156**

[134] *CICA v Hutton* (n 4) [72]–[75].

[135] Courts and Tribunals Judiciary, *Criminal Injuries Compensation Tribunal—Rules and Legislation, Practice and Guidance Statement (C-16)*.

[136] *MM v CICA* (n 10) [8].

[137] Judiciary for England and Wales, *The Administrative Court Judicial Review Guide 2017* para 5.6.2.1; CPR 1998 (n 83) Pt 54.1.

[138] The First-tier Tribunal and Upper Tribunal (Chambers) Order 2008, SI 2008/2684 arts 6 and 7; The Supreme Court of England And Wales Direction—Classes of Cases Specified under Section 18(6) of the Tribunals, Courts and Enforcement Act 2007.

[139] 2008, SI 2008/2698 (L 15) (21 August 2015).

Administrative Court: '[T]he Upper Tribunal must apply the principles that the High Court would apply in deciding whether to grant judicial review (s 15(4))'.[140]

6.157 These principles govern the entire range of judicial review hearings conducted by the Upper Tribunal; the discussion here deals only with their application to the review of decisions concerning the scheme. As in the case of the FTT Rules, the Upper Tribunal is under an obligation to give effect to the UT Rules' overriding objective, and to the parties' obligation to cooperate with the tribunal; that is, 'to enable the Tribunal to deal with cases fairly and justly'. Rule 2 specifies the same considerations and obligations on the tribunal and the parties as appear in FTT rule 2.

6.158 Where the alleged criminal injury occurred in England or Wales, but the application was made in Scotland (or vice versa) the common law doctrine *forum non conveniens* applies to the question of whether English or Scottish courts have jurisdiction to hear a judicial review. This was the issue in the joined three judge panels in *R (MB) v First-tier Tribunal* and *NF v First-tier Tribunal and Criminal Injuries Compensation Authority*. The panel held that TCEA 2007 did not provide for mutually exclusive review jurisdictions in England and Wales on the one hand, and Scotland on the other, and that the doctrine applied in determining whether the High Court (and the Upper Tribunal), or the Court of Session, should determine a review of a decision when both have jurisdiction to do so. As the doctrine applied, the convenient forum in this case was the Upper Tribunal.[141]

B Application for permission to bring a judicial review

1 Grounds for a judicial review

6.159 A judicial review is the only way to challenge an FTT decision in a criminal injuries compensation case, which is otherwise an 'excluded decision', thus precluding the normal route of a statutory appeal (TCEA 2007, section 11(5(a)).[142] Because there is no provision for an appeal to the Upper Tribunal (which would otherwise be of right or subject to leave) the party seeking the review of the FTT's decision must apply to the Upper Tribunal for permission (TCEA 2007 section 16(2)). This may be the victim, a qualifying relative, or the CICA, any one of whom is, by Upper Tribunal rule 1(3)), for these purposes, an 'applicant', that is 'a person who applies for permission to bring, or does bring, judicial review

[140] *Criminal Injuries Compensation Authority and First-Tier Tribunal (SEC) v Kenneth Mailer and Lewis Haigh* [2018] EWCA Civ 1175, 2018 WL 02338152, [6]–[7] (CA), (*CICA v Mailer and Haigh*).

[141] [2012] UKUT 286 (AAC), [2013] AACR 10, [2012] UKUT 287 (AAC), [2013] AACR 11, respectively (Charles J, Lord Brailsford, and Judge Levenson).

[142] An FTT decision concerning the Victims of Overseas Terrorism Compensation Scheme in compliance with the Crime and Security Act 2010 s 52(3) is also an 'excluded decision' within s 11; (ch 3.09).

proceedings before the Upper Tribunal and, in judicial review proceedings transferred to the Upper Tribunal from a court'.

The FTT's Practice and Guidance Statement (CI-6) gives extensive guidance to parties who are contemplating making application to bring judicial review proceedings.[143] Along with her personal details and details of the decision being challenged, the applicant must state the outcome that she seeks, and the facts and grounds on which she relies (UT rule 28(4)(f)–(g)). These grounds will be based on the FTT's public law obligations to direct itself correctly as to matters of law; that is, the proper interpretation and application of the scheme's provisions, of any other relevant legislation, and of applicable judicial decisions. In the case of questions of fact, its *Wednesbury* obligation is not to reach any findings that no reasonable tribunal, properly directed, could reach. These obligations extend also to the standard public law matters of procedural irregularity, fairness, and natural justice, and to the recognition of legitimate expectations.[144] **6.160**

The applicant must send the Upper Tribunal copies of any written record of the decision she may have, and of any other documents on which she intends to rely. This will be the written statement of reasons that she may request under FTT rule 34(3) where the FTT decision was given orally. There is nothing to prevent an application for judicial review being made without a full statement of reasons, but in its absence the applicant might well find it impossible to show why the FTT's decision was wrong. There is therefore a clear imperative on the applicant to obtain that record; the Upper Tribunal holding in *BN v CICA* that the applicant's letter to the Upper Tribunal asking for permission could not be construed as impliedly also asking for that statement.[145] **6.161**

Upon receipt, the tribunal must send a copy of the application and any accompanying documents 'to each person named in the application as a respondent or interested party' (UT rule 28(8)). Rule 28(4) requires the applicant to identify, in addition to the respondent 'any other person whom the applicant considers to be an interested party'; that is, by UT rule '1(a) a person who is directly affected by the outcome sought in judicial review proceedings'. The interested party is entitled to receive any documents relating to the review, the tribunal's acknowledgement of service (UT rule 28(8)), and its decision to grant or refuse permission (UT rule (30)). By UT rule 30(1), the tribunal must send **6.162**

> to the applicant, each respondent and any other person who provided an acknowledgement of service to the Upper Tribunal, and may send to any other person who may have an interest in the proceedings, written notice of— (a) its decision in

[143] Courts and Tribunals Judiciary, *Appeals on error of law against final decision of the Tribunal, Practice and Guidance Statement CI-6*.

[144] *Associated Provincial Picture Houses Ltd v Wednesbury Corporation* [1948] 1 KB 223 (CA), *Council of Civil Service Unions v Minister for the Civil Service* [1983] UKHL 9, [1985] AC 374 (HL).

[145] *BN v CICA* (n 51) [18]–[19].

relation to the application for permission; and (b) [the reasons for any—(i) refusal of the application or refusal to admit the late application, or (ii) limitations or conditions on permission.

Where the applicant is the CICA seeking a review of the FTT's decision the interested party will be the victim or the qualifying relative; where it is they who are seeking the review, it will be the CICA.

C Time limit for seeking a judicial review

6.163 The application is made on the Judicial Review claim form (Criminal Injuries Compensation Case) under the terms of UT rule 28;[146] it must be made 'promptly', and no later than three months of the FTT's decision (UT rule 28(2)). This time limit applies equally to applications made by the CICA. Rule 28(3) provides for an extension of time if the application 'is made within 1 month after the date on which the First-tier Tribunal sent—(a) written reasons for the decision; or (b) notification that an application for the decision to be set aside has been unsuccessful, provided that that application was made in time'.

6.164 The application of UT rule 28 was extensively reviewed in *CICA v CB*, a case that revealed a factually convoluted chronology involving two separate FTT decisions (*FTT1* and *FTT2*), and a three year gap between the first and the second of these.[147] In summary, the CICA had rejected the claimant's application arising from an attack on her own dog by two Rottweilers, which caused her to develop symptoms consistent with a stroke, on the ground that her injury was not the result of a crime of violence. *FTT1* allowed her appeal and adjourned the case for a decision on the causal link between the attack and the stroke, which was heard by *FTT2* eighteen months later, and decided in her favour. Within a month of that decision, the CICA asked the FTT office for its written reasons, and also for those of *FTT1*, a request clearly well outside the one month statutory limit (FTT rule 34(4)). The FTT office itself sent both sets of reasons within one month of receiving those requests, following which the CICA applied within the succeeding month for permission to seek a judicial review.

6.165 The first procedural issue was whether the CICA's application for judicial review of *FTT1*'s decision was late. The CICA argued that it was not, because its application did comply with UT rule 28(2) in respect of *FTT2*'s decision. The Upper Tribunal rejected this argument. So far as it provides for an extension of time, UT rule 28(3) must be read as referring in this case to the decision in *FTT1*, in respect of which the CICA was well out of time, and not to *FTT2*.[148]

---

146 HM Courts & Tribunals Service, *Form JRC1: Judicial review claim form—criminal injuries compensation cases, England and Wales.*

147 *CICA v CB* (n 120).

148 ibid [48]–[55].

The second procedural issue was whether, accepting that the application was late, the Upper Tribunal should extend the time limit in the exercise of paragraph 5(3)(a) of its case management powers, which is in identical terms to FTT rule 5(3)(a). Judge Wikeley concluded that the general and specific considerations relevant to that question, when they were all taken together, were more than outweighed by 'the very lengthy delay, the inadequate justification for CICA not acting sooner to challenge the decision by *FTT1* and the prejudice to the claimant and more particularly the detriment to good administration caused by CICA's conduct of this case'.[149] **6.166**

These reasons are consistent with the Upper Tribunal's decision in *R (Criminal Injuries Compensation Authority) v First-tier Tribunal*. This concerned the CICA's application in respect of the FTT's decision to allow an appeal in the case of a lorry driver who suffered a psychiatric injury when witnessing a man committing suicide by running into his lorry. The ground of the CICA's application was that the FTT had failed to follow the clear guidance in *Jones* concerning the question of whether the claimant's injury was caused by a crime of violence (Chapter 2.07–2.08). Refusing permission, the application being eight months late, Judge Rowland observed that, while rule 28(3) must be construed as extending the time limit in rule 28(2), 'despite its literal meaning' it should not be read as interfering 'with the need for an application to be made promptly'.[150] **6.167**

D Costs in respect of an application for judicial review

By section 29(1) of the TCEA 2007, 'the costs of and incidental to—(a) all proceedings in the First-tier Tribunal, and (b) all proceedings in the Upper Tribunal shall be in the discretion of the Tribunal in which the proceedings take place', and by section 28(2) and (3), subject to their rules, 'the relevant Tribunal shall have full power to determine by whom and to what extent the costs are to be paid'. UT rule 10(3) provides that the Upper Tribunal may not make an order for costs or expenses except (a) in judicial review proceedings ... or (d) if it considers that a party or its representative 'has acted unreasonably in bringing, defending or conducting the proceedings'. This was the issue in *H v First-tier Tribunal and Criminal Injuries Compensation Authority*, a claim that had a complicated history.[151] **6.168**

In short, the applicant had been subjected to a serious sexual assault in 2006 but did not report it until 2008, making her application in 2011, and attributing the delay to her continuing trauma. Without an oral hearing, the FTT upheld the CICA's rejection of her claim as being out of time, but shortly before the oral hearing ordered by the Upper Tribunal, the CICA agreed that the two-year time **6.169**

149 ibid [56]–[62]; TCEA 2007 s 16(4) and (5).
150 [2015] UKUT 299 (AAC) [30].
151 [2014] UKUT 338 (AAC) (*H v CICA*).

limit for making the original claim should have been waived, with which the FTT agreed. The claimant then sought her £25,000 costs incurred prior to this 'late concession' as 'evidence of their unreasonable behaviour' in refusing the initial appeal.

6.170 The Upper Tribunal refused the application for costs, holding that while it did not preclude an order for costs in judicial review proceedings, UT rule 10(3) did not require it. On this point, the tribunal adopted its confirmation by the cross-chamber three judge panel in *R (LR) v First-tier Tribunal and Hertfordshire County Council (Costs)*.[152] As to its jurisdiction under UT rule 10(d), Judge Levenson held that it could not be invoked against the FTT, which clearly had not 'acted unreasonably in bringing, defending or conducting the proceedings'.[153]

E Hearings

6.171 The provisions governing hearings are contained in Part 5 of the UT Rules. Each party is entitled to attend (UT rule 35), and by UT rule 37 the hearing must be in public, but the tribunal may direct that it, or part of it, be held in private, and determine who may attend; by UT rule 37(4) it may exclude any person from attending the hearing on the same grounds as in FTT rule 30. By UT rule 36, the tribunal must give the parties 'reasonable notice of the time and place of the hearing', that is, at least fourteen days, and of any adjourned or postponed hearing or changes to the time and place of the hearing; this may be shorter with the parties' consent or in urgent or exceptional circumstances (UT rule 36(b)). If the appellant (or, which is unlikely, the CICA) fails to attend, the tribunal may proceed with the hearing if it is satisfied that they have been notified or that reasonable steps have been taken to notify them of the hearing, and it considers that it is in the interests of justice to proceed (rule 31). Rules 15 and 16 governing the number and summoning of witnesses, and whether expert witnesses are permitted or required, are to the same effect as the equivalent FTT rules, including those relating to child, vulnerable adult, and sensitive witnesses.[154]

6.172 Assuming the preceding provisions are met, UT rule 34 provides that the tribunal 'may make any decision without a hearing', but only after it has had 'regard to any view expressed by a party whether to hold a hearing to consider any matter, and the form of any such hearing'. If a party fails to attend a hearing, the Tribunal may proceed if it (a) is satisfied that the party has been notified of the hearing or that reasonable steps have been taken to notify the party of the hearing; and (b) considers that it is in the interests of justice so to proceed (UT rule 38).

152 [2013] UKUT 294 (AAC), [2013] AACR 27.
153 *H v CICA* (n 151) [23]–[27].
154 Tribunals Judiciary, Sensitive Witnesses (n 117).

F Decisions

1 Decision alternatives

The Tribunal may, first, decide against the applicant on judicial review. Where it decides for them, section 15(1) of the TCEA 2007 provides the full range of judicial review remedies: a mandatory order, a prohibiting order, a quashing order, a declaration and an injunction. When making a quashing order under section 15(1)(c) it may, by section 17(1)(a) remit the matter for a fresh hearing by a differently composed FTT panel, with a direction to reconsider, and to reach a decision in accordance with its findings. As many of the cases discussed in this book illustrate, this is a routine outcome where the Upper Tribunal finds that the reasons for the FTT's decision were not adequately set out in its written statement of reasons. This may result in a finding for the claimant, but it may equally be the case that, properly directed, the new FTT panel reaches the same decision as its predecessor. Alternatively, the Upper Tribunal may, by section 17(1)(b) and (2), substitute its own decision, but only if the FTT decision is quashed on the ground that there has been an error of law, *and* (emphasis added) without the error, there would have been only one decision that the court or tribunal could have reached. **6.173**

The statutory alternatives that are open to the Upper Tribunal where it has quashed the FTT's decision are exhaustive of its jurisdiction. In *CICA v Mailer and Haigh* the Court of Appeal held that, having found that there was a material error of law in the FTT's decision in an appeal concerning the proper test for assessing what could amount to 'an exceptional risk' in paragraph 5 of the 2012 Scheme (Chapter 2.113–2.116), the tribunal had, in substituting its own decision, acted unlawfully, there being, on the facts of the claim as judged on the basis of that test, more than one possible decision open to the FTT. In the circumstances of this case, the Upper Tribunal 'did not have the power to do anything other than quash the original decision and remit the case to the FTT'.[155] **6.174**

While allowing the CICA's appeal in the firefighter's case,[156] the Court understood 'the frustration that a judge feels in a judicial review case when he or she concludes that the decision-maker made an error of law, but considers that the right answer is plain, and wants to save time and resources by correcting the error and providing that answer'. But, Coulson LJ continued: 'It is important that a proper and fair process is maintained: it is only that can provide the necessary certainty, consistency and clarity in the decisions of the Tribunal Services'.[157] **6.175**

---

155 *CICA v Mailer and Haigh* (n 140) [18] (CA).

156 In the case of the linked appeal concerning the police officer's claim, the Court held that the Upper Tribunal was justified when it upheld the FTT's decision; (ch 2.116).

157 *CICA v Mailer and Haigh* (n 140) [19]–[20] (CA).

2 Decision formalities and appeal

6.176 With the parties' consent, but only if it considers it appropriate, the tribunal may by UT rule 39 make a consent order disposing of the proceedings and making such other appropriate provision as the parties have agreed. Where it does so, it does not need to hold a hearing; if it does it may give its decision orally at the hearing (UT rule 40(1)). By UT rule 40(2) it must, 'as soon as reasonably practicable' after making its final decision issue the parties with '(a) a decision notice stating the Upper Tribunal's decision; and (b) notification of any rights of review or appeal against the decision and the time and manner in which such rights of review or appeal may be exercised'.

6.177 These rights are provided for in Part 7 of the UT Rules. Put shortly, an Upper Tribunal decision:

- may be set aside if the Tribunal considers that it is in the interests of justice to do so and there was a procedural irregularity (UT rule 43)
- may, with leave, be appealed to the Court of Appeal (UT rules 44 and 45), or
- on an application to appeal, be reviewed if when making the decision the Tribunal overlooked a legislative provision or binding authority which could have had a material effect on the decision, or since its decision, a court has made a decision which is binding on the Upper Tribunal and which, had it been made before the Upper Tribunal's decision, could have had a material effect on the decision (UT rule 46).

In addition, from April 2015 it has been possible for a leapfrog appeal to the Supreme Court to be initiated in the Upper Tribunal under the same conditions as appeals from the High Court.[158]

G The role of the Upper Tribunal

6.178 A central aspect of the Upper Tribunal's function in respect of the interpretation and application of this 'specialised statutory scheme' is 'to develop structured guidance on the use of expressions which are central to the scheme, and so as to reduce the risk of inconsistent results by different panels at the First-tier level'. This was, Lord Carnwath noted in *Jones*, part of the thinking behind the recommendations of the Leggatt committee for the restructuring of the tribunal service and the establishment of a new tier of appellate tribunals.[159]

6.179 In recognizing the need for 'particular deference' to be given to specialist tribunals, there is here a balance to be struck between the Upper Tribunal's performance of that role, and of its function in the assessment of the accuracy of the

[158] Criminal Justice and Courts Act 2015 s 64, inserting ss 14A to 14C into the TCEA 2007; Supreme Court, Revised Practice Directions.

[159] *Jones* (n 129) [41]; before his appointment to the Supreme Court, Lord Carnwath was Senior President of the Upper Tribunal, and 'Tribunal Justice: a New start' [2009] PL 48.

FTT's understanding and application of the scheme in any case. Echoing Lord Hope's comments in *Jones*,[160] the Court of Appeal observed in *Criminal Injuries Compensation Authority v First-Tier Tribunal (SEC) v TS*, that FTT decisions should be 'read benevolently', and that 'both the Upper Tribunal and the Court of Appeal should be cautious about interfering with its decisions, even when they are less fully expressed than might be desirable'.[161] These cautionary observations are partly about deference to specialist expertise, but also about not being too demanding of the standards expected of very busy tribunals when setting out all of the reasons for their decisions.

They also constituted a clear restraint on the Upper Tribunal's analysis of the FTT's approach to the contested factual circumstances in *MJ (No 1)*, where the Upper Tribunal observed that 'it would clearly be right not to be too ready to second-guess a value judgment, or the expression of the factors that have led to it'. But, Judge Ward continued, **6.180**

> that does not mean that 'anything goes'. There is a world of difference between not being over-hasty to infer that a tribunal has failed to consider particular parts of the evidence, to second-guess its value judgments on the evidence it found, or to pick holes in the expression of the tribunal's reasons, and 'finding a tribunal to have erred in law where, on the face of its reasons, it either must have failed to take incontrovertibly important evidence into account or has reached a conclusion which, on that part of the evidence, was one that no reasonable tribunal could reach.[162]

In *CICA v Hutton* the Court of Appeal considered at length the *dicta* in *Jones* concerning the proper role of the Upper Tribunal in relation to the FTT. It drew particular attention to Lord Hope's remark that 'a pragmatic approach should be taken to the dividing line between law and fact, so that the expertise of tribunals at the first tier and that of the Upper Tribunal can be used to best effect',[163] and to Lord Carnwath's extra-judicial comments that favour 'expediency' or 'policy' influencing the division between law and fact, so as to permit a specialist appellate tribunal to range more widely and thus ensure that its "... expertise should be used to best effect, to shape and direct the development of law and practice in the field" '.[164] **6.181**

Pulling these threads together the Court held: **6.182**

> (i) First, this Court should exercise restraint and proceed with caution before interfering with decisions of specialist tribunals. Not only do such tribunals have the

---

[160] *Jones* (n 129).

[161] [2014] EWCA Civ 65, [2014] PIQR P10 (CA) [20] (Moore-Bick LJ).

[162] *MJ (No 1)* (n 15) [36]–[37].

[163] *Jones* (n 129) [16]. In similar vein, see the comments of the Outer House of the Court of Session in *MM v CICA* (n 10) [32].

[164] *CICA v Hutton* (n 4) [56] (Gross LJ). In both *Jones* (n 129) and *Hutton v CICA* (n 2) the courts' starting point was Baroness Hale's observations in *AH (Sudan) v Home* Secretary [2007] UKHL 49, [2008] 1 AC 678 [30] (HL).

expertise which the 'ordinary' courts may not have but when a specialised statutory scheme has been entrusted by Parliament to tribunals, the Court should not venture too readily into their field.

(ii) Secondly, if a tribunal decision is clearly based on an error of law, then it must be corrected. This Court should not, however, subject such decisions to inappropriate textual analysis so as to discern an error of law when, on a fair reading of the decision as a whole, none existed. It is probable, as Baroness Hale said, that in understanding and applying the law within their area of expertise, specialist tribunals will have got it right. Moreover, the mere fact that an appellate tribunal or a court would have reached a different conclusion, does not constitute a ground for review or for allowing an appeal.

(iii) Thirdly, it is of the first importance to identify the tribunal of fact, to keep in mind that it and only it will have heard the evidence and to respect its decisions. When determining whether a question was one of 'fact' or 'law', this Court should have regard to context, as I would respectfully express it ('pragmatism', 'expediency' or 'policy', *per Jones*), so as to ensure both that decisions of tribunals of fact are given proper weight and to provide scope for specialist appellate tribunals to shape the development of law and practice in their field.

(iv) Fourthly, it is important to note that these authorities not only address the relationship between the courts and specialist appellate tribunals *but also* between specialist first-tier tribunals and appellate tribunals'.[165]

6.183 It is notoriously the case that the common law provides no definitive account of the conceptual basis on which questions of law and questions of fact may be differentiated, with the result that there are no settled criteria for determining whether a question is one of law or fact in any particular context. As it has traditionally proved difficult to predict how the courts will classify any given question, some may regard the purpose of the classification as the determining factor. Those issues that are thought suitable for a jury or a First-tier Tribunal to decide might for that reason be regarded as questions of fact, as might issues thought unsuited to be the subject of an appeal or to give rise to precedents.

6.184 Determining what is suitable entails an assessment of the advantages and disadvantages of such treatment. Treating a question as one of fact allows the law to reflect standards as they vary across time and place; in this context to be applied relatively easily by the CICA's claims officers or the FTT. To counter the criticism that the scheme will be uncertainly and inconsistently applied, a question may instead be treated as one of law. This increases judicial control over the FTT's decisions and so ensures a greater degree of uniformity in adjudication. It is the balance between expediency and policy on the one hand, and, in Gross LJ's words, 'the desire to shape the development of law and practice' in the interpretation and application of the 2012 Scheme, that it is the Upper Tribunal's task to strike.

[165] *CICA v Hutton* (n 4) [57]–[58] (Gross LJ).

Part II

7

COMPENSATION ORDERS
Eligible Injuries and Persons

I Introduction

For many years courts of criminal jurisdiction possessed powers to require offenders convicted of offences causing personal injury to compensate their victims as an order ancillary to a probation order, or to an absolute or conditional discharge, to pay 'damages for injury'.[1] The Advisory Council on the Penal System concluded in 1970 that a combination of such factors as the offender's youth or lack of means, the presence of other penal objectives when sentencing, and the absence of any clear basis upon which the loss or injury could be assessed, meant that 'in practice the prospects of a victim receiving compensation in pursuance of an order of a criminal court are remote'.[2] Many of these factors remain live. **7.01**

Following this review, the ancillary order was transmuted into a sentencing option in its own right, taking precedence over fines and confiscation orders, and requiring the court to give reasons why it had not made an order where it had **7.02**

[1] Criminal Justice Act 1948 s 11(2). The earlier legislation was reviewed in the Report of the Hodgson Committee, *The Profits of Crime and Their Recovery* (Heinemann 1984) (Hodgson, *Profits of Crime*).

[2] Advisory Council on the Penal System (1970) para 24.

power to do so. Until the amendments made by the Crime and Courts Act 2013, orders made by magistrates' courts were limited to level 5 of the standard scale (£5,000), but they are now unlimited, as has always been the case in the Crown Court; but before making an order both courts must have regard to the offender's means. A second signal advance is the duty imposed by section 63 of the Legal Aid, Sentencing and Punishment of Offenders Act 2012 (LASPOA 2012), requiring the court to consider making a compensation order in any case where it has power to do so. These powers and duties are consolidated in sections 130–134 of the Powers of Criminal Courts (Sentencing) Act 2000 (PCC(S)A 2000).[3]

7.03 These developments were, as in the case of state compensation, the product of the government's broader concern that the criminal justice system was neither meeting its objectives with regard to the rehabilitation of offenders nor recognizing the interests of victims of crime (Chapter 1.01–1.03). But as the Ministry of Justice's 2012 consultation, *Getting it Right for Victims and Witnesses* makes clear,[4] this concern was tempered by a desire to reduce the burden on the public finances. Putting a 'much stronger emphasis on compensation for victims of crime' does not necessarily imply that it is the taxpayer who foots the bill. The government's object was to bring about 'a fundamental shift in approach in which offenders play a significantly greater role in making financial reparation, in repairing the damage their criminal activity has caused, and, where appropriate, in helping victims come to terms with the harm that has been done to them', moving away 'from a culture of state compensation towards one of offenders making direct reparation for the harm they cause'.[5]

7.04 In addition to 'any personal injury', sections 130–134 of the PCC(S)A 2000 provide that compensation may be ordered in respect of 'loss or damage' resulting from the offence. Many of the authorities relate to offences against property, but I do not address those offences directly. Nor do I deal directly with the range of restitution, reparation, deprivation, and confiscation orders that the court may make, save that as sentencing options they may have an impact on the making of a compensation order. The discussion assumes that the offender is an adult; particular reference is made where the offence is committed by a young offender.

[3] The Criminal Justice Acts 1972, 1982, and 1988, and the Powers of Criminal Courts Act 1973 (PCCA 1973). Unless there are substantive differences between the repealed provisions and ss 130–134 of PCC(S)A 2000, the text refers only to the latter.

[4] Ministry of Justice (2012a).

[5] Ministry of Justice (2012a) paras 10 and 14; (2012c) para 16; Home Office (2010) para 82.

II The Liability of the Offender

A Criminal liability

The operative provision of PCC(S)A 2000 is section 130(1): **7.05**

> A court by or before which a person is convicted of an offence, instead of or in addition to dealing with him in any other way, may, on application or otherwise, make an order (in this Act referred to as a 'compensation order') requiring him
>
> (a) to pay compensation for any personal injury, loss or damage resulting from that offence or any other offence which is taken into consideration by the court in determining sentence; or (b) to make payments for funeral expenses or bereavement in respect of a death resulting from any such offence, other than a death due to an accident arising out of the presence of a motor vehicle on a road.

The criminal liability of the offender is a condition precedent to a compensation order, which may follow conviction or be formally admitted as an offence taken into consideration (TIC). Where it is made in respect of TIC offences, the order may only be made for the amount set out on the indictment, or stipulated in respect of other TIC offences. It is not open to the court to make a compensation order arising from sample or specimen counts even where they have been admitted by the defendant, unless the defendant has been charged, or they have been taken into consideration. An order that includes such offences will to that extent be reduced.[6] **7.06**

Where the order is made in respect of a personal injury it will frequently follow a conviction for an offence against the person under sections 18, 20, or 47 of the Offences Against the Person Act 1861 (OAPA 1861), or an offence of racially or religiously aggravated offences of wounding and assault (Crime and Disorder Act 1998 section 29).[7] **7.07**

A person who has been trafficked within the meaning of section 2 of the Modern Slavery Act 2015, or who has been held in conditions of slavery in which he has been required to perform forced or compulsory labour (section 1), may well have suffered injurious treatment that does not amount to an offence under the OAPA 1861 (although it may), but could constitute 'personal injury' for the purpose of section 130(1). That Act creates its own regime for making 'slavery or trafficking reparation orders', which in many respects mirrors the conditions that apply to compensation orders; these are reviewed in Chapter 9.59–9.61. **7.08**

---

[6] *Crutchley and Tonks* (1994) 15 Cr App R (S) 627; applied *Whitbread* [2002] EWCA Crim 1523, No 2001/5151/Y1 (CA), *Hose* (1995) 16 Cr App R (S) 82, *Revenue & Customs Prosecutions Office v Duffy* [2008] EWHC 848 (Admin) [2008] 2 Cr App R (S) [24]–[25].

[7] *Engen* [2004] EWCA Crim 1536, 2004 WL 1372293 (CA).

7.09 Section 130(1) of the PCC(S)A 2000 does not, however, require the offence in respect of which the order is made itself to be an offence against the person. As the Sentencing Council indicates, an order could be made against the dog's owner on a conviction of the aggravated offence in section 3(1) of the Dangerous Dogs Act 1991 in respect of the victim's injury.[8] This is a 'criminal injury' under the 2012 Criminal Injuries Compensation Scheme (the 2012 Scheme) only if the dog was used 'with intent to cause injury to a person' (Chapter 2.78–2.86).[9] Assuming the offender has means, a compensation order is a realistic option in such cases, and may be made in sums lower than the scheme's £1,000 minimum.

7.10 A compensation order may be made in respect of a personal injury caused by the commission of a crime against property, and as illustrated by *Bond v Chief Constable of Kent*,[10] may be made independently of any order in respect of the property that was stolen or criminally damaged. The offender was convicted under section 1 of the Criminal Damage Act 1971, and was ordered to pay compensation to cover the cost of replacing the window of the house through which he had thrown a stone. Given the clear terms of section 35(1) of the PCCA 1973, the Divisional Court expressly approved the magistrates' additional order in respect of the distress and anxiety suffered by the occupier, who had feared a sustained attack on himself and his family.

7.11 Shock is a common reaction where the victim's house has been burgled, and may have a lasting impact on elderly and vulnerable victims;[11] the more so if they were present at the time. This is not a criminal injury, but a compensation order may recognize that impact. The Magistrates' Court Sentencing Guidelines indicate that, in assessing the victim's pain and suffering, the court should take account of 'the victim's age and personal circumstances'.[12]

7.12 Assuming a sufficient causal link between the offender's behaviour and the victim's injury, an order may be made for *any* criminal offence, other than injuries arising 'from the presence of a motor vehicle on a road'. The Advisory Council had recognized that the proposed extension to the court's powers could include regulatory offences resulting in personal injury, but considered that compensation orders should be confined to offences that, broadly speaking, involve the intentional or reckless infliction of injury (or loss or damage). Injuries caused by offences of strict liability or of negligence were better suited to civil proceedings.[13]

---

[8] Sentencing Council, *Dangerous Dog Offences*, Definitive Guideline.

[9] *Criminal Injuries Compensation Authority v First-tier Tribunal (SEC) and TS* [2014] EWCA Civ 65, [2014] PIQR P10 [11] (CA).

[10] [1983] 1 WLR 40, 41 (QBD).

[11] Ronald Clarke and Tim Hope, *Coping with burglary: Research perspectives on policy* (Springer Science & Business Media vol 4 2012) 234–38; *Berry v Cooper* (1983) WL 880104 (CA) is an example.

[12] Sentencing Council, *Magistrates' Court Sentencing Guidelines, Explanatory Materials, Fines and Financial Orders* (MCSG *Guidelines) Compensation 1* para 8.

[13] Advisory Council on the Penal System (n 2) para 60.

But given clear evidence of their impact (Chapter 8.01), such offences may fall within the scope of section 130(1);[14] for example, under the Consumer Protection from Unfair Trading Regulations,[15] and in *Pola,* for personal injury caused by an offence under section 33(1)(a) of the Health and Safety at Work Act etc 1974.[16] An order may also be apt for injuries caused by offences under sections 36 and 37 of the Fire Safety and Safety of Places of Sport Act 1987, and section 7 of the Food Safety Act 1990.

B Civil liability

The Advisory Council envisaged that compensation orders would only be made where civil liability was unproblematic, as in the typical case of an injury caused by an offence under sections 18, 20, or 47 of the OAPA 1861. In what continues to be a leading case on the interpretation of sections 130–134, *Inwood,* the Court of Appeal observed: **7.13**

> Compensation orders were introduced into our law as a convenient and rapid means of avoiding the expense of resort to civil litigation when the criminal clearly has means which would enable the compensation to be paid. One has to bear in mind that there is always the possibility of a victim taking civil proceedings, if he be so advised. Compensation orders should certainly not be used when there is any doubt as to the liability to compensate.[17]

The courts have repeatedly affirmed this final remark, usually in connection with the issue of quantifying the extent of the victim's injury. Judicial opinion had differed about the possibility of a compensation order 'where it is at least arguable whether any civil liability arises from the commission of an offence',[18] but the matter was authoritatively settled by the Court of Appeal in *Chappell.*[19] The defendant had been convicted of offences in relation to the VAT returns of the company of which he was a director, and was ordered to pay compensation in respect of the unpaid tax. On appeal, he argued that in the absence of any fraud he was not personally liable for any unpaid tax, and thus the order was unlawful. Dismissing his appeal, the Court held that to require civil liability as a precondition necessitated reading the word 'actionable' into the operative section. The legislative framework may have envisaged that in many, or indeed most, cases the criminal remedy would be exercised against the background of a potential civil proceedings, but it did not follow that Parliament intended 'to make that remedy conditional on the existence of a civil cause of action'.[20] **7.14**

---

[14] *Briscoe* (1994) 15 Cr App R (S) 699 (CA) (an offence under the Town and Country Planning Act 1990).

[15] *Connors* [2012] EWCA Crim 2106, [2013] CTLC 32 (CA) (aggressive commercial practices).

[16] [2009] EWCA Crim 655, [2010] 1 Cr App R (S) 6 (CA).

[17] (1974) 60 Cr App R 70, 75 (CA) (Scarman LJ).

[18] *Lester* (1975) 63 Cr App R 144, 146 (CA) (Bridge LJ).

[19] (1985) 80 Cr App R 31 (CA).

[20] ibid 34 (Lord Lane CJ).

7.15 A compensation order may short-circuit 'the expense of resort to civil litigation', but it is not, as Hughes LJ observed in *Jawad*,[21] the equivalent of a civil judgment in favour of the loser. Its enforcement depends on powers to be exercised by the magistrates' court, and before it is made, the sentencing court must take into account the offender's means. Even if they are sufficient, and civil liability does exist, it has discretion whether to make the order, despite an agreed or proved injury to the victim.

III Eligible Personal Injuries

A Scope

7.16 The personal injuries that fall within the scope of section 130(1) will in many cases be of the same kind as those constituting a 'crime of violence' for the purposes of the 2012 Scheme: actual or grievous bodily harm and wounding caused by the use of weapons, acid, or the offender's own head or limbs. As illustrated by *Bond*,[22] and *Smith v Chief Superintendent, Woking Police Station*,[23] where the offender had deliberately frightened the victim by staring at her through her bedroom window, an order may be apt where the victim suffers anxiety or a nervous condition as a result of acts or words that cause the victim to apprehend that immediate unlawful violence will be used against her.[24] Similarly, an order may be apt following a conviction for an offence under sections 20 or 47 of the OAPA 1861 in respect of silent phone calls, text messages, and emails,[25] or for other forms of harassment constituting the offence of stalking.[26] These possibilities illustrate three general points concerning the potential for compensation under sections 130–134 of the PCC(S)A 2000 when compared with the 2012 Scheme.

7.17 First, as the examples concerning harassment indicate, not every offence that results in personal injury will constitute 'a crime of violence' under the 2012 Scheme (Chapter 2.35–2.37), but on conviction may fall within the scope of section 130(1). Injury caused by poisoning is no longer explicitly within its scope, but a conviction under section 24 of the OAPA 1861 could trigger an order. Neither is bigamy 'a crime of violence',[27] but in *Sones* an order was made against the complainant's 'husband' on conviction under section 57 of the OAPA 1861 for the 'significant distress' that she suffered upon discovering that her marriage was bigamous.[28] Injuries sustained by the victims of sexual offences may in many

---

21 [2013] EWCA Crim 644, [2013] 1 WLR 3861 [16] (CA).
22 *Bond* (n 10).
23 (1983) 76 Cr App Rep 234 (CA).
24 *Chan-Fook* (1994) 99 Cr App Rep 147 (CA); ch 2.40.
25 *Ireland, Burstow* [1988] AC 147 (HL), Malicious Communications Act 1988 s 1(1)(a).
26 Protection from Harassment Act 1997, s 2(A).
27 *Gray v Criminal Injuries Compensation Board* (1999) SC 137.
28 [2012] EWCA Crim 1377, 2012 WL 2191447 (CA).

cases be compensable under the 2012 Scheme, but some, such as voyeurism, are not.[29] However, a compensation order can be made on conviction of an offence under section 67 of the Sexual Offences Act 2003, and if it were a criminal offence, might cover the circumstances of 'upskirting'.[30]

Secondly, a personal injury may potentially fall within the 2012 Scheme, but be excluded because it does not meet its more restrictive provisions. A victim who suffers a psychiatric injury caused by witnessing a crime of violence being committed against another might benefit from a compensation order. This would not constitute 'a criminal injury' unless the victim feared that violence might be used against himself (Chapter 2.30–2.33). In these circumstances, or where the victim was directly threatened with a weapon, the court could make an order in respect of 'terror, shock or distress', as an aspect of the assessment of the pain and suffering the victim suffered as a result of her injury.[31] In *Godfrey* the Court of Appeal confirmed the use of compensation orders where the defendants were convicted of affray in which they had directly threatened the victim.[32] Orders could also be apt where persons who are unwilling and proximate spectators to a street fight or other behaviour that results in convictions under Part 1 of the Public Order Act 1986 (POA 1986). **7.18**

Thirdly, the victim may have sustained a personal injury, but not one that is sufficiently serious to meet the 2012 Scheme's £1,000 threshold. By contrast, compensation orders can, and typically are, made for lower sums. This is of particular relevance for victims who suffer those 'minor multiple injuries' that were excluded as a result of the changes to the tariff in 2012 (Chapter 5.42–5.44). For example, the 2012 Scheme excludes compensation for 'temporary mental anxiety' (Chapter 5.39), an injury having a suggested starting point in the MCSG Guiidelines of £500 (Chapter 8.21). **7.19**

B Injuries caused by road traffic offences

As section 35(3) of the PCCA 1973 also provided that no order could be made in respect of loss suffered 'by the dependants of a person in consequence of death' arising from the offence for which the offender was convicted, neither were fatal accidents caused by road traffic offences compensable. As in the case of the 2012 Scheme (Chapter 2.69), the factors that weighed in favour of their exclusion were that compensation would be provided by the driver's insurance or under the arrangements made by the Motor Insurers' Bureau (MIB).[33] **7.20**

---

[29] *Criminal Injuries Compensation Authority v First-tier Tribunal and BW* [2017] UKUT 97 (AAC) [21]; (ch 2.35).

[30] The Law Commission (2015) para 3.109. This would be an offence under s 9(4A) of the Sexual Offences (Scotland) Act 2009.

[31] MCSG *Guidelines* (n 12) *Compensation 1* para 8.

[32] (1994) 15 Cr App R (S) 536.

[33] Advisory Council on the Penal System (n 2) para 63.

7.21 Their exclusion where personal injury was caused was criticized by the Hodgson Committee,[34] and remedied by the amendments made to the Criminal Justice Act (CJA 1988). With the continuing exclusion of fatal injuries, section 130(6) of the PCC(S)A 2000 provides that a compensation order can be made if it is in respect of an injury for which the offender was uninsured and for which compensation is not payable by the MIB, or the defendant has been charged with an offence under the Theft Act 1968 or the Fraud Act 2006. Thus in *Paymai*,[35] where, following a minor road traffic accident, the defendant drove at the victim, knocking him off his motor bike and injuring him, a compensation order might have been appropriate were it not for the fact that the injury did not result from an offence of theft or fraud, and the defendant was insured. Unlike the 2012 Scheme, a compensation order may be made whether or not 'the vehicle was used with intent to cause injury to a person'. Where the conditions in section 130(6) apply, an order could be made in respect of injuries caused by an offence under section 1A (causing serious injury by dangerous driving) or section 3ZD (causing serious injury by driving: disqualified drivers) of the Road Traffic Act 1988.

7.22 As section 130(6) only applies to motor vehicle accidents, there would seem to be no objection to a compensation order on conviction of an offence under section 35 of the OAPA 1861 where a cyclist causes personal injury, as to which, compare the position under the 2012 Scheme (Chapter 2.70–2.75).

C Causation

7.23 The 'personal injury' must be one 'resulting from' the offence for which the offender was convicted, or was TIC. This causal question is one of fact, which the Divisional Court held in *Bond* should be approached 'in a broad common sense way' that does not 'become enmeshed in the refined questions of causation which can sometimes arise in claims for damages under the law of contract or tort'.[36] The leading authority remains *Thomson Holidays Ltd*, where the Court of Appeal approved a test in which the court 'must ask itself whether loss or damage can fairly be said to have resulted to anyone from the offence for which the accused has been convicted or which has been taken into consideration'.[37]

7.24 While easily stated the test is not always easily applied, particularly in cases where a number of defendants are involved. In allocating causal responsibility to one or more of them for the purpose of making an order on conviction of affray under section 3 of the POA 1986, in which a non-participant is injured, the Court of Appeal distinguished two broad sets of circumstances. In the first, *Taylor*, where 'the events take place so close to each other in time and are so linked with each

[34] Hodgson, *Profits of Crime* (n 1) 56.
[35] [2013] EWCA Crim 1383, 2013 WL 3878945 [5] (CA).
[36] *Bond* (n 10) 44 (McCullough J).
[37] [1974] QB 592, 599 (CA) (Lawton LJ) (*Thomson Holidays*).

other that it would be both artificial and unjust to look narrowly at the physical acts of each defendant relied upon by prosecution',[38] the order may be made against any one of them. But if, as in *Derby*, there is a break in those events, and it is clear that the injuries were inflicted by one of the other participants, it would be wrong to make an order against the appellant.[39]

7.25 These two decisions have become clear reference points in cases of affray, and will include the offence of violent disorder under section 2 of the POA 1986. In reaching its decision in *Taylor*, the Court expressly referred to *Thomson Holidays*, and in *Derby* it emphasized that 'there is authority in this Court that the strict views of causation in tort and contract are not to be applied [in these cases]. But it is also entirely clear that there must be evidence of causation before the order can be made'.[40] No order could be made in *Deary*,[41] where there was no 'proven causal link' between the defendant's participation in the affray and the victim's injury, or in *Woolmer*, where it was clear that the defendant had not herself inflicted any injury.[42] Nor, in *Wenzel*, could the injury have resulted 'from the simple possession or carrying of [an article with a blade or a point] in a public place' contrary to section 139(1) of the CJA 1988.[43]

7.26 Where, as in *Bond*,[44] the offender's behaviour is 'the only cause' of the victim's injury, there will clearly be a sufficient causal link, but it does not have to be the sole cause.[45] In this respect, the Court of Appeal's approach to causation reflects its decision in *R v Criminal Injuries Compensation Board, ex parte Ince*, where Megaw LJ held that, for the purposes of the scheme, a personal injury could be 'directly attributable' to a crime of violence or an act of law enforcement if either of these was a substantial cause of the injury; it did not need to be the sole cause (Chapter 3.32–3.35). The question was whether 'a reasonable person, applying his common sense, would fairly and seriously regard [the incident] as being a cause'.[46]

7.27 A compensation order may be appropriate, as in the case of the 2012 Scheme, where the victim is injured when seeking to escape a violent situation, for example, by jumping out of a moving car (Chapter 3.43–3.45).[47] This may be so notwithstanding that the offence expressly contemplates a personal injury other than the one sustained by the victim. An offender who fires a weapon intending

---

38 (1993) 14 Cr App R (S) 276, 280 (CA) (Waterhouse J).

39 (1990–91) 12 Cr App R (S) 502 (CA).

40 ibid 503 (Tudor Evans J).

41 (1993) 14 Cr App R (S) 648 (CA).

42 [2004] EWCA Crim 2690, 2004 WL 2700817 [15] (CA) (Tugendhat J).

43 [2001] EWCA Crim 335, 2001 WL 172080 (CA); further Archbold, *Criminal Pleading, Evidence and Practice 2018* (Sweet & Maxwell 2018) para 5-675.

44 *Bond* (n 10).

45 *Rowlston v Kenny* (1982) 4 Cr App R (S) 85, 88 (CA) (McCullough J); and *Corbett* (1993) 14 Cr App R (S) 101 (CA).

46 [1973] 3 All ER 808, 812, 815 (CA) (Megaw LJ).

47 *Roberts* (1971) 56 Cr App Rep 95 (CA); and *Lewis* [1970] Crim LR 647 (CA).

to kill or cause the victim grievous bodily harm but misses, could, on conviction of an attempt, be ordered to pay compensation for the shock the victim suffered.

IV Eligible Persons

A Non-fatal injuries

7.28 The majority of persons in whose favour a compensation order may be made will be those whose injuries comprise the external element of an offence under the OAPA 1861; that is, a person whom the 2012 Scheme would treat as the 'direct victim'. This was certainly what was contemplated when the legislation was enacted in 1972, but the operative provisions did not restrict the class of eligible persons to those *directly* injured by the offence. As Lawton LJ confirmed in *Thomson Holidays,* the power to order compensation 'for any personal injury' is unqualified; an order may be made for an injury (or loss or damage) that 'can fairly be said to have resulted to *anyone* from the offence' (emphasis added).[48]

7.29 It was suggested earlier that an order may be apt where a person suffers shock who is not the 'direct' victim of the offence, but a bystander, for example of a robbery or a shooting, or who witnesses a house she knows to be occupied being the subject of an arson attack. These are hypothetical possibilities, but in *Vaughan* the Court of Appeal contemplated the possibility that the witnesses to acts of criminal damage who had suffered shock could properly be compensated.[49] It emphasized that the person suffering shock would need to be identified separately from the direct victim of the offence, and with clear evidence of the alleged shock being available to the court.

B Fatal injuries

7.30 The CJA 1988 gave the court power to make an order requiring the offender 'to make payments for funeral expenses or bereavement in respect of a death' resulting from the offence for which he was convicted or was TIC. This power is now contained in section 130(1)(b) of the PCC(S)A 2000, save where the death was 'due to an accident arising out of the presence of a motor vehicle on a road'.

7.31 In common with the 2012 Scheme, an order in respect of funeral expenses 'may be made for the benefit of any one who incurred the expenses' (section 130(9)). The basic funeral payment under the 2012 Scheme is £2,500 (Chapter 5.105–5.107), but the amount of the compensation order is not fixed. This is because the court must take account of the offender's means to pay it, and even where his means are sufficient, the order is at its discretion.

---

[48] *Thomson Holidays* (n 37) 599.
[49] (1990–91) 12 Cr App R (S) 46 (CA).

By section 130(10), an order in respect of bereavement may be made 'only for the benefit of a person for whose benefit a claim for damages for bereavement could be made under section 1A of the Fatal Accidents Act 1976', and 'shall not exceed the amount for the time being specified in section 1A(3) of that Act', that is, £12,980. As a conventional sum, payment for bereavement requires no assessment of the dependant's loss, but even where the offender has means it is unlikely that he would be able to pay this amount, which is why this order is also not fixed. **7.32**

V The Sentencing Court's Duties

In its review of the pre-1972 arrangements, the Advisory Council doubted the wisdom of imposing on the victim an obligation to apply for compensation. Apart from the obvious point that the victim is a third party who has no *locus* in criminal proceedings, 'arguments during a criminal trial about the desirability of awarding compensation, and the amount, would distract the courts from their primary function'; that is, determination of the offender's guilt. 'Save in cases where liability and quantum are clear the courts would be well advised not to order compensation'.[50] **7.33**

Its conclusions did not, however, answer the problem that it had earlier identified as being one of the primary obstacles to the making of compensation orders; that is, whose was the responsibility for adducing and verifying evidence of the victim's injury? Its recommendations, enacted in 1972 and consolidated in section 35(1) of the PCCA 1973, provided only that the court could make an order 'on application or otherwise', without specifying who could or should make it. In practice, this meant that an order would follow representations by the prosecution or the defence, or 'otherwise' of the court's own motion, as in *Bond*.[51] A sufficient basis could emerge during the trial, or where there was a guilty plea, in a *Newton* hearing,[52] but specific evidence of the extent of the victim's injury depended on the detail with which the police completed the administrative routines that were developed during the 1970s and 1980s for checking whether the victim wished to receive compensation, and for verifying the victim's loss.[53] **7.34**

There was, however, little consistency in the extent to which police forces complied with these routines; some did not fully accept that the issue of victim compensation was 'their job', but was that of the magistrates and their clerks. Following a **7.35**

---

[50] Advisory Council on the Penal System (n 2) para 78.

[51] *Bond* (n 10).

[52] (1982) 77 Cr App R 13 (CA).

[53] Joanna Shapland and David Cohen, 'Facilities for Victims: the role of the police and the courts' [1987] Crim L R 28–38; Tim Newburn, *The Use and Enforcement of Compensation Orders in Magistrates' Courts* (Home Office Research Study 102 1988).

parliamentary review in 1984,[54] the government proposed that the court should be obliged to give reasons why it had not made an order in any case in which it had power to do so. This took effect as section 104(1) of the CJA 1988, now section 130(3) of the PCC(S)A 2000: 'A court shall give reasons, on passing sentence, if it does not make a compensation order in a case where this section empowers it to do so'. This additional duty is important, as judicial review does not lie in respect of the Crown Court's failure to make a compensation order; nor is there a prosecution right of appeal in such a case.[55]

7.36 The legislative and administrative rules governing criminal trials now place much greater emphasis on the criminal justice agencies' responsibilities for recognizing the victim's interest in obtaining compensation. In the case of both the magistrates' and the Crown Court, the Criminal Procedure Rules 2015 (CPR 2015) state that the prosecutor must

> provide information relevant to sentence, including any statement of the effect of the offence on the victim, the victim's family or others; and (d) where it is likely to assist the court, identify any other matter relevant to sentence, including—(i) aggravating and mitigating factors, (ii) the legislation applicable, and (iii) any sentencing guidelines, or guideline cases.[56]

The Sentencing Council's sentencing 'Steps' indicate that the court should, as a matter of routine, consider whether to make a compensation order; for example, in its updated 'sentencing guidelines and offences involving corrosive substances', made in response to reports of increased assaults and robberies involving the use of acid.[57]

7.37 Where they wish to use one, a Victim Personal Statement (VPS) gives victims a formal opportunity to say how the offence has affected them 'physically, emotionally, psychologically, financially or in any other way', and whether they wish to claim compensation.[58] In its guidance on compensation orders, the Crown Prosecution Service (CPS) indicates that the role of the prosecutor is 'to draw the court's attention to its powers to award compensation and inviting them to make such an order where appropriate', for which purpose the VPS 'and any evidence in support should be considered and taken into account by the court prior to passing sentence'.[59] A VPS is presented to the court as an expert's report or a witness statement made under section 9 of the Criminal Justice Act 1967 as part of the judge's papers, and must be served in good time on the defendant's solicitor

---

[54] Home Affairs Select Committee (1985) para 46.

[55] *Faithfull v Ipswich Crown Court* [2007] EWHC 2763, [2008] 1 WLR 1636 (DC).

[56] Ministry of Justice (2015b), *Rules and Practice Directions, Trial,* Part 24 rule 24.11.3 and Part 5 rule 25.16.3.

[57] Sentencing Council, *Sentencing Guidelines and Offences Involving Corrosive Substances.*

[58] Crown Prosecution Service, *Victim Personal Statements.*

[59] Crown Prosecution Service, *Sentencing, Ancillary Orders, The Role of the Prosecutor in Compensation Applications.*

or the defendant if he is not represented.[60] However, 'except where inferences can properly be drawn from the nature of or the circumstances surrounding the offence, a sentencing court must not make assumptions unsupported by evidence about the effects of an offence on the victim'.[61]

A VPS can 'fulfil an important role, either in terms of calibrating the seriousness of the offence or in identifying compensation for the crime victim',[62] as is illustrated by *Sones*[63] and *Malik*.[64] Research on its use in Scottish courts has also shown an association between its presence and court ordered compensation.[65] Reviewing in 2012 the use of compensation orders since their introduction thirty years earlier, the government noted that there had been 'significant variations in the proportion of offenders required by the courts to pay compensation. The 1990s saw a gradual decline in the use of compensation orders'; in 2001 the proportion (13%) was the same as in 1988, a figure that had risen to 18 per cent in 2010.[66] **7.38**

The government attributed what it regarded as an unsatisfactory incidence and level of offender compensation to a variety of factors. Some were particular to the applicable law, but many reflected the difficulties identified in this chapter. Nor have the courts necessarily fully taken on their duty to give reasons why they have not made an order where empowered to do so. Research conducted in the 1990s showed that in some 70 per cent of cases in which magistrates made no order, no reason was given, contrary to the express terms of the legislation.[67] 'We strongly suspect', the Court of Appeal said in *Jones,* that section 130(3) 'is seldom in the minds of judges when sentencing, unless they have cause to recall it from bitter experience'. In order 'to avoid this pitfall, judges and the Bar should make sure' that this duty 'is considered at the time of sentencing'.[68] **7.39**

In 2008, compensation orders to the value of £31.5 million were issued, but in order to 'encourage a much greater use' of the 'tried and tested' compensation order as a way of ensuring that offenders provide reparation to their victims,[69] **7.40**

---

60 *Perkins and Others* [2013] EWCA Crim 323, [2013] 2 Cr App R (S) 72 [9C]–[9D] (CA).

61 The evidential and other formalities are set out in Criminal Practice Directions [2013] EWCA Crim 1631, [2013] 1 WLR 3164; Sentencing F: Victim Personal Statements; Consolidated Criminal Practice Direction III.28.2(a).

62 Julian Roberts and Marie Manikis, *Victim Personal Statements: A Review of Empirical Research* (Report for the Commissioner for Victims and Witnesses in England and Wales 2011) 4.

63 *Sones* (n 28) [8].

64 [2013] EWCA Crim 1703, 2013 WL 5336583 [16] (CA).

65 Fiona Leverick, James Chalmers, and Peter Duff, *An Evaluation of the Pilot Victim Statement Schemes in Scotland* (Scottish Executive Social Research 2007).

66 Ministry of Justice (2012d) para 134.

67 Claire Flood-Page and Alan Mackie, *Sentencing Practice: An Examination of Decisions in Magistrates' Courts and the Crown Court in the Mid-1990s* (Home Office Research Study 180 1998).

68 [2003] EWCA Crim 1631, [2004] 1 Cr App R (S) 23 [18] (CA) (The Recorder of London).

69 Home Office (2010) 20; Ministry of Justice (2010) para 32; (2012c) para 162; (2012d) para 135.

LASPOA 2012 added section 130(2A) to the PCC(S)A 2000, imposing the additional duty on the court that it 'must consider making a compensation order in any case where this section empowers it to do so'. The lexical ordering of sections 130(2A) and (3) present the court with a clear sequence of sentencing decisions: first, to consider whether to make an order when it has power to do so, and secondly, where that power exists, to give reasons where it does not. By rule 28.1(b)(ii) of the CPR 2015, where it decides not to make a compensation order where it could, 'the court must explain why it has so decided, when it explains the sentence that it has passed'.[70]

7.41 Assuming a proper consideration of the circumstances, good reasons for not making an order will relate to the kinds of cautionary matters that the Court of Appeal has identified, and, as discussed in Chapter 8, difficulties concerning the assessment of the victim's injury, and the sufficiency of the offender's means. It may be, as their VPS indicates, that the victim does not wish to be compensated by the offender or, because of an existing relationship between them, it would be inappropriate to make an order. A victim who is 'aggrieved by the conviction, order, determination or other proceeding of the court' may by section 111 of the Magistrates' Courts Act 1980 appeal to the High Court by way of case stated, but it is suggested that where the magistrates' decision not to make an order conforms to the advice that the senior courts have repeatedly given, such an appeal is unlikely to be successful.

7.42 At the time when the government was considering the proposal that became section 130(2A), the number of compensation orders made between 2006/2007 and 2012/2013 in all courts against all offenders fell from 165,874 to 148,906. This gradual decline masks a much starker profile in the case of violent offences against the person; the numbers in the magistrates' courts fell from 8,068 to 2,902, and in the Crown Court from 2,690 to 1,205.[71] In the case of sexual offences, there was a slight increase in the magistrates' courts, from 368 to 430 offenders, but a slight decline in the Crown Court, from forty-six to forty orders. Whether these procedural changes have increased the incidence and level of offender compensation remains to be seen.

70 Ministry of Justice (2015b), Pt 28 r 28.1(1)(b)(ii).
71 Ministry of Justice (2017a), Table Q5.1a and Q5.3.

8

COMPENSATION ORDERS

Assessment of Compensation

I Introduction

Assuming that the victim's injury falls within the scope of section 130(1) of the Powers of Criminal Courts (Sentencing) Act 2000 (PCC(S)A 2000), and the sentencing court considers it appropriate to make a compensation order, it is then necessary to determine its amount. In *Stapylton v R*, the Court of Appeal reviewed the key elements of the principles that the courts have established since the compensation order powers were widened in 1972, consolidated in the Powers of Criminal Courts Act 1973 (PCCA 1973).[1] First, the court has no jurisdiction to make an order where there are real issues as to whether those to benefit have suffered any, and if so, what loss.[2] Secondly, because compensation orders are for 'simple and straightforward cases',[3] a court should not embark on a detailed **8.01**

[1] [2012] EWCA Crim 728, [2013] 1 Cr App R (S) 12 [12] (CA) (Cranston J).
[2] *R v Horsham Justices, ex parte Richards* [1985] 1 WLR 986 (QBD) (*ex parte Richards*); *Watson* (1990–91) 12 Cr App R (S) 508 (CA).
[3] *Kneeshaw* [1975] QB 57, 60 (CA) (Lord Widgery CJ).

inquiry as to the extent of any injury, loss, or damage. If the matter demands such attention it is better left for civil proceedings.[4] Thirdly, compensation orders must not be made unless there is a realistic possibility of compliance,[5] and should not be made if they will be protracted in effect, although much will turn on the nature of the offence and the offender.[6] These principles, and the issues to which they give rise, are the subject matter of this chapter.

II Financial Evaluation of the Victim's Injury

A Evidence of injury

8.02 Whether the conviction is for an offence against the person, property, or public order, or was an offence taken into consideration (TIC), it has been authoritatively held on a number of occasions that the fact of the injury, and the extent of any medical or financial consequences (or loss or damage) that the victim sustained, must be agreed by the defendant or established by evidence. The Court of Appeal's observation in *Amey,* that proof of injury 'means proof by evidence and not by inference or guesswork',[7] succinctly confirmed earlier *dicta,* that if there is no evidence of injury no order can be made.[8] In the absence of any information as to the extent of the victim's injuries, it would, as the Court has also held on many occasions, be more appropriate for the victim, 'if he sees fit, to bring proceedings in the county court', where 'proper medical reports could be considered'.[9]

8.03 As a consequence of what the government thought to be an unnecessarily restrictive interpretation of the legislation in *Vivian,*[10] the Criminal Justice Act 1982 added section 35(1A) to PCCA 1973, now section 130(4) of the PCC(S) A 2000, providing that compensation 'shall be of such amount as the court considers appropriate, having regard to any evidence and to any representations that are made by or on behalf of the accused or the prosecutor'. This, the Court of Appeal held in *Baker-Owens and Brennan,* means 'that a court must take account of, but need not necessarily be bound by, a basis of plea, provided that the basis of plea has been properly accepted in the way that it is dealt with in the Consolidated Practice Direction.[11] When the Court interpreted section 130(4) in *Swann,* it concluded that the amendment's effect was to 'ease slightly the requirement' that

4 *Donovan* (1981) 3 Cr App R (S) 192 (CA); *Briscoe* (1994) 15 Cr App R (S) 699, 701 (CA).
5 *Webb* (1979) 1 Cr App R (S) 16 (CA).
6 *Olliver* (1989) 11 Cr App R (S) 10 (CA).
7 [1983] 1 WLR 345, 347 (CA) (Kilner Brown J).
8 *Vivian* [1979] 1 WLR 291, 293 (CA); *Vaughan* (1990–91) 12 Cr App R (S) 46, 48–49 (CA).
9 *Cooper* (1982) 4 Cr App R (S) 55, 57 (CA) (Stocker J).
10 *Vivian* (n 8); Hansard, HC Debs vol 16 col 302 (20 January 1982).
11 [2013] EWCA Crim 2315, 2013 WL 6229730 [22] (CA) (Aikens LJ).

there must be evidence or agreement as to the 'correct' amount of compensation.[12] It had not eliminated any need for the victim's injury and its impact to be established to the court's satisfaction; rather it expressly gave what had (arguably) earlier been implied, namely a discretion to fix the amount of the order in the light of the evidence.

But section 35(1A) did not license proof by inference or guesswork. Where the cause or nature of the injury, its impact, the offender's liability, or what would be an 'appropriate' amount of compensation are in doubt, the matter cannot, Neill LJ held in *ex parte Richards*, be determined 'merely by representations'.[13] The Court of Appeal has regularly cited this *dictum* with approval, and as section 130(4) is in identical terms to section 35(1A), it continues to be authoritative on the court's approach to its application.[14] **8.04**

Where there has been a conviction following a not guilty plea to an offence against the person, some evidence of the injury will have emerged during the trial, although this is likely to be less well established where shock or distress is occasioned by an offence against property, or by a bystander witness to a public order offence. The legal guidance of the Crown Prosecution Service (CPS) on ancillary orders requires the prosecution to provide the court with up-to-date and detailed information concerning the extent of the injury: **8.05**

> This will usually involve medical reports and photographs. As a general rule, the more serious the injury, the more information will be needed by the court including details of the injury itself, treatment, time lost from work and the likely prognosis. Details of expenses such as dentists or opticians should be available.[15]

These observations apply with greater force where sentence follows a guilty plea or the injury is the result of a TIC offence. As a general matter, the Court of Appeal has stressed that the effect of the offence on the victim must be demonstrable by potentially admissible evidence, and where they open a case on a plea of guilty, counsel should not refer to the effect of the offence on the victim, unless appropriate evidence has been served on the defendant.[16] In practice, evidence of the effects of an offence on the victim is most likely to be provided in a Victim Personal Statement (VPS),[17] but it is also possible for the defendant to offer to pay compensation by way of mitigation. In this case, counsel must be able to verify the source from which payment will be made,[18] as to which the court should **8.06**

---

[12] (1984) 6 Cr App R (S) 22 (CA).

[13] *Ex parte Richards* (n 2) 993.

[14] *James* [2003] EWCA Crim 811, [2003] 2 Cr App R (S) 97 [9] (CA); *Stapylton* (n 1) [12].

[15] Crown Prosecution Service, *Sentencing, Ancillary Orders, Legal Guidance* (CPS, *Ancillary Orders*) *The Role of the Prosecutor in Compensation Applications.*

[16] *Hobstaff* (1993) 14 Cr App R (S) 605, 607 (CA) (Ognall J).

[17] Crown Prosecution Service, *Victim Personal Statements.*

[18] Archbold, *Criminal Pleading, Evidence and Practice 2018* (Sweet & Maxwell 2018) para 5-683.

make further enquiries if the offer of compensation appears 'more aspirational than realistic'.[19]

8.07 Where information is incomplete, the court has some discretion to make an assessment of the amount to be awarded. However, if the claim is challenged, as *ex parte Richards* confirmed,[20] and the CPS advises,[21] the court must hear evidence to determine liability. Where there is a dispute, prosecutors should avoid going beyond available information in pressing a victim's case. The Magistrates' Court Sentencing Guidelines indicate that 'where it is difficult to ascertain the full amount of the loss suffered by the victim, consideration should be given to making a compensation order for an amount representing the agreed or likely loss. Where relevant information is not immediately available, it may be appropriate to grant an adjournment for it to be obtained'.[22] But, as Watkins LJ said in *Hyde v Emery*, '[t]he process of making compensation orders should be a very simple one. Courts should not be invited, and if invited, should decline the invitation, to endeavour to proceed to make compensation orders upon evidence out of which arise questions difficult to resolve of either fact or law or both'.[23] This is especially the case where, as in *Bewick*, there was 'headlong conflict between the two competing witnesses'.[24]

B Sufficiency of evidence as to the extent of injury

8.08 The two leading early authorities dealing with the making of compensation orders both stressed that they were 'intended for clear and simple cases', to be used 'as a convenient and rapid means of avoiding the expense of resort to civil litigation'. They 'should certainly not be used when there is any doubt as to the liability to compensate, nor should they be used when there is a real doubt as to whether the convicted man can find the compensation'. An order 'made by the court of trial can be extremely beneficial as long as it is confined to simple, straightforward cases and generally cases where no great amount is at stake', but 'it must always be remembered that the civil rights of the victim remain', and in 'a great majority of cases the appropriate court to deal with the issues raised by matters of this kind is in the appropriate civil proceedings'.

8.09 These cautionary remarks, drawn from *dicta* by Lord Widgery CJ in *Kneeshaw* and Scarman LJ in *Inwood*,[25] set the repeated context in which the Court of Appeal

---

19 *Carrington* [2014] EWCA Crim 325, [2014] 2 Cr App R (S) 41 [9] (CA) (Turner J); *James* (n 14) [4].

20 *Ex parte Richards* (n 2).

21 CPS, *Ancillary Orders* (n 15) *The Role of the Prosecutor in Compensation Applications.*

22 Sentencing Council, *Magistrates' Court Sentencing Guidelines, Explanatory Materials, Fines and Financial Orders* (MCSG *Guidelines*) *Compensation 1* para 8.

23 (1984) 6 Cr App R(S) 206, 210 (CA).

24 [2008] 2 Cr App R (S) 31 [12] (CA) (Sir Michael Astill); *Thames Water Utilities* [2010] EWCA Crim 202, [2010] 2 Cr App R (S) 90 [39 xi] (CA) (Moore Bick LJ).

25 *Kneeshaw* (n 3) 60; *Inwood* (1974) 60 Cr App R 70, 75 (CA).

has dealt with appeals against the making of a compensation order. The quantity and quality of the evidence that the court considers will be sufficient for an assessment of the victim's injury will of course vary according to a number of factors, principally the nature and extent of the injury and its long-term effects. It may be, as in *Welch*, that there is 'enough information about the nature of the assault and the consequences' that the victim experienced to justify the order,[26] but that does not relieve the court from making a proper assessment of the amount that is payable to reflect the victim's experience. In *Godfrey* the Court of Appeal agreed that a compensation order was an entirely appropriate response to the defendants' racist threats against the victim, but fundamental to that response 'is a secure basis upon which the compensation order can be based, namely an assessment of precisely what it is that has been suffered by the victim and then an appropriate determination of its value in money terms'.[27]

The sentencing court's task was analysed in some detail by Hedley J in *Pola*,[28] and **8.10** *Sones*,[29] which also illustrate the scope of section 130(1) of the PCC(S)A 2000 (Chapter 7.16–7.19). In *Pola* the victim had sustained severe brain injuries as the result of an accident at work in respect of which the builder had been convicted of an offence under section 33(1)(a) of the Health and Safety at Work etc Act 1974, and which left him with permanent disabilities.[30] The Crown Court judge made a compensation order in his favour in the sum of £90,000; had this been a criminal injury, a comparable tariff award under the Criminal Injuries Compensation Scheme 2012 (2012 Scheme) of £110,000 for 'moderately severe brain damage' might be appropriate. The difficulty was that the evidence of the victim's injuries was incomplete and medically complex, which raised the question whether they were outside the ambit of cases for which compensation orders are designed. Nevertheless, Hedley J concluded that the judge 'was not only entitled to make the order that he did but was right to do so'.[31]

1. There was a clear causal link between the conviction and the injury.
2. The judge had available to him sufficient evidence of the gravity of the injury to demonstrate that it was worth far in excess of anything that he was minded to award.
3. The judge had satisfied himself that there was no more convenient or practicable alternative route of which [the victim] might avail himself.
4. The judge had satisfied himself that the appellant had the means to satisfy the order that he had in mind.

---

[26] (1984) 6 Cr App R (S) 13, 15 (CA) (Ackner LJ).
[27] (1994) 15 Cr App R (S) 536, 537 (CA) (Latham J).
[28] [2009] EWCA Crim 655, [2010] 1 Cr App R (S) 6 (CA).
[29] [2012] EWCA Crim 1377, 2012 WL 2191447 (CA).
[30] Pola (n 28).The live issue in the appeal, decided in his favour, was whether the victim was an employee of the building firm, [1]–[25] (CA) (Moses LJ).
[31] ibid [31]–[32] and [35].

5. The order was compliant with both with the policy of section 130 and its practice in that he gave priority to the compensation order over any other financial order.
6. The order was just and proper in the context of the appellant's proven culpability.

8.11 In *Sones* Hedley J returned to point 3 of his analysis, the relevance of the viability or otherwise of the victim's civil remedy in cases where there is some doubt about the evidential basis on which a proper assessment of the injury may be made. The difficulty in this case lay in quantifying the victim's losses upon the discovery that her marriage was bigamous.[32] While drawing attention to the Court of Appeal's repeated caution that the sentencing court should not involve itself in detailed analysis of remoteness, causation, and of the appropriate compensation, Hedley J noted that the Court has also been clear that it 'should not hesitate to use its powers of compensation where it is possible to achieve substantial justice between the parties and saving the rather protracted process of County Court proceedings'. It was important in such cases 'properly to strike the necessary balance'.[33]

8.12 In *Inwood* Scarman LJ had concluded that as the legislation left 'a considerable area of judgment', requiring only that it should have regard to the offender's means, the sentencing court 'must follow a common sense course' in its application.[34] A more nuanced conclusion may be seen in *Pola*, where the Court commented that 'it may be that the very cautious approach adopted in the early cases needs some modification and full weight to be given to the words of Scarman LJ'.[35] A 'common sense course' might therefore be sufficient to support an order that addresses that element of the victim's injuries or losses that the court can properly assess. As it was clear in *Sones* that the complainant had suffered both stress and lost work opportunities, and equally plain that the appellant was in a position to pay some compensation, the Court's confirmation of the order sought to strike 'the necessary balance' between the early authorities' strictures, and achieving 'substantial justice' between the parties.[36]

C Determining the quantum of compensation

1 Introduction

8.13 The MCSG Guidelines indicate that:

> The court should consider two types of loss: financial loss sustained as a result of the offence such as the cost of repairing damage or, in case of injury, any loss of earnings

---

32 *Sones* (n 29) [15].
33 ibid [13].
34 *Inwood* (n 25) 75.
35 *Pola* (n 28) [33].
36 *Sones* (n 29) [18]–[19].

or medical expenses; and pain and suffering caused by the injury (including terror, shock or distress) and any loss of facility. This should be assessed in light of all factors that appear to the court to be relevant, including any medical evidence, the victim's age and personal circumstances.[37]

2 Financial loss

Earlier guidelines for magistrates indicated that such items as loss of earnings, expenses incurred in obtaining dental treatment, replacing spectacles or damaged clothing, or in travelling to hospital, were properly compensable where they were supported by documentary evidence of these losses, and of payments made by or on the victim's behalf.[38] The provision to the court of payslips, receipts, bills, and the like is now the responsibility of the CPS,[39] but as the Court of Appeal confirmed in *Flinton,* where the victim claimed that he had been off work as a result of the assault, in the absence of any documentary evidence to that effect, no order for loss of earnings could be made.[40] **8.14**

Where, as in *Smith,* there is insufficient evidential basis on which to make an assessment of the injury, or the evidence as to the financial loss is disputed or complex, the victim's remedy is, as the Court of Appeal has frequently restated, 'if so minded and if advised, to bring a civil claim'.[41] Where matters are contentious, this expectation may, as it observed in *James*, 'be wholly unrealistic'. But in a comment that presaged Hedley J's preference for 'a necessary balance' between the parties' interests, the Court held that notwithstanding their apparently irreconcilable differences, it would be 'good practice' to make a compensation order where the calculation of the victim's minimum loss was comparatively simple, rather than to decline on grounds of complexity.[42] **8.15**

3 Pain and suffering

Two aspects of the process of assessing the victim's pain and suffering stood as initial obstacles to the routine making of compensation orders in magistrates' courts following the widening of their scope in 1972. The first was magistrates' lack of training and of preparedness to place a monetary value on what was often the victim's self-reported experience of the injury. These factors were instrumental in the appellate courts' strong advice that magistrates should not engage in anything other than the simplest assessments of injury. **8.16**

---

[37] MCSG *Guidelines* (n 22) *Compensation 1* para 8.

[38] 'Compensation for injury' (1980) *Justice of the Peace* 698.

[39] CPS, *Ancillary Orders* (n 15) *The Role of the Prosecutor in Compensation Applications.*

[40] [2007] EWCA Crim 2322, [2008] 1 Cr App R (S) 96 [4]–[5] (CA) (Mitting J).

[41] [1998] 2 Cr App R (S) 400, 402 (CA) (Keene J); *Ukueku* [2015] EWCA Crim 184, 2015 WL 685487 [12] (CA).

[42] *James* (n 14) [7] and [15] (Henriques J).

8.17 The second was that the guideline figures prepared by the Magistrates' Association were generally at a lower level than the injury would attract in a civil action. This was an effect of magistrates' common experience that, having taken account of their means, the majority of offenders could not meet those levels. This is necessarily a systemic issue in the implementation of section 130(1); there will frequently be a disparity between the amount that the court might ideally wish to order the offender to pay, what might be called an 'ideal assessment' of the injury, and the requirement that it must take the offender's means into account before making the order.

8.18 A 1985 parliamentary review had concluded that it was not 'desirable that two different standards of compensation should apply depending on the victim's choice (or lack of it) of remedy',[43] recommending that the Criminal Injuries Compensation Board prepare a new set of guidelines for use by magistrates and in the Crown Court. Because the scheme was then based upon them, these guidelines would reflect common law general damages. This was first published in 1988.[44] But, as the government later observed, the underlying tension between the ideal assessment of the victim's injury, and the reality of what the offender can afford to pay remained unresolved, exacerbated by widespread variation in the incidence and levels of awards made in magistrates' courts.[45]

8.19 Its proposed remedy was that the Sentencing Council should adapt the MCSG Guidelines to support a more consistent approach to fixing the value of compensation, to be based upon the tariff in the 2012 Scheme, and developed by the Criminal Injuries Compensation Authority (CICA). This does not mean that compensation orders would necessarily be made at its levels, since many injuries would fall below the £1,000 threshold, and of course the offender's means would have to be taken into account, but the guidelines would provide a uniform reference point for the court.

8.20 The two sets of MCSG Guidelines comprising '*suggested starting points for physical and mental injuries*' are set out in full below.[46] Table 8.1 suggests starting points for compensating those injuries that are commonly encountered in a magistrates' court. The definition of a 'disabling' mental injury is that used in Part A of Annex E to the 2012 Scheme (Chapter 3.60–3.63). The CICA tariff makes no award for minor injuries which result in short-term disability; the suggested starting points for these injuries are adapted from an earlier tariff.

[43] Home Affairs Select Committee (1985) para 51.

[44] Home Office Circular No 85/1988, *Guidelines on Compensation in the Criminal Courts.* Annex (*Home Office Circular*).

[45] Ministry of Justice (2012d) paras 142–43.

[46] MCSG *Guidelines* (n 22) *Compensation 2.*

Table 8.1 Physical injury

Type of injury	*Description*	*Suggested starting point*
Graze	Depending on size	£75
Bruise	Depending on size	£100
Cut: no permanent scar	Depending on size and whether stitched	£100–£300
Black eye		£125
Eye	Blurred or double vision lasting up to 6 weeks	£500
	Blurred or double vision lasting for 6 to 13 weeks	£1,000
	Blurred or double vision lasting for more than 13 weeks (recovery expected)	£1,500
Brain	Concussion lasting one week	£1,500
Nose	Undisplaced fracture of nasal bone	£1,000
	Displaced fracture requiring manipulation	£2,000
	Deviated nasal septum requiring septoplasty	£2,000
Loss of non-front tooth	Depending on cosmetic effect	£750 per tooth
Loss of front tooth	Depending on cosmetic effect	£1,500 per tooth
Facial scar	Minor disfigurement (permanent)	£1,000
Arm	Fractured humerus, radius, ulna (substantial recovery)	£1,500
Shoulder	Dislocated (substantial recovery)	£900
Wrist	Dislocated/fractured—including scaphoid fracture (substantial recovery)	£2,400
	Fractured—Colles type (substantial recovery)	£2,400
Sprained wrist, ankle	Disabling for up to 6 weeks	£500
	Disabling for 6 to 13 weeks	£800
	Disabling for more than 13 weeks	£1,000
Finger	Fractured finger other than index finger (substantial recovery)	£300
	Fractured index finger (substantial recovery)	£1,200
	Fractured thumb (substantial recovery)	£1,750
Leg	Fractured fibula (substantial recovery)	£1,000
	Fractured femur, tibia (substantial recovery)	£1,800
Abdomen	Injury requiring laparotomy	£1,800
Temporary mental anxiety	(including terror, shock, distress) not medically verified	£500
Disabling mental anxiety	lasting more than 6 weeks, medically verified	£1,000
Disabling mental illness	lasting up to 28 weeks, confirmed by psychiatric diagnosis	£1,500

8.21 Table 8.2 suggests starting points for compensating physical and sexual abuse. The MCSG observes that it will be rare for cases involving this type of harm to be dealt with by magistrates, such offences being more commonly dealt with in the Crown Court; in these cases they should consult their legal adviser for guidance.

8.22 The starting points in these two tables are consistent with the CICA's 2012 tariff values, and in the more serious cases are their equivalents; but it is essential to recognise that the 'suggested' figures are *guidelines* only. They do not, as is their function in the 2012 Scheme, specify in categorical terms the award that is to be made should the injury fit the relevant descriptor. In the application of the tariff to a claimant's injury there is no discretion: it is a binary choice between the two closest descriptors (Chapter 5.19).

8.23 Nor can the suggested figures displace the court's discretion to determine as section 130(4) provides, the amount of compensation that it 'considers appropriate'; that is, at, above or below that point, depending on the medical evidence of the extent and impact of the injury. Earlier guidance given to magistrates indicated that 'the amount of compensation should be determined in the light of the medical evidence, the victim's sex and age, and any other factors which appear to the court to be relevant in the particular case',[47] guidance that is substantially repeated in the current guidelines.

8.24 In assessing the victim's pain and suffering, the court may alternatively refer to or rely on the Judicial College's Guidelines, formerly published by the Judicial Studies Board.[48] This reliance is seen in *Smith*,[49] *Akman*,[50] and *Best*,[51] all of which concerned facial scarring and disfigurement. If the court does rely on these Guidelines, it is essential that it does so explicitly, explaining how, on the basis of the medical evidence, it arrived at its chosen figure. In *Saunders* the court made an order for £10,000 payable over twenty months at £500 per month, where the victim 'had been left scarred for life, physically and psychologically' as the result of being 'glassed' in an offence under section 20 of the Offences Against the Person Act 1861 (OAPA 1861).[52] Reducing the order to £5,000, payable at £250 per month, the Court of Appeal acknowledged that 'awarding compensation orders in criminal cases in circumstances such as these is not an easy task', but was critical of the court's failure to meet these essentials, where the medical evidence placed the injury within a bracket between £2,900 and £10,100.

---

47 *Home Office Circular* (n 44).

48 Judicial College, *Guidelines for the assessment of General Damages in Personal Injury* (14th edn, Oxford University Press 2017).

49 *Smith* (n 41) [402].

50 [2009] EWCA Crim 1087, 2009 WL 1321746 [11] (CA).

51 [2004] EWCA Crim 483, 2004 WL 343812 [6] (CA).

52 [2014] EWCA Crim 2272, 2014 WL 5797373 [9]–[11], [16]–[17] (CA).

Table 8.2 Physical and sexual abuse

Type of injury	*Description*	*Suggested starting point*
Physical abuse of Adult	Intermittent physical assaults resulting in accumulation of healed wounds, burns or scalds, but with no appreciable disfigurement	£2,000
Physical abuse of Child	Isolated or intermittent assault(s) resulting in weals, hair pulled from scalp etc	£1,000
	Intermittent physical assaults resulting in accumulation of healed wounds, burns or scalds, but with no appreciable disfigurement	£1,000
Sexual abuse of adult	Non-penetrative sexual acts over clothing	£1,000
	Non-penetrative sexual act(s) under clothing	£2,000
Sexual abuse of child (under 18)	Non-penetrative indecent physical act(s) over clothing	£1,000
	Non-penetrative frequent assaults over clothing or non-penetrative indecent act under clothing	£1,500 or £2,000
	Repetitive indecent acts under clothing	£3,300

The assessment is to be made 'in light of all factors that appear to the court to be relevant'. In *Flinton* that factor was the victim's unlawful conduct in striking the first blow in the assault in which he was injured. On appeal against the order to pay the victim £1,500, the Court of Appeal first took the view that what might constitute an 'appropriate' amount within section 130(4) should not exceed the sum which would be awarded by a court in civil proceedings, which, on a full liability basis was £1,000.[53] **8.25**

The Court also concluded that the words, 'such amount as it considers appropriate', are 'plainly wide enough to encompass the reduction of an award on account of the unlawful conduct of the victim of an assault', at least where that conduct contributes to its occurrence. The 2012 Scheme's earlier provisions concerning the victim's conduct were noted (Chapter 4.22–4.36), but provided limited guidance, 'because it is the taxpayer and not the assailant who is being required to provide compensation to the victim'.[54] Unlike the 2012 Scheme, the Court thought it appropriate to strike a balance between the victim's unprovoked assault, and the offender's subsequent assault against him, reducing the order by 25 per cent. But where the relevance of and weight to be attached to the victim's conduct is less clear, it may be appropriate, as in *Cooper*, that the matter be decided in civil proceedings.[55] **8.26**

53 *Flinton* (n 40) [4]–[5].
54 ibid [8].
55 *Cooper* (n 9) 57.

D Financial limits on compensation orders

8.27 In its 2012 consultation paper, *Punishment and Reform: Effective Community Sentences,* the government observed:

> The mean value of [a] compensation order imposed in 2010 was £306. In real terms, this average has remained stable over the last decade. This is in contrast to the real terms increase in the average value of fines over the same period. As with fines, these averages also hide variation beneath the surface. In the magistrates' courts, the mean value of compensation awarded in 2010 (excluding summary motoring offences) was £240. However, nearly a quarter of all compensation orders imposed by magistrates are for £1,000 or more. In the Crown Court, by contrast, the mean value was £1,454: but nearly two-thirds of all compensation orders imposed were for less than £100.[56]

8.28 There are no limits on the amount of compensation that a Crown Court may order, and until its removal in the Crime and Courts Act 2013 (CCA 2013), section 131 of the PCC(S)A 2000 capped single compensation orders imposed in the magistrates' courts at £5,000. The government was critical of this limit, which it argued unnecessarily hindered magistrates in meeting their obligations under section 130.[57] Noting that in 2010, a small but not insignificant proportion of compensation orders that they imposed were within the region of £4,000 to £5,000, it concluded that it would be desirable to lift the £5,000 cap to bring compensation orders into line with changes that it was making to fines.[58]

8.29 The effect of the amendment made by the CCA 2013 is that there is now no limit on the value of a single compensation order that magistrates may impose on an adult offender. The former limit in section 131(2) concerning TIC offences is maintained in the case of a young offender (Chapter 9.36–9.38).

E Multiple offences, defendants, and victims

1 Multiple offences

8.30 Where there are convictions for multiple offences or multiple TIC offences, 'it is important to bear in mind that what the Act empowers the court to do is to make an order requiring the accused to pay compensation for any personal injury, loss or damage resulting from *that offence or any other offence*' (original emphasis). Lawton LJ added: 'It seems to us that it is clear from the wording of the Act that any order for compensation must be related to a specific offence whether that offence be in the indictment or be an offence taken into consideration'.[59] Similarly, in setting out in *Inwood* the basis for the requirements noted in the following paragraphs, Scarman LJ said: 'A compensation

[56] Ministry of Justice (2012d) para 143.
[57] Ministry of Justice (2012a) para 165.
[58] Ministry of Justice (2012d) para 145.
[59] *Oddy* [1974] 1 WLR 1212, 1216 (CA).

order must be related to a particular sum of money owing to a particular person, firm or other body ... A single compensation order when there are different offences and different victims contravenes good practice, and is, perhaps, even a nullity'.[60]

An omnibus order is proper only if there is one victim and one offender and, where there are multiple offences, only if they were all committed against the same victim. Otherwise, it is, as Lawton LJ said in *Oddy*, 'a grave defect' to make an order for a global sum not related to any specific offence or any specific loser, adding, 'and not merely on legalistic grounds, because if any loser does seek to proceed by way of civil action how is he to know what he is going to get out of the compensation order?'[61] Similarly, in the case of payment by instalments, the order 'must specify the instalments—only if this is done can the loser's rights at civil law be adequately protected'.[62] **8.31**

2 Multiple defendants

Whether it is appropriate to order compensation against one defendant and not another depends, first, as the Court of Appeal's decision in *Lovell* to reduce the order against the second defendant shows,[63] on their degrees of responsibility for the offence and resulting injury. In *Godfrey* the two defendants had been ordered to pay differing amounts, which the Court of Appeal reduced on the ground, first, that the court had made no proper assessment of what was payable in respect of the victim's experience, and secondly, that it had no material upon which it could properly differentiate between them in terms of their responsibility. The resulting figure was therefore divided between them.[64] If two or more defendants are equally responsible for the victim's injury, as in *Cooper and Cooper*, each of whom has sufficient means, it is 'clearly appropriate to make the same order in respect of all of them'.[65] **8.32**

The second consideration depends on their relative capacity to pay.[66] Equal contributions for equal culpability would have been appropriate in *Priestly*, save that the appellant had no means of paying his half of the order.[67] But in offences against public order or joint enterprise, it may be difficult to determine exactly who did what, and consequently who ought to pay compensation in respect of the injury. Referring to *Taylor* (Chapter 7.24–7.25), the CPS's advice repeats Lawton LJ's test in *Thomson Holidays*, that the court may make an award 'where it can **8.33**

60 *Inwood* (n 25) 74; *Henry* [2012] EWCA Crim 1265, 2012 WL 1933524 [6] (CA).
61 *Oddy* (n 59) 1218.
62 *Miller* (1979) 68 Cr App R 56, 58 (CA) (Peter Pain J).
63 [2012] EWCA Crim 1564, 2012 WL 2500572 [5] (CA).
64 *Godfrey* (n 27) 537.
65 [2017] EWCA Crim 262, 2017 WL 01084444 [9] (CA) (Sir John Griffith Williams).
66 *Beddow* (1987) 9 Cr App R (S) 235 (CA).
67 [2013] EWCA Crim 1883, 2013 WL 5826267 [3] (CA).

fairly be said that a particular loss results from an offence, without having regard to the technical issues of causation'.[68]

3 Multiple victims

8.34 Where there are competing claims by more than one victim, but the defendant has insufficient means to pay them all in full, the CPS' advice is that the court should decide on an appropriate figure and apportion it on a pro rata basis.[69] Where there are several claimants and one of them has a large claim which is much greater than those of others, apportionment on a pro rata basis 'may lead to one or more small claimants being compensated to a wholly inadequate degree', for example in the case of an article of relatively small intrinsic value but of importance to the individual:

> In theory the civil remedy is still there, but in reality this may be either impossible or futile ... In such a case the court should exercise its inherent discretionary power to see that justice was done and select one or more claimants to the exclusion of others.[70]

III Financial Evaluation of What the Defendant Can Pay

A Introduction

8.35 A distinguishing feature of the law on compensation orders is the relevance of the offender's means to the decision to make an order, and for how much. This consideration is of course wholly absent from an action in damages for personal injury where, if there is liability, the defendant's financial status is, so far as the formal judgment goes, neither here nor there. The court's obligation to consider the defendant's means is set out in section 130(11) of the PCC(S)A 2000. 'In determining whether to make a compensation order against any person, and in determining the amount to be paid by any person under such an order, the court shall have regard to his means so far as they appear or are known to the court'.

8.36 This obligation has two main implications for the theory and practice of compensation orders. The offender's means are relevant, first, because a financially onerous order may lead to further offending to meet its requirements, or in some other way may be incompatible with the sentencing objectives appropriate in his case. The sentencing court's concern not to impose an order that would in this sense be counter-productive, is one element of the Court of Appeal's long-held view that the order must be 'realistic'.[71]

68 CPS, *Ancillary Orders* (n 15) *Compensation in Cases Where There Is More Than One Defendant*; *R v Thomson Holidays* [1974] QB 592, 599 (CA).
69 ibid.
70 *Amey* (n 7) 347.
71 *Miller* (n 62) 58; *Webb* (1979) 1 Cr App R (S) 16, 18 (CA).

The desirability of an order that does not induce the offender 'to go back to crime' may be tempered by a robust view of what she can reasonably be expected to pay. Merely to base an appeal on the ground that she might commit further offences will not be persuasive if the amount is, relative to her means, not large and the offender is fit for work. The demands of such penal models as just deserts or modern retributivism may suggest that a compensation order is apt, notwithstanding that the offender may experience difficulty in complying with it.[72] In *Bradburn* Lord Widgery CJ observed: 'There are good moral reasons for making compensation orders which will in measure hurt the defendant's pocket and act to remind him of what he has done'.[73] Referring to these observations, the Court of Appeal commented in *Wing* that: 'It is not right to restrict orders to cases where the defendant can easily pay'.[74] **8.37**

The obligation 'to have regard to [the offender's] means so far as they appear or are known to the court' is relevant, secondly, because many offenders will have insufficient means to comply with a compensation order that reflects an ideal assessment of the injury, even by way of instalments, a consideration that underlines its limited potential to meet the victim's interests. It may be, as in *Best*, where it was indicated by the JSB Guidelines,[75] that the order does meet that assessment, or as in *Jhally* where, although it was reduced on appeal, it was nevertheless in line with what a civil court would order.[76] But it is also clear that any limitations on the offender's ability to pay may mean that the order will be for an amount that is significantly less. For example, in *Stancombe*, the victim's scarring would have been valued at £5,000 in general damages, but as the offender was earning no more than £5 an hour the order was reduced to £1,500, to be paid at £30 a week.[77] **8.38**

B Assessing the offender's capacity to pay the order

1 *The offender's current and future means*

In *Khokhar* the Court of Appeal stressed that: 'It is elementary that no [compensation] order should be made unless there are assets or some prospect of it being met'.[78] The purpose of a means enquiry 'is to ensure that the compensation award in any given case is realistic and to avoid the possibility of making an order which is an impossible financial burden unable to be met by a defendant', in particular **8.39**

72 Andrew Ashworth, *Sentencing and Criminal Justice* (Cambridge University Press 2015) 93–96; Susan Easton and Christine Piper, *Sentencing and Punishment* (Oxford University Press 2016) section 2.6.

73 *Bradburn* (1974) 57 Cr App R 948, 953.

74 [2017] EWCA Crim 633, 2017 WL 02978782 [10] (CA) (Henriques J).

75 *Best* (n 51) [6].

76 [2015] EWCA Crim 791, 2015 WL 2190629 [10] (CA).

77 [2005] EWCA Crim 1139, 2005 WL 1459180 [10]–[14] (CA).

78 [2006] EWCA Crim 1538, 2006 WL 2469701 [24] (CA) (Tuckey LJ).

where the defendant will be released from prison with no established means.[79] Failure to conduct this enquiry may result in the order being quashed, but if on appeal it appears that the offender does have means, for example good prospects of employment, an order may then be made.[80]

8.40 It is clear, first, that present inability to pay is not conclusive against making an order. A person who is without capital or income is not necessarily a person without 'means' for the purpose of section 130(11). If he enjoys good health and has reasonable prospects of employment, as in *Bradburn*,[81] an offender may be ordered to pay compensation, although the amount and the period over which it is payable may be limited. In determining what it is reasonable, the court will take account of the offender's outgoings by way of rent and utilities' bills, and the demands on his income presented by his dependants.

8.41 There is no objection in principle to the inclusion of state benefits as an element of the offender's income, as for example in *Williams*,[82] but it would be inappropriate where the offender is entirely dependent on a disability benefit, and without any other means to pay the order.[83] But where the offender was properly in receipt of accumulated and backdated benefits on which the offender and her family could rely, she had the means by which to pay the compensation order that was made in respect of her earlier fraudulent claims.[84]

8.42 By section 162(1) and (2) of the Criminal Justice Act 2003, the court has power, before sentencing the offender, to make a financial circumstances order that will, by section 162(3) as amended by the CCA 2013, include a statement of his 'assets'. This amendment was intended 'to make it clear that courts can, where appropriate, take account of an offender's assets when fixing the value of a financial penalty. This will allow courts to impose proportionate and equitable fines and compensation orders in cases where offenders may be cash-poor but have property of significant value'.[85] The power in section 162(1) reaffirms the courts' longstanding view that it is not unreasonable to require an offender to sell his assets to enable him to pay compensation,[86] in which case the sentencing court should take steps to enquire as to their value.[87]

8.43 Those assets could include the offender's car, against which a 'clamping order' may be made should he default on payment of the order,[88] and perhaps more

79 *Gray* [2011] EWCA Crim 225 [15] (Irwin J).
80 *Cooper and Cooper* (n 65) [16].
81 (1974) 57 Cr App R 948, 952 (Lord Widgery CJ).
82 [2004] EWCA Crim 1911, 2004 WL 1808742 (CA).
83 *Djouma* [2004] EWCA Crim 351, 2004 WL 412941 [7] (CA).
84 *Beyter* [2016] EWCA Crim 134, 2016 WL 01129812 [10] (CA).
85 Ministry of Justice (2012e) para 10.
86 Ashworth, *Sentencing* (n 72) 343; *Chambers* (1981) 3 Cr App R (S) 318 (CA).
87 *Cooper and Cooper* (n 65) [14].
88 Courts Act 2003 s 97, Sch 5, Pt 9 para 38(2).

controversially could comprise the equity in the offender's flat,[89] or the sale of the matrimonial home. The Court of Appeal considered this latter possibility at length in *Parkinson*,[90] a case concerning the making of a compensation order with a confiscation order where the offender's means were insufficient to pay both in full. For the purposes of section 9 of the Proceeds of Crime Act 2002 (POCA 2002), the offender's share in the matrimonial home constituted 'free property', and was thus available for disposal by the court. Where the offender cannot pay both orders, section 13(6) of the POCA 2002 provides that the shortfall in compensation must be met from the confiscation order (Chapter 9.52–9.54). In this case, the value of the offender's interest in the home was 'in principle capable of being regarded as means potentially available for the purposes of meeting and satisfying a compensation order'.[91]

The offender had challenged the judge's order, referring to a number of earlier decisions of the Criminal Division,[92] but the Court was persuaded by its more recent decision in *Maguire*,[93] where it 'firmly rejected the notion that there was some general principle that a compensation order should not be imposed if the effect would be to force the sale of the family or matrimonial home'.[94] The reluctance to require the sale of the matrimonial home stems from the basis that a family should not be made homeless but, as illustrated by *Khokhar*, this is not 'an absolute rule'. The Court of Appeal agreed that making a compensation order in the council's favour, where the defendant had been convicted of offences with regard to housing and council tax benefit, was 'one of those exceptional cases in which it is right to make such an order'.[95] **8.44**

Moreover, as the Court observed in *Parkinson*, it may not be thought exceptional where a half share in the matrimonial home might be worth a great deal of money: 'Why should there be any general principle operating to prevent a compensation order being made when, even if the property in consequence had to be sold, the defendant and his family may be able to acquire a cheaper property as a family home with the remaining equity?' No such principle was to be found in section 130 of the PCC(S)A 2000, which, as Scarman LJ indicated in *Inwood*,[96] while requiring the court to have regard to the offender's means, **8.45**

---

[89] *Dorton* (1987) 9 Cr App R (S) 514, 516.

[90] [2015] EWCA Crim 1448, [2016] 1 Cr App R (S) 6 (CA).

[91] ibid [21]–[22] (Davis LJ).

[92] *Blackmore* (1984) 6 Cr App R (S) 244 (CA); *Hackett* (1988) 10 Cr App R (S) 388 (CA); *Holah* (1989) 11 Cr App R (S) 282 (CA).

[93] (1991) 13 Cr App R (S) 332, 334 (CA).

[94] *Parkinson* (n 90) [28]; the Court also distinguished on its facts *Beaumont* [2014] EWCA Crim 1664, [2015] 1 Cr App R (S) 1 (CA), a two judge decision that had followed these earlier decisions of the Criminal Division.

[95] *Khokhar* (n 78) [28].

[96] *Inwood* (n 25).

'otherwise essentially leaves unfettered the exercise of the discretion of the judge in this kind of situation'.[97]

8.46 Apart from her employment and receipt of state benefits, an offender may claim to have other sources of income, but the Court of Appeal has insisted that vague assertions about unliquidated sums being available at some point in the future are to be treated with caution.[98] The offender's claim that she may obtain the money from a third party by way of gift or loan is not 'automatically' to be disregarded,[99] but in *Patsalos* the Court emphasized that the judge must be satisfied that the offender will be able to pay, and, if she proposes to borrow the money, that she will be able to repay the loan.[100]

8.47 These *dicta* follow earlier authorities, notably *Phillips*, in which the Court emphasized the need for 'most careful enquiry' into such third-party sources.[101] Noting the imposition of the duty on the court to take the defendant's means into account, in *Carrington* the Court observed that: 'what steps are appropriate to discharge this duty will vary from case to case. But where, as here, there are grounds to suspect that any offer of compensation may be unrealistic, further enquiries involving, if necessary, the taking of evidence will be apt'.[102] Where they put information about the offender's means before the court, counsel similarly have a clear duty to satisfy themselves of their existence and sufficiency, and must themselves make appropriate enquiries of the offender.[103]

2 Payment by instalments

8.48 'There is nothing wrong with an order for compensation of a relatively high amount',[104] but 'the key considerations are whether the order will impose an undue burden (e.g. will it constitute too severe a punishment given the offender's means) and whether the judge reached a figure for compensation on a supportable basis'.[105] One way of suiting the offender's means to the ideal assessment of the victim's injury is to order him to pay in instalments. In the magistrates' court, this power is provided by section 75 of the Magistrates' Courts Act 1980 (MCA 1980), 'a magistrates' court by whose conviction or order a sum is adjudged to be paid may, instead of requiring immediate payment, allow time for payment'. In the Crown court, it is provided by section 141 of the PCC(S)A 2000. Where

---

97 *Parkinson* (n 90) [29].
98 *Johnstone* (1982) 4 Cr App R (S) 141 (CA); *Inwood* (n 25); and *Ferreira* [2003] EWCA Crim 2073, 2003 WL 21729193 [4] and [10] (CA).
99 *Carrington* (n 19) [13].
100 [2016] EWCA Crim 768, 2016 WL 03564044 [12].
101 (1988) 10 Cr App R (S) 419 (CA).
102 *Carrington* (n 19) [16].
103 Archbold (n 18) para 5-685; *Engen* [2004] EWCA Crim 1536, 2004 WL 1372293 [14] (CA).
104 *Patsalos* (n 100) [7].
105 *Saunders* (n 52) [13].

it makes an order against an accused for the payment of compensation, the court may '(a) allow time for the payment of the sum due under the order; (b) direct payment of that sum by instalments of such amounts and on such dates as the court may specify'. Thus, as in *Patsalos*,[106] and in *Lovell*,[107] an order that is excessive may be both reduced in its amount, and the period over which it is to be paid increased.

Like the question, *how much* should the offender be required to pay, the question *for how long* a period should he be required to pay is relative to his particular circumstances. In *Williams* the Court of Appeal observed that '[T]he need to avoid excessively long periods of payment by instalments has been considered by this Court on a number of occasions',[108] quashing periods of four,[109] six,[110] and a 'wildly excessive' payment of seven and a half years.[111] In *Webb* it had approved the principle that a compensation order should not be made in such an amount that the offender will have no prospect of paying within the foreseeable future,[112] and in *Broughton* indicated that, as a general guideline, the court should follow 'much the same principles as those for fines, namely a period of 12 months or thereabouts', coinciding with the 1988 Home Office circular.[113] **8.49**

But, as the Court emphasized in *Williams*, 'there is, of course, no set formula. Every case must be determined upon the circumstances of the defendant. Regard must be made to his age, his prospects of employment and his liabilities'.[114] Revisiting the case law at length in *Olliver*, a decision concerning the imposition of both fines and compensation orders, Lord Lane CJ held that there was nothing wrong in principle in a period of payment longer than one year, providing it is not an undue burden and so too severe a punishment having regard to the nature of the offence and the nature of the offender: 'Certainly it seems to us that a two-year period will seldom be too long, and in an appropriate case three years will be unassailable'.[115] **8.50**

Olliver has been applied many times; for example in *Favell*,[116] and in *Yehou*, where an appropriate order 'would have been one which ran for three years only, to pay £25 a week in respect of an order for £3,900, not £9,000'.[117] But in *Ganyo* the **8.51**

[106] *Patsalos* (n 100) [17], *Stancombe* (n 77).
[107] [2012] EWCA Crim 1564, 2012 WL 2500572 [11]–[13] (CA) (Henriques J).
[108] ibid [8].
[109] *Bradburn* (n 73) 952.
[110] *Daly* [1974] 1 WLR 133 (CA).
[111] *Makin* (1982) 4 Cr App R(S) 180 (CA).
[112] (1979) 1 Cr App R (S) 16 (CA) (Cantley J).
[113] (1986) 8 Cr App R (S) 379, 381 (Saville J); *Home Office Circular* (n 44).
[114] *Williams* (n 82) [13].
[115] *Olliver* (n 6) 15.
[116] [2010] EWCA Crim 2948, 2010 WL 5093968 [12] (CA).
[117] [1997] 2 Cr App R(S) 48, 50 (CA) (Hidden J). In *Khokhar* (n 78) the period of payment was increased from 3 months to 2 years.

Court said that: 'neither *Oliver* [sic] nor *Yehou* are authority for a bright line rule imposing an outer limit for the period of repayment of a compensation order'. In effect restating the Court's long-held view on section 130(4), Cranston J held that when making a compensation order, the sentencer

> must ask whether it is appropriate. That requires an enquiry into whether the compensation order will be oppressive or an undue burden given the offender's means, whether realistically the offender can be expected to repay in the terms proposed and whether the compensation order accords with the nature of the offence and the nature of the offender.[118]

8.52 The MCSG Guidelines state: 'Where the offender has little money, the order may have to be scaled down or additional time allowed to pay; the court may allow compensation to be paid over a period of up to three years in appropriate cases'.[119] Referring to *Ganyo*, where it held that because the offender would have sufficient earnings to meet the order, it was not 'unrealistic to expect that she can continue to pay over a period of [eight] years',[120] the Court confirmed in *Hossain* its view that the authorities 'did not support the proposition that there was any outer limit on the period over which a compensation order could be made to be repayable'. But the order must always be subject to a realistic appraisal of what the defendants could pay.[121]

C The sufficiency of the offender's means and the assessment of the victim's injury

8.53 Between 2006/2007 and 2012/2013 the average compensation for indictable offences of violence against the person ordered by magistrates was £285, and for sexual offences £229. At the Crown Court, the average payments were £797 and £925 respectively.[122] Assuming an offender with some means, the matters discussed in the preceding sections raise two questions concerning their sufficiency.[123]

8.54 The first involves a judgment about the relationship between the offender's means and the ideal assessment of the victim's injury. Given their underlying purpose, and the statutory duties on the court in sections 130(2A) and (3) of the PCC(S) A 2000, where the offender does have sufficient means in this first sense, an order should, absent any prior sentencing considerations, be routinely made. There may be many cases in which the offender can pay, as a lump sum or in instalments,

---

118 *Ganyo* [2011] EWCA Crim 2491, [2012] 1 Cr App R (S) 108 [9] (CA).
119 MCSG, *Guidelines* (n 22) *Compensation 1* para 9.
120 *Ganyo* (n 118) [10]–[11].
121 *Hossain* [2016] EWCA Crim 1099, 2016 WL 04446426 [16]–[18] (CA).
122 Ministry of Justice (2013a), Table A5.17.
123 The discussion draws on David Miers, *Compensation for Criminal Injuries* (Butterworths 1990) 243–48.

an order that meets that assessment. Their sufficiency in this instance is not an absolute matter, but is relative to the injury that the offender caused. Where an assault results in a cut leaving no permanent scar, the MCSG Guidelines suggest a bracket of £100–£300, depending on its size and whether it was stitched. An offender with only £60 disposable weekly income could, by analogy with the guidelines on the payment of fines, be ordered to pay at a rate of £5 a week over forty weeks in respect of a cut assessed at £200.[124]

Insufficiency in this first sense arises where the offender does not have the means to pay, even in instalments within the normal twelve-month period, a sum that is either commensurate with, or in the court's view, appropriate to the ideal assessment. The Advisory Council thought that 'the unpalatable fact' that an order may be 'derisory in comparison with the victim's loss' would be 'a strong incentive' not to make one.[125] In *Priestly* the Court of Appeal noted that 'whilst there may be a practice of requiring those on benefits to pay a sum of £5 a week for 52 weeks to ensure that they make some compensation', such a small sum against an order for £800 over twelve months would be inappropriate.[126] **8.55**

The question of whether the court should refrain from making an order where the payment would be so out of proportion to the ideal assessment of the injury so as to minimize or trivialize it, necessarily engages the relevance of the victim's interest in compensation. As the Court of Appeal commented in *Normanton*, while no amount of compensation may properly recompense her for a serious injury, the victim should not regard the reduction it had to make to reflect the offender's means as downplaying her injury.[127] The victim may have indicated in her VPS that she is prepared to accept what might amount to no more than a token recognition of the harm done. Alternatively, as past research, confirmed in later interviews, indicates, many victims do not wish to prolong their contact with the offender, in particular by receiving delayed or what they perceive to be derisory compensation payments.[128] The MCSG Guidelines indicate that 'compensation should benefit, not inflict further harm on, the victim', cautioning that 'any financial recompense from the offender may cause distress'.[129] The issue is therefore not whether the offender *can* pay, but whether he *should* pay, and if so how much, issues that are implicit in the appellate courts' frequent justification for not making an order: that the victim is free to pursue her civil remedy. **8.56**

[124] MCSG *Guidelines* (n 22) *Approach to the assessment of fines 12.*
[125] Advisory Council on the Penal System (1970) para 28.
[126] *Priestly* (n 67) [7].
[127] [2003] EWCA Crim 959, 2003 WL 21236388 [12]–[14] (CA) (Gross J).
[128] Commissioner for Victims and Witnesses in England and Wales (2011), 18–23; and David Miers, 'Offender and State Compensation for Victims of Crime: Two Decades of Development and Change' (2014) 20 *International Review of Victimology* 145, 149–50.
[129] MCSG *Guidelines* (n 22), *Compensation 1* para 6.

8.57 Sufficiency may, secondly, involve a judgment about the relationship between the offender's means and the likelihood of his compliance with the order, irrespective of its commensurability with the ideal assessment of the victim's injury. Here the issue is not whether he *should* pay, but whether he *can* pay. Frequently, an offender will have insufficient means in both senses, and so it is considered appropriate that no order is made, that it is substantially reduced, or that the period of payment is increased. But where only one sense is apt in any case, it is important that the right reason for these variations is given, or where no order is made, is a reason that satisfies section 130(3) of the PCC(S)A 2000.

8.58 Good reasons for not making an order where the offender's means are insufficient in the first sense concern the court's perception of its commensurability with the victim's injury and any views he has expressed. Where the offender's means are insufficient in the second sense, good reasons concern its perception of the relationship between them and the likelihood of the offender being able to comply with the order without frustrating any individualized or general sentencing objectives: 'The crux of the matter is, of course, that while reparation remains an integral part of sentencing the criminal courts must have regard to the other objectives of sentencing, and the needs of prevention of crime, and the treatment of the offender may often be the dominant consideration'.[130]

8.59 In summary, as the Victim Support website indicates:

> If the court decides that an offender must pay you compensation, it will be limited to what they can afford and may depend on the sentence the court has given them. For example, the court will not usually order an offender to pay compensation if they're being sent to prison. The compensation may not cover the full cost of your damage or loss and often the offender will be able to pay it in instalments.[131]

It is in part for these various considerations that it has in the past been suggested that a better option would be for court funds to pay the compensation order, later recovering the amount from the offender.

8.60 This suggestion was closely examined and recommended by the Hodgson Committee,[132] but it presents a number of difficult theoretical and operational issues. These centre on the role of the state, in effect as a lender of last resort for impecunious offenders, of the potential for a perverse incentive as courts set compensation orders in the knowledge that the shortfall will be made up from public funds, and where such an arrangement envisages that there will be financial recovery from the offender, similar challenges as are associated with the collection of fines.[133]

---

130 Advisory Council (n 125) para 28.

131 https://www.victimsupport.org.uk/help-and-support/what-you-can-do/compensation (last accessed 10 June 2018).

132 Report of the Hodgson Committee, *The Profits of Crime and their Recovery* (Heinemann 1984).

133 Ashworth (n 72) para 10.5.8; Easton and Piper (n 72) para 10.2.4.

There is, however, nothing in the government's more recent consultations to indicate that it may pursue this idea. One of the driving forces behind the changes to the statutory conditions governing compensation orders is to fix financial responsibility for their offending more securely on offenders, and the changes made to the 2012 Scheme are expressly intended to reduce the financial burden on public funds. Faced with obstacles to the making of compensation orders, the courts have remarked on the possibilities of a civil action or, more recently, of a claim under the 2012 Scheme.[134] But the MCSG Guidelines are clear that these possibilities should not deflect the court from exercising its section 130(1) power: 'The court must order compensation wherever possible and should not have regard to the availability of other sources such as civil litigation or the Criminal Injuries Compensation Scheme'.[135] 8.61

IV Other Financial Recovery by the Victim

A Introduction

It is always possible that the victim may recover some or all of the financial and non-financial losses that she sustains otherwise than by virtue of the compensation order. The sources may include personal accident insurance, occupational sick pay, Department of Work and Pensions benefits, CICA awards, damages, and other payments by the offender. With the exception of the CICA awards and a civil judgment against the offender for damages, where there are statutory answers to the question, there is no direct authority on what the impact of these other payments upon the making of a compensation order should be. 8.62

Where the injury caused loss of earnings in respect of which the victim has received state benefits that fall within the scope of the Social Security (Recovery of Benefits) Act 1997, the court might take the view that she ought not to be able to recover twice from the offender for that injury. It should also be noted that by section 1(2) of and paragraph 2 of Part I of Schedule 1, any payment made to or for the injured person under section 130 is an 'exempted payment' for the purpose of that Act. 8.63

But this would not hold for the pain and suffering payments represented by the MCSG guideline figures. The matter might be further complicated where the victim has recovered under an occupational or a personal accident insurance policy where, notwithstanding the potential application of analogies drawn from personal injury actions, the court might simply heed the Court of Appeal's repeated caution, that criminal courts should not engage in issues concerning the 8.64

[134] *Ferreira* (n 98) [11].
[135] MCSG *Guidelines* (n 22) *Compensation 1* para 4.

measure of damages. But whatever the details of any statutory or common law recognition of the relevance of these collateral benefits, they variously give effect to one or both of two aspects of their underlying policy: that the victim should be precluded from double recovery either from the offender or from the taxpayer in respect of the same injury.

B Compensation orders and civil damages

8.65 The Advisory Council took the view that, in general, a victim should not be able to recover, in the two sets of civil and criminal proceedings, more than the amount of his injury, loss, or damage.[136] It is indeed difficult to envisage circumstances in which it would be right for an offender to be required to pay damages in excess of the ideal assessment of the victim's injury. Assuming that the objective is to ensure that the victim receives from the offender no more than that assessment as reached by a civil court, the two main factors that are relevant to the question, what effect should the order have upon an award of damages, and vice versa are, first, whether the damages exceed or are less than the order and, secondly, whether the order has been fully complied with. The powers and duties of the civil and criminal courts with respect to this question were contained in sections 37 and 38 of the PCCA 1973, re-enacted with some amendments in sections 133 and 134 of the PCC(S)A 2000.

8.66 Section 133(1) provides that 'the magistrates' court for the time being having functions in relation to the enforcement of a compensation order (in this section referred to as "*the appropriate court*") may, on the application of the person against whom the compensation order was made, discharge the order or reduce the amount which remains to be paid'. One of the three grounds only on which the court may exercise this power is where it appears to the court (s 133(3)(a)), 'that the injury, loss or damage in respect of which the order was made has been held in civil proceedings to be less than it was taken to be for the purposes of the order'.

8.67 Section 134(1) provides that where a compensation order has been made

> in favour of any person in respect of any injury, loss or damage and a claim by him in civil proceedings for damages in respect of the injury, loss, or damage subsequently falls to be determined, the damages in the civil proceedings shall [section 134(2)] be assessed without regard to the order, but the plaintiff may only recover an amount equal to the aggregate of the following—(a) any amount by which they exceed the compensation; and (b) a sum equal to any portion of the compensation which he fails to recover, and may not enforce the judgment, so far as it relates to a sum such as is mentioned in paragraph (b) above, without the leave of the court.

[136] Advisory Council (n 125) para 38.

8.68 The general effect of these two sections, and of their predecessors, is to give formal recognition to any amounts paid by the offender in compliance with the civil judgment, and to give the appropriate court power to discharge or reduce the order where the civil court makes a more modest assessment of the victim's injury than did the sentencing court. The particular effect of sections 133 and 134 may be explained by reference to the four situations that arise from the two factors mentioned above. The examples are drawn from the MCSG *Guidelines*' suggested starting points for physical and mental injuries.

1 Compensation order made and fully paid: damages for a greater sum

8.69 The simplest case is one where an order for an amount less than the ideal assessment of the victim's injury is made payable as a lump sum or in instalments payable over a short period of time and which, by the date of the civil judgment, the offender has fully met. But, as the Court of Appeal observed in *Berry v Cooper*, even here 'the question of further civil rights has to be dealt with very carefully'.[137]

8.70 By section 134(2), the civil court must assess the damages without regard to the order, but the victim may only recover an amount equal to the aggregate of 'any amount by which they exceed the compensation'. A knife injury to the abdomen requiring laparotomy attracts a guideline figure of £1,800, but damages for such injury could well exceed that figure. Suppose the civil court assessed the injury at £5,000, and the sentencing court, having conducted a means enquiry, made an order for £2,000, now fully met. In recovering £3,000, offender's 'contribution' to the civil judgment is recognized, and the victim/claimant prevented from recovering twice for some of the injury.

2 Compensation order made but not fully paid: damages for a greater sum

8.71 Here again the civil court must assess the damages payable without regard to the compensation order. Suppose, in the previous example, that at the date of judgment the offender had paid £1,000 of the order. The victim/claimant may recover £3,000 from the offender, and by section 134(2)(b) an amount equal to the aggregate of 'a sum equal to any portion of the compensation which he fails to recover'; that is £1,000. But section 134(2) also provides that the victim/claimant may not enforce the judgment, 'so far as it relates to a sum such as is mentioned in paragraph (b) above, without the leave of the court'.

8.72 The purpose of section 134 in this case is both to recognize the contribution the offender has made or may make under the order to the satisfaction of the judgment in damages, and to ensure that the enforcement of any remaining liability to meet that judgment takes account of the offender's liability under the

---

[137] (1983) WL 880104 (CA) (Purchas LJ).

two processes. As the Court of Appeal observed in *Osbourne v Kendrick,* 'thus the court retains control over the enforcement even of a judgment obtained in separate civil proceedings, in respect of any amount relating to the original compensation order'.[138]

3 Compensation order made but not fully paid: damages for a lesser sum

8.73 Suppose the victim has been involved in a fight in which he sustained an undisplaced fracture of his nasal bone, for which the court ordered the offender to pay the starting point guideline figure, £1,000. Having conducted a means enquiry of an offender with a weekly income of £200 it ordered him to pay £25 a week, completing the order within twelve months. In the subsequent civil proceedings, by which time the offender has paid £600, the court addresses evidence of the victim's contributory negligence and assesses damages at £800. As in the cases just discussed, the court will have made that assessment without reference to the compensation order, but as that exceeds the damages, the victim/claimant is precluded by section 134 from enforcing the civil judgment. This will leave the offender/defendant liable to pay the £400 remaining in respect of the compensation order, being £200 more than the damages assessment. It is then for the offender to seek a review of the order under section 133(3)(a); if successful, he would pay only a further £200.

4 Compensation order made and fully paid: damages for a lesser sum

8.74 Unlike the three preceding cases there is no provision permitting recognition of the offender's *excessive* payment to the victim. Section 134 ensures that the victim cannot recover twice for the same injury, but does nothing, as in the preceding case, where, by the time of the civil judgment, the offender has fully paid the order; in that case the victim may retain the full £1,000 in respect of an injury the civil court assessed at £800. Nor does the appropriate court have any jurisdiction under section 133 to review the order. It has power only (section 133(2)) where

> (a) at a time when (disregarding any power of a court to grant leave to appeal out of time) there is no further possibility of an appeal on which the compensation order could be varied or set aside; and (b) at a time before the person against whom the compensation order was made has paid into court the whole of the compensation which the order requires him to pay.

8.75 The Advisory Council considered that, in these circumstances, 'it would be impracticable to disturb the situation', and it may also be surmised that the inclusion of provisions enabling the offender to recover the discrepancy between the order and the civil judgment would be both legally and politically difficult.[139] But it might also be said that, given that the criminal court's assessment is a broad one,

---

[138] [2001] EWCA Civ 690, 2001 WL 483083 [14] (CA) (Butterfield J).

[139] Advisory Council (n 125) para 40.

with guidance rather than a prescriptive tariff, and with less prescriptive rules in relation for example to causation, there is nothing intrinsically wrong with the criminal court's assessment resulting in a higher figure than that of a civil court or of the CICA's suggested starting points.

C An award under the Criminal Injuries Compensation Scheme

By paragraph 85(1) of the 2012 Scheme, 'An award under this Scheme will be **8.76** withheld or reduced if in respect of the criminal injury to which the award relates the applicant, whether in any part of the United Kingdom or elsewhere: . . . (d) receives a compensation order or offer made during criminal proceedings'. The scope of this provision was discussed in Chapter 5.136–5.138. It is important to note that, as paragraph 91(c) requires the applicant to inform the claims officer of any claim or other proceedings which may give rise to an award or payment mentioned in paragraph 85 and the progress of the claim or proceedings, the victim will need to alert the CICA to an order that involves payment by instalments, and the progress of the offender's compliance with that order. The object of this paragraph is not to prevent double recovery from the same source but to relieve the taxpayer where the victim can obtain compensation from the offender.

9

COMPENSATION ORDERS AS A SENTENCE OF THE COURT

I Introduction

Compensation orders are intended to benefit the victim, but they are also sentences of the court,[1] and as such must attract some consideration based on current sentencing theory and practice. From this perspective, the single most significant development in their history was the amendment introduced in the Criminal Justice Act 1982 that permits the court to impose a compensation order instead of, and not as was formerly the case, only in addition to dealing with the offender in any other way. That Act introduced a second important change, requiring the court to give priority to a compensation order over the imposition of a fine where the offender's means are insufficient to meet both, a priority that continues to apply to confiscation orders. **9.01**

Compensation orders may also be seen as having a number of beneficial impacts upon the offender: depriving him of assets to pay for the harm done; reparative, **9.02**

[1] *Faithfull v Ipswich Crown Court* [2007] EWHC 2763 (Admin), [2008] 1 WLR 1636 (CA); Archbold, *Criminal Pleading, Evidence and Practice 2018* (Sweet & Maxwell 2018) ch 5 Pt VIII.

by requiring him to compensate the victim for the injuries he caused; and rehabilitative, 'to bring home to a defendant that what he has done has affected somebody who needs to be and should be appropriately compensated'.[2] The offender's realization may, however, seriously constrained by the court's statutory duty to have regard to his means, and is especially problematic where he is either very poor or very wealthy.

9.03 This chapter discusses the issues raised in these paragraphs, dealing first with procedural matters concerning appeals against, and the review of, a compensation order, and its enforcement.

II Procedure: Appeal, Review, and Enforcement

A Appeal

9.04 An offender against whom a compensation order has been made by magistrates or the Cown Court may appeal that decision alone, or together with some other aspect of the sentence. During this time, the order is enforceable and she must make payments, but by section 132(1) of the Powers of Criminal Courts (Sentencing) Act 2000 (PCC(S)A 2000), the victim 'shall not be entitled to receive the amount due to him until (disregarding any power of a court to grant leave to appeal out of time) there is no further possibility of an appeal on which the compensation order could be varied or set aside'. Section 132(2) states that the Criminal Procedure Rules may make provision regarding the way in which the enforcing magistrates' court is to deal with money paid in satisfaction of the order, but it appears that none has been made.

9.05 By section 132(3) of the PCC(S)A 2000, the Court of Appeal may annul or vary any compensation order made by the court of trial. The conviction is not quashed; the order, if annulled, shall not take effect and, if varied, shall take effect as varied. The Supreme Court may, by section 132(4), make any compensation order which the court of trial could have made in a case where it restores a conviction quashed by the Court of Appeal.

9.06 Where a compensation order has been made against any person in respect of an offence taken into consideration (TIC), section 132(5) provides that:

> (a) the order shall cease to have effect if he successfully appeals against his conviction of the offence or, if more than one, all the offences, of which he was convicted in the proceedings in which the order was made; (b) he may appeal against the order as if

[2] *Godfrey* (1994) 15 Cr App R (S) 536, 537 (CA) (Latham J).

it were part of the sentence imposed in respect of the offence or, if more than one, any of the offences, of which he was so convicted.

B Review

On application by the person against whom the compensation order was made, section 133(1) of the PCC(S)A 2000 permits the magistrates' court that is enforcing it (known as 'the appropriate court') to discharge the order or reduce the amount which remains to be paid. As section 133(2)(b) provides, this power may only be exercised 'at a time before the person against whom the compensation order was made has paid into court the whole of the compensation which the order requires him to pay'. That 'person' may include the parents where the order was made against a young offender (9.36–9.38). Secondly, the same time limit applies to its exercise as applies to an appeal under section 133(2)(a). **9.07**

The only grounds on which the court may exercise this power are set out in section 133(3). By section 133(3)(a), the first of these is where the injury, loss or damage has been held in civil proceedings to be less than it was taken to be for the purposes of the order (section 134 (Chapter 8.73–8.74). A second is where, by section 133(3)(d), the person against whom the compensation order was made has suffered a substantial reduction in his means, which was unexpected at the time when the order was made, and that his means seem unlikely to increase for a considerable period (Chapter 8.35–8.47). **9.08**

Section 133(3)(c) provides for three further cases in which 'the means of the person against whom the compensation order was made are insufficient to satisfy in full both the order and any or all of the following orders made against him in the same proceedings'. They are: (i) a confiscation order under Part 6 of the Criminal Justice Act 1988 (CJA 1988) or Part 2 of the Proceeds of Crime Act 2002 (POCA 2002); (ii) an unlawful profit order under section 4 of the Prevention of Social Housing Fraud Act 2013 (PSHFA 2013); and (iii) a slavery and trafficking reparation order under section 8 of the Modern Slavery Act 2015 (MSA 2015). Finally, the order may be discharged or reduced where 'in the case of a compensation order in respect of the loss of any property, the property has been recovered by the person in whose favour the order was made' (section 133(3)(b)). **9.09**

Where the compensation order was made by the Crown Court the appropriate court shall not exercise any power in the cases specified in section 133(3)(c) or (d) unless it has first obtained that court's consent (section 133(4)). Where it was made on appeal from a magistrates' court, the order shall be deemed for the purposes of section 133(4) to have been made by that court, or if made on an appeal **9.10** brought from the Crown Court, or from the Criminal Division of the Court of Appeal, to have been made by the Crown Court (section 133(5)).[3]

C Enforcement

9.11 One of the principles enumerated by the Court of Appeal in *Miller*, and which remains authoritative, is that the order must be precise in its terms: 'It must be related to an offence in respect of which the defendant has been convicted or to an offence which he has asked to have taken into account. It must specify the amount and if there is to be payment by instalments it must specify the instalments'.[4] Compensation orders are enforced by magistrates' courts in substantially the same manner as fines.[5] By section 41(1) of the Administration of Justice Act 1970 (AJA 1970), a compensation order made by the Crown Court

> [s]hall be treated, for the purposes of collection and enforcement, as if it had been adjudged to be paid on a conviction by a magistrates' court, being—(a) where the order is made by a magistrates' court, that court; and (b) in any other case, such magistrates' court as may be specified in the order.

The Victim Support website advises victims that 'the court has to make sure that the offender pays the compensation. If you have any questions about this, you should speak to the clerk of the court or the court manager—you shouldn't discuss this with the offender'.[6]

9.12 Like fines, compensation orders are sums 'adjudged to be paid' and are payable on the day they are imposed. But by section 75 of the MCA 1980, a magistrates' court, and by section 141 of the PCC(S)A 2000), the Crown Court, may allow time for payment or direct payment by instalments, normally for a period not exceeding twelve months (Chapter 8.48–8.52). The Courts Act 2003 created a fines collection scheme that provides for greater administrative enforcement of fines, and of compensation orders. Unless it would be impracticable or inappropriate to do so, the court must make an attachment of earnings order (AEO) or application for benefit deductions (ABD) whenever compensation is imposed.[7]

9.13 While the order would (should) not have been made when he was sentenced unless the offender had means, it does not follow that they will subsist by the

---

[3] Ministry of Justice (2015b), *Rules and Practice Directions, Sentencing,* Pt 28 rule 28.5.

[4] (1979) 68 Cr App R 56, 57 (CA) (Peter Pain J).

[5] Magistrates' Courts Act 1980 (MCA 1980) Pt III; Ministry of Justice (2015b), *Rules and Practice Directions, Sentencing,* Pt 30 r 30.1.

[6] https://www.victimsupport.org.uk/help-and-support/what-you-can-do/compensation (last accessed 10 June 2018).

[7] Courts Act 2003, Sch 5, Collection of Fines, Pt 4 Making of Collection Orders; Sentencing Council, *Magistrates' Court Sentencing Guidelines, Explanatory Material, Fines and Financial Orders* (MCSG *Guidelines*), *Approach to the assessment of fines 13.*

enforcement stage. There are three options available to the magistrates' court in the event that the offender defaults on his payments. Least used are those methods available in respect of a judgment of the High Court or County Court, where it is enforceable 'as if the sum were due to the clerk of the magistrates' court ... It does not become so enforceable in the hands of the beneficiary'.[8] Alternatively, the court may issue a warrant of distraint, but in common with civil enforcement action, this is, as Hughes LJ observed in *Jawad*, of limited effect unless relevant assets have been identified following a means enquiry under section 87(3) of the MCA 1980.[9]

The third option, to be used only as a matter of last resort, is a warrant of commitment to prison, governed by sections 82–88 of the MCA 1980. This requires the court to conduct a means enquiry, following which it may give the offender further time to pay, arrange payment by or reduce the amounts of instalments, or to remit or reduce the order. In the limited circumstances set out in section 82(4), the court may order immediate imprisonment, where the default is due to the offender's wilful refusal or culpable neglect, and having considered or tried all other methods of enforcing payment of the sum, it appears that they are inappropriate or likely to be unsuccessful. As in the case of a fine, the effect of an order for commitment in default is to bring to an end the obligation to pay the compensation order, the default affecting the payment of the sum ordered to a person (the victim), rather than to an inanimate institution (the court).[10] **9.14**

The maximum terms of imprisonment that the magistrates' court may impose are the same as apply to fines, and are set by section 76 of and Schedule 4 to the MCA 1980; they range from seven days in respect of an amount not exceeding £200 to no more than twelve months in respect of an amount exceeding £10,000, although the court has discretion to fix a lower term. Unlike fine default, the Crown Court has no power to fix a term of imprisonment for default in the payment of a compensation order.[11] But by section 41(8) of the AJA 1970, if it 'thinks that the period for which the person subject to the order is liable apart from this subsection to be committed to prison for default under the order is insufficient', it may substitute a longer period, but with any modification, being a reduction in the substituted period for part payment at the date of imprisonment. By section 41(8A), the Crown Court may not specify 'a period of imprisonment longer than that which it could order a person to undergo on imposing on him a fine equal in amount to the sum required to be paid by the order'. **9.15**

---

[8] *Osbourne v Kendrick* [2001] EWCA Civ 690, 2001 WL 483083 [14] (CA) (Butterfield J).

[9] [2013] EWCA Crim 644, [2013] 1 WLR 3861 [16] (CA).

[10] *R (Evans) v North Somerset Magistrates Court* [2012] EWHC 2382 (Admin), 2012 WL 3492007 (QBD); *R (Hopkins) v Bristol Magistrates' Court* [2013] EWHC 4760 (Admin), 2013 WL 8467456 (QBD).

[11] PCC(S)A 2000 ss 139 and 141(1); *Komsta* (1990–91) 12 Cr App R (S) 63, 64 (CA); *Beyter* [2016] EWCA Crim 134, 2016 WL 01129812 [11] (CA).

III Compensation Orders, Sentencing Theory, and Practice

9.16 Compensation orders may be imposed together with custodial and non-custodial sentences, with fines, or with discharge. In making an order the court must, by section 125(1) of the Coroners and Justice Act 2009:

> (a) follow any sentencing guideline which is relevant to the offender's case, and (b) must, in exercising any other function relating to the sentencing of offenders, follow any sentencing guidelines which are relevant to the exercise of the function, unless the court is satisfied that it would be contrary to the interests of justice to do so.

These are set out in the Sentencing Council's Magistrates' Court Sentencing Guidelines (MCSG) and its Definitive Guidelines for the Crown Court, to which reference is made as appropriate.

9.17 As to their beneficial impact on the victim, compensation orders give express effect to the purposes of sentencing set out in section 142(1)(e) of the Criminal Justice Act 2003 (CJA 2003), 'the making of reparation by offenders to persons affected by their offences'. On this basis compensation is apt, at least as an ancillary order, whenever the offender has, in the first sense described in Chapter 8.53–8.56, sufficient means to meet some or all of the ideal assessment of the victim's injury. As to the second objective, it remains an open question whether they do have a beneficial impact on the offender. What is clearer is that they do not always sit comfortably with other sentencing principles.

9.18 Where the offence meets the threshold for custody or for a community sentence,[12] and it is minded also to impose a compensation order to which the offender can make only a limited contribution, the court must resist the temptation to increase the period of custody or of a suspended sentence, or to impose a more onerous community sentence, as a means of 'compensating' for the shortfall in actual compensation; a compensation order is not an alternative to a sentence.[13] The principle of equality before the law implies that a poor offender who is unable to pay the fine or the level of compensation that the court considers appropriate to the offence, or to the victim's injury, ought not to be treated less favourably than an offender who is wealthy enough to pay them.[14]

---

12 CJA 2003 ss 152 and 148; Archbold (n 1) ch 5 Pts V and VI); Andrew Ashworth, *Sentencing and Criminal Justice* (Cambridge University Press 2015) 9.4.1 and 10.6.2; Susan Easton and Christine Piper, *Sentencing and Punishment* (Oxford University Press 2016) 3.1.3 and 10.3.

13 *Miller* (n 4) 57.

14 Ashworth (n 12) 7.5.

The value of ensuring even-handed justice as between poor and wealthy offenders may also be compromised where the offender is very wealthy in relation to the victim's injury. On the same principle of equality, he ought not to be able to avoid a custodial or community sentence because he can readily pay an order. Scarman LJ's emphatic observation in *Inwood*, that 'compensation orders were not introduced into our law to enable the convicted to buy themselves out of the penalties for crime',[15] has been regularly followed. In *Copley* Lord Lane LJ 'observed—if it needs observing—that it is not open to persons who participate in crime and plead guilty to try to buy their way out of prison, or to buy shorter sentences by offering money in the way of compensation'.[16] Similarly, in *Malik*, the Court rejected the proposition that the trial judge should have taken the compensation order into account in assessing whether the prison term was excessive: 'In particular, an offender cannot "buy" a reduced sentence by the payment of compensation that, in any event, is properly due to the victim whether or not it is made the subject of a compensation order in the criminal court'.[17] **9.19**

Where the offender can readily pay, the court might be tempted to increase the amount, in this instance to avoid the criticism that the offender is purchasing her freedom, or a relative degree of it. This is impermissible: 'A compensation order is not a punishment but rather a convenient summary means of putting right all or some of the damage done by a criminal offence'.[18] It should not be used as a means of penalizing the offender in the absence of any injury,[19] in an amount in excess of its ideal assessment 'by way of additional punishment',[20] or, in the absence of a realistic appraisal of the offender's means, simply to make the offender repay in full the amounts she had fraudulently obtained.[21] **9.20**

The order should therefore have no bearing on the sentence that is imposed. But where, despite the serious nature of the incident, the judge considered it appropriate to suspend the sentence of imprisonment given the impact custody would have on the appellant's family, it may, by means of a compensation order, be appropriate 'to demonstrate to the complainant, whose suffering continued, that justice had been done'.[22] **9.21**

---

15 (1974) 60 Cr App R 70, 73 CA).
16 (1979) 1 Cr App R (S) 55, 57 (CA).
17 [2013] EWCA Crim 1703, 2013 WL 5336583 [20] (CA) (Hickinbottom J).
18 *Jorge* [1999] 2 Cr App R (S) 1 (CA) (Hughes LJ); *Dorton* (1987) 9 Cr App R (S) 514 (CA).
19 *Vaughan* (1990–91) 12 Cr App R (S) 46 (CA).
20 *Dorton* (n 18).
21 *Hossain* [2016] EWCA Crim 1099, 2016 WL 04446426 [16]–[18] (CA) (Laing J).
22 *Saunders* [2014] EWCA Crim 2272, 2014 WL 5797373 [6] (CA) (Fulford LJ).

IV Compensation as an Ancillary Sentence

A Introduction

9.22 The nature of the sentence is initially determined by reference to section 152(2) of the CJA 2003, which specifies the custody test: 'the court must not pass a custodial sentence unless it is of the opinion that the offence, or the combination of the offence and one or more offences associated with it, was so serious that neither a fine alone nor a community sentence can be justified for the offence'. It is not necessary here to examine this test,[23] save to note that, as an ancillary sentence, a compensation order can be made either with a custodial or with a non-custodial sentence imposed on an adult offender.

B Custodial sentences

1 Immediate custody

9.23 A prison sentence is of itself no bar to making a compensation order. The Court of Appeal has frequently held that it may be combined with a sentence of immediate custody where the offender is clearly able to pay, or has good prospects of employment on his release from custody.[24] But while it may, as Scarman LJ observed in *Inwood*, appear to the offender at the trial 'to be a life line', the order may 'become a millstone round his neck' when released from prison. In this respect, the order must be realistic and not counter-productive; it should not impose such a financial burden as may force the offender 'back into crime to find the money'.[25] The longer the sentence the more certain the court should be that the offender will be able to comply with the order, bearing in mind also that compliance is backed by imprisonment for default.

9.24 For these reasons, the Sentencing Council advises that there will be few circumstances in which it is appropriate to impose both a fine and a custodial sentence for the same offence, 'particularly where the custodial sentence is to be served immediately ... combining these sentences is most likely to be appropriate only where the custodial sentence is short and/or the offender clearly has, or will have, the means to pay'.[26] *Normanton* was, 'unusually perhaps', a case where a reduced compensation order could be made on conviction for a road rage incident that crossed the custody threshold, the offender being in secure employment and having indicated to the court that he had put money aside to compensate the victim. The court reiterated the standard advice, that immediate custody does

23 Sentencing Council, *Imposition of Community and Custodial Sentences, Definitive Guideline*.
24 *Love* [1999] 1 Cr App R (S) 484, 487 (CA) (Hughes J); *Panayiotou* (1989) 11 Cr App R (S) 535 (CA) (Hodgson J); *Henry* [2012] EWCA Crim 1265, 2012 WL 1933524 [6] (CA).
25 *Inwood* (n 15) 73.
26 MCSG *Guidelines* (n 7) *Approach to the assessment of fines 11*.

not necessarily mean that a compensation order should not be imposed, but 'for obvious practical reasons' an order should not be made 'either unless the offender has assets from which to pay or is reasonably assured of income on his release'.[27]

Equally, if the offence is so serious that it merits an immediate custodial sentence, the court should not suspend it so that a poor offender would then be able to work and to compensate the victim. This puts the cart before the horse: the question is whether, in passing that sentence, as the court must, it is realistic also to impose a compensation order to be met on release.[28] In *Woodman*, a Royal Mail employee was convicted of theft, for which he was sentenced to eight months' imprisonment and ordered to pay nearly £1,200 compensation over twelve months. Had the sentence been suspended, the offender may have had clear means of being able to meet such an order, but noting the Sentencing Council's guidance, the court quashed it, adding 'that if Royal Mail Plc chooses to take civil proceedings, it has that right'.[29] **9.25**

In *Wing* the Court observed that: **9.26**

> It is pointless to make such an order if the offender does not have the means to pay it, as may often be the position for so long as the offender is incarcerated. An order may be made to take effect after release, with a view to payment out of income receivable at that point in time; but of course the court needs to consider whether there is likely to be a suitable income.[30]

But in exercising this caution, the Court also observed in *Love* that:

> Those important considerations, however, should not be understood to mean that a compensation order is inappropriate in those cases where there is evidence that the defendant has assets, or will have sufficient earning capacity. On the contrary, where either of those things is true, it is very often right that the defendant should compensate someone who has lost by his offence.[31]

2 Suspended sentence orders

The offence may satisfy the threshold test for custody but the court may order by section 189 of the CJA 2003 that the term of imprisonment shall not take effect, unless during the period of suspension the offender commits another offence.[32] A suspended sentence order (SSO) carries with it one or more of the community requirements specified by section 19 of the CJA 2003. These do not include compensation of the victim, but provided that it is satisfied that the offender has **9.27**

---

[27] [2003] EWCA Crim 959, 2003 WL 21236388, [9] (CA) (Gross J); *MD* [2012] EWCA Crim 1647, 2012 WL 2922803 [26] CA).

[28] *Panayiotou* (1989) 11 Cr App R (S) 535 (CA).

[29] [2016] EWCA Crim 640, 2016 WL 01377196 [4]–[5] (CA) (McGowan J).

[30] *Wing* [2017] EWCA Crim 633, 2017 WL 02978782 [17] (CA) (Warby J); *Gray* [2011] EWCA Crim 225, 2011 WL 441793.

[31] *Love* (n 24) 487.

[32] Sentencing Council, *Imposition of Community and Custodial Sentences* (n 23) 9.

means, the court may make a compensation order on the basis of the offender's present and future ability to pay from income or capital (Chapter 8.39–8.47). If, during the period of suspension, the basis on which the court made the order against the offender is compromised, for example, she loses or is otherwise unable to continue her job, she should seek a review under section 133(3)(d) of the PCC(S)A 2000 (9.07–9.08).

C Community sentences

9.28 An offence that does not meet the custody threshold but which is 'serious' may warrant a community sentence, which must carry one or more of the twelve 'requirements' listed in section 177 of the CJA 2003 as a 'community order'. These do not specifically include compensation, but as a compensation order can be combined with them, community orders 'can be an effective means of providing reparation while also leaving the courts capacity to select appropriate punitive, protective or rehabilitative requirements'. The great majority of compensation orders are issued alongside non-custodial sentences; in 2010, one-third of community orders had a compensation order issued alongside them.[33]

9.29 A compensation order made together with a community sentence 'will remind the defendant of the evil he has done … and may apply particularly in the case where a non-custodial penalty is imposed and the compensation which is appropriate is a sum which is not too great'.[34] But, as detailed in Chapter 8.48–8.52, care must be taken to avoid excessively long periods of payment by instalments, and where there is no evidence that the offender will be able to pay even the minimum amount the order should be quashed.[35] Similarly, the court should be cautious about basing a substantial weekly order on present but irregular earnings. Where there is an unforeseen interruption of earnings, the offender may, as in the case of an SSO, seek a review under section 133(3)(d) of the PCC(S)A 2000, but caution may nevertheless justify a smaller amount to be paid.[36]

9.30 When imposing a community order the court must, by section 177(2A) of the CJA 2003, include at least one requirement imposed for the purpose of punishment, impose a fine for the offence in respect of which the community order is made, or comply with both of paragraphs (a) and (b) of section 177(1). The second alternative raises a point concerning the priority of a compensation order over a fine. If the court were minded to make that order in the case of an offender with limited means, it would be required by section 130(12) of the PCC(S)A 2000 to prefer the compensation order, in which case section 177(2A) could be satisfied

---

[33] Ministry of Justice (2012d) para 136.
[34] *Miller* (n 4).
[35] *Priestly* [2013] EWCA Crim 1883, WL 5826267 [7] (CA).
[36] *Stancombe* [2005] EWCA Crim 113, 2005 WL 1459180 [13]–[14] (CA).

only by its compliance with the first alternative, or by including in the community order an unpaid work requirement or a rehabilitation activity requirement.

D Fines and discharge

The court has power to impose a fine in addition to any other penalty, including custodial and non-custodial sentences.[37] If the custody threshold has not been passed, and the offence is not serious enough to warrant a community order, the court should consider a fine or discharge; in either case a compensation order may be made as an ancillary order. **9.31**

By section 164(2) of the CJA 2003 the amount of a fine must reflect the seriousness of the offence. Before fixing the amount to be paid in full or in instalments the court must 'inquire into his financial circumstances', and when fixing it 'must take into account the circumstances of the case including, among other things, the financial circumstances of the offender so far as they are known, or appear, to the court' (section 164(1) and (3) of the CJA 2003).[38] **9.32**

These inquiries apply whether they have the effect of increasing or reducing the amount of the fine (section 164(4)). An increase may be justified provided that it remains proportionate to the seriousness of the offence,[39] but as indicated earlier, where the offence has passed the custody threshold, that increase must not permit the offender to purchase his freedom:[40] 'A modest fine is no problem for a rich offender'.[41] However, if the offender is sufficiently wealthy to pay the appropriate fine, there is surely a strong argument from section 130(2A) of the PCC(S)A 2000 that any 'increase' should, assuming the victim's injury meets section 130's other qualifying conditions, instead be used to meet an appropriate level of compensation; where it is not, section 130(3) requires the court to give its reasons for not doing so (Chapter 7.40). **9.33**

The Sentencing guidelines' aim is 'for the fine to have an equal impact on offenders with different financial circumstances; it should be a hardship but should not force the offender below a reasonable 'subsistence' level'; reduction may therefore be appropriate, and normally be capable of being paid within twelve months.[42] Where the offender has limited means, and the court considers '(a) that it would be appropriate both to impose a fine and to make a compensation order, but (b) that the offender has insufficient means to pay both an appropriate fine and appropriate compensation', section 130(12) of the PCC(S)A 2000 provides **9.34**

[37] In the Crown Court, CJA 2003 s 163; in the magistrates' court, MCA 1980 s 32.
[38] Archbold (n 1) ch 5 Pt VII; Ashworth (n 12) 10.5; Easton and Piper (n 12) 10.2.
[39] *Jerome* [2001] 1 Cr App R (S) 316 (CA).
[40] *Markwick* (1953) 37 Cr App R 125 (CA); *Copley* (n 16).
[41] Ministry of Justice (2012d) para 94.
[42] MCSG *Guidelines* (n 7) *Approach to the assessment of fines 1 and 5.*

that 'the court shall give preference to compensation (though it may impose a fine as well)'. This priority does not affect sentences other than fines, but it means that the fine should be reduced or, if necessary, dispensed with altogether, to enable the compensation to be paid. However, when set alongside them, in 2010 less than 10 per cent of all cases in which fines were imposed also attracted a compensation order.[43]

9.35 In a case of low culpability that did not meet the threshold for custody, a community sentence or a fine, the remaining option available to the court, subject to PCC(S)A 2000 section 12(1A), is an absolute or a conditional discharge. By section 12(7), these may be combined with a compensation order, and in such a case a court may be inclined to make an order for a sum that reflects the offender's limited means, but also signal a possible future punitive response by discharging the offender conditionally.

E Young offenders

9.36 When sentencing a young offender CJA 2003 section 142A makes similar provision for the sentencing objectives in their case as section 142(1) does for adults; that is, including reparation, for which reparation orders are possible in their case (Chapter 10.37–10.38). Where it has power to do so, the court may impose a compensation order if, by section 137 of the PCC(S)A 2000, it is of the opinion that the case would best be met by its imposition, whether with or without any other punishment. Section 137(1) provides that the court has a duty to order the parent or guardian to pay instead of the child or young person unless they cannot be found or, having regard to the circumstances of the case, it would be unreasonable to make an order for payment. By section 137(3), that duty becomes a power where the offender is 'a young person aged 16 or over'. In short, 'any order for compensation *must* be made against the parents of a young person under 16 years of age and may be made against the parents of a young person under 18 years of age, unless the parent cannot be found or it would be unreasonable to do so'.[44] These provisions also apply to local authority having parental responsibility for the young person (ss 137(8) and (9)).

9.37 Before making any order under section 137, the court may first make a financial circumstances order under section 136 of the PCC(S)A 2000 with respect to the parent or guardian. Nor may the order be made without giving the parent or guardian an opportunity of being heard; but it may be made against them if, having been required to attend for that purpose, failed to do so (section 137(4) and (5)). These provisions also apply where under section 137(1) the court makes

---

[43] Ministry of Justice (2012d) para 137.

[44] Crown Prosecution Service, *Sentencing, Ancillary Orders, Legal Guidance, Compensation Orders and Young Offenders.*

an order for costs (9.62–9.64) or, under section 137(1A) orders the young offender to pay a victim surcharge (9.55–9.58).

The £5,000 limit on compensations orders that previously applied to magistrates' courts (Chapter 8.27–8.29), now applies only to young offenders (PCC(S)A 2000 section 131(A1)). The provision in section 131(2) relating to TIC offences is also retained in their case. The compensation **9.38**

> shall not exceed the difference (if any) between—(a) the amount or total amount which under subsection (1) above is the maximum for the offence or offences of which the offender has been convicted; and (b) the amount or total amounts (if any) which are in fact ordered to be paid in respect of that offence or those offences.

V Compensation Orders and Other Financial Payments

A Confiscation orders

Originating in the Drug Trafficking Offences Act 1986 and expanded in Part VI of the CJA 1988, the making of confiscation orders is governed by POCA 2002. In common with restitution and deprivation orders, which return property to the victim or realize it to the public finance,[45] confiscation orders were intended to show that 'crime doesn't pay'. The POCA 2002 signalled a substantial effort to widen their reach, notably by introducing the notion of 'a criminal lifestyle' as a source from which the offender's assets, in particular those of professional criminals engaged in serious organized crime, derive.[46] Its 'dominant purpose' is the confiscation of those assets.[47] The complex matters concerning the mandatory application of its provisions and of their relationship with Convention rights under the European Convention on Human Rights (ECHR) go beyond the scope of this section,[48] which concentrates on the relationship between confiscation and compensation orders. **9.39**

Given the nature and scale of the offences that can trigger the section 6 process under POCA 2002, confiscation orders are typically made in respect of the loss of property or other assets. In respect of offences of theft or fraud, compensation orders are intended to restore the victim's 'loss' under section 130(1) of the PCC(S)A 2000, and there may also be an 'injury' to be compensated where its **9.40**

[45] That is, by the Police Property Act 1897, and ss 143–44 of the PCC(S)A 2000.

[46] Cabinet Office (2000).

[47] *Guraj* [2016] UKSC 65, [2017] 1 WLR 22 [31] (SC) (Lord Hughes).

[48] Peter Alldridge, *Money Laundering* (Hart Publishing 2013); Sutherland Williams, Michael Hopmeier, and Rupert Jones, *Trevor Millington & Sutherland Williams, On Proceeds of Crime* (Oxford University Press 2017); Archbold (n 1) Pt IX; Ashworth (n 12) 11.5.1; Easton and Piper (n 12) 7.2.2.

impact falls within the Sentencing Council's guidelines, the victim suffering stress or anxiety as a result of that loss. (Chapter 8.20, Table 8.1). Where the court is considering both a confiscation and a compensation order, 'it has been held on several occasions in the past that there is no obstacle to making both orders in the same case where the offender has sufficient assets to meet both'.[49]

9.41 As Hughes LJ said in *Jawad*:

> [a] compensation order and a POCA confiscation order are two very different things. They derive from quite separate statutes and they serve different purposes ... A POCA confiscation order is designed to remove from the defendant the fruits of crime. A compensation order has a different purpose; it is designed as a limited and summary method of ordering the defendant to repay the loser and is available to short-circuit a civil action against the defendant in a straightforward case.[50]

This last observation reflects the Court of Appeal's long-standing views concerning the inadvisability of making a compensation order where the offender has no or very few assets (Chapter 8.55–8.57), seen also in the CPS' guidance in confiscation cases.

9.42 Because the court needs to know the amount of the confiscation order before it makes any other financial orders, it should not make a compensation order until the confiscation proceedings that have commenced are concluded,[51] or by section 15(2)(c) of the POCA 2002, where those proceedings have been postponed following an application under section 14. The CPS guidance notes that postponed confiscation proceedings give rise to a risk that compensation may be overlooked if it is subsequently decided that it is not appropriate to proceed with confiscation: 'Accordingly, prosecutors should ensure the court explicitly deals with compensation claims separately from confiscation and gives reasons why a compensation order is not being imposed at the point of sentencing'.[52]

9.43 The POCA 2002 is designed to ensure that compensation for victims and losers takes precedence over confiscation; as the Court of Appeal said in *Mitchell*, 'it was the clear intention of Parliament that the victim should come first'.[53] Put briefly, the court must first make the confiscation order and then determine such amount of compensation as the court considers appropriate under section 130(4) of the PCC(S)A, but without regard to that order (POCA 2002 section 13(3)(a) and (3A(a)) (9.52–9.54). This process gives rise to three issues, discussed in the following sections.

---

49 *Jawad* (n 9) [12] (Hughes LJ).
50 [2013] EWCA Crim 644, [2013] 1 WLR 3861 [12] (CA).
51 *Firmager and Annett* [2013] EWCA Crim 2756, 2013 WL 8182378 [10] (CA).
52 Crown Prosecution Service, *Proceeds of Crime, Legal Guidance* 4.
53 *Mitchell* [2001] 2 Cr App R (S) 29 [18] (CA) (Kennedy LJ).

1 The meaning of 'proceedings' in POCA 2002 section 6(6)

Where it has decided that the offender has benefited from his general or particular criminal conduct, the court *must* by section 6(5) decide the recoverable amount (emphasis added), and make a confiscation order, but 'only if, or to the extent that, it would not be disproportionate' to require them to pay that amount' (section 6(5)(b)). If it believes that 'any victim of the conduct has at any time started or intends to start proceedings against the defendant in respect of loss, injury or damage sustained in connection with the conduct', the court must by section 6(6) treat the duty in section 6(5) as a power. In this event, as was the case in *Davenport v R*,[54] the court is entitled to decide for itself whether to make a confiscation order and, if so, for what amount. **9.44**

In its reference to the victim's actions or intentions section 6(6) means what it says. In *Jawad* the offender argued that because the bank he defrauded had asked the prosecution to make an application for a compensation order, it had 'started proceedings' against him in respect of its 'loss', and thus section 6(6) applied. The Court of Appeal emphatically rejected this argument: 'The court is under a duty to consider [a compensation order] whether the loser seeks it or not. The "proceedings" in which it is considered and, if appropriate, made, are the criminal proceedings brought by the Crown by way of indictment, not civil proceedings brought by the loser'.[55] **9.45**

2 'Double counting': disproportionate orders

In *Neill*, a decision made under the equivalent provisions of the CJA 1988, the court, satisfied that the offender had sufficient assets, and that his 'benefit' entirely comprised the loss to the victim, imposed both a confiscation and a compensation order. Noting that the judge had been concerned about the possibility of double counting, the Court of Appeal observed that what may at first appear to be the case fails 'to take account of the two distinct jurisdictions which are in play, namely a confiscation order which is made in the criminal courts, and the civil liability which exists to make good to a victim ... in damages or compensation for the loss that has been sustained'.[56] **9.46**

Broadly speaking, the same principles apply to the POCA 2002, reflected in Hughes LJ's *dicta* in *Jawad* concerning the purposes of the two orders.[57] But, as Davis LJ observed in *Davenport*, while the statutory provisions plainly give the court this dual jurisdiction, there has been some unease at their potential for the injustice of double counting.[58] These circumstances are now governed by the Supreme Court's **9.47**

---

[54] [2015] EWCA Crim 1731, [2016] 1 WLR 1400 [27].

[55] *Jawad* (n 9) [24].

[56] *Neill* [2005] EWCA Crim 3282, 2005 WL 3605729 [7] (CA) (Moses LJ).

[57] *Jawad* (n 9) [12].

[58] *Davenport* (n 54) [49], citing *Morgan & Bygrave* [2009] 1 Cr App R(S) 60 (CA), where the Court held that this result could be an abuse of process.

decision in *Waya*.[59] Where the benefit obtained by the defendant has been wholly restored to the loser, a confiscation order which requires him to pay the same sum again 'does not achieve the object of the legislation of removing from the defendant his proceeds of crime, but amounts simply to a further pecuniary penalty—in any ordinary language a fine'.[60] This would be disproportionate, and an infringement of Article 1 of Protocol 1 to the ECHR (A1P1), an outcome that led to the amendment made in the POCA 2002 as section 6(5)(b).[61]

9.48 In *Jawad* the Court of Appeal conducted a detailed review of *Waya*, concluding that a confiscation order that requires the offender to pay twice where they have fully restored the loser will generally be disproportionate.[62] But it also held that 'the mere fact that a compensation order is made for an outstanding sum due to the loser, and thus that that money *may* be restored' (original emphasis), is not enough to render disproportionate a confiscation order which includes that sum'. The Court continued: 'what will bring disproportion is the certainty of double payment. If it remains uncertain whether the loser will be repaid, a confiscation order which includes the sum in question will not ordinarily be disproportionate'.[63]

9.49 The key is whether there has been or is an assured payment.[64] Full restoration of the victim's loss is not guaranteed since a compensation order is not the equivalent of a civil judgment; it therefore remains uncertain whether such restoration will be made. In general, CPS advises that a restraint order under POCA 2002 section 40 should be considered if there are identified assets that may be required to satisfy a compensation order, in circumstances in which the compensation order is likely to be paid out of the monies enforced in respect of the confiscation order.[65]

9.50 *Jawad* was itself considered at length by the Court of Appeal in *Davenport*. The judge had found that the offender could, in time, have sufficient assets to pay the two orders, and therefore sections 13(5) and (6) of the POCA 2002 did not apply. These provide that where the defendant has insufficient means to satisfy both orders in full, the court 'must direct' that the shortfall is to be met from the confiscation order. But, having considered *Waya* and *Jawad*, the judge concluded that as the payment of compensation was not 'cut and dried and certain', they should both be made in full. The Court of Appeal agreed that restitution to the victims must be 'assured' or 'certain', but that in this case there were tangible, valuable, and identified assets in the United Kingdom to be derived from the sale of property; accordingly, it confirmed the compensation order and reduced the confiscation order by that amount.[66]

---

59 [2012] UKSC 51, [2013] 1 AC 294 (HL).
60 ibid [29] (Lord Walker and Sir Anthony Hughes).
61 *Davenport* (n 54) [50].
62 *Axworthy* [2012] EWCA Crim 2889, 2012 WL 6774645 [12]–[17] (CA).
63 *Jawad* (n 9) [11]–[23].
64 *Goodenough* [2004] EWCA Crim 2260, [2005] 1 Cr App R (S) 88 [32]–[34] (CA).
65 CPS, *Proceeds of Crime* (n 52) 7.
66 *Davenport* (n 54) [66]–[74].

The Court agreed with Hughes LJ's lament in *Jawad* that the POCA 2002 does not, where the available assets *are* sufficient, give the court the same power to direct that compensation be paid out of any sums recovered under the confiscation order as it does where they are insufficient.[67] In the absence of that power, it listed a series of pointers, neither prescriptive nor exhaustive, to which Crown Courts should have regard where the prosecution seeks both a compensation order and a confiscation order in circumstances where sections 13(5) and (6) of the POCA 2002 are not applicable: **9.51**

> '(1) The court is empowered to make both a confiscation order and a compensation order.
> (2) However, the court should be alert to any risk of double counting inherent in such a combination of orders and should be alert to the risk of making a confiscation order which is disproportionate
> (3) The court ordinarily should not make both a compensation order and a confiscation order representing the full amount of the benefit where there has been actual restitution to the victims prior to the date of the confiscation hearing: *Waya; Jawad.*
> (4) Where it is asserted by a defendant that there will be restitution made after the date of the hearing then the court should scrutinize very carefully and critically the evidence and arguments raised in support of such assertion.
> (5) If the court remains uncertain whether the victims will be repaid under the compensation order then a confiscation order which includes that amount will not ordinarily be disproportionate: *Jawad.*
> (6) However, mathematical certainty of restitution is not required. The court should approach matters in a practical and realistic way in deciding whether restitution is assured.
> (7) Restitution to the victims in the future is capable of being properly assessed as assured, depending on the particular circumstances, notwithstanding that such restitution will not be immediate, or almost immediate, at the time of the confiscation hearing. Obviously the longer the time frame the greater force there will be to an argument that restitution is not assured: but a prospective period of delay in realization is not of itself necessarily a conclusive reason for proceeding to make a combination of such orders without adjusting the amount of the confiscation order.
> (8) Whilst a defendant who is truly intent on making restitution in full to his victims ordinarily should be expected to have arranged such restitution prior to the date of the confiscation hearing there may sometimes be cases where that is not possible. If, in such a case, the court has firm and evidence-based grounds for believing that restitution may nevertheless be forthcoming, albeit that cannot be taken as "assured" at the time of the hearing, the court has power in its discretion to order an adjournment to enable matters to be ascertained.
> (9) Finally, to state the obvious, each case must be decided on its own facts and circumstances.'[68]

[67] *Jawad* (n 9) [23].
[68] *Davenport* (n 54) [75].

3 Priority of the compensation order

9.52 Section 13 of the POCA 2002 creates two rules in cases where the court is considering both a confiscation and a compensation order. First, sections 13(2) and (3) provide that where it is minded to impose a financial penalty in addition to the confiscation order, being a fine or 'a payment by the offender', which includes deprivation and forfeiture orders, the court must 'take account of the confiscation order' before it makes those decisions; that is, it may have to reduce the fine or other order.

9.53 This does not, however, apply to 'priority orders' (section 13(3A)); that is a compensation order under section 130 of the PCC(S)A, the victim surcharge, an unlawful profit order under the PSHFA 2013, or a slavery and trafficking reparation order made under the MSA 2015. As Hughes LJ observed in *Jawad*, section 13(2) 'is easily misread because of its rather convoluted structure, and it is easy to think that a compensation order is an order within section 13(2) via section 13(3)(a), but in fact the statute says the opposite'. In short, there is no duty under the POCA 2002 to take the confiscation order into account when deciding on a compensation order.[69] Subject to section 13(2), the court must also leave it out of account in deciding the appropriate sentence for the defendant (section 13(4)).

9.54 The second rule concerns a case where the court believes the offender will not have sufficient means to satisfy both (or other priority) orders in full (section 13(5)). In this case the court 'must direct' that so much of the compensation order that would otherwise not be paid is to be met out of the sum recovered under the confiscation order (section 13(6)). These two rules

> can co-exist with the general provision in [s 130(11) of the 2000 Act] which requires a court to have regard to the means of the defendant when determining whether to make a compensation order and, if so, for how much. The prospect of a compensation order which is rendered unpayable by a POCA confiscation order which has taken everything the defendant has is avoided by sections 13(5) and (6).[70]

As is the case with the application of section 130(11) of the PCC(S)A 2900, the issue for the application of section 13(6) of the POCA 2002 is the identification of the offender's means (Chapter 8.35–8.47).

B The victim surcharge

9.55 A confiscation order may benefit victims directly who have suffered 'loss, damage or injury' caused by the offence. A more recent, general, application

[69] *Jawad* (n 9) [13].
[70] ibid.

of the belief that offenders should be accountable to victims for their crimes is the victim surcharge, used in England and Wales to support services for victims of crime. It is a levy on all offenders, including corporate bodies, imposed on conviction for any offence, including one that may or may not have harmed any victim or, indeed, may not contemplate causing any harm. It raises about £10 million annually towards the government's Victim and Witness General Fund; the 2012 increases in both its scope and payment levels reflected its desire to redress the balance between its own spending on victim services and that made by offenders, and to make savings on the costs of the Criminal Injuries Compensation Scheme.[71]

The surcharge was introduced by section 14(1) of the Domestic Violence, Crime and Victims Act 2004, inserting sections 161A and 161B of the CJA 2003. Subject to sections 161A(2) and (3), the court must, when dealing with a person for one or more offences, order them to pay a surcharge. The amount to be levied varies according to the offender's age (over or under 18), the date on which the offences were committed (before, or after 8 April 2016),[72] and the sentence that was imposed (section 161B). In the case of an adult offender whose offence was committed in 2017, the surcharges are: conditional discharge: £20; fine: 10 per cent of the fine value with a £30 minimum and a £170 maximum; community sentence: £85; suspended sentence order: £115 (six months or less); and immediate custody £115 (six months or less).[73] **9.56**

It can be seen that, while these surcharges may be thought modest, there will inevitably be cases in which the offender's means are so limited that she will not be able to meet both the relevant surcharge and a compensation order that meets some or all of the ideal assessment of the victim's injury. Where it considers that the offender has insufficient means to pay both, the court must, by section 161A(3), reduce the surcharge, 'if necessary to nil'. Section 161A does not permit the court to order that it be paid as compensation; in *Hare and Purse*, the court erred when it ordered compensation to be paid to the victims 'from the victim surcharge'.[74] A reduction must also be made where the court has made an unlawful profit under the PSFHA 2013 or a slavery and trafficking reparation order under the MSA 2015. But where the court is fixing a fine to be imposed on an offender (section 164(3)), it must not reduce the amount of the fine on account of any surcharge it orders the offender to pay, 'except to the extent that he has insufficient means to pay both' (section 164(4A)). **9.57**

---

71 Ministry of Justice (2012c) paras 130–61; Roger Bowles, *International development of victims' funds and their use in victim related initiatives* (Northern Ireland Office Criminal Justice Policy Division 2010) 4.

72 These variations have led to difficulties; *Holden* [2013] EWCA Crim 2017, 2013 WL 5905548 [4]–[7] (CA); *Hossain* [2016] EWCA Crim 1099, 2016 WL 04446426 [3] (CA).

73 MCSG *Guidelines* (n 7) *Victim surcharge*.

74 [2016] EWCA Crim 1355, 2016 WL 04721343 [18] (CA).

9.58 Section 132(4A) of the PCC(S)A provides that where the Court of Appeal varies a compensation order, or the Supreme Court makes one when restoring a conviction, they shall make such order for the payment of a victim surcharge or such variation of the Crown Court's order 'as is necessary to secure that the person's liability under that section is the same as it would be if he were being dealt with by the Crown Court'.

C Slavery and trafficking reparation orders

9.59 By section 8 of the MSA 2015, the court may make a slavery or a trafficking reparation order (STRO), where there has been a conviction under sections 1, 2, or 4 of the Act, and a confiscation order made against the offender. When the MSA 2015 was enacted, confiscation orders could only be made in the Crown Court; by section 97 of the Serious Organised Crime and Police Act 2005, and section 40 of the Serious Crime Act 2015, they can now be made by a magistrates' court, subject to a limit of £10,000.

9.60 STROs are orders requiring the offender to pay compensation 'to the victim for any harm resulting from that offence' (section 9). Although it was previously possible, few compensation orders were made against persons convicted of a modern slavery offence; the government's purpose was to create a specific remedy enabling courts to order them to pay reparation to their victims in these cases. For this purpose, by reason of section 10(3)(c), which applies sections 132–134 of the PCC(S)A 2000 to them, 'harm' means 'injury, loss or damage', and the discussion in Chapter 7.16–7.19 on the scope of 'personal injury' in section 130(1) will be relevant to its interpretation. In consequence, by section 10(1), a compensation order under section 130 of the PCC(S)A 2000 cannot be made in respect of the same offence for which an STRO has been made.

9.61 The MSA 2015 specifies a number of requirements to the making of an STRO that are for the most part substantively equivalent to those in section 130 of the PCC(S)A 2000. It is convenient simply to list them, noting their similarity or otherwise with a compensation order:

- Subject to the limitation in section 10(1) of the MSA 2015, the court may make a STRO against the offender in addition to dealing with him in any other way, and may do so (section 8(4)) even if he was sentenced for the offence before the confiscation order was made. In this event that sentence is, for the purpose of any relevant appeal time limits, to be regarded as being imposed on the day on which the reparation order is made (section 10(2)).
- Section 8(7) requires the court to consider making the order in any case where it has power to do so, even where an application is not made, and to give reasons if it does not do so (section 130(2A) and (3)).
- By section 9(3), the amount of the compensation to be ordered is such amount as the court considers appropriate having regard to any evidence and to any

representations made by or on behalf of the person or the prosecutor (section 130(4)), and by section 9(4) the amount of compensation must not exceed the amount the person is required to pay under the confiscation order.

- By section 9(5), in determining that amount the court must have regard to the person's means (section 130(11)), and where it considers that it would be appropriate to impose a fine and make a STRO, but the defendant has insufficient means to pay both, section 8(6) requires priority to be given to the STRO (section 130(12)).
- Section 10(3) modifies sections 132 to 134 of the PCC(S)A 2000 so that their provisions concerning appeals and review (9.04–9.10) apply to an STRO. Sections 10(4)–(9) enable a court that varies, so as to increase, reduce, quash, or discharge a confiscation order in accordance with Part 2 of the POCA 2002, also to vary, quash, or discharge any STRO.

D Prosecution costs

Where an offender has been convicted of an offence before a magistrates' court or the Crown Court, or the Crown Court has dismissed an appeal against such a conviction or against the sentence imposed on that conviction, the court may by section 18 of the Prosecution of Offences Act 1985 (POA 1985) order the accused to pay such of the prosecution's costs as it considers just and reasonable. It is not necessary here to examine the procedural and other details of a costs order, but the Sentencing Council's guidelines indicate that 'where the court wishes to impose costs in addition to a fine, compensation and/or the victim surcharge, but the offender has insufficient resources to pay the total amount, the order of priority is: 1. compensation; 2. victim surcharge; 3. fine; 4. costs'.[75] **9.62**

It is therefore relevant to note that the good reasons for the prosecution not applying for costs include a consideration of the offender's means. If there is 'firm information' that the offender's financial circumstances are 'dire', the court is likely to consider the award of costs as oppressive. If their means are of this kind, a compensation order may be unlikely, but the court 'will regard payment of compensation as a higher priority than prosecution costs if a defendant has limited means'.[76] This was the reason why the Court of Appeal quashed the judge's order for costs in *Lovell*,[77] and in *Bunn*, because having been sentenced to a term of immediate imprisonment, the compensation order could only have been paid by money the offender borrowed from his family (Chapter 8.46–8.47).[78] **9.63**

[75] MCSG *Guidelines* (n 7) *Prosecution costs*.

[76] Crown Prosecution Service (2018), *Costs, Legal Guidance, Good reasons for not applying for costs under section 18*.

[77] [2012] EWCA Crim 1564, 2012 WL 2500572 [10]–[15] (CA).

[78] [2013] EWCA Crim 1636, 2013 WL 5336067 [15]–[17] (CA).

9.64 By contrast, where, in *Flinton*, the court had reduced the compensation order from £2,000 to £750 because the victim had provoked the attack in which he was injured, it was then possible to make the order for costs that the trial judge had, given that initial amount, declined to do.[79] And in *Campbell*, where it doubled the rate at which the orders for compensation and costs were to be paid, the Court of Appeal commented:

> [i]t is only right, in our judgment, that the appellant pays the money that she stole back and repays the public purse for the costs of this trial. The learned sentencing judge was right to take that approach. Only then will she have made amends and gone some way to rehabilitating herself.[80]

E Criminal court charge

9.65 The Criminal Court Charge was introduced by section 54 of the Criminal Justice and Courts Act 2015 as sections 21A to 21F of Part IIA of the POA 1985. Section 21A imposed a mandatory charge on offenders convicted of a criminal offence, intended to help cover the 'relevant court costs' of the proceedings. The charge was in addition to the other financial orders, but unlike them, it was fixed, regardless of the offence or the offender's financial circumstances.[81] Being mandatory the charge was not part of the court's sentence, and was unaffected by any guidance issued by the Sentencing Council. Its report to the Justice Select Committee's inquiry into the impact of the charge was of reduced levels of fines and prosecution costs, and that 'it was probable that orders of compensation for victims of crime were being similarly affected'.[82]

9.66 The government's response to the Committee's critical report was to announce a review to 'consider alternative ways of ensuring that criminals pay their fair share'; meanwhile, an amending order was made omitting regulation 3 of the 2015 regulations, which set the charge levels.[83]

F Unpaid financial orders

9.67 Unpaid financial orders are a detriment to victims directly (compensation orders) and indirectly (the victim surcharge), and to the public finances (fines, confiscation orders). In 2003/2004, the proportion of all financial penalties recovered from offenders was 74 per cent, which had increased by 2009/2010 to

[79] [2007] EWCA Crim 2322, [2008] 1 Cr App R (S) 96 [11] (CA) (Mitting J).

[80] *Campbell* [2015] EWCA Crim 1876, 2015 WL 7692915 [12] (CA) (Haddon-Cave J).

[81] Prosecution of Offences Act 1985 (Criminal Courts Charge) Regulations 2015/796, *Explanatory Memorandum* para 7.4.

[82] House of Commons, Justice Committee (2015a), Summary and paras 13 and 38–39.

[83] House of Commons, Justice Committee (2015b); Prosecution of Offences Act 1985 (Criminal Courts Charge) (Amendment) Regulations 2015 (SI 2015/1970).

80 per cent excluding administrative cancellations, in round numbers £214 million of £313 million.[84] But three years later the Public Accounts Committee noted that the amount of fines collected had failed to keep pace with the volume of impositions, with an outstanding balance of over £600 million. There had also been 'a startling growth' in the level of confiscation orders outstanding, over £1.3 billion by the middle of 2011–2012.[85]

In 2015, the government reported annual increases in the preceding three years, collecting 'an all-time high of £290 million at the end of 2013/14', the total outstanding balance of financial impositions being reduced by £26 million (5%) in the year. This was based on the table it published showing the value outstanding at the end of the financial years 2010/2011 to 2013/2014 for the impositions made in the same year, broken down into (a) fines, (b) compensation orders, (c) victim surcharge orders, and (d) prosecution costs.[86] **9.68**

Year	Fines	Compensation	Victim Surcharge	Prosecution Costs	Total
2010/11	£413,158,000	£70,122,000	£10,488,000	£131,427,000	£625,195,000
2011/12	£388,292,000	£68,484,000	£9,877,000	£130,102,000	£596,755,000
2012/13	£370,591,000	£67,564,000	£12,084,000	£128,289,000	£578,528,000
2013/14	£335,377,000	£67,918,000	£21,110,000	£126,861,000	£551,266,000

VI Compensation Orders as the Sole Sentence

By section 130(1) of the PCC(S)A, the court by or before which a person is convicted of an offence may, subject to sections 130(2) and (2ZA), make a compensation order against him 'instead of or in addition to dealing with him in any other way'. The exceptions are, by section 130(2), where the offence is one for which the sentence is fixed by law, or is an offence listed in section 130(2ZA).[87] In these cases a compensation may be ordered, for example for funeral expenses or bereavement (section 130(1)(b)) in the case of murder, but in none of them is that the only possible way of dealing with the offender. **9.69**

[84] Hansard HC vol 530 col 174W (21 June 2011).

[85] House of Commons, Committee of Public Accounts (2012) paras 1–2.

[86] http://www.parliament.uk/business/publications/written-questions-answers-statements/written-question/Commons/2015-01-14/220833 (last accessed 10 June 2018).

[87] These are (a) ss 1(2B) or 1A(5) of the Prevention of Crime Act 1953; (b) s 51A(2) of the Firearms Act 1968; (c) ss 139(6B), 139A(5B), or 139AA(7) of the Criminal Justice Act 1988; (d) ss 110(2) or 111(2) of PCC(S)A 2000; (e) ss 224A, 225(2), or 226(2) of the Criminal Justice Act 2003; and (f) s 29(4) or (6) of the Violent Crime Reduction Act 2006.

9.70 The central issue is whether, notwithstanding its statutory independence, a compensation order can be regarded as a credible single sentencing option. Compensation orders can, as the Court of Appeal held in *Bradburn*, serve a penal function 'to hurt the offender's pocket and acting to remind him of what he has done',[88] a 'good moral reason' that similarly supports its later observation that the order may demonstrate to the complainant that justice had been done.[89]

9.71 But at the time that the single option was introduced in 1982 there had been no consideration of the criteria by which compensation orders might be used as the sole sentence, and there has been no appellate guidance. Nor do the MCSG's sentencing guidelines offer much assistance. Its 'Introduction to Compensation' notes that a compensation order can 'either be an ancillary order or a sentence in its own right', but Step Seven of its guidelines for the court's sentencing tasks for all offences refers only to its use as an ancillary order, as do its explanatory materials. As the sole sentence the MCSG guidelines note only that a compensation order does not attract the victim surcharge.[90]

9.72 It may be that it would be inappropriate to order compensation as the sole sentence where the offender has insufficient means to meet the ideal assessment of the victim's injury. But where the offender's means are sufficient it is difficult to see how a single monetary order can serve both the function of compensation and punishment. If the offender can readily pay £1,000 for an injury resulting in a facial scar causing minor disfigurement, or £2,400 for a Colles fracture of the wrist with substantial recovery (MCSG Guidelines Chapter 8.20, and Table 8.1), can it be said that the order hurts the offender, or imposes any sanction that would not otherwise be equivalent to an award of damages?

9.73 Where it is the sole sentence, or is combined with an absolute discharge, the public aspect of the offence is in effect concluded, as Hughes LJ observed in *Jorge*, as 'a convenient summary means of putting right all or some of the damage done by a criminal offence'.[91] In short, if they have no function other than compensation, it may be objected that where the offender has sufficient means to meet an ideal assessment of the victim's loss, no formal sanction has been imposed to reflect the public aspect of his offence, save the stigma of a conviction. Since in these circumstances the order is in effect a surrogate for the victim's civil action, the offender's public wrong has been rectified by the private cost set upon it.

9.74 Considerations of this kind may explain the very limited use magistrates have made of compensation as the sole sentence. Newburn's research in the 1980s showed that its frequency did not exceed 5 per cent of all cases in which compensation

[88] *Bradburn* (1974) 57 Cr App R 948, 953; *Wing* (n 30).
[89] *Saunders* (n 22).
[90] MCSG *Guidelines* (n 7) *Compensation 1* para 1.
[91] *Jorge* (n 18).

was ordered, and in many magistrates' courts the numbers ordered were in single figures. This situation appears to be unchanged. Between 2007 and 2017, the number of compensation orders made as the 'principal' sentence for all persons convicted of an offence of violence against the person fell from 519 to 105, and from seventeen to thirteen in the case of sexual offences.[92]

Newburn found that magistrates shared a strongly held belief that compensation **9.75**
and punishment were not interchangeable responses to crimes of violence, and could not be realized in a single order. Later research carried out by the Home Office showed only a small overall increase following the 1988 amendment that imposed on the court the duty to give reasons where it had not made an order.[93] Magistrates strongly sensed that some punitive response other than the compensation order, even though it might be minimal, was both natural and desirable.[94] The government's view is that the compensation order is 'essentially reparative rather than punitive' and 'should not count towards the 'punitive weight' of a sentence'. But where an offender does not have the means to pay both compensation and a fine, such that the only option is to make a compensation order, then it may bear some punitive emphasis.[95]

---

[92] Ministry of Justice (2017a) Table Q5.3.

[93] David Moxon, John Corkery, and Carol Hedderman, *Developments in the use of compensation orders in magistrates' courts since October 1988* (Home Office Research and Planning Unit 1992).

[94] Tim Newburn, *The Use and Enforcement of Compensation Orders in Magistrates' Courts* (Home Office Research Study 102 1988) 10–12.

[95] Ministry of Justice (2010) para 137.

10

COMPENSATION AND RESTORATIVE JUSTICE

I Restorative Justice and Criminal Justice Policy

In its 2012 consultation, *Punishment and Reform: Effective Community Sentences,* the government observed that: **10.01**

> [v]ictims and communities also want offenders to face up to the consequences of their actions. Through restorative processes, victims and offenders can come together to collectively resolve how to deal with an offence. The outcome of this process may be reparation, but it may also involve a range of other outcomes including the offender accepting responsibility for their crime, giving the victim an opportunity to have their say and helping the victim to move on from the offence committed against them.[1]

As a process for achieving better (more inclusive, better accepted, and more robust), outcomes for unwanted conflicts, restorative justice can be seen as a better response to offences causing criminal injuries because it is intrinsically good: it treats victims and offenders as valuable in themselves and apart from any system or community benefits that may accrue. Alternatively (and sometimes, in addition), it is a better response because it can be seen as being instrumentally good. The legal guidance of the Crown Prosecution Service (CPS) on restorative justice describes these outcomes as principally comprising 'victim satisfaction: to reduce the fear of the victim and ensure they feel "paid back" for the harm that has been done to them', 'engagement with the perpetrator: to ensure that they are aware of **10.02**

[1] Ministry of Justice (2012d) para 111.

the consequences of their actions, have the opportunity to make reparation, and agree a plan for their restoration in the community', and 'creation of community capital; to increase public confidence in the criminal justice system and other agencies with a responsibility for delivering a response to anti-social behaviour'.[2]

10.03 The government's approach to its objective, that restorative justice can 'help put the power back in the victims' hands, rehabilitate those that offend, and bring down reoffending rates',[3] has been largely pragmatic: does it work? This question was to the fore when the Home Office funded its two major evaluations of restorative justice schemes, in 1999/2000,[4] and in 2001/2008.[5] Since then successive governments have committed to a gradual implementation of a restorative justice agenda throughout England and Wales, including pre-sentence provision, and, commencing in 2012, a sequence of annual restorative justice action plans for the criminal justice system.[6]

10.04 These initiatives also give effect to Article 14 of the 2012 Victims Directive,[7] transposed on 16 November 2015 as a revised Code of Practice for Victims of Crime.[8] A principal change broadened the definition of 'victim' to mean 'a natural person who has suffered harm, including physical, mental or emotional harm or economic loss which was directly caused by a criminal offence', and 'a close relative of a person whose death was directly caused by a criminal offence'.[9]

10.05 Section 7 of the Victims' Code sets out the core features of the purpose and the procedures for the implementation of restorative justice, which it defines as 'the process of bringing together victims with those responsible for the harm, to find a positive way forward'. A defining and universal characteristic of restorative justice is its requirement that there is explicit mutual consent on the part of both the victim and the offender to engage in its procedures.[10] It follows that in its absence there can be no voluntary compensation. But it should also be emphasized that while victims must be consulted about any pre- or post-trial restorative justice, reparation or compensation proposals, they have no veto over the disposal or sentence save in respect of its direct impact upon them.

---

[2] Crown Prosecution Service, *Restorative Justice* (CPS, *Restorative Justice*) *General Principles*.

[3] Ministry of Justice (2012f) 3.

[4] David Miers, Mike Maguire, Shelagh Goldie, Karen Sharpe, Chris Hale, Ann Netten, Kate Doolin, Steve Uglow, Jill Enterkin, and Tim Newburn, *An Exploratory Evaluation of Restorative Justice Schemes* (Home Office 2001).

[5] Joanna Shapland, Gwen Robinson, and Angela Sorsby, *Restorative Justice in Practice: Evaluating What Works for Victims and Offenders* (Routledge 2011).

[6] The most recent is Ministry of Justice (2017b).

[7] *Directive 2012/ 29/ EU of the European Parliament and of the Council of 25 October 2012 establishing minimum standards on the rights, support and protection of victims of crime, and replacing Council Framework Decision 2001/ 220/ JHA* [2012] OJ L315.

[8] Ministry of Justice (2015a) (the Victims' Code).

[9] ibid *Introduction* para 4.

[10] ibid ch 2, Pt B, s 7; ch 3, Pt A, s 7.

Restorative justice now comprises a range of administrative and statutory pre- and post-trial measures having a variety of purposes. It is managed directly by the Ministry of Justice, by statutory bodies—principally the CPS and the Youth Justice Board (YJB), the statutory body responsible for overseeing the youth justice system—and by the voluntary sector, in particular the Restorative Justice Council (RJC). The RJC is a pressure group that does not of itself offer restorative justice services, but collates information on their development, and has published a highly respected Statement of Restorative Justice Principles.[11] The following sections identify the main provisions governing its use as pre-trial and post-conviction options in respect of adult, and secondly, of young offenders, noting any opportunities for offender compensation that they provide. The text does not deal with the much wider and more complex statutory arrangements for non-custodial sentences of which these provisions form part. **10.06**

II Adult Offenders

A Pre-trial: the caution

1 The 'simple caution'

'Simple cautions' administered by the police 'are primarily intended for low level, mainly first time offending', now governed by the Ministry of Justice's 2013 Guidance. This provides that before it is given, 'it is important to establish where appropriate and possible what the victim's views about the offence are and the proposed method of disposal. It will be important to consider the nature and extent of the harm caused and whether any form of compensation could be paid'. In that case a conditional caution 'might be preferable'.[12] **10.07**

2 Conditional cautions

Introduced for adult offenders by sections 22–27 of the Criminal Justice Act 2003 (CJA 2003), a 'conditional caution' is 'a caution that is given in respect of an offence committed by the offender, having conditions attached to it with which by section 22(2) the offender must comply.[13] The Code of Practice for Adult Conditional Cautions provides that its purpose is to provide an opportunity to offer a proportionate response to low level offending, for offenders to make swift reparation to victims and communities, and to be diverted at an early opportunity **10.08**

---

[11] Restorative Justice Council https://restorativejustice.org.uk/ (last accessed 10 June 2018).

[12] Crown Prosecution Service, *Cautioning and Diversion* (CPS, *Cautioning and Diversion), Views of the Victim.*

[13] Indictable only offences and offences involving hate crime and domestic violence must be referred to the CPS; Crown Prosecution Service, *Adult Conditional Cautions (The Director's Guidance)* ss 3 and 6.

into rehabilitative services thereby reducing the likelihood of reoffending, and to punish an offender by means of a financial penalty.[14]

10.09 Section 23 imposes five requirements for a conditional caution to be given; these include a signed document containing the offender's consent to the caution and to its conditions. One of those requirements is ensuring that the person makes reparation for the behaviour or offence in question: 'Reparative conditions may include apologizing, repairing or otherwise making good any damage caused, provided this is acceptable to the victim. Specific financial compensation may be paid'.[15] Where the offence comprises anti-social behaviour under section 2 of the Anti-social Behaviour, Crime and Policing Act 2014 (ABCPA 2014), the local policing body may, by sections 101–103, instead of the offender being dealt with 'without court proceedings', order him to carry out one or more 'actions' drawn from its 'community remedy document', which actions serve any of those same conditions. By section 102(6), ' "action" includes the making of a payment to the victim'.

10.10 Before 'a relevant prosecutor or an authorised person' attaches any conditions to a conditional caution or orders the offender to carry out any community remedy,[16] the person making that decision must, by the CJA 2003 section 23ZA(1) 'make reasonable efforts to obtain the views of the victim (if any) of the offence, and in particular the victim's views as to whether the offender should carry out any of the actions listed in the community remedy document'. For the purpose of a conditional caution, 'victim' means 'the particular person who seems to [the decision-maker] to have been affected, or principally affected, by the offence' (section 23ZA(4)).

10.11 The same duty to consult applies where an out of court disposal based on an action listed in the community remedy document is being considered; in this case with the particular person who seems to have been affected, or principally affected, by the anti-social behaviour or offence (ABCPA 2014 sections 102(3)–(5)). The victim's views 'will be important but cannot be conclusive'; they must be taken into account but not acted upon if it would be inappropriate to do so (ABCPA 2014 section 102(4) and section 23ZA(3) of the 2003 Act).

10.12 The Code of Practice is very clear that the victim's consent must be obtained in any case where the conditions attached to a caution will have a direct impact on her, for example where compensation is to be paid, or work intended to benefit her is undertaken.[17] Similarly, the CPS Guidance provides that the views of the

---

[14] Ministry of Justice (2013b) para 1.4.

[15] ibid para 2.16.

[16] An 'authorised person' is a police officer not below the rank of sergeant or any person specifically authorized to do so by the Director of Public Prosecutions; CJA 2003 ss 22 and 27(4).

[17] Ministry of Justice (2013b) paras 2.47–2.49.

victim as to any restorative or reparative conditions and details of any compensation to be considered should be recorded in writing and included in the MG5 Report,[18] in particular if victims 'do not wish to participate in any meeting or have any contact, direct or indirect, with the offender or have any harm made good or compensation paid'.[19]

There are no restrictions in the CJA 2003 on the offences for which a compensation payment can be given as part of a reparative condition, or on its amount. The relevant prosecutor for each CPS area may set guidelines on the use of compensation payment as part of a reparative condition, but its guidance indicates that it will be appropriate only where the impact of the injury is limited. Its table of injuries and awards, up to £75 for a graze and £100 for a bruise (depending on size), and up to £125 for a black eye, reflect those indicated by the Sentencing Council as starting points for compensation orders (Chapter 8.20), but are in other respects more modest, £100–£200 for a minor cut with no permanent scar (depending on size and whether stitched), and £100–£200 for a sprain (depending on loss of mobility).[20] **10.13**

As is the case with compensation orders, the CPS guidance acknowledges that where the offender's means are limited any compensation payable as part of a reparative condition may well be less than an ideal assessment of the victim's injury. This does not preclude the use of a conditional caution if the offender and victim can agree an amount, but compensation is not a principal objective of a restorative justice meeting, and disagreement about the amount might well subvert the realization of that objective. **10.14**

Disparity between the offender's means and the extent of the victim's injury is exacerbated by the fact that the compensation 'must be capable of being paid within a reasonable period of time'; for this reason, the guidance suggests that the decision-maker should consider whether a compensation order payable by instalments 'would be a more suitable response',[21] a response that necessarily precludes a conditional caution. Where the offender is of limited means, compensation paid in compliance with a conditional caution may therefore comprise little more than a token recognition of the injury. **10.15**

A compensation payment as part of a reparative condition is one instance of a conditional caution that includes a financial element. The two others are costs **10.16**

[18] The MG5 document is a case summary prepared by the police and disclosed to the defence and the court. It is a National File Standard (NFS, May 2015) Pre-Charge Report for CPS Charging Decision for the First Magistrates Court Hearing; CPS, *Adult Conditional Cautions* (n 13) *Practical arrangements for the referral of cases* paras 16.4 and 16.5.

[19] CPS, *Restorative Justice* (n 2) *Views of the Victim.*

[20] CPS, *Adult Conditional Cautions* (n 13) *Annex B: Guidance for the Selection of Appropriate Conditions, Compensation for personal injuries; Annex A: Case Studies.*

[21] Ministry of Justice (2013b) paras 2.43–2.44.

associated with reparative, rehabilitative, punitive, or foreign offender conditions, and a financial penalty as part of a punitive condition. This penalty may only be used in respect of those offences prescribed by order made under section 23A(1) of the CJA 2003, for which maximum amounts of £50, £100, and £150 are set according to their level on the standard scale.[22] The decision-maker should determine the level of a financial penalty, taking into account the means of the offender and the circumstances of the case, including the seriousness of the offence, and apply the standard penalty unless she is satisfied that there is substantial mitigation, or the offender is in receipt of state benefit as his main or only source of income.[23] As in the case of compensation orders where the offender is of limited means, in cases where she is considering a condition with a financial element, the decision-maker 'should always prioritise compensation for the victim ahead of any costs associated with other conditions and any financial penalty condition'.[24]

B Post-trial

1 Deferment of sentence

10.17 Sentencing courts have since 1972 had power to defer sentence for up to six months in order to have regard to the offender's conduct after conviction. This initially merely permitted the court to 'take account of' any reparation the offender may have made, but appears to have seldom been relied upon. By section 1(1)(a) of the Powers of Criminal Courts (Sentencing) Act 2000 (PCC(S)A 2000) the court may defer passing sentence on an offender for the purpose of enabling the court to have regard to his conduct after conviction, 'including, where appropriate, the making by him of reparation for his offence'. For this purpose, the offender must consent and undertake to comply with any requirement as to their conduct or to making reparation the court considers it appropriate to impose (section 1(3)).

10.18 The Crime and Courts Act 2013 added, by section 1ZA of the PCC(S)A 2000, a requirement that the offender participate in 'restorative justice activities', defined in section 1ZA(2). In common with all statutory and other provisions concerning restorative justice, participation in these activities requires, in addition to the offender's consent and undertaking, 'the consent of every other person who would be a participant in the activity concerned' (section 1ZA(3)). For this purpose, 'victim' means 'a victim of, or other person affected by, the offending concerned' (section 1ZA(7)).

---

[22] Criminal Justice Act 2003 (Conditional Cautions: Financial Penalties) Order 2009, SI 2009/2773.

[23] CPS, *Adult Conditional Cautions* (n 13) *Annex B: Guidance for the Selection of Appropriate Conditions.*

[24] Ministry of Justice (2013b) para 2.42.

The Magistrates' Court Sentencing Guidelines suggest that 'deferred sentences will be appropriate only in very limited circumstances',[25] and the government's guidelines for 'pre-sentence restorative justice (RJ)' made under section 1ZA(6) contain only one reference to making 'some sort of reparation', and no reference to compensation.[26] Those guidelines focus on the purposes of the restorative justice activity specified in section 1ZA(2), which, as its philosophy emphasizes, comprise its defining characteristics. These are to maximize the offender's awareness of the impact of the offending concerned on the victim, and gives an opportunity to a victim or victims to talk about, or by other means express experience of, the offending and its impact. Compensation for the victim's personal injury may be a welcome by-product, but is not a primary objective. Where an offender is in a position fully to compensate the victim, it might be objected that he is buying his way out of any penalty (Chapter 9.19), an outcome that would be at odds with what restorative justice contemplates for the participation of the victim and the offender. Even where the defendant is genuinely remorseful, the issue of principle is one of equity as between offenders, pointedly illustrated in *Crosby and Hayes*.[27] Each sought to compensate the victim, but only one had sufficient means to do so. Invited to give him a lower sentence, the Court of Appeal refused, holding that it was wrong in principle to differentiate between them if the only difference was that one had the means to pay and the other did not. **10.19**

2 *Restorative justice as a sentencing condition*

When dealing with an adult offender, section 142(1)(a)–(e) of the CJA 2003 requires the court to have regard to the purposes of sentencing, in particular to the reform and rehabilitation of offenders, and the making of reparation by offenders to persons affected by their offences. In *Rahman* the Court of Appeal was faced with a question concerning sentencing equity where one of the two offenders could, and the other could not, make reparation, The court had sentenced them to the same terms of imprisonment, possibly, although this was not explicit, because it thought that the co-accused's inability to provide reparation to the victim was balanced by his lower level of culpability, whereas the appellant's ability to do so was balanced by his higher level of culpability. While this speculative line of reasoning might indicate an equilibrium between the two offenders, a basic difficulty was that the court had not addressed section 142(1)(e) of the CJA 2003. The Court of Appeal held that, in taking its requirement into account, the principle of sentencing equity was not compromised if the offer of reparation was reflected in a reduction in the term of imprisonment.[28] **10.20**

---

[25] Sentencing Council, *Magistrates' Court Sentencing Guidelines, Explanatory Materials, Deferred Sentences*.

[26] Ministry of Justice (2014b) para 1.21.

[27] (1974) 60 Cr App R 234 (CA).

[28] [2015] EWCA Crim 320, [2015] 2 Cr App R (S) 10 [14–[15] (CA) (Jeremy Baker J).

10.21 Reparation may, in the case of offences against property, be met by ancillary orders for restitution (PCC(S)A 2000 sections 148–149), deprivation (PCC(S) A 2000 sections 143–145), confiscation (Chapter 9.39–9.43), and, in the case of personal injury, by compensation orders. Reparation is also specifically provided for as a 'community requirement' that may be imposed when the court makes a suspended sentence order (SSO) (CJA 2003 section 189(1A)), or as a 'community order' when it imposes a community sentence (CJA 2003 section 147), being, by sections 190(1)(aa) and 177(1)(aa) of the CJA 2003 respectively, 'a rehabilitation activity requirement'. By section 200A(7)(b) of the CJA 2003, this includes activities 'whose purpose is reparative, such as restorative justice activities'.

10.22 These activities are defined in the same terms as section 1ZA(2) of the PCC(S)A 2000 in respect of the deferment of sentence, as is the definition of a 'victim', and as in that case there is also little guidance concerning reparation and compensation. The Sentencing Council's guidance observes that community orders are a means of 'ensuring that the offender engages in reparative activities',[29] and the RJC's information pack for magistrates notes that 'a number of rehabilitation activity requirements can be made as part of a community order, along with other elements, such as rehabilitation and compensation'.[30] Both community orders and SSOs can involve the imposition of an 'unpaid work requirement' (CJA 2003 sections 177(1)(a) and sections 199 and 200 respectively), broadly having a reparative object, such as removing graffiti, clearing wasteland, or decorating public places and buildings, commonly known as Community Payback.[31] These do not engage the victim, and may be regarded as some way removed from accepted notions of restorative justice.

III Young Offenders

A Pre-trial

1 Youth cautions

10.23 Many of the early restorative justice initiatives took the form of diversionary procedures for first time young offenders. The formal procedures of reprimands and warnings introduced by sections 65 and 66 of the Crime and Disorder Act 1998 (CDA 1998) were replaced with effect from 8 April 2013 by the youth caution (sections 66ZA and 66ZB of the CDA 1998). This is a formal out-of-court

[29] Sentencing Council, *Imposition of Community and Custodial Sentences, Definitive Guideline* 3.

[30] RJC, *Restorative justice in the magistrates' court* (2014) 4; https://restorativejustice.org.uk/sites/default/files/resources/files/1bbm_info_packs%20%282%29%20mags_0.pdf (last accessed 11 June 2018).

[31] GOV.UK, Community sentences.

disposal to be used as an alternative to prosecution for offenders aged 10 to 17. In terms of its impact on the offender, it sits in an offence seriousness hierarchy comprising: no further action, community resolution, youth caution, youth conditional caution, and charge. The 'Youth Out-of-Court-Disposal: Guide for Police and Youth Offending Services' provides an overview of the entire of-court disposal framework,[32] and the Association of Chief Police Officers (ACPO)'s 'Youth Offender Case Disposal Gravity Factor Matrix' provides guidance as to the selection of those options.[33]

The criteria that apply to the giving of a youth caution and the procedures that the police and the youth offending team (YOT) must follow are set out in statutory guidance made under section 66ZA(5) of the CDA 1998, 'Youth Cautions: Guidance for Police and Youth Offending Teams', prepared jointly by the government and the YJB.[34] Youth cautions aim to provide a proportionate and effective resolution to offending and support the principal statutory aim of the youth justice system of preventing offending by children and young people. Unlike adult simple cautions, the young person does not 'consent' to receiving a youth caution; it is a matter for the police to decide the appropriate disposal in accordance with section 66ZB of the CDA 1998. The young offender must then be referred to the specified YOT; its task is to assess the likelihood and suitability of the young person engaging with a YOT intervention, which may explore the possibility of participation in restorative justice for the delivery of the caution. **10.24**

This participation necessarily requires the YOT to obtain the victim's informed consent, as it must in respect of any aspect of the youth caution,[35] or, if the matter had not reached this point, any community resolution, which may be delivered either with or without the use of restorative justice techniques.[36] The statutory guidance deals extensively with the use of restorative justice for these various out-of-court disposals,[37] which, in a youth caution, 'may involve direct reparation if the victim wishes it'.[38] The interventions attached to a youth caution are not conditions with which the offender must comply, but they may be cited in criminal proceedings (CDA 1998 section 66ZB(7)); if compliance is required, a youth conditional caution is to be preferred. But monetary compensation is not a possible option either for a youth caution or community resolution. **10.25**

---

32 Ministry of Justice/Youth Justice Board (MoJ/ YJB) (2013a) (MoJ/YJB) 3.2.

33 Association of Chief Police Officers (2013); Crown Prosecution Service, *Prosecution Guidance, Minor Offences.*

34 Ministry of Justice/Youth Justice Board (MoJ/ YJB) (2013b).

35 ibid 8.12.

36 Ministry of Justice/ Youth Justice Board (MoJ/ YJB) (2014a) paras 3.7–3.9.

37 Ministry of Justice/ Youth Justice Board (MoJ/ YJB) (2014b) section 9; MoJ/YJB (2014a) paras 3.23–3.27.

38 MoJ/YJB (2014a) section 9.10.

2 Youth conditional cautions

10.26 Youth conditional cautions are governed by sections 66A–66G of the CDA 1998. They largely mirror the provisions in sections 22–27 of the CJA 2003 in respect of adult conditional cautions, and broadly speaking serve the same purposes. Reflecting the early history of the informal disposal of young offenders, their purpose is also to divert young offenders at an early opportunity into rehabilitative services in order to reduce the likelihood of reoffending. The conditions for their use are set out in guidance published by the CPS,[39] and by the government under section 66G of the CDA 1998.[40]

10.27 Youth conditional cautions may enable offenders 'to make swift reparation to victims and communities', that is, including conditions 'which serve to repair the damage done either directly or indirectly by the young person', and which provide reparation or compensation to any victim or relevant neighbourhood or community'. 'Compensation' has the same significance as in the case of an adult conditional caution, that is, a payment as part of a reparative condition. The one other condition having a financial element is the financial penalty, governed by section 66C of the CDA 1998, for which the maximum amounts vary between £3 and £50 depending on offence procedure, the age of the offender between 10–14 or 15–18, and whether the amount has been mitigated.[41] The compensation levels, however, are the same as for adult conditional caution,[42] in respect of which, as where reparation is proposed, the victim's expectations should not be unrealistically raised.[43]

B Post-trial

10.28 When sentencing a young offender the court must have regard to the Sentencing Council's Definitive Guideline. This provides that 'while the seriousness of the offence will be the starting point, the approach to sentencing should be individualistic and focused on the child or young person, as opposed to offence focused. For a child or young person the sentence should focus on rehabilitation where possible'.[44] Among the factors that the court must consider when sentencing is the harm that the offence caused, in respect of which it should encourage reparation to the victims. This may be possible as an element in either of the two principal non-custodial sentences, referral orders and youth rehabilitation

[39] Crown Prosecution Service, *Youth Conditional Cautions (The Director's Guidance)* (CPS, *Youth Conditional Cautions*).

[40] Ministry of Justice (2013b).

[41] Crime and Disorder Act 1998 (Youth Conditional Cautions: Financial Penalties) Order 2-2013, SI 2013/608.

[42] CPS, *Youth Conditional Cautions* (n 39), *Annex B: Financial penalty conditions banding*.

[43] MoJ/YJB (2013a) para 9.3.

[44] Sentencing Council, *Sentencing Children and Young People, Definitive Guideline* (June 2017) para 1.2.

orders (YRO). In addition, the court may also make a compensation order as a sole or an ancillary sentence (Chapter 9), possibly with an absolute or conditional discharge, and a reparation order under sections 73–75 of the PCC(S)A 2000 (10.37–10.38).[45]

1 *Referral orders*

Referral orders were introduced in 1989 and are now contained in sections 16–31 of the PCC(S)A 2000. They are a 'first tier' response whose broad purpose is 'to prevent young people reoffending and provide a restorative justice approach within a community context'.[46] The order is mandatory for most young offenders who have not previously been convicted and who plead guilty in a youth court or a magistrates' court (not the Crown Court) to an imprisonable offence. The Act also provides for its discretionary use (sections 16 and 17). Among other prohibitions, a referral order cannot be made where the court imposes a sentence which consists of or includes a YRO or a fine, makes a reparation order, or conditionally discharges the young offender; but it may discharge her absolutely in respect of a 'connected offence' (section 19). **10.29**

The court determines the length of the order (between three and twelve months), but the action to be taken is decided by a youth offender panel established by the YOT specified in the order (section 21). In assessing the young offender and determining the content of the contract, the panel uses the YJB's 'scaled approach', a framework for the assessment of all young people involved in the criminal justice system, and of the corresponding interventions. This approach applies when a young person is subject to a referral order, a YRO, or during the community element of a custodial sentence. It distinguishes standard, enhanced, or intensive levels of intervention that reflect the offender's low, medium, or high likelihood of reoffending. **10.30**

All three interventions may involve victim (or community) reparation, but in the case of a low risk offender the referral order will primarily seek to repair the harm caused by the offence.[47] It should be noted that the terms of the mandatory referral order mean that the offence was serious enough to have met the custody threshold; in this case 'a robust and credible sentencing option' should involve 'a referral order intensive contract',[48] which may include the full range of intensive community intervention options. **10.31**

The selected options constitute the content of the 'youth offender contract' agreed by the young offender and implemented by the panel (PCC(S)A 2000 section **10.32**

---

[45] ibid paras 6.13–6.16.
[46] Ministry of Justice/Youth Justice Board (MoJ/YJB) (2015) para 1.1.
[47] Youth Justice Board, *The Scaled Approach* (2010).
[48] MoJ/YJB (2015) para 7.4.

23(1)). The MoJ/YJB *Referral Order Guidance* provides that the contract must include 'two core elements: reparation/restoration to the victim or wider community, and a programme of interventions/activities to address reoffending risk'.[49] By definition, a youth offender contract requires the offender's agreement (in the presence of his parents if under 16 (section 20)); failing which he may be referred back to the appropriate court for sentencing (sections 25 and 28). The panel is responsible for monitoring its progress and for the final meeting with him. If the panel decides that the contract has been, or by the time it expires will have been, satisfactorily completed, the conviction will be spent (PCC(S)A 2000 sections 24, 26, and 27).

10.33 The first of the nine terms of the contract (section 23(1)(a)) requires the offender 'to make financial or other reparation' to any person falling within section 22(4). As is the case with youth conditional cautions and with restorative justice interventions generally, 'it is essential that youth offending teams facilitate the involvement of victims. The involvement of victims must be entirely voluntary and based on informed consent'.[50] This applies to any term of the contract that contemplates engagement between the victim and the offender: 'Reparation to individual victims should, as far as possible, be determined by the wishes of the victim, whilst having regard to proportionality, and may include an explanation, an apology, verbal or written, and practical recompense, including financial compensation, for the harm that has been caused'. But direct reparation, or a letter to the victim, should not be considered where there is any possibility that the victim might be put at risk by further contact with the offender, or 'without his or her express prior consent'.[51]

10.34 When making a referral order, the court may also impose a compensation order against the young offender, subject to the provisions in section 137 of the PCC(S)A 2000 concerning payment by her parent or guardian (Chapter 9.36–9.38). There is also the option of including financial reparation into the contract, for which purpose 'it is essential that the YOT has financially sound and robust procedures in place to ensure the reparation is carried out in a secure and efficient manner'.[52] It is not clear, however, to what extent this option has figured in youth offender contracts. A systematic review published in 2016 showed that in 2014/2015 there were 12,039 referral orders, but while it commented at length on their restorative justice and reparation arrangements, there was no information on the use or impact of any financial reparation of the victim.[53]

---

[49] ibid para 1.8.
[50] ibid para 6.2.
[51] ibid para 8.23.
[52] ibid paras 8.21–8.23.
[53] HM Inspectorate of Probation, *Referral orders—do they achieve their potential? An inspection by HM Inspectorate of Probation* (2016) (HMIP, *Referral Orders*).

2 Youth rehabilitation orders

A YRO is a 'second tier' sentence for young offenders introduced by sections 1–4 of the Criminal Justice and Immigration Act 2008, and may be used where the offence is 'serious enough' to warrant it (sections 1(3) and 1(4)).[54] It creates one generic community sentence comprising all community sentences that existed when it came into effect. The court can choose from a 'menu' of fifteen different requirements designed to provide a variety of options for punishment, protection of the public, reducing reoffending, reparation, and rehabilitation. In determining which, and what combination of requirements is to be completed within the maximum three-year period, the YOT uses the YJB's scaled approach. **10.35**

As in the case of referral orders, reparation, which may be included in 'an activity requirement', can be a requirement at all three intervention levels. Any contact between the young person and the victim, including any proposals concerning restorative justice, must be based on the victim's consent.[55] **10.36**

3 Reparation orders

By PCC(S)A 2000 section 73, in addition to any sentence other than a custodial sentence, a new or continuing YRO or a referral order (sections 73(4) and (4A)), the court may order a young offender to make reparation to a person or persons 'identified by the court as a victim of the offence or a person otherwise affected by it', or to the community at large (section 73(1)). A reparation order is an intervention that lies below the YRO in the sentencing hierarchy, and may in particular be used for lower level offending that would not meet the 'serious enough' threshold for a YRO. **10.37**

The type of work to be included in the reparation order must be suitable for the offender, and the report considered by the court must indicate 'the attitude of the victim or victims' to those requirements (section 73(5)). In common with section 130(3) of the PCC(S)A 2000, the court must give reasons if it does not make a reparation order in a case where it has power to do so. The purpose of section 130(3) was to encourage magistrates in particular to make greater use of compensation orders; a similar purpose may be assumed to underlie section 73(8) in respect of reparation. But whatever the requirements are (section 74)), they may not include 'the payment of compensation' (section 73(3)). **10.38**

---

54 Sentencing Council, *Sentencing Children* (n 44) paras 6.23–6.41.

55 Ministry of Justice (2015a) para 6.33.

IV Compensation and Restorative Justice

10.39 In the case of adult offenders, compensation possibilities will be limited either because, as with compensation orders, they will have insufficient means, or because there are competing pre-trial constraints on the arrangements governing cautioning, and, post-trial, on the court's sentencing powers. In the case of young offenders, the overarching principles governing their treatment by the criminal justice system necessarily inhibit the scope for their direct compensation or reparation of the victim.[56] In the case of the simple reality of their limited means, these principles find particular expression in section 137 of the PCC(S)A 2000, which, in addition to its application to the parents' or guardian's payment of a compensation order against a young offender, requires any fine for the offender's breach of a reparation order to be paid by them (section 137(2)(d)), subject to the same terms as to their liability.

10.40 In 2016/17 'around 17,500 children and young people (68%) were given community sentences, of which 64% were Referral Orders (around 11,200), 35% were Youth Rehabilitation Orders (around 6,200) and 1% were Reparation Orders (just under 120)'.[57] Community sentences are the most commonly imposed sentences on young offenders, but so far as these concern their victims it is not clear to what extent they achieve their objectives.

10.41 The very thorough review carried out by HM Inspectorate of Prisons on the implementation of referral orders found that almost half the victims who had been interviewed had not been asked for their views on what reparation should be undertaken, and less than half were offered the opportunity to request direct reparation via a referral order.[58] The review also found that while there was widespread commitment to restorative justice among YOTs, the opportunity to deliver it 'was severely restricted by the small proportion of victims who had engaged with the YOT'.[59]

10.42 These conclusions are echoed in a Crime Survey for England and Wales' report on victims' experience of potential restorative justice meetings, based on 2016/2017 data. Its findings, which largely reflect the previous survey years, were that only 4 per cent of victims were given the opportunity to meet the offender, while, if the offer had been made, 24 per cent would have accepted. In 2014/2015 (the sample for later years was too small) 44 per cent of victims did accept the offer, but only 5 per cent of victims received reparation in 2016/2017.[60]

---

56 Sentencing Council, *Sentencing Children* (n 44) section 1: *General approach*.
57 Youth Justice Board/Ministry of Justice (2018) 20.
58 HMIP, *Referral Orders* (n 53) para 8.11.
59 ibid paras 8.1–8.3.
60 Office for National Statistics (August 2017).

In its 2016 reviews,[61] the Victims' Commissioner attributed victims' very low take up to a variety of factors. These centred on inconsistent messaging about the purpose of restorative justice and its impact on the offender, victims' concerns about their own role in any restorative meeting, and more generally about their entitlements under the Victims' Code. These reviews were, nevertheless, more positive than the Commissioner's finding in 2014, that too much emphasis was being placed on the needs of offenders, and of the outcome that restorative justice would bring for them.[62] **10.43**

Despite the universal presence of restorative justice in the pre- and post-trial arrangements discussed in this chapter, there are only two reported Court of Appeal decisions that have considered its relevance to sentencing decisions. However, both were positive. Noting that it was 'by no means a soft option', the Court in *Collins* held that it was to the appellant's credit 'that he took part in [a restorative justice] programme and that [it] is a factor properly to be taken into account',[63] a stance also in taken in *Barci,* where the appellant had shown 'an express and genuine willingness' to attend such a programme.[64] **10.44**

These were adult offenders, but the underlying obstacle to its wider use for young offenders, the group for whom restorative justice has been especially promoted, is, simply, that 'not enough victims became involved in restorative justice, or benefited from referral order work'.[65] A notable element of the HMIP *Referral Orders* report is the resonance between its findings of 'confusion about what constitutes restorative justice', and the conclusions that the Home Office's first research exercise reached two decades ago,[66] a matter that continues to resonate in the restorative justice literature.[67] **10.45**

[61] Victims' Commissioner (2016a) and (2016b) paras 1.1–1.2.

[62] Victims' Commissioner (2014).

[63] [2003] EWCA Crim 1687, 2003 WL 1610401 [7] (CA) (Moses J).

[64] [2003] EWCA Crim 2816, 2003 WL 22358414 [6]–[7] (CA) (Penry-Davey J).

[65] HMIP, *Referral Orders* (n 53) paras 8.1–8.3.

[66] Miers and others (n 4) 30.

[67] David Miers, 'Restorative Justice as a Boundary Object: Some Critical Reflections on the Rise and Influence of Restorative Justice in England and Wales' in Sandra Walklate and Dale Spencer (eds), *Critical Victimology: Reconceptualizations, Interventions, and Possibilities*. (Lexington Books 2016) 95–110.

BIBLIOGRAPHY

All web addresses were accessed in March 2018

1 THE CRIMINAL INJURIES COMPENSATION STATUTORY SCHEMES AND GUIDES

http://hmctsformfinder.justice.gov.uk/HMCTS/GetForms.do?court_forms_category=criminal%20injuries%20compensation

1.1 The schemes

The 1996 Scheme, *Criminal Injuries Compensation Scheme 1996*; https://formfinder.hmctsformfinder.justice.gov.uk/criminal-injuries-compensation-scheme-1996-eng.pdf

The 2001 Scheme, *Criminal Injuries Compensation Scheme 2001*; https://formfinder.hmctsformfinder.justice.gov.uk/criminal-injuries-compensation-scheme-2001-eng.pdf

The 2008 Scheme, *Criminal Injuries Compensation Scheme 2008*; https://www.justice.gov.uk/downloads/tribunals/criminal-injuries-compensation/Criminal-Injuries-Compensation-Scheme-2008.pdf

The 2012 Scheme, *Criminal Injuries Compensation Scheme 2012*; https://formfinder.hmctsformfinder.justice.gov.uk/criminal-injuries-compensation-scheme-2012-eng.pdf

1.2 The Guides

References to 'the 2012 Guide' are references to the online 'guide to applying for compensation under the Criminal Injuries Compensation Scheme', updated to November 2016. This guide reproduces much of what was contained in the paper *Guide to the 2012 Scheme* published in 2012, updated to June 2013. The digital guide does not entirely supersede the paper guide, which contains a number of indicators to the CICA's application of the scheme that are not repeated in the online version. Where appropriate, the text refers to this as the 'paper 2012 Guide', and also to the CICA's Guides to the earlier tariff schemes.

CICA (1996 Guide), *Victims of Crimes of Violence: A Guide to the Criminal Injuries Compensation Scheme 1996*; http://hmctsformfinder.justice.gov.uk/HMCTS/GetLeaflet.do?original_id=4496

CICA (2001 Guide), *Guide to the 2001 Compensation Scheme*; http://hmctsformfinder.justice.gov.uk/HMCTS/GetLeaflet.do?original_id=4497

CICA (2008 Guide), *Guide to the 2008 Compensation Scheme*; http://hmctsformfinder.justice.gov.uk/HMCTS/GetLeaflet.do?original_id=4498

CICA (paper 2012 Guide), *Guide to the 2012 Compensation Scheme*; https://www.citizensadvice.org.uk/Global/Migrated_Documents/adviser net/04370105-ews-a-guide-to-the-criminal-injuries-compensation-scheme-2012-pdf-6.pdf

CICA (2012 Guide), *Guide to the 2012 Compensation Scheme*; https://www.gov.uk/guidance/criminal-injuries-compensation-a-guide

1.3 Other CICA Documents

About our services; https://www.gov.uk/government/organisations/criminal-injuries-compensation-authority/about/about-our-services

CICA 2020 and 2017-18 Business Plan; https://assets.publishing.service.gov.uk/government/uploads/system/uploads/attachment_data/file/658742/bp_2017_2020.pdf

CICA statistics for 2016–1; https://www.gov.uk/government/uploads/system/uploads/attachment_data/file/655967/transparency_data_2016-17.csv/preview

Claim compensation for a criminal injury; https://www.gov.uk/claim-compensation-criminal-injury

Compensation if you're a victim of crime abroad; https://www.gov.uk/compensation-victim-crime-abroad

Criminal injuries compensation: residency and nationality; https://www.gov.uk/guidance/criminal-injuries-compensation-residency-and-nationality

Victims of human trafficking and the Criminal Injuries Compensation Scheme; https://www.gov.uk/government/publications/victims-of-human-trafficking-and-the-criminal-injuries-compensation-scheme

2 ANNUAL REPORTS OF THE CRIMINAL INJURIES COMPENSATION AUTHORITY (CICA) AND THE CRIMINAL INJURIES COMPENSATION APPEALS PANEL (CICAP)

In describing the application of the 2012 Scheme's provisions, the text refers for illustrative purposes to decisions reached by the CICA. These will be references to the end date of the financial year to which the relevant Annual Report and Accounts refers, irrespective of the date of publication. For example, CICA (2004) refers to the Criminal Injuries Compensation Authority's Eighth Report: *Annual Report and Accounts 2003/04* (House of Commons Paper 1196, June 2006).

Appeals from the CICA have since 2008 been heard by the First-tier Tribunal, replacing the Criminal Injuries Compensation Appeal Panel. Where the text refers for illustrative purposes to CICAP's decisions, they are identified by reference to the end date of the financial year to which the relevant Annual Report and Accounts refers, irrespective of the date of publication. For example, CICAP (1999) refers to the Criminal Injuries Compensation Appeal Panel's Third Report, *Annual Report and Accounts for the year ended 31 March 1999* (Cm 4670, April 2000).

Chapters 1–6 also occasionally refer to decisions of the Criminal Injuries Compensation Board made under the common law Scheme. These are identified in the text by reference to its annual report, Command Paper, and year of publication; for example, CICB, 24th Report (Cm 536 1988).

2.1 Annual Reports of the Criminal Injuries Compensation Authority

Criminal Injuries Compensation Authority; https://www.gov.uk/government/organisations/criminal-injuries-compensation-authority

CICA (1997), Criminal Injuries Compensation Authority: *First Report; Accounts for the year ended 31 March 1997* (House of Commons Paper 631, March 1998)

CICA (1998), Criminal Injuries Compensation Authority: *Second Report; Accounts for the year ended 31 March 1998* (House of Commons Paper 131, January 1999)

CICA (1999), Criminal Injuries Compensation Authority: *Third Report; Accounts for the year ended 31 March 1999* (House of Commons Paper 353, March 2000)

CICA (2000), Criminal Injuries Compensation Authority: *Fourth Report; Annual Report and Accounts 1999-2000* (House of Commons Paper 356, March 2001)
CICA (2001), Criminal Injuries Compensation Authority Fifth Report: *Annual Report and Accounts 2000-01* (House of Commons Paper 705, May 2002)
CICA (2002), Criminal Injuries Compensation Authority Sixth Report: *Annual Report and Accounts 2001-02* (House of Commons Paper 450, September 2003)
CICA (2003), Criminal Injuries Compensation Authority Seventh Report: *Annual Report and Accounts 2002-03* (House of Commons Paper 451, March 2004)
CICA (2004), Criminal Injuries Compensation Authority Eighth Report: *Annual Report and Accounts 2003-04* (House of Commons Paper 1196, June 2006)
CICA (2005), Criminal Injuries Compensation Authority Ninth Report: *Annual Report and Accounts 2004-05* (House of Commons Paper 1427, July 2006)
CICA (2006), Criminal Injuries Compensation Authority Tenth Report: *Annual Report and Accounts 2005-06* (House of Commons Paper 214, June 2007)
CICA (2007), Criminal Injuries Compensation Authority Eleventh Report: *Annual Report and Accounts 2006-07* (House of Commons Paper 950, July 2007)
CICA (2008), Criminal Injuries Compensation Authority Twelfth Report: *Annual Report and Accounts 2007-08* (House of Commons Paper 877, July 2008)
CICA (2009), Criminal Injuries Compensation Authority Thirteenth Report: *Annual Report and Accounts 2008-09* (House of Commons Paper 728, July 2009)
CICA (2010), Criminal Injuries Compensation Authority Fourteenth Report: *Annual Report and Accounts 2009-10* (House of Commons Paper 115, July 2010)
CICA (2011), Criminal Injuries Compensation Authority Fifteenth Report: *Annual Report and Accounts 2010-11* (House of Commons Paper 1246, July 2011)
CICA (2012), Criminal Injuries Compensation Authority Sixteenth Report: *Annual Report and Accounts 2011-12* (House of Commons Paper 296, July 2012)
CICA (2013), Criminal Injuries Compensation Authority Seventeenth Report: *Annual Report and Accounts 2012-13* (House of Commons Paper 222, June 2013)
CICA (2014), Criminal Injuries Compensation Authority: *Annual Report and Accounts 2013–14* (House of Commons Paper 155, June 2014)
CICA (2015), Criminal Injuries Compensation Authority: *Annual Report and Accounts 2014–15* (House of Commons Paper 200, June 2015)
CICA (2016), Criminal Injuries Compensation Authority: *Annual Report and Accounts 2015–16* (House of Commons Paper 470, July 2016)
CICA (2017) Criminal Injuries Compensation Authority: *Annual Report and Accounts 2016–2017* (House of Commons Paper 256, July 2017)
CICA (2018) Criminal Injuries Compensation Authority: *Annual Report and Accounts 2017–2018* (House of Commons Paper 1337, July 2018)

2.2 Annual Reports of the Criminal Injuries Compensation Appeals Panel

https://www.gov.uk/government/organisations/criminal-injuries-compensation-appeals-panel
CICAP (1997): First Report, *Annual Report and Accounts for the year ended 31 March 1997* (Cm 3840, February 1998)
CICAP (1998): Second Report, *Annual Report and Accounts for the year ended 31 March 1998* (Cm 4184, January 1999)
CICAP (1999): Third Report, *Annual Report and Accounts for the year ended 31 March 1999* (Cm 4670, April 2000)
CICAP (2000): *Fourth Report, Annual Report and Accounts for the year ended 31 March 2000* (Cm 5081, March 2001)

CICAP (2001): Fifth Report, *Annual Report and Accounts for the year ended 31 March 2001* (House of Commons Paper 722, April 2002)
CICAP (2002): Sixth Report, *Annual Report and Accounts for the year ended 31 March 2002* (House of Commons Paper 960, July 2003)
CICAP (2003): Seventh Report, *Annual Report and Accounts for the year ended 31 March 2003* (House of Commons Paper 450, March 2004)
CICAP (2005) Ninth Report, *Annual Report and Accounts 2004-05* (House of Commons Paper 849, February 2006)
CICAP (2006) Tenth Report, Annual *Report and Accounts 2005-06* (House of Commons Paper 1428, July 2006)

3 OFFICIAL REPORTS

Association of Chief Police Officers (2013), *ACPO Youth Offender Case Disposal Gravity Factor Matrix*; https://static1.squarespace.com/static/579fce76d2b857f883038fa5/t/57a485bf725e25acf934d438/1470399936178/Gravity+Matrix+May09.pdf
Advisory Council on the Penal System (1970), *Reparation by the Offender*
Cabinet Office (2000), *Recovering the proceeds of crime*; http://webarchive.nationalarchives.gov.uk/+/http:/www.cabinetoffice.gov.uk/media/cabinetoffice/strategy/assets/crime.pdf
Commissioner for Victims and Witnesses in England and Wales (2011), *Victims' Views of Court and Sentencing: Qualitative research with WAVES victims. London: UK*; https://www.justice.gov.uk/downloads/news/press-releases/victims-com/victims-views-court-sentencing1011.pdf
Courts and Tribunals Judiciary, *Criminal Injuries Compensation Tribunal—Rules and Legislation*; https://www.judiciary.gov.uk/publications/criminal-injuries-compensation-tribunal-rules-and-legislation/
Practice Guidance CI-1 Claims for Financial Loss—Loss of Earnings, Loss of Earning Capacity, Special Expenses, State Benefits, Pension Payments
Practice Statement CI-2—Listing of appeal hearings: eligibility issues
Practice Statement CI-3—Specialist evidence
Practice Guidance CI-4, cap on loss of earnings 10June
Practice Statement CI-5—Listing of appeal hearings; postponement of hearings
Practice and Guidance Statement CI-6)—Appeals on error of law against final decision of the Tribunal
Practice Direction, First Tier and Upper Tribunal Child, Vulnerable Adult and Sensitive Witnesses
Crown Prosecution Service (2013), *Adult Conditional Cautions (The Director's Guidance)*; https://www.cps.gov.uk/legal-guidance/adult-conditional-cautions-directors-guidance#a06
Crown Prosecution Service, *Cautioning and Diversion*; https://www.cps.gov.uk/legal-guidance/cautioning-and-diversion
Crown Prosecution Service, *Costs*; https://www.cps.gov.uk/legal-guidance/costs
Crown Prosecution Service, *Human Trafficking, Smuggling and Slavery*; https://www.cps.gov.uk/legal-guidance/human-trafficking-smuggling-and-slavery
Crown Prosecution Service (12 March 2018), *Proceeds of Crime. Legal Guidance*; https://www.cps.gov.uk/sites/default/files/documents/legal_guidance/Proceeds%20of%20Crime.pdf
Crown Prosecution Service, *Prosecution Guidance, Minor Offences*; http://www.cps.gov.uk/legal/l_to_o/minor_offences/
Crown Prosecution Service, *Restorative Justice*; https://www.cps.gov.uk/legal-guidance/restorative-justice

Crown Prosecution Service, *Sentencing, Ancillary Orders*; https://www.cps.gov.uk/legal-guidance/sentencing-ancillary-orders

Crown Prosecution Service, *Special Measures*; https://www.cps.gov.uk/legal-guidance/special-measures

Crown Prosecution Service, *Victim Personal Statements*; https://www.cps.gov.uk/legal-guidance/victim-personal-statements

Crown Prosecution Service, *Youth Conditional Cautions (The Director's Guidance)*; https://www.cps.gov.uk/legal-guidance/youth-conditional-cautions-directors-guidance

Department for Business, Energy & Industrial Strategy (2018), *Gig economy research*; https://www.gov.uk/government/publications/gig-economy-research

Department for Work and Pensions, *Capability for work questionnaire*; https://www.gov.uk/government/publications/capability-for-work-questionnaire

Department of Work and Pensions (2017), *Recovery of benefits and lump sum payments and NHS charges: technical guidance*; https://www.gov.uk/government/publications/recovery-of-benefits-and-or-lump-sum-payments-and-nhs-charges-technical-guidance/recovery-of-benefits-and-lump-sum-payments-and-nhs-charges-technical-guidance

Government Actuary's Department, *Ogden tables: actuarial compensation tables for injury and death*; https://www.gov.uk/government/publications/ogden-tables-actuarial-compensation- tables-for-injury-and-death

Government Equalities Office (2010), *The Stern Review: An independent review into how rape complaints are handled by public authorities in England and Wales* (Cabinet Office 2010); http://webarchive.nationalarchives.gov.uk/20110608162919/http:/www.equalities.gov.uk/pdf/Stern_Review_acc_FINAL.pdf

GOV.UK, *Carers and disability benefits*; https://www.gov.uk/browse/benefits/disability

GOV.UK, *Community sentences*; https://www.gov.uk/community-sentences/community-payback

GOV.UK, *Criminal injuries compensation tribunal*; https://www.gov.uk/criminal-injuries-compensation-tribunal

HM Courts & Tribunals Service, *Form JRC1: Judicial review claim form—criminal injuries compensation cases, England and Wales*; https://formfinder.hmctsformfinder.justice.gov.uk/jrc1-eng.pdf

HM Inspectorate of Probation (2016), *Referral orders—do they achieve their potential? An inspection by HM Inspectorate of Probation*; https://www.justiceinspectorates.gov.uk/hmiprobation/wp-content/uploads/sites/5/2016/07/Referral-orders-do-they-achieve-their-potential.pdf

Home Office (1959), *Penal Practice in a Changing Society* (1959 Cmnd 645); http://www.butlertrust.org.uk/wp-content/uploads/2015/07/RAB-white-paper-1959.pdf

Home Office (1961), *Compensation for Victims of Crimes of Violence* (1961 Cmnd 1406)

Home Office (1964), *Compensation for Victims of Crimes of Violence* (1964 Cmnd 2323); http://discovery.nationalarchives.gov.uk/details/r/C1689757

Home Office (1978), *Review of the Criminal Injuries Compensation Scheme: Report of an Interdepartmental Working Party*

Home Office (1986), *Criminal Injuries Compensation: A Statutory Scheme*

Home Office (1993), *Compensating victims of violent crime: Changes to the criminal injuries compensation scheme* (1993 Cm 2434); https://www.gov.uk/government/uploads/system/uploads/attachment_data/file/271990/2434.pdf

Home Office (1999), *Compensation for Victims of Violent Crime: Possible Changes to the Criminal Injuries Compensation Scheme*)

Home Office (2000), *Setting the Boundaries: Reforming the law on sex offences;* http://webarchive.nationalarchives.gov.uk/+/http:/www.homeoffice.gov.uk/documents/volmmain.pdf?view=Binary

Home Office (2005), *Rebuilding Lives: supporting victims of crime* (2005 Cm 6705); https://www.gov.uk/government/uploads/system/uploads/attachment_data/file/272209/6705.pdf

Home Office (2006), *Rebalancing the criminal justice system in favour of the law-abiding majority*; http://webarchive.nationalarchives.gov.uk/20061209024625/http://www.homeoffice.gov.uk/documents/CJS-review.pdf/CJS-review-english.pdf?view=Binary

Home Office, *Nationality policy: assessing ordinary residence Version 2* (2017); https://www.gov.uk/government/uploads/system/uploads/attachment_data/file/655489/Nationality-policy-assessing-ordinary-residence-v2.0EXT.pdf

Home Affairs Select Committee (1985), *Compensation and Support for Victims of Crime* (House of Commons Paper 43 198485)

Home Affairs Select Committee (1990), *Compensating Victims Quickly: The Administration of the Criminal Injuries Compensation Board* (House of Commons Paper 92 1989–1990)

House of Commons, Committee of Public Accounts (2012), *Ministry of Justice Financial Management* (Seventy-fifth Report of Session 2010–12, HC 1778, 20 March 2012) https://publications.parliament.uk/pa/cm201012/cmselect/cmpubacc/1778/1778.pdf

House of Commons, Justice Committee (2015a), *Criminal courts charge* (Second Report of Session 2015–16 HC 586, 17 November 2015); https://publications.parliament.uk/pa/cm201516/cmselect/cmjust/586/586.pdf

House of Commons, Justice Committee (2015b), *Criminal courts charge: Government Response to the Committee's Second Report of Session 2015–16* (Second Special Report of Session 2015–16, HC 667, 9 December 2015); https://publications.parliament.uk/pa/cm201516/cmselect/cmjust/667/667.pdf

The Law Commission, *Simplification of Criminal Law: Public Nuisance and Outraging Public Decency* (Law Com No 358 HC 213 2015); https://www.gov.uk/government/uploads/system/uploads/attachment_data/file/438194/50076_Law_Commission_HC_213_bookmark.pdf

Ministry of Justice (2010) *Breaking the Cycle: Effective Punishment, Rehabilitation and Sentencing of Offenders* (2010 Cm 7972); http://webarchive.nationalarchives.gov.uk/20111206103817/http://www.justice.gov.uk/consultations/docs/breaking-the-cycle.pdf

Ministry of Justice (2012a), *Getting it Right for Victims and Witnesses* (2012, Cm 8288); https://consult.justice.gov.uk/digital-communications/victims-witnesses/supporting_documents/gettingitrightforvictimsandwitnesses.pdf

Ministry of Justice (2012b), *Getting it right for victims and witnesses: The Government response* (2012, Cm 8397); https://www.gov.uk/government/uploads/system/uploads/attachment_data/file/236100/8397.pdf

Ministry of Justice (2012c), *Reform of the Criminal Injuries Compensation Scheme, Equality Impact Assessment*; https://consult.justice.gov.uk/digital-communications/victims-witnesses/results/eia-criminal-injuries-comp-scheme.pdf

Ministry of Justice (2012d), *Punishment and Reform: Effective Community Sentences* Consultation (Paper CP8/2012, Cm 8334); https://www.gov.uk/government/uploads/system/uploads/attachment_data/file/228573/8334.pdf

Ministry of Justice (2012e), *Punishment and Reform: Effective Community Sentences Government Response*; https://www.gov.uk/government/uploads/system/uploads/attachment_data/file/228560/8469.pdf

Ministry of Justice (2012f), *Restorative Justice Action Plan for the Criminal Justice System*; http://www.iars.org.uk/sites/default/files/58w4_rjactionplan-1.pdf

Ministry of Justice (2013a), *Sentencing Statistics: England and Wales 2013, Sentencing Tables*; https://www.gov.uk/government/statistics/criminal-justice-statistics-quarterly-december-2013

Ministry of Justice (2013b), *Code of Practice for Adult Conditional Cautions*; https://www.gov.uk/government/publications/code-of-practice-for-adult-conditional-cautions

Ministry of Justice (2013b), *Code of Practice for Youth Conditional Cautions*; https://www.gov.uk/government/uploads/system/uploads/attachment_data/file/243443/9780108512179.pdf

Ministry of Justice (2014a), *Guidance on the Rehabilitation of Offenders Act 1974*; https://www.gov.uk/government/uploads/system/uploads/attachment_data/file/299916/rehabilitation-of-offenders-guidance.pdf.

Ministry of Justice (2014b), *Pre-sentence Restorative Justice (RJ)*; https://www.gov.uk/government/publications/pre-sentence-restorative-justice

Ministry of Justice (2015a), *Code of Practice for Victims of Crime*; https://www.gov.uk/government/uploads/system/uploads/attachment_data/file/476900/code-of-practice-for-victims-of-crime.PDF

Ministry of Justice (2015b), *Rules and Practice Directions*; https://www.justice.gov.uk/courts/procedure-rules/criminal/rulesmenu-2015

Ministry of Justice (2017a), *Criminal Justice Statistics Quarterly Update September 2017, Overview Tables*; https://www.gov.uk/government/statistics/criminal-justice-system-statistics- quarterly- september-2017

Ministry of Justice (2017b) *Restorative Justice Action Plan for the Criminal Justice System for the Period to March 2018*; https://www.gov.uk/government/publications/restorative-justice-action-plan-november-2016-to-march-2018

Ministry of Justice/Youth Justice Board (2013a), *Youth Out-of-Court-Disposal: Guide for Police and Youth Offending Services*; https://www.gov.uk/government/uploads/system/uploads/attachment_data/file/438139/out-court-disposal-guide.pdf

Ministry of Justice/Youth Justice Board (2013b), *Youth Cautions: Guidance for Police and Youth Offending Teams*; https://www.gov.uk/government/uploads/system/uploads/attachment_data/file/354050/yjb-youth-cautions-police-YOTs.pdf

Ministry of Justice/Youth Justice Board) (2015) *Referral Order Guidance*; https://www.gov.uk/government/uploads/system/uploads/attachment_data/file/418443/revised

National Audit Office (2000), *Compensating Victims of Violent Crime* (House of Commons Paper 398 1999–2000)

National Audit Office (2007), *Compensating victims of violent crime* (House of Commons Paper 100, 2007–2008); https://www.nao.org.uk/wp-content/uploads/2007/12/0708100.pdf

Office for Disability Issues (2011), *Equality Act 2010 Guidance*; https://www.gov.uk/government/uploads/system/uploads/attachment_data/file/570382/Equality_Act_2010-disability_definition.pdf

Office for National Statistics (2016), *Focus on Violent Crime and Sexual Offences: Year ending March 2015*, chapter 1 section 15; http://tinyurl.com/zv5cm2t

Office for National Statistics (August 2017), *Restorative Justice, year ending March 2011 to year ending March 2017 Crime Survey for England and Wales*; https://www.ons.gov.uk/peoplepopulationandcommunity/crimeandjustice/adhocs/007298restorativejusticeyearendingmarch2011toyearendingmarch2017crimesurveyforenglandandwales

Sentencing Council, *Dangerous Dog Offences*; https://www.sentencingcouncil.org.uk/wp-content/uploads/Dangerous-dog-offences-Definitive-Guideline-web.pdf

Sentencing Council, *Imposition of Community and Custodial Sentences, Definitive Guideline*; https://www.sentencingcouncil.org.uk/wp-content/uploads/Definitive-Guideline-Imposition-of-CCS-final-web.pdf

Sentencing Council, *Magistrates' Court Sentencing Guidelines, Explanatory Material*; https://www.sentencingcouncil.org.uk/explanatory-material/

Sentencing Council, *Sentencing Children and Young People Overarching Principles and Offence Specific Guidelines for Sexual Offences and Robbery Definitive Guideline*; https://www.sentencingcouncil.org.uk/wp-content/uploads/Sentencing-Children-and-young-people-Definitive-Guide_FINAL_WEB.pdf

Sentencing Council, *Sentencing Guidelines and Offences Involving Corrosive Substances*; https://www.sentencingcouncil.org.uk/news/item/sentencing-guidelines-and-offences-involving-corrosive-substances/

Supreme Court, *Revised Practice Directions*; https://www.supremecourt.uk/news/revised-practice-directions-april-2015.html

Tribunals Judiciary, Practice Statement (2014), *Composition of Tribunals in Relation to Matters that Fall to be Decided by the Administrative Appeals Chamber of the Upper Tribunal on or After 26th March 2014*; https://www.judiciary.gov.uk/wp-content/uploads/JCO/Documents/Practice+Directions/Tribunals/admin-appeals-chamber-upper-trib-on-or-after-260314.pdf

Victims' Commissioner (2014), *The Potential Benefits of Restorative Justice for Victims*; http://victimscommissioner.org.uk/app/uploads/2014/11/Restorative_Justice.pdf

Victims' Commissioner (2016a), *A Question of Quality: A Review of Restorative Justice, Part 1—Service Providers* http://victimscommissioner.org.uk/app/uploads/2014/10/A-question-of-quality_RJ-review-part-1-service-providers.pdf

Victims' Commissioner (2016b), *A Question of Quality: A Review of Restorative Justice, Part 2—Victims*; https://s3-eu-west-2.amazonaws.com/victimscomm-prod-storage-clhgxgum05k1/uploads/2016/11/VC-review-into-restorative-justice-services-part-2_November-2016.pdf

Youth Justice Board (2010), *The Scaled Approach*; https://www.gov.uk/government/uploads/system/uploads/attachment_data/file/682536/Youth_Justice_the_Scaled_Approach_-_A_framework_for_assessment_and_interventions.pdf

Youth Justice Board/Ministry of Justice (2018), *Youth Justice Statistics 2016/17*; https://www.gov.uk/government/uploads/system/uploads/attachment_data/file/676072/youth_justice_statistics_2016-17.pdf

4 EUROPEAN DOCUMENTS

4.1 Council of Europe

Council of Europe (1983), *European Convention on the Compensation of Victims of Violent Crimes*; https://rm.coe.int/1680079751

Council of Europe (2005), *Convention on Action against Trafficking in Human Beings, Council of Europe Treaty Series—No 197*; https://rm.coe.int/168008371d

4.2 European Union

Anti-Trafficking Directive (2001), *Directive 2011/36/EU of the European Parliament and of the Council of 5 April 2011 on preventing and combating trafficking in human beings and protecting its victims, and replacing Council Framework Decision 2002/629/JHA* [2011] OJ L101/1; https://eur-lex.europa.eu/legal-content/en/TXT/?uri=CELEX%3A32011L0036

Compensation Directive (2004), *Council Directive (EC) 2004/80/EC relating to compensation to crime victims* [2004] OJ L261/15; http://eur-lex.europa.eu/legal-content/EN/TXT/?uri=uriserv:OJ.L_.2004.261.01.0015.01.ENG&toc=OJ:L:2004:261:TOC

European Commission Directorate-General Justice Freedom & Security (2008), *Analysis of the application of Directive 2004/80/EC relating to compensation to crime victims Synthesis Report* (Matrix Insight, 12 December 2008); http://ec.europa.eu/civiljustice/publications/docs/study_application_directive_compensation_synthesis_report_en.pdf

Victims' Directive (2012), *Directive 2012/29/EU of the European Parliament and of the Council of 25 October 2012 establishing minimum standards on the rights, support and protection of victims of crime, and replacing Council Framework Decision 2001/220/JHA* [2012] OJ L315; https://eur-lex.europa.eu/legal-content/en/TXT/?uri=CELEX%3A32012L0029

INDEX